VICARIOUS KINKS

S/M in the Socio-Legal Imaginary

Who decides where "normal" stops and "perverse" begins? In *Vicarious Kinks*, Ummni Khan looks at the mass of claims that film, feminism, the human sciences, and law make about sadomasochism and its practitioners, and the way those claims become the basis for the legal regulation of sadomasochist pornography and practice. Khan's audacious proposal is that for film, feminism, law, and science, the constant focus on taboo sexuality is a form of "vicarious kink" itself.

Rather than attempt to establish the "truth" about sadomasochism, *Vicarious Kinks* asks who decides that sadomasochism is perverse, examining how various fields present their claims to truth when it comes to sadomasochism. The first monograph by a new scholar working at the juncture of law and sexuality, *Vicarious Kinks* challenges the myth of law as an objective adjudicator of sexual truth.

UMMNI KHAN is an associate professor in the Department of Law and Legal Studies at Carleton University.

UMMNI KHAN

Vicarious Kinks

S/M in the Socio-Legal Imaginary

UNIVERSITY OF TORONTO PRESS
Toronto Buffalo London

Library and Archives Canada Cataloguing in Publication

Khan, Ummni, author
Vicarious kinks : s/m in the socio-legal imaginary / Ummni Khan.

Includes bibliographical references and index.
ISBN 978-1-4426-4740-4 (bound). – ISBN 978-1-4426-1551-9 (pbk.)

1. Sadomasochism – Social aspects – Canada.   2. Sadomasochism – Law and legislation – Canada.   3. Sadomasochism.   I. Title.

HQ79.K43 2014   306.77'50971   C2014-900693-4

This book has been published with the help of a grant from the Federation for the Humanities and Social Sciences, through the Awards to Scholarly Publications Program, using funds provided by the Social Sciences and Humanities Research Council of Canada.

University of Toronto Press acknowledges the financial assistance to its publishing program of the Canada Council for the Arts and the Ontario Arts Council.

University of Toronto Press acknowledges the financial support of the Government of Canada through the Canada Book Fund for its publishing activities.

This book is dedicated to Brian Smith

Contents

Acknowledgments

Thank you to Brenda Cossman, Brian Smith, Bobby Noble, Bill Miller, Carl Stychin, Charles Moser, Chris Bruckert, Corinn Columpar, Duncan Kennedy, Ed Morgan, Gayle Rubin, Janet Halley, Jenny Nedelsky, Kate Sutherland, Lorne Goldstein, Marianne Valverde, Peggy Kleinplatz, Simon Stern, Trish Salah, Varda Burstyn, Alan Young, Alex Dymock, Alexandre Baril, Ashleigh Gardner, Adrian Smith, Betina Kuzmarov, Bruce Ryder, Bryan Thomas, Christiane Wilke, Corrie Scott, Dana Phillips, Daniel Rosenblatt, Danielle DiNovelli-Lang, David Gurnham, David Sealy, Dawn Moore, Deborah Conners, Diana Majury, Diana Young, Dianne George, Doris Buss, Emilie Cameron, Evelyn Maeder, George Rigakos, Hila Shamir, Jena McGill, Jackie Kennelly, Kathryn Trevenen, Kim Stanton, Kristin Bright, Lara Karaian, Leslie Robertson, Lisa Forman, Melanie Adrian, Michael Orsini, Neil Sargeant, Patrizia Gentile, Paul Saurette, Priya Watson, Radha Jhappan, Rena Bivens, Robert Smith, Rosemary Warskett, Seema Khan, Sheryl Hamilton, Shoshana Magnet, Stacy Douglas, Stuart Murray, Suzanne Bouclin, Vincent Kazmierski, Zoran Oklopcic, participants of the Law and Humanities Junior Scholar workshop, and the many other colleagues, friends, and family for their support and willingness to delve into these s/m matters with me. Your insights, debates, and downright disagreements were so helpful.

Thank you to Mama, Papa, Virna, Reema, and the rest of the Jamshed-Trunnell-Khan clan, Aloo Gobi (the cat, not the dish), Ken, Karen, and the rest of the Smith-Chan clan.

Thank you to Daniel Quinlan, Wayne Herrington, and Ian MacKenzie for outstanding editorial support and encouragement.

Thank you to Amanda Murphyao for invaluable feedback and indexing.

Thank you to SSHRC's Awards to Scholarly Publications Program (ASPP) for generous funding.

VICARIOUS KINKS

S/M in the Socio-Legal Imaginary

Prelude

A Screenplay:
my own private sex wars

INT. MCGILL UNIVERSITY WOMEN'S CENTRE – MIDDAY – 1992
Two young women, Marie and Ummni, are sitting on mismatched lumpy fur-
niture, engaged in heated, but not angry, discussion. A third woman – self-
chosen name Dragyn – is boiling water. The walls are covered with political
posters advocating women's rights.

DRAGYN, *scrutinizing one box of tea.* Who bought this spiced chai? The
    centre is officially boycotting products from India
    until the government does something about
    dowry killings.
UMMNI (voice-over). Although I began my undergraduate studies
    towards the end of the sex wars, I was
    completely unaware at the time of any "war"
    between feminists on the issues of pornography
    or sadomasochism (s/m). It was self-evident that
    a feminist would be against porn and s/m, just
    as a human rights activist would be against
    torture and killings.
UMMNI, *retrieving the box of tea from Dragyn with a sheepish look.*
    Sorry. My mom sent it to me.
UMMNI (voice-over). The Women's Centre was my favourite haunt.
    After I had finished classes for the day, I'd hurry
    over to the university centre to meet up with my
    Soul sisters and debrief our daily encounters

with the patriarchy in a safe, "womyn-only"
space. Sexuality was our most treasured topic of
discussion. Not so much swapping stories of hot
encounters, of course, as dissecting its power
dynamics: sex as a weapon against women; sex
as the linchpin to patriarchy.

MARIE. I can't believe the film society sponsored a screening of *Bitter
Moon*. The man is a paedophile rapist.

UMMNI. What do you expect? The art-house crowd considers Polanski
"ground-breaking" (*making scare quotes with her
fingers*).

DRAGYN, *handing each woman a mug of tea and joining them at the
couch.* Don't you mean the *andro* house crowd?

MARIE, *sarcastically.* Yeah, sadomasochistic misogyny. Really
ground-breaking!

DRAGYN. He cast his *own wife* as the femme fatale.

UMMNI. The film itself is evidence of domestic violence.

DRAGYN. We should organize a feminist film festival in response.

UMMNI (voice-over). In protest to the Polanski screening, The
Woman's Centre screened *Not a Love Story: A
Film about Pornography*, a documentary that
features hardcore pornographic footage to
demonstrate the sex industry's harmful effects.
Afterwards, I remember being giddy with
outrage.

DISSOLVE TO:

INT. CONCORDIA UNIVERSITY ART GALLERY – 1993

*A vernissage at the University Art Gallery. Students and professors mingling.
Ummni is talking to Daphne, a woman slightly older than she, but still clearly
a student.*

UMMNI (voice-over). In my sophomore year, I transferred to
Concordia University to enrol in its Creative
Writing program. That's where I met Daphne.
And that's where my feminism started to
become undone. She seemed really cool: a
graduate student working on a manuscript
that retold *Snow White* through a series of
interlinking poetry and prose.

UMMNI. So, it's a feminist retelling?
DAPHNE. You could say that.
UMMNI. I'd love to read it. Do you ever show your work in progress?

*(Ummni turns to look at a painting, as if she doesn't care what Daphne's answer
would be.)*

DAPHNE. I'm a bit of an exhibitionist; I'll share my work at anytime.

CUT TO:
*A small one-bedroom apartment, clearly furnished with hand-me-downs and
sidewalk finds. Daphne is holding a bottle of cheap dépanneur wine and heads
to the kitchen in search of a corkscrew. Ummni is sitting at the dining table in
awe of all the books scattered around. An anthology catches her eye:* The Girl
Wants To: Women's Representations of Sex and the Body *(Crosby 1993).
Daphne walks over to the table with two mugs brimming with wine. She no-
tices the book Ummni is holding and says:*

DAPHNE. Check out the Trish Thomas poem at the end. It's intense.

*The book opens naturally towards the end at the poem by Trish Thomas called
"Fuck Your Ex-Lover."*
CLOSE UP: on the stanza that Ummni is reading:
*"Don't get me wrong./I've intellectualized up the/feminist ass/with the best of
them./But all that theoretical masturbation/never got me a warm body in my
bed" (Crosby 1993, 181).*

UMMNI. What is this? *(Ummni turns away awkwardly, as if she had just
  been got caught reading a secret diary.)*
DAPHNE. Inspiration.
UMMNI. Right *(taking a gulp of wine)*. This book is part of that whole
  backlash thing, huh?
DAPHNE, *with a look of amusement.* Here's one of my poems. *(Daphne
  hands Ummni a spiral notebook.)*

*Ummni's eyes bulge out as she reads the text. She gets to the bottom of one page
and then abruptly closes it and hands the book back to Daphne.*

UMMNI. It's really ... vivid.
DAPHNE. What do you write?

UMMNI. I'm working on a story about sexual abuse in the context of an
    immigrant family. I'm using a postcolonial
    critique in my narrative.
UMMNI (voice-over). I thought the words "postcolonial critique" would
    impress Daphne. She was a TA; I was an
    undergrad.
DAPHNE. I bet it's brilliant.
UMMNI, *pleased and shy*. Oh, I don't know about that … Your poem, I
    guess, deals with abuse stuff too?
DAPHNE. It's about the vicissitudes of pleasure.
UMMNI (*to herself*). "Vicissitudes" must mean something bad. Maybe
    she means distortions of pleasure.

CUT TO:

EXT – MONTREAL SIDEWALK – THE NEXT MORNING

Dragyn and Ummni walking and talking.

DRAGYN. Do you think she was coming on to you with that poem?
UMMNI. Goddess! I hope not.
DRAGYN. You're so naive. What do you think the title "Fuck Your Ex-
    Lover" means? She's saying forget your ex and
    (*cringing as she says the word*) "fuck" her.
UMMNI. I don't think I'm her type.
DRAGYN. What about Daphne's poem, was it just as offensive?
UMMNI. It was good … (*noticing Dragyn's look of disgust*) … from a
    technical perspective, that is. But it creeped me
    out.

MONTAGE:

*A sequence of arguments between Ummni and Daphne at quintessential
    Montreal landmarks as the season turns from summer to fall to winter.*

UMMNI (voice-over during montage). That's how I entered the
    sex wars. At first, I approached my
    conversations with Daphne and the books she
    gave me the way a litigator approaches the
    opposing party's factum. Study it and find any
    weaknesses in the reasoning, or any vulnerable
    spots you can exploit.

1. Ummni's wild gesticulating hands as she tries to persuade Daphne of some-
thing by the illuminated cross at the top of Mount Royal.
2. Daphne handing Ummni a pile of books in front of the Saint Joseph's Ora-
tory, the leaves in full autumnal colour display.
3. Ummni and Daphne in heated discussion in front of the Biosphère as snow
falls on their faces.

MONTAGE:
A continuing sequence of arguments between Ummni and Dragyn at quint-
essential Montreal landmarks as the season turns from winter to spring to
summer again.

UMMNI (voice-over during montage). At some point, I defected
and became Daphne's willing protégé. Part of it
might have had to do with the fights I had with
Dragyn. Her accusations that Daphne was
colluding with the patriarchy. An implication that
I was getting contaminated as well.

1. Dragyn covering her face, as if in disbelief of what Ummni is telling her in
front of the Cathedral-Basilica on a dreary grey night.
2. Dragyn emphasizing her point to Ummni by drawing her attention to the
display at a sex shop on Saint Catherine Street. The leaves are just starting to
come out on the sidewalk trees.
3. Ummni and Dragyn staring at each other with cold stone faces at the back
patio of the Café Santropol, a copy of The Story of O (Réage 1965) *between*
them on the table.

DRAGYN. I'm not going to read that woman-hating book.
UMMNI. But it was written by a woman.
DRAGYN:Women are just as capable of spreading misogynist lies as
their andro counterparts. (*Pregnant pause.*) And
it's worse when they do it. They legitimate
patriarchy.

CUT TO:
INT. DAPHNE'S APARTMENT – THE NEXT DAY
Daphne and Ummni on the couch, facing each other and grinning mischie-
vously. On the scuffed coffee table in front of them are piles of books with titles

that denote kinky erotica, sex-positive feminism, and postmodern theory. A flyer for a fetish night is sticking out of one of the books.

                                                            CUT TO:
                            INT. A DARK SMOKY CLUB – NIGHT
Daphne and Ummni holding hands as they walk downstairs and enter the club. Daphne is sporting leather pants and a tiger print bra, Ummni is teetering on hazardously high stiletto heels.

                    PAN SHOT OF THE PEOPLE AT THE CLUB:
In one corner are foot fetishists sucking hairy toes and massaging tired insteps. In another an adult man is in diapers, holding a baby bottle in one hand and a beer in the other. By the window, a woman outfitted in the classic kinky nurse costume is leading her "patient" around on a dog leash. In the centre are two men taking turns whipping a very butch woman tied to some hooks in a crucifixion pose.

UMMNI (voice-over). Their audacity was stunning. Was heart-
    breaking. People who are hated and mocked by
    movies, by laws, by feminists, by conversations
    that begin with "What would you do if your
    boyfriend turned out to be a …?" – gathered
    together. In a safe and dangerous space. They –
    we – were not united by mutual desire. In the
    underworld of sexual deviance, I discovered
    stark differences in sexual practices, desires,
    aesthetics, and ethos, ranging from the classic
    s/m leather-dom to the animal-emulating furries.
    But there we were, bound together by our non-
    normative sexuality and the disgust we evoked
    in others.

    Ummni watches another patron teaching Daphne how to flick a whip.

                                                        DISSOLVE TO:
INT. OSGOODE HALL LAW SCHOOL LIBRARY – NIGHTIME – 2001
Ummni is conducting legal research on the computer. The book, Bad Attitude/s on Trial: Pornography, Feminism and the Butler Decision, *is propped open next to the keyboard (Cossman, Bell, Gotell, and Ross 1997). She finds a case*

*that she has apparently been looking for. As she reads the judgment, her face
registers a memory and she looks out the window, lost in the past.*

UMMNI (voice-over). I was reading a critique of *R. v. Butler*
   (1992), the Supreme Court decision that upheld
   the obscenity provisions of the *Criminal Code*. As it
   turns out, that precedent-setting case was first
   applied to criminalize a lesbian s/m magazine. I
   looked up that trial decision to discover that the
   magazine was deemed obscene because of a
   short story it contained by Trish Thomas, the
   writer of that poem I had read eight years ago in
   Daphne's living room.
UMMNI (*to herself*). Fuck your ex-lover.

Introduction

Getting to the Truth of the Matter: Narratives of the Real

I begin this book with an origin story to hint at my stakes in the topic at hand. Hoping that my confessional will have a seductive effect on the reader, I wrote a dramatization of a micro-battle in which I engaged (both internally and externally) during the so-called feminist sex wars. Both personal and biographical, the impact of the narrative relies on memory to project the past onto a screen of truth. Yet such a documentation of past experiences, as Hayden White has pointed out, "arises out of a desire to have real events display the coherence, integrity, fullness, and closure of an image of life that is and can only be imaginary" (White 1987, 24). The chronology of my screenplay offers a classic narrative, complete with the initial set-up (establishing my affiliation with the feminist community), catalyst (meeting Daphne, who challenges my feminist understandings of sexuality), rising action (arguments with Daphne and then Dragyn about the meaning of s/m), climax (attending a fetish night), and denouement (doing legal research on sexual rights). As White observes, "Where in any account of reality, narrativity is present, we can be sure that morality or a moralizing impulse is present too" (24). The story romanticizes sexual alterity, with an underlying critique of the ideological constraints around sexual citizenship.[1] In short, accounts of s/m – including my own – always involve normative storytelling. This book investigates some of the stories society spins about the truth of s/m.

Practitioners tell us that s/m rests on appropriating social hierarchies, restaging power imbalances, and/or re-signifying pain within a consensual context. As such, s/m desires are based on the drive to retell a particular story, to replay a particular scene, but in a way that seeks to transmute the social scripts from which it borrows (McClintock 1993, 89). But my focus here is not on s/m itself. Rather, I examine how three major cultural discourses and frameworks about s/m – science, feminism, and film – interact with one another, and with law's construction of s/m as an object of knowledge.

In order to properly understand the legal regulation of s/m, I situate law in the context of cultural production. Debates and discussions about the meaning of s/m reverberate through multiple fields. Consider, for example, the etymology of *sadism* and *masochism*. These sexual terms are rooted in the names of two notorious authors, Marquis de Sade and Leopold von Sacher-Masoch, who chronicled their sexual fantasies and philosophies in the eighteenth and nineteenth centuries. In the latter nineteenth century, pioneering sexologist Richard von Krafft-Ebing classified the dialectic syndromes of sadism and masochism out of the two novelists" names (Krafft-Ebing 1965). In the current moment, the law relies on psychiatric evidence to decode these desires, grapples with s/m in concert with feminist legal advocates, and represents s/m alongside pop cultural enactments of its dangers and allure. In considering these intertwining conceptions of s/m, my point of departure is to understand the construction of s/m as a narrative product made up of multidisciplinary, overlapping, and sometimes conflicting stories.

But beyond navigating this intertextual labyrinth, one of the hazards faced by those who seek to establish the *true* story of s/m is the possibility of contagion. Ann Coughlin has argued that when a scholar proposes to make pornography her subject of inquiry, she is confronted with the dilemma of how to address the topic without *becoming* the topic. "Porn must be identified before it can be isolated, seized, and destroyed" (Coughlin 2002, 2153). Similarly, the identification of s/m and its aetiology, its pleasures and its harms, can involve a complex and parasitic relationship with the sexual practice under examination.

To understand some of these complexities, consider, for example, the film referred to in my screenplay prologue: *Not a Love Story: A Film about Pornography*. Produced by the National Film Board of Canada in 1981, this classic anti-porn feminist documentary has received much attention. The organizational structure of the narrative relies on two contrasting "guides" whose exploration of the peepshow and pornography industries demonstrates the misogyny and violence that purportedly inhere in these practices. The first guide is a committed anti-porn feminist and director of the film, Bonnie Sher Klein; the other, an ambivalent stripper, Linda Lee Tracey, who eventually comes to embrace Klein's perspective. The narrative invites the viewer to undergo a similar conversion, with explicit footage of women gagged, tied up, spreadeagled, and exposed operating as a classic feminist consciousness-raising strategy.

And yet the film's parasitic relationship to the practices it seeks to condemn has generated surprising responses that go against the semantic grain of the narrative. Soon after its release, the now defunct Ontario Censor Board withheld approval of the commercial exhibition of *Not a Love Story*, thereby effectively banning it. Thus the movie was tacitly classified as "obscene," as government officials apparently found its sexual content inappropriate for public viewing. Another irony of the film is that some sadomasochists have taken pleasure in *Not a Love Story*, as it provides excerpts of some exceptional, hard-to-get-your-hands-on hardcore footage (Sasha 2003). The filmmakers may have intended to provide a "worst of" porn collection, but ended up providing a "best of" collection for the kinky community. Judith Butler provides insight into the dynamics of this semiotic slippage: "Language that is compelled to repeat what it seeks to constrain invariably reproduces and restages the very speech that it seeks to shut down" (Butler 1997, 129). In this way, a highly polemical documentary bent on denouncing a sexual arena can end up doubly defeated. Those who sympathize with its cause may find its affective impact too powerful for general consumption, while those who stand in opposition to its normative claims may choose to view it because of its (unwitting) affective power – that is, the power to arouse them.

Not a Love Story can thus be understood as a form of vicarious pornography. In order to give the "real" story of the harms of hardcore pornography, the film was compelled to excerpt the original pornographic material and move it into the documentary genre. There is a discursive affinity between the narrative and the object of knowledge, which both the censors and the kink community evidently recognized. Furthermore, if hardcore pornography is hot and enticing because it captures in explicit detail "real" bodies having "real" penetrative sex (Williams 1999, 49), then vicarious porn, like *Not a Love Story*, also gets its emotive power from its trafficking of "the real."

I explore this vicarious dynamic between s/m sexuality and investigations of s/m sexuality throughout the book. Specifically, the production of s/m in law and society, whether by a psychiatrist, radical feminist, film director, or judge, creates a vicarious dynamic that reproduces the taboo sexuality. Unquestionably, this book also participates in vicarious kinks, including its reproduction of taboo sexuality in my analysis of s/m truth-claims, as well as through teaser tidbits that imply a personal investment in the topic. This does not mean that about-s/m narratives are fundamentally or straightforwardly pornographic. The vicarious relationship of s/m investigations to s/m text entails both an affinity to the original s/m artefact and a mediating distance imposed through the conventions of the particular genre in use. Interestingly, while each genre has its own narrative trajectory in its vicarious dealings with s/m, certain consistent truth-claims and tropes reappear in different guises, from empirical studies in psychiatry to imaginative creations in movies, and from the counterculture of radical feminism to the conservative culture of legal discourse.

Getting to the Heart of the Matter: What Is S/M?

Today, s/m pornography is viewed as one of the hardest of hardcore pornographies. But this was not always the case. Initially, the jurisprudence of the United States and Canada measured the *hardness* of a sexual representation by the level of sexual explicitness. Beginning in the mid-1980s, however, judges began to adopt a more liberal attitude towards sexual explicitness, a shift that came at the cost of scapegoating sexual minorities (Williams 1993, 46). As Linda Williams argues, "In the definition of obscenity, explicitness has given way to the deviant sexuality of the 'other,' defined in relation to a presumed heterosexual, non-sadomasochistic norm" (49). S/m pornography is hardcore, not because it necessarily shows explicit sexuality (e.g., a whipping scene need not involve any overt sexual content or nudity), but because it seeks to arouse the viewer with non-normative activities.

A further complication in discerning s/m pornography is brought up by the debates on the semantics of the term. There is much controversy about the question of how to classify and identify divergent representations that depict the eroticization of power exchange or abuse – depending on your perspective.

In his discussion of the limits of free expression, L.W. Sumner exemplifies the difficulties in pinning down what makes a text s/m, and what makes it unadulterated violence (Sumner 2004). Sumner offers a comparison between the representation of what he calls a "gang-rape scenario" and a "BDSM scenario" (191–2). The first scenario features a woman being violently gang-raped who protests and resists her attackers but, after a certain period of time, comes to welcome the onslaught. Sumner describes the second scenario as two women engaged in consensual "sadomasochistic" sex involving bondage and "mild" torture. The "bottom"[2] is represented as relishing her position and capable of halting the activities whenever she likes. Sumner posits, "In both cases the activity depicted is violent and the depiction has the purpose of sexual arousal. Both therefore fall within the category of violent pornography" (192). Yet Sumner insists that the scenarios can be distinguished, because "only the first expresses an attitude of hatred and contempt toward women; in eroticizing forced sexual violence against them it degrades them to the status of objects or things" (192). In his categorization of the two texts, Sumner thus assumes that each has a singular meaning that is self-evident and stable and that he can determine what kind of "attitude" is being expressed.

Consider how Sumner stacks the deck in favour of the second scenario. The activity takes place between a couple (because group sex is more suspect?) who are women (because women cannot degrade other women?) who engage only in "mild" torture (who gets to define what constitutes "mild"?), where the "bottom" (Sumner chooses this neutral label used by the s/m community) appears to be enjoying her submissive status the whole time. Sumner further oversimplifies the issue by pre-emptively labelling the second scenario as sadomasochistic, thereby associating it with a sexual subculture.

Sumner takes a middle pathway between anti-porn advocates, who are usually anti-s/m, and anti-censorship advocates, who usually defend s/m. In his view, porn that matches up to the conventions of what *he* perceives to be a contrived s/m scene, particularly if it occurs between two women, is not harmful or degrading to women. Yet anti-porn advocates as well as anti-censorship advocates might interpret both scenes as sadomasochistic. They both clearly depict parties who are in dominant positions meting out aggressive sexual treatment to constrained individuals who sooner or later enjoy it.

An anti-porn advocate might characterize both scenarios as not only sadomasochistic, but also hateful and degrading, therefore warranting censorship. Both configure pain and submissiveness as a source of pleasure, a concept that anti-porn theorists generally regard as a fundamental distortion of human sexuality. An anti-censorship advocate might view both scenes as harmless fantasy materials that stage power imbalances for the sake of arousal. Indeed, the first "gang-rape" scenario that Sumner indicts as misogynist matches up with a short story by Patrick Califia, a prominent s/m advocate who has written erotica, how-to books, and passionate opinion-pieces on the topic.

In Califia's "The Surprise Party," a butch lesbian is abducted by renegade male cops who assault her, rape her, and sodomize her – all the while launching homophobic and degrading epithets at her (Califia 1988b, 211). The heroine is portrayed as resistant most of the time, but the reader is aware that she is secretly and shamefully enjoying much of the "violence." Only in the last paragraph is the reader informed that the "cops" were actually friends enacting a pre-arranged scene that was orchestrated by the protagonist's girlfriend. How would Sumner interpret this story? Is it saved by the surprise ending in the last paragraph that places the "violence" within a consensual s/m context?

Questions and controversies about how to characterize pornographic representation are at the heart of s/m controversy. Practitioners, advocates, and critics struggle over the meaning of concepts like violence, pleasure, and consent in an attempt to pin down the essence of s/m.

Pro-s/m literature usually (but not always) dissociates s/m from the term *violence*, as the standard usage of the term suggests an absence of consent and agency, factors that, according to practitioners, should be present in every s/m encounter and implied in every s/m representation.[3] Anti-s/m literature understands s/m porn to be an unabashed promotion of violence that not only depicts sexual aggression as a turn-on, but also portrays such violence as consensual and pleasurable – thus justifying the aggression, encouraging it, and normalizing it.[4]

The sexual practice of s/m is fraught with concerns similar to those arising from its representation in pornography. How can someone consent to being forced? Isn't pain by definition something one seeks to avoid? If a woman enjoys sexual submissiveness with a dominant man, is this patriarchal indoctrination or postmodern reinscription? Questions such as these highlight the instability of "s/m" as a category; for its defenders it is a delicious paradox, for its detractors, a euphemism for violence.

Approaching the Matter: The Theoretical Framework

Sexual sadism and sexual masochism conspicuously stand out in the nomenclature of the authoritative handbook of mental disorders, the *Diagnostic and Statistical Manual of Mental Disorders V* (*DSM-V*), as the only two paraphilias that derive their root meanings from the names of two individuals (American Psychiatric Association, 2013). The etymological origins of the names of all the other sexual disorders within this section relate directly to the perversities being described. For example, exhibitionism denotes exhibiting one's genitals to non-consenting strangers, while fetishism denotes the sexualization of a non-human object, i.e., a fetish. Perhaps even more significant is the fact that sadism and masochism do not reference the names of doctors or psychologists who "discovered" the mental illnesses, or of patients who brought the perversions to the attention of the mental health profession. Instead, as mentioned, two storytellers provided their namesakes: Marquis de Sade and Leopold von Sacher-Masoch.[5]

What can be drawn from the fact that sadism and masochism are perversities that emerge out of the objectification of two authorial figures? Admittedly, there is evidence that de Sade enjoyed "sadistic" acts with some men and women, while Sacher-Masoch enacted "masochistic" scenes with his female lovers. Yet it was the narrativizing of their sexual predilections that caught the attention of the mental health profession and catapulted their names into sexual infamy. The texts were taken as confessions of clandestine acts and abnormal desires. The psychiatric disorders of sadism and masochism thus materialized from a removal and redistribution of discursive products; the erotic writings of de Sade and Sacher-Masoch were rendered into evidence of sexually abnormal types within an emerging classificatory system of pathologies in the nineteenth century. This multiplication of discourses demonstrates what Foucault has identified as "an excess, a redoubling … an interference between two modes of production of truth: procedures of confession, and scientific discursivity" (1990, 64–5). The "redoubling" of the novels of de Sade and Sacher-Masoch into confessional discourse, and then in turn into medico-juridical typology, opened up further avenues to speak of sex within a system, which Foucault has dubbed the power-knowledge-pleasure regime.

In *The History of Sexuality*, Foucault argues that power does not stand in the way of sexual pleasure, but rather that power constructs knowledge, and that this process itself is both sexual and pleasurable. He counters the once established notion that the nineteenth century was marked exclusively by the repression, censorship, and prohibition of sexuality. Rather, the scientific and juridical realms opened up multiple spaces for sexuality to be discussed, analysed, and parsed in infinite detail. The new scientific authority on sexuality engaged in a production of truth, whereby it "multiplied, intensified, and even created its own intrinsic pleasures" (Foucault 1990, 71). Foucault later elaborates that the empirical method of obtaining "objective" evidence of the "true" nature of human sexuality was, in fact, itself a pleasure-creating apparatus: "pleasure in the truth of pleasure, the pleasure of knowing the truth, of discovering and exposing it, the fascination of seeing and telling it, of captivating and capturing others by it, of confiding it in secret, of luring it out in the open – the specific pleasure of the true discourse on pleasure" (71). The Foucauldian spotlight on the triangulated system of power-knowledge-pleasure helps bring into focus how, and to what purpose, sadism, masochism, and s/m have been "put into discourse" in the socio-legal imaginary.[6]

While Foucault's theory of sexual discursivity will provide an overarching frame to my analysis, theories of abjection, disgust, and expulsion will help distinguish the nuances of power and pleasure that occur in particular institutional and discursive realms that produce knowledge of s/m sexuality.

My use of abjection to theorize responses to and articulations of s/m revolves around two theorists, Julia Kristeva and David Halperin. In her book *Powers of Horror: An Essay on Abjection* (1982), Julia Kristeva surveys the "abject," an unstable terrain between subject and object where the borders around identities and categories are most susceptible to leakage, permeability and violation. Kristeva describes this shaky ground as "the in-between, the ambiguous, the composite" (4). Within the socio-legal imaginary, perversion can amplify this shaky ground into an earthquake, where the civilized individual falls into the chasm of destructive carnality. Investigations of s/m frequently find that the fault line between normal sexuality and pathological sexuality is fragile and in need of reinforcement from psychological diagnosis, criminal investigation, feminist education, and moralizing stories. Abjection instils anxiety about the collapse of categories, order, and meaning, but it is also associated with jouissance – an enjoyment that derives from the shattering of a unified self. David Halperin describes – and celebrates – the jouissant antisocial power of abjection in the context of gay male subjectivity as "the alchemical transmutation of social humiliation into erotico-religious glorification" (2007, 75). Abjection is thus a site of defiant thrill as well as uncertainty, oppression, and harm. With its resignification and sexualization of hierarchical relationships and painful sensations, and its use of orifices and bodily fluids for non-reproductive purposes, s/m – regardless of sexual orientation – provokes abject disorientation and incites taboo delights. In this way, sadomasochists are particularly adept at harnessing abjection for their own purposes. As Halperin states, "In the unpredictable course of its efforts to abject the pariah, society suddenly loses its annihilating power over its victim; his fear and horror are turned into resistance, even into desire" (76). As I will demonstrate, particularly in chapter 3, anti-s/m discourse and strategies provided s/m practitioners with intensified narratives from which to construct their own fantasies of desire and resistance.

In response, those who seek to contain s/m deploy the rhetoric of disgust to ward off the abject and reinforce the edges of normality. This book draws upon a number of theorists who have analysed the work accomplished by disgust. From a psychological perspective, Paul Rozin has provided foundational analyses on the cultural psychology and development of disgust. Rozin and his co-authors argue that the emotion originates as a biological drive to avoid oral incorporation of a bad-tasting contaminant, but has evolved to encompass much broader ideological strategies to avoid and condemn spiritual, moral, or social contaminants (Rozin, Haidt, and McCauley 2000, 637). Mary Douglas's *Purity and Danger* (1984) provides an anthropological and transcultural account of the ways in which boundaries, both literal and discursive, are maintained through conceptions of pollution and taboo. With a normative agenda, Martha Nussbaum argues in *Hiding from Humanity: Disgust, Shame, and the Law* (2004) that disgust and shame should not influence what gets criminalized or how criminals get punished. Nussbaum conceives of disgust as part of a coping method by which people hide from and displace onto others the ontological reality of our material selves: our bodies, our animality, and our mortality. Finally, of most relevance is William Miller's *Anatomy of Disgust* (1997). In this trans-disciplinary study, Miller argues that disgust is a "culture-creating passion" that ranks people into hierarchal order and protects the boundaries of our bodies, our identities, and our communities (xii).

When confronted with the s/m abject, disgust-implying labels like "monster" or "misogynist" are employed by those who seek to establish who belongs in the community, and to eradicate the "in-between," to clarify the "ambiguous," and to pull apart the "composite." Yet as Miller points out, "Disgust is a recognition of danger to our purity" (1997, 204). In its very utterance, disgust acknowledges the instability of categories and demonstrates the necessity to police their frontiers.

Furthermore, articulations of disgust spoken from a position of relative power (whether a judge ruling on the legality of s/m, or a renowned scholar condemning "patriarchal" sexuality) do not eradicate pleasure. As Foucault reminds us, "Pleasure and power do not cancel or turn back against one another; they seek out, overlap, and reinforce one another. They are linked together by complex mechanisms and devices of excitation and incitement" (1990, 48).

When power speaks the language of sexual disgust, the judgment operates as a device of excitation and incitement. When one is disgusted with a sexual other, one is captivated, shocked, and entertained (Miller 1997, 17). The bearer of disgust buttresses her own humanity by erasing it from another (17). Yet when the frontiers between the normal and the perverse are threatened, or worse, breached, utterances of disgust will often not suffice; rejection and expulsion become the compulsory measures to sanctify the community of normalcy.

Julia Kristeva's reinterpretation of Freud's anal stage will frame my analysis of the pleasures activated from expelling sexual deviancy from the community. To understand the social expulsion of sadomasochists, it is helpful to turn to Freud, who analysed the psycho-sexual significance of the most basic act of human expulsion: defecation. Freud designated the anal phase as the second stage in ego and libidinal childhood development, following the oral phase. Each stage involves a physical site where sensation is localized to the particular body part and corresponds with a psychic component that triggers emotive satisfaction.

Freud proposed that in the second phase of infantile sexuality, the anal orifice becomes a primary site of pleasure and fixation. Here defecation, especially when it is withheld for a period of time, creates both painful and pleasurable sensations through "violent muscular contractions" and "powerful stimulation of the mucous membrane" (Freud 1975, 52). Yet, as mentioned, the pleasures associated with this stage are not just physical, they are conjunctively psychological. The second stage initiates a process of psychic separation where the infant begins to recognize, in a preliminary fashion, the contours of her own body. In addition, Freud argues, "The instincts for looking and for gaining knowledge (the scopophilic and epistemophilic instincts) are powerfully at work" (1973, 370). Interestingly for our purposes, Freud called this the *sadistic* anal stage, because it is marked with the desire to control and imprint oneself on the outside.

While Kristeva provides us with the language of abjection to understand the anxieties provoked by s/m, her elaboration on the anal stage assists us in understanding the psychological pleasure rooted in the scene of rejection. In *Revolution in Poetic Language* (1994, 149), Kristeva revises the chronology of Freud's theory by proposing that when a subject enters into language, a "reactivation of anality" must occur. She argues that there is "pleasure underlying the symbolic function of expulsion" and that "this pleasure derives from the anal drive – anal rejection, anality" (149). In other words, when the subject expels what has been symbolically designated as "waste," she derives a satisfaction that is informed by the pleasures of the anal stage. Furthermore, the symbolic pleasure in expulsion does not simply negate an unwanted element from the individual or social body; it simultaneously produces identity. Kristeva later elaborates on the constructive aspects of rejection: "Rejection reconstitutes real objects, 'creates' new ones, reinvents the real, and re-symbolizes it" (155). The repeated use of the prefix *re-* in her statement points to the cyclical nature of rejection. It is part of an ongoing repetitive and reiterative process that discerns the subject from the other, even as it betrays the instability of borders.

Bearing in mind Freud's anal theory and Kristeva's update on its psychic and social uses, I explore the epistemic pleasures embedded in understanding and exposing the sexual deviant, and the cathartic pleasures of expelling or destroying her. The community of normalcy recognizes itself through the rejection of the sexual other and through its fortification of the boundaries around sexual citizenship. I thus recast infantile sexual impulses as socio-legal drives to see, know, master, and eliminate the sadomasochist as social waste. These expulsion pleasures inform the satisfaction, indeed the sexual satisfaction that vicarious kinks can generate in the socio-legal imaginary.[7]

Outlining the Matter: Summary of the Following Chapters

In examining how the incitement to sexual discourse produces its own abject, disgust, and expulsion pleasures, I deconstruct narratives from institutional and cultural spheres of power that have interrogated s/m. In the process of interrogation, each narrative must re/move the stories, confessions, descriptions, and depictions of this deviant sexuality into a "serious" field of discourse, with the ostensible purpose of exploring the truth of human nature. This transplantation creates its own intrinsic pleasures that traffic in the affective impact of s/m itself.

Chapter 1 begins by addressing the medico-psychiatric discourse that first spawned the perversions of sadism and masochism. It explores how Krafft-Ebing, Sigmund Freud, Havelock Ellis, and the *DSMs* have reckoned with the notion that pleasure can be extracted from inflicting or receiving pain. In these discursive formations, abjection is managed through the clinical gaze that proffers empiricism and diagnosis as devices that unlock the secrets of human sexuality. I further consider challenges to this pathologizing gaze, paying particular attention to the counter-hegemonic work of Charles Moser and Peggy Kleinplatz, who have advocated for a removal of sexual sadism and sexual masochism from the *DSM*, pointing to the lack of empirical evidence to support their status as sexual disorders.

The book begins with the scientists in part because their narratives chronologically precede the other discursive fields, but also because the medico-psychiatric authorities that formulated the pathologies of sadism and masochism in the late nineteenth and early twentieth centuries involved certain governing assumptions that continue to be perpetuated or contested in feminist, pop cultural, and legal truth-claims. These include assumptions that sexuality is dangerous and corrupting, that animals provide a blueprint for what is inherently natural, that civilized society must engage rules and codes to curb our animal sexuality, and that sadism and masochism are inescapably gendered as masculine and feminine, respectively. With these assumed subtexts, modern medicine set the stage upon which the feminist, cinematic, and legal engagements with sadism, masochism, and s/m would be played out.

Chapter 2 addresses s/m as a political minefield that erupted in the feminist sex wars in the 1980s and early 1990s. During this time, abjection fears about the significance of s/m became most magnified, as certain feminists were confronted with the identity-shattering issue that other self-styled feminists were "infecting" the movement with what had previously been unanimously regarded as patriarchal sexuality. In other words, some feminists were disgusted to find the "enemy" was lying (and fucking!) in their midst. In the lesbian-feminist community, there was a passionate drive to expel sadomasochists from lesbian spaces, as if s/m lesbians amounted to nothing more than double agents who vacillated between feminist sexual identity and patriarchal sexual practice. For their part, s/m lesbians understood themselves as a persecuted minority in both mainstream and feminist communities. Their self-construction as outcasts and outlaws against feminist repression and societal rejection generated pleasures through discourses of rebellion and opposition.

The third discursive field that I examine is pop culture, specifically mainstream cinematic treatment of s/m. Although I characterize all narratives that take s/m as their subject of inquiry as vicarious kink, pop culture most directly extracts voyeuristic and parasitic pleasures. In movies like *Nine and a Half Weeks*, the audience is given full licence to explore the allure of s/m sexuality. However, the sexiness of s/m is usually confined to the first half of the narrative. Historically, movies that address s/m have tended to depict the protagonists as falling down a slippery slope of unwholesome sexuality, often ending with the s/m practitioners receiving karmic punishment for having given in to temptation. In *Nine and a Half Weeks*, for example, the heroine just barely escapes from what had amounted to an escalating abusive relationship. However, some more recent fictional depictions of s/m have offered a lenient, even romanticized portrayal of its practitioners, particularly if they adhere to other hetero-normative strictures. The 2001 film *Secretary*, and more recently, the novel trilogy *Fifty Shades* exemplify this sympathetic portrayal, where an s/m couple overcome internalized kinkphobia and defy societal disapproval to enjoy a fairy tale ending of marriage and domestic bliss. Such narrative tolerance of heterosexual couples that dabble in s/m – particularly if the s/m is mild and they are in long-term relationships – is in affinity with some recent legal trends.

The next two chapters examine the juridical realm, where s/m is put on trial under the scrutiny of the judicial gaze. Through close textual analysis, I consider the ways in which the previously examined discourses of psychiatry, feminism, and pop culture inform the legal truthclaims on s/m. Chapter 4 focuses on s/m in the context of obscenity cases. An examination of the treatment of pornography in Canadian law highlights the semantic tensions between s/m and violence, and the debates regarding whether s/m sexuality is premised on consent or coercion. This analysis demonstrates that when the Canadian legal system applies obscenity law to s/m pornography, it relies primarily upon anti-s/m feminist discourse (although seldom acknowledging any feminist influence) to justify censorship. Anti-pornography feminists (whose agenda could be said to overlap with anti-s/m feminists) hijacked the "progressive" voice in the legal debate, allowing the courts to refocus their censorship justification on the issue of equality (for women) and to defocus on the issue of morality (against sexual minorities). This is dramatically illustrated in the reasoning of the Supreme Court of Canada's *Butler* precedent on pornography, which took its cue from anti-pornography feminism, sentimentalizing female sexuality and dismissing s/m imagery as necessarily harmful to all women (*R. v. Butler* 1992, 452). Gay and lesbian s/m sexuality is also interpreted as harmful and is particularly subject to regulation and censorship through border control mechanisms. However, recent case law on s/m reveals a more lenient judicial treatment, particularly if the imagery is heterosexual.

To begin the consideration of s/m practice in chapter 5, I take a brief journey to England to deconstruct and compare three cases where assault charges were laid for consensual s/m activities. A key issue that emerges from this comparison is the extent to which hetero-normative identity can purchase credibility for one's consent to submissive sexuality. In Canada, the issue of s/m practice has come up in cases that deal with sexual assault, manslaughter, child custody, prostitution, human rights, and workplace codes of conduct. I demonstrate that in these cases, consensual s/m is often conflated with non-consensual sadism, and that "psy experts" (meaning psychiatrists, psychologists, psychoanalysts, counsellors, and therapists), in addition to feminist theorists, often perpetuate this view. Furthermore, s/m desire, in and of itself, is commonly understood in these cases as a sign of mental illness, despite the fact that the last two editions of the *DSM* – the *DSM-IV* and the *DSM-V* – do not necessitate this conclusion. I end this chapter by examining the regulation of s/m practitioners outside of the criminal legal process. Of particular note is how s/m practitioners are beginning to appropriate the law to defend their sexual rights. In the *Hayes* human rights case, for example, an s/m practitioner asserted his right to be free from discrimination based on his s/m "sexual orientation" (*Hayes v. Vancouver Police Department and Barker* 2008). In the 2008 *Mosley v. News Group Newspapers Limited* decision, Max Mosley, president of the Fédération Internationale de l'Automobile, successfully sued the *News of the World* because of its sensationalist coverage of his involvement with several female sex workers in an s/m encounter. Such cases reveal the ways sadomasochists are taking up particular legal discourses and normative frameworks to assert their subjectivity and establish their entitlement to be included in the community of rights-bearers.

In the legal regulation of both practice and pornography, abjection fears abound, particularly about the uneasy boundaries between human and animal, and between person and object. Disgust plays a prominent role in the jurisprudence to castigate the dominant sexual partners and to discredit the viability of submissive sexuality. The courts, of course, wield the ultimate power of expulsion, as sadomasochists can be evicted from the public sphere through a jail sentence, allowing the law to reconstitute societal identity in opposition to those who practise non-normative sexuality.

Although my focus is on the Canadian socio-legal imaginary, the texts I will be deconstructing come from Europe and the United States, as well as Canada. In order to grasp the complexity of the discursive formations that support Canadian regulation of s/m, it is critical to understand the ways that sexual regulation is produced by intercultural and interdisciplinary narratives that bleed into one another. This is particularly true for Canada as a postcolonial nation with its jurisprudential roots in England, and as a North American country influenced strongly by the neighbouring United States.

In the chapter on medico-scientific discourse, I look almost exclusively at European and American texts (with the exception of the articles by Peggy Kleinplatz, a professor at the University of Ottawa). This is because European doctors formulated the early psychiatric discourse on the perversions of s/m, and because the current definitive text used in Canada for mental disorders is the *DSM-V* produced by the American Psychiatric Association. My chapter on the feminist sex wars also draws primarily upon literature from the United States and Britain, with less reliance on Canadian texts. This is because in the United States and Britain, s/m, specifically lesbian s/m, became a hotbed of controversy that appeared to rupture through the feminist communities, producing numerous texts that battled over its meaning. In Canada, there is less literature that addresses s/m as such, likely because the sex wars in this nation were centred primarily on the broader issue of pornography censorship. My chapter on popular culture focuses almost exclusively on Hollywood productions, reflecting my understanding of Hollywood's hegemony over cinematic culture and the popular imagination in Canada. One exception to this social fact is world-famous Canadian film-maker David Cronenberg, whose movies often engage with sadomasochistic themes. Out of all of his films, however, I chose to deconstruct *Videodrome*, because its plot most explicitly addresses s/m practice and pornography. In addition, I consider the art-house Canadian film *Walk All Over Me*, to address how independent Canadian filmmakers have taken up recent iterations of the dominatrix figure and s/m culture. In the two chapters concerning the law, I focus mostly on Canadian legal texts that invoke or hint at s/m sexuality, and consider a handful of British cases and one American case to demonstrate either their contrasting or shared agendas. Throughout the book, I point out conspicuous overlapping or conflicting perspectives among the psychiatric, feminist, cinematic, and legal-discursive constructions and truth-claims of s/m.

In all of the chapters, I reckon with two kinds of texts. The first and most frequent are the psy, feminist, cinematic, or legal texts that appeared to me to be the most characteristic of their ilk – the most hegemonic, the most classic, the most prominent, the most influential, the most exemplary, and/or the most cited. But s/m is a site of contestation, and so the second kind of text examined runs against the grain of the first. These are texts that undermine any easy structuralist conclusions about the construction of s/m in vicarious kink. Either they are explicitly counter-hegemonic, or they are simply atypical, evidence that hegemonic norms are never monolithic, seamless, all-pervasive, or omnipotent. My method of close textual reading allows for a detailed deconstructive and semiotic analysis of both kinds of texts, but it means that depth has been gained at the expense of total comprehensiveness.

The ultimate goal of this book is to analyse what variety of truth-claims and vicarious kinks are produced when s/m is rendered an object of knowledge. I recognize that there will be multiple desired aspirations in the texts: harm reduction, sex equality, sexual well-being, or a moral objection to violence, to name a few. I argue that alongside these well-intentioned goals are discursive and epistemic pleasures that have a vicarious relationship with s/m. Thus Foucault's observation that the analysis of sexuality is itself a sexual practice gives us our starting point for getting to the bottom of the matter.

1

Who's Your Daddy?
S/M's Founding Fathers

The pathologies of sadism and masochism trace their genealogical origins to the nineteenth century, where medico-psychiatric discourse sought to taxonomize sexual practices and identities, and differentiate normal and pathological behaviour. This is not to say that before the classification of these "perversions," activity that one might term today as sadomasochistic did not exist, but rather to emphasize that the act of consolidating such behaviour with a clinical diagnosis was a creative endeavour. As Deleuze has pointed out in his treatise on Sacher-Masoch, "Symptomatology is always a question of art" (1991, 14).

This chapter analyses the "art" of medicine in its construction of sadism and masochism. The identification of these two perversions formed part of a larger trend in which the emerging sexual sciences of the nineteenth and early twentieth centuries pioneered new knowledge of human subjectivity in conversation with larger evolutionary, social, and biological theories. Of particular influence were Charles Darwin's evolutionary theories that animals, both human and non-human, compete not just to survive (natural selection), but also to procreate (sexual selection), and that this contest produced and amplified differences between males and females over time (Darwin 1871). Patrick Geddes and J. Arthur Thomson countered that sex difference was a product of essential biology, not evolution (Geddes and Thompson 1889). The scientists constructed male and female libidos as metabolically different, as reflected in the "active" sperm and the "passive" egg, and argued that this corresponded to the generalized behaviour of men and women. These productions of sex difference (whether through discourses of evolution or biology) provided sexologists with scientific theories from which to naturalize and gender sadism and masochism in some forms, while pathologizing it in others. As Foucault notes, science sought to "take sex 'into account,' to pronounce a discourse on sex that would not derive from morality alone but from rationality as well" (1990, 24). Through case studies, empirical observation, analysis, and theorization, scientific experts in fields such as medicine, psychiatry, psychoanalysis, and psychology probed sexuality as an objective and knowable phenomenon. This reification centralized sexuality as a core element of human subjectivity and generated a multitude of distinct types of abnormal sexual identity. In this context, the sadist and masochist appeared as members in a diverse cast of pathological sexual characters, which also included the homosexual, the invert, the fetishist, the paedophile, the prostitute, and many more. Though each form of perversity had its own distinguishing features, it also generally shared certain recurrent epistemological foundations. As Lucy Bland and Laura Doan explain (1998, 6), sexology's taxonomy of perverse identity in the nineteenth and early twentieth century generally rested on hierarchical binaries, racialized classifications, and eugenic logics. Despite the claims of scientific rationality, sexologists perpetuated an essentialist, moralistic, and racialized conception of human sexuality.

Bearing this historical context in mind, this chapter begins by performing a close-text deconstruction of three of the most well-known scientific theorists on sadism and masochism in early sexology: Richard von Kraft-Ebing (1840–1902), Sigmund Freud (1856–1939), and Havelock Ellis (1859–1939). I then turn to the American Psychiatric Association's *Diagnostic and Statistical Manual of Mental Disorders* (*DSM*), the major classificatory system used in Canada and the United States, that pinpoints sadism and masochism as sites of sexual abnormality and potential danger. The chapter ends with an overview of counter-hegemonic studies on s/m, paying particular attention to the current work of Peggy Kleinplatz and Charles Moser, two doctors and scholars who have advocated for the de-pathologization of sadism and masochism, and their removal from future editions of the *DSM*.

Krafft-Ebing: The Unending Struggle of Reason over Passion (1886)

"It is from the search of truth that the exalted duties and rights of medical science emanate," proclaims Krafft-Ebing in the preface of *Psychopathia Sexualis*, first published in 1886 (Krafft-Ebing 1965). As such, it was in the name of "truth" that the prominent psychiatrist appropriated the literary imagination of de Sade and Sacher-Masoch to coin the pathologies of sadism and masochism for his book of case studies of sexual aberrations. De Sade and Sacher-Masoch's novels provided a framework to augment the truth-value of Krafft-Ebing's scientific "discovery" that some people derive sexual pleasure from their pain, or that of others. Yet one of the fascinating "truths" alleged by Krafft-Ebing is that sadism and masochism are not so much unnatural sexual perversions, but are rather hyper-natural atavistic manifestations of an untamed instinct. In the introductory chapter of *Psychopathia Sexualis*, Krafft-Ebing sets out a general theory of the psychology of human sexual life that informs his later writings on sadism and masochism, and indeed will continue to reverberate in twenty-first-century engagements with non-normative sexuality. In his analysis, he reifies hierarchal polarities between man and beast, man and woman, and what he calls "civilized" and "savage" cultures. Yet these divisions between opposites are revealed to be permeable, vulnerable, and open to disintegration. Positioned between these contrasting ontologies is an abject and dangerous space that can lure a civilized man to cross over to beastly, uncivilized, or gender-transgressive sexuality. Appropriate education, breeding, socialization, and legal codification must be in force in order to shore up the boundaries between these unstable categories.

In the first paragraph of his treatise, Krafft-Ebing addresses the animal that lurks inside the man: "Man puts himself at once on a level with the beast if he seeks to gratify lust alone, but he elevates his superior position when by curbing the animal desire he combines with the sexual functions ideas of morality, of the sublime, and the beautiful" (1965, 1). Man is constructed as above animals, yet animalism is shown to be an abject but nonetheless inherent part of his nature. As Kristeva puts it, "It [the abject] is something rejected from which one does not part" (1982, 4). Later in his chapter, Krafft-Ebing confirms this notion that man can never fully segregate his animal nature from his humanity: "Life is a never-ceasing duel between the animal instinct and morality. Only will-power and a strong character can emancipate man from the meanness of his corrupt nature" (1965, 5). Krafft-Ebing's ontological dualism perpetuates the long-standing philosophical tradition that casts the body as a corrupt, carnal, and volatile thing in tension with the mind: the exalted, spiritual, and moral realm of existence.[1] Man is always at war with himself; he must exert significant mental effort in order for his humanity to overcome his bestiality.

If man fails to constrain his sexual appetites, Krafft-Ebing warns of dire consequences: "Love unbridled is a volcano that burns down and lays waste all around it; it is an abyss that devours all – honour, substance and health" (1965, 2). These statements evince ambivalence towards sexuality and its perversions. The naturalized sexual instinct is constructed as a voracious force that relentlessly seeks gratification. Our nature must be "bridled"; our willpower must be strong, otherwise "sensual power may easily degenerate into the lowest passion and the basest vice" (2). The perversity that Krafft-Ebing later classifies in his casebook is shown to be our own animal instinct gone unchecked by civilizing forces. Consequently, perversity, defined as sexuality that exceeds the boundaries of heterosexual monogamous procreative activity, is revealed as our *natural* animal state. And as Martha Nussbaum has argued, "Disgust has been used throughout history to exclude and marginalize groups of people who come to embody the dominant group's fear and loathing of its own animality" (2004, 14). Krafft-Ebing exemplifies this tendency by employing a rhetoric of disgust towards "base" sexuality to marginalize those who appear to have succumbed to their animal side.

The refining and sublimating power of civilization is also credited with fostering superior social dynamics that protect men and women from subverting their assigned gender roles. However, Krafft-Ebing is quick to point out that proper gender roles are always in danger of slipping into exaggerated or inverted manifestations. For example, the doctor asserts that woman's ultimate virtue rests in her sexual passivity, which is expressed through her modesty and her faithfulness. Yet he concedes that, "among all races, the women are fond of toilet and finery" (1965, 16). Krafft-Ebing further explains that such female vanity is rooted in an unconscious impulse to entice men, an admittedly immodest objective. This is a danger zone for women that must be managed with proper socialization and breeding: "So long as woman seeks only self-gratification in personal adornment, and so long as she remains unconscious of the psychological reasons for thus making herself attractive, no objection can be raised against it, but when done with the fixed purpose to please men it degenerates into coquetry" (17). Woman must be saved from self-knowledge of her own desire to attract men, lest she transgress her proper passive role in courtship and abandon all pretensions of modesty.

For men, their own lustful masculine nature can ironically undermine their gendered role as active pursuer and head of the household. "In the sexual demands of man's nature will be found the motives of his weakness towards woman. He is enslaved by her, and becomes more and more dependent upon her as he grows weaker, and the more he yields to sensuality" (Krafft-Ebing 1965, 15). Accordingly, man's allegedly stronger libido can lead him into a position of weakness. If he prioritizes sensual gratification, his natural role as the one in charge is inverted, and he becomes subservient to his beloved. As with the taming of the inner beast, the abject space between genders is managed through the proper religious, moral, legal, and social constraints; without these safeguards, women might partake in active sexual conduct, and men might yield to a passive sexual position.

Conversely, Krafft-Ebing warns that masculine activity and feminine passivity must not become too extreme, or else civilized society will come to resemble its heathen neighbours. In illustrating this point, he compares Christianity with Islam by considering their respective treatment of women. He states, "The Mohammedan woman is simply a means for sensual gratification and propagation of the species; whilst in the sunny balm of Christian doctrine, blossom forth her divine virtues and her qualities of housewife, companion and mother" (1965, 5). Krafft-Ebing's characterization of Muslim women as mere sexual objects to their male partners places them closer to the animal world. In contrast, he credits the Christian faith for providing women with dignity, humanity, and a place of respect in the social fabric. Yet further in his analysis, Krafft-Ebing admits that even when the proper cultural constraints are engaged, the civilized Christian man still frequently succumbs to savage sexual yearnings: "In spite of the aid which religion, law, education and the moral code offer him, the Christian (to subdue his sensual inclination) often drags pure and chaste love from its sublime pedestal and wallows in the quagmire of sensual enjoyment and lust" (5). No one is ever fully immunized from the lure of sexual hedonism. Abject sexual yearnings continually threaten to overcome the religious teachings of Christianity.

The threat posed by the instability of boundaries separating man from beast, man from woman, and Christian from savage informs and ignites the instability between healthy civilized sexuality and perverse sadomasochistic (s/m) sexuality. Moreover, in Krafft-Ebing's analysis of s/m, he associates the "pathological behaviour" with animal sexuality, gender exaggerations or inversions, and uncivilized sexual practice. As such, he presents sadism and masochism as extreme expressions that emerge from naturalized gender imperatives where men are essentially aggressive and women essentially submissive.

Drawing on both biological and evolutionary theories, Krafft-Ebing postulates that these gender roles are now hardwired into the sex of each individual. For man, sadistic tendencies facilitate his ability to woo and win a woman: "Under normal conditions man meets obstacles which it is his part to overcome, and for which nature has given him an aggressive character" (1965, 85). Krafft-Ebing identifies "the natural shyness and modesty of women" as one such obstacle that man must overcome to achieve sexual union (81). It follows that nature has embedded a sadistic tendency in man to facilitate procreation. However, Krafft-Ebing asserts that through human progress and social evolution, sadism's affects have become subdued. "In the civilized man today, in so far as he is untainted, associations between lust and cruelty are found, but in a weak and rudimentary way" (80–1). As a normal expression in civilized society, sadistic manifestations should take the form only of mild aggression, i.e., "horseplay" in Krafft-Ebing's terms, which includes wrestling, pinching, and biting between couples.

To complement man's inherent aggression, woman is bestowed with an inherent submissiveness that provides masochistic satisfaction. Krafft-Ebing explains that, "owing to her passive role in procreation and long-existent social conditions, ideas of subjection are, in women, normally connected with the idea of sexual relations" (1965, 195). Here, Krafft-Ebing offers two explanations for women's "normal" masochism. He first casts women's role in heterosexual intercourse as inherently "passive," reflecting the biological essentialist characterization of heterosexual union and conception as man (and sperm) actively penetrating and woman (and egg) passively receiving. (Of course one could interpret the act in a different light: woman actively envelops while man is passively engulfed).[2] The second explanation invokes the social conditions of women, which, he implies, have placed them in an inferior position to men. Thus nature and nurture work in tandem to create the normal passive woman. Further, the masochistic instinct is sexually satisfying: "Woman no doubt derives pleasure from her innate coyness and the final victory of man affords her intense and refined gratification" (81). Masochism is to woman what sadism is to man. Custom and nature have worked together to create these complementary instinctual pleasures for the survival of the species.

In support of this view of male–female dynamics, Krafft-Ebing turns to the animal world for confirmation. "Among animals it is always the male who pursues the female ... Playful or actual flight of the female is not infrequently observed; and then the relation is like that between the beast of prey and the victim" (1965, 85n3). This homogeneous and Darwinian portrayal of animal courtship provides a gender-normative blueprint for man's latent sexual inclinations.[3] Although Krafft-Ebing bemoans the tenacious force of man's animal nature, he also positions animalism as the epitome of man's most natural self.

Similarly, Krafft-Ebing turns to "savage" culture to find further proof of sadism and masochism's natural claims on male and female sexuality. "From the history of civilization and anthropology we know that there have been times, as there are savages today that practice it, where the brutal force, robbery, or even blows that rendered woman powerless, were made use to obtain love's desires" (1965, 85). In addition, some foreign women – who Krafft-Ebing implies are less civilized than those in his own society – enjoy their masochistic role as well. "Many women like nothing better than to kneel before their husbands or lovers. Among the lower classes of the Slavs it is said that the wives feel hurt if they are not beaten by their husbands. A Hungarian official informs me that the peasant women of the Somogyer Comitate do not think they are loved by their husbands until they have received the first box on the ear as a sign of love" (197). Here Krafft-Ebing relies on unsubstantiated ethnographic anecdotes as proof that a lower-class woman who comes from a "less civilized" nation will typically display overtly masochistic behaviour. This association of s/m with racialized and working-class sexuality will later be repeated in some cinematic renditions of s/m sexuality (while in others, s/m will be associated with the "filthy" rich).

Within his own society, Krafft-Ebing does not doubt that civilized women also hold some masochistic tendencies. He posits that the reason that science has found few cases of perverse female masochism is again twofold: "Intrinsic and extraneous restraints – modesty and custom – naturally constitute in woman insurmountable obstacles to the expression of perverse sexual instinct" (1965, 197). Nature and nurture have generated masochism in woman, and nature and nurture restrain her from expressing it overtly in civilized societies.

Krafft-Ebing, then, naturalizes a particularly gendered vision of s/m, even as he pathologizes its manifestations in case studies. S/m desire is not inherently perverse. Rather, in the context of an enlightened and civilized society, cultivated citizens are socialized to control and transform animalistic urgings, thereby attenuating s/m instincts. Its occurrence among citizens is explained by individual biological weaknesses that Christian culture has been unable to correct. In particular, Krafft-Ebing subscribed to eugenic explanations where "improper breeding" can produce "psychical degeneration" that unleashes sexual atavistic impulses.

Sigmund Freud: Deriving Sadism and Masochism from Biological Drives

Sigmund Freud, a contemporary of Krafft-Ebing, continued the work of theorizing the origins and effects of sadism and masochism. While his work on sadism replicated the essential thrust of Krafft-Ebing's, his work on masochism was more troubled and unsure. Freud's account for masochistic desire would undergo several different and contradictory versions over a span of twenty-five years, during which he struggled to determine whether masochism was a reverse-formation of sadism, or its own primary instinct.

Freud's theory of sadism, like that of Krafft-Ebing, starts by looking to nature – and in particular naturalized categories of gender – to explain the existence of a primary sadism in men. In his 1910 essay "The Sexual Aberrations," Freud draws on Darwinian explanations of sex selection: "The sexuality of most male human beings contains an element of *aggressiveness* – a desire to subjugate; the biological significance of it seems to lie in the need for overcoming the resistance of the sexual object by means other than wooing" (Freud 1962, 23–4). As with Krafft-Ebing, Freud draws on evolutionary and biological theories to gender sadism as a masculine force, driven by the instinct to procreate. Freud understood pathological sadism as an exaggeration of this aggressive instinct, whereby dominance supplants the "normal sexual aim" of procreative activity and becomes itself a source of pleasure, rather than a means to a pleasurable end (i.e., to sexual intercourse).

Masochism, on the other hand, was a conundrum that Freud would revisit in different contexts, attempting to rationalize how pleasure could be wrought from pain. In 1900, Freud published *The Interpretation of Dreams*, in which he put forth the notion that sexuality and cruelty often work in concert. In this early treatment, Freud made sense of masochism as a derivative of sadism in which the primary sadistic drive is repressed by the ego and undergoes a reversal into masochism. A decade-and-a-half later, in his 1915 essay "Instincts and Their Vicissitudes," Freud reiterated the notion that masochism is, in fact, a "vicissitude," that is, a variation of a primary instinct (1981c). As such, masochism was considered a reworking of primary sadism, with activity transformed into passivity. He dismisses the possibility of a "direct masochistic satisfaction" as "highly doubtful" (128). In 1919, Freud again addressed masochism, this time by analysing the dreams of six patients in "A Child Is Being Beaten" (1981a, 175) . Freud was struck by a recurring theme in their dreams: a child (other than the patient) was being beaten. But later in the lives of these patients, the dream shifts into a scene where the child who is being beaten has become the patient himself or herself. From this transformation of watching another child getting beaten, to becoming the very child getting beaten, Freud found confirmation that masochism is not a primary instinct, but an inverted form of sadism (186). He surmised that the first dream of gazing upon another child's pain was sadistic, but that guilt reverses this pleasure into a masochistic dream.

However, Freud shifted his theory of masochism in later works, understanding its role as a primary drive where the death instinct is directed towards the self. In 1920, Freud wrote *Beyond the Pleasure Principle*, in which he tentatively modified his previous assessment of masochism, stating, "The account that was formerly given of masochism requires emendation as being too sweeping in one respect: there *might* be such a thing as primary masochism – a possibility which I had contested at that time" (1961, 49). While Freud chose not to hypothesize what might characterize a "primary masochism," this admission reveals that masochism was proving to be an enigma for psychoanalytic theory.

Four years later, Freud's 1924 essay "The Economic Problem of Masochism" revamps his previous analysis, postulating that the fusion and diffusion of a life instinct and a death instinct generates a primary instinctual masochism (1981b, 156). The essay enumerates three interconnecting forms of masochism: erotogenic, feminine, and moral. Erotogenic masochism denotes simply the obtaining of sexual pleasure from pain, and thus underlies the latter two types. Feminine masochism occurs when the masochistic individual wants to be treated "like a small and helpless child, but particularly, like a naughty child" (162). Freud conflates femininity with infantilism, asserting that "the wish, which so frequently appears in phantasies, to be beaten by the father stands very close to the other wish, to have a passive (feminine) sexual relation to him and is only a regressive distortion of it" (169). Freud explains that this form of masochism is "feminine" because it ultimately signifies "being castrated, copulated with, or giving birth to a baby" (162). This tautological explanation, which never fully elaborates on why there is a parallel between being beaten by the father, being castrated by the father, having sexual intercourse with the father, and having a baby (although, of course, biological theory at the time did link passivity with femininity), recalls Krafft-Ebing's insistence on gendering masochism as an inherently feminine trait, despite its disproportionate occurrence in men in his case studies.

The specific desire to be "copulated with by the father" leads to the third form of masochism: moral masochism. This last form stems from unconscious guilt over incestuous desire, and a corresponding wish for punishment from an authoritative source (Freud 1981b, 169). Freud saw grave dangers for people who are lured by this masochistic impulse: "Masochism creates a temptation to perform 'sinful' actions which must then be expiated by reproaches of the sadistic conscience … or by chastisement from the great parental power of Destiny. In order to provoke punishment from this last representative of the parents, the masochist must do what is inexpedient, must act against his own interests, must ruin the prospects that open out to him in the real world and must, perhaps, destroy his own real existence" (169–70). This notion of the "self-destructive" masochist whose submissive sexual pleasure bleeds into generalized self-sabotaging behaviour is perpetuated in later s/m discourses, in particular pop cultural ones. It also reflects Krafft-Ebing's dire warning that "love unbridled" is a dangerous force with the potential to annihilate those involved.

It is worth noting that Freud's most developed and forceful essay on masochism, "The Economic Problem of Masochism," still presents the phenomenon as a "problem." As with Krafft-Ebing, Freud seemed quite complacent to explain sadism as an inherently masculine drive grounded in biological urges towards pleasure and procreation. Yet masochism remained a convoluted issue that demanded more explication. Three different shades of masochism – erotogenic, feminine, and moral – were necessary to illustrate its complexity. The apparent senselessness of masochism will later be at issue when feminists and legal practitioners grapple with people, whether male or female, who consent to pain, bondage, or humiliation in pursuit of their own pleasure.

Havelock Ellis: Sadism and Masochism? It's the Same Difference

Writing during the same time period as Freud, the British doctor, social reformer, and sexual psychologist Havelock Ellis was also grappling with sexuality and its attendant perversities. In 1933, ten years after

Freud had published "The Economic Problem of Masochism," Ellis wrote the *Psychology of Sex: A Guide for Students* (1972), in which he addressed sadism and masochism as two versions of the same phenomenon. Indeed, Ellis specifically repudiated Freud's final theory of masochism as a primary instinct, finding it an "ingeniously constructed elaborate hypothesis" that he deemed unnecessary and unhelpful (206). Instead, Ellis preferred the term *algolagnia* to unite sadism and masochism under one rubric that conveyed "the connection between sexual excitement and pain" (198). While sadism denoted the "active form" and masochism the "passive form," for Ellis they together represented two sides of the same perversity.

Like Krafft-Ebing, Ellis located algolagnia in a naturalized discourse of human sexuality. Interestingly, in Ellis's version, both the active and the passive form are experienced by males and females, during what he calls the "primitive phase of courtship" (Ellis 1972, 203). At the beginning of this phase, Ellis contends that men suffer to win their beloved's heart. "The lover is his mistress's servant; he must be ready to undertake all sorts of risks, to encounter many dangers, to fulfill many unpleasant duties, in order to serve her and to gain her favor" (203).[4] In "savage" societies, the lover's trials manifest in extreme and violent ways, as compared to the mild and symbolic ways found in "civilized" societies. To further this savage/civilized binary, Ellis appoints nonhuman animals as the epitome of savage culture: in the animal kingdom, the male suitor often "returns maimed and bleeding from contests with a successful rival" (203). Again, Krafft-Ebing's utilization of the savage/civilized binary is reproduced, as is the use of animal behaviour to stand in for man's most primitive self.

Where Ellis departs from Krafft-Ebing is in his portrayal of the female role during the courtship. While male suffering is represented as the passive form of algolagnia (i.e., masochism), a form of female satisfaction with such suffering is represented as the active form of algolagnia (i.e., sadism). Ellis states, "In the process of courtship the wooer is her slave and she is able to view with pleasure the sufferings she is the cause of, alike to successful and unsuccessful wooers" (1972, 203). In the early stages of courtship, when the female has not yet acquiesced to any particular suitor, Ellis describes her gaze upon her bruised suitors as sadistic.

This power dynamic does not last long. As the courtship progresses to coupledom, Ellis insists that the female will soon be on the passive end of algolagnia. After one suitor triumphs over the others, "she in turn becomes subjugated to her mate and later to her offspring, receiving her full share of the pain which the sexual process allows" (1972, 203). Ellis elaborates on the painful aspects of "mating" by once again drawing a simile between humans and animals. He points out that sometimes "the male at mating time falls into a state of sexual frenzy, and the more passive female suffers … The love bite, again, is an animal as well as human device, and horses, donkeys etc., gently bite the female before coitus" (23). As with Krafft-Ebing, Ellis draws inspiration from the animal kingdom, imposing a particularized view of heteronormative gender roles, as a way to map the most innate sexual tendencies of humans.

The final piece of evidence that Ellis proffers for his thesis are written accounts, both fiction and nonfiction, that verify his claim that love and cruelty often overlap, specifically male cruelty towards a beloved female object. He quotes Lucian from the second century CE, who claimed (through one of his female characters), "He who has not rained blows on his mistress and torn her hair and her garments is not yet in love" (1972, 23). Ellis then takes an example from the seventeenth century, suggesting "the same idea, that for a man to beat his sweetheart is an appreciated sign of love, occurs in one of Cervantes's *Exemplary Novels*" (ibid.). Finally, Ellis jumps to the modern era, quoting Pierre Janet (1859–1947), a French colleague working in psychology, who claimed that one of his female patients said of her husband, "He does not know how to make me suffer a little. One cannot love a man who does not make one suffer a little" (ibid.). Interestingly, in these examples there is no indication that the mistreatment is situated in a sexual context. Rather, it is simply a man assaulting or abusing a woman that is considered a sign of love, not lust. Furthermore, Ellis provides examples where it is the woman, and not the man, who insists females require cruelty from their male lovers in order to feel loved. This recalls Freud's understanding of "moral masochism," where masochistic satisfaction associated with sexual gratification becomes a more generalized yearning to suffer at the hands of one's lover. Ellis's literary examples also resonate with Krafft-Ebing's appropriation of the novels of de Sade and Sacher-Masoch where, in Foucauldian terms, works of fiction were *redoubled* as proof of an ontological claim of the sexual and gendered essence of humans.

Like Krafft-Ebing, Ellis understands the phenomena of sadism and masochism as resting on a solid bed of normal sexual and gendered tendencies. When these tendencies exceed the boundaries of "mild" cruelty and pain, then pathology has set in. Yet unlike Krafft-Ebing, Ellis does not view algolagnia as representative of overexcited atavistic impulses that have overcome civilizing forces; rather, they are indications of physiological weakness in the individual. Those who succumb to algolagnic impulses are hypo-, not hyper-, sexual. Ellis states, "The sadist and the masochist alike merely use pain as a method of drawing on a great reservoir of primitive emotion, which imparts energy to a feeble sexual impulse" (1972, 205). In other words, those who are less sexual, less virile, and less healthy must use algolagnia to stimulate a fledgling libido. This is contrasted to Krafft-Ebing's classification of sadism and masochism as subsets of *hyperesthesia sexualis*, that is, "abnormally increased sexual desire" (Krafft-Ebing 1965, 69).

The Diagnostic and Statistical Manuals

Concurrent with the research of Krafft-Ebing, Freud, and Ellis, and that of many other doctors and psychologists of sexuality were institutional responses to the emerging discourses of sexuality. By the middle of the nineteenth century, the notion that "madness" could be clinically diagnosed and parsed into separate pathologies was gaining momentum (Foucault 1990, 51). It became apparent, however, that there was confusion about the exact definitions and criteria for each specific mental disease. Official endeavours were undertaken in the United States to clarify and unify nomenclature of mental illness and to provide statistical data on its frequency. In 1918, the Committee on Statistics of the American Psychiatric Association (then called the American Medico-Psychological Association), along with the National Committee on Mental Hygiene, created the *Statistical Manual for the Use of Hospitals for Mental Diseases* (American Psychiatric Association 1942). In 1952, this was followed by the first edition of the *DSM* (the "*DSM-I*") published by the American Psychiatric Association Committee on Nomenclature and Statistics (American Psychiatric Association 1952). Right from its inception, the *DSM-I* identified sexuality as a site where deviations from the norm were to be ascertained and treated. In its definition of the diagnosis of sexual deviation, the manual states, "This diagnosis is reserved for deviant sexuality which is not symptomatic of more extensive syndromes, such as schizophrenic and obsessional reactions. The term includes most of the cases formerly classed as 'psychopathic personality with pathologic sexuality.' The diagnosis will specify the type of the pathologic behavior, such as homosexuality, transvestism, pedophilia, fetishism and sexual sadism (including rape, sexual assault, mutilation)" (38–9). The definition thus seeks to carve out a specific arena for sexual deviations. With sexual deviation no longer piggy-backing on other diagnoses like schizophrenia, the incitement to discourse called for it to have its own specified place in the manual, where it could be analysed and defined on its own terms.

The *DSM-I* also catalogues a non-exclusive list of sexual deviancies, which includes sadism. Masochism had yet to make its appearance in the literature, but sadism was specified and is further elaborated parenthetically with examples of its form. Yet despite the fact that the diagnosis for sexual deviancy takes up only six lines, its description indicates the escalating textuality of sexuality. It is also worth noting that the *DSM-I* had more than tripled in size from its predecessor, the *Statistical Manual for the Use of Hospitals for Mental Diseases*. Hence Foucault's observation becomes apparent, in that the compulsion to speak sex in the mental health field was indeed proliferating, demanding more detail in its relentless pursuit of the "truth" of the human psyche.

In the next edition published in 1968, the *DSM-II* further elaborated on the category of sexual deviancy (American Psychiatric Association 1968). Not only would the length of its description increase, but it would offer subsections of specific forms of sexual deviation:

> This category is for individuals whose sexual interests are directed primarily toward objects other than people of the opposite sex, toward sexual acts not usually associated with coitus, or toward coitus performed under bizarre circumstances as in necrophilia, pedophilia, sexual sadism, and fetishism …

    302.0 Homosexuality
    302.1 Fetishism
    302.2 Pedophilia
    302.3 Transvestism
    302.4 Exhibitionism
    302.5 Voyeurism
    302.6 Sadism
    302.7 Masochism
    302.8 Other sexual deviation (44)

The section has thus propagated subsections that offer more precision in diagnosis. Masochism finally appears on the sexual deviancy stage as a verifiable mental disorder. However, none of the enumerated sexual deviations are defined. Those consulting the *DSM-II* would have to look to other scientific literature to understand the substance of the specific disorders. The most that can be gleaned about s/m at this point in the *DSM* series is that sadism involves "coitus ... performed under bizarre circumstances" (44).

Despite the postulation of scientific objectivity, the subjective descriptor "bizarre" invokes both abjection and disgust. Such acts have become *abjectified* as they transgress the normal procreative boundaries of "coitus" and infect it with a grotesqueness worthy of medical intervention. To deem it "bizarre" further draws up disgust-driven emotion to distance normal coitus from these deviations, and to justify the pathologization of the sexual practice by mental health authorities.

While both the *DSM-I* and the *DSM-II* came in at roughly 130 pages, the *DSM-III*, published in 1980, jumped to 494 pages (American Psychiatric Association 1981). In addition, the section on sexual deviancy was redubbed "Paraphilias," and went from half a page in the *DSM-II* to eleven pages. The *DSM-III* states that the term *paraphilia* was consciously chosen over *sexual deviation* because "it correctly emphasizes that the deviation (para) lies in that to which the person is attracted (philia)" (279). In other words, the problem is found in the trajectory of desire, not with the sexual response cycle itself. This latter category of mental disorders would now fall under the newly added category of "sexual dysfunctions." The *DSM-III* further nuances the category of sexual pathology, parsing it into multiple sections and subsections, and offering more avenues for analysis, pathologization, and diagnosis. The proliferation of sexual discourse had again gone through a rapid growth spurt.

The rhetoric of the *DSM-III* also strives for more objectivity than earlier editions. The laden word *bizarre* is dropped for a more clinical understanding of sexual abnormality. The manual describes paraphilias as "characterized by arousal in response to sexual objects or situations that are not part of normative arousal-activity patterns and that in varying degrees may interfere with the capacity for reciprocal, affectionate sexual activity" (279). This characterization of paraphilias is layered with both detachment and disapproval. Instead of classifying sexual paraphilias as inherently "bizarre," the manual acknowledges that society has created normative standards applicable to arousal and sexuality.

Beneath this anti-essentialist gloss, however, the *DSM-III* goes on to offer an ideologically based explanation for why society must be concerned: these paraphilias that defy normative standards may detract from "reciprocal, affectionate sexual activity." The underlying message is that sexuality *should* involve reciprocity and affection, i.e., it should be emotionally connected with another person and not merely a tool for physical pleasure.

In terms of the specific diagnoses of sadism and masochism, the *DSM* series went from merely enumerating these mental disorders in the second edition, to offering pages of explanation and specific criteria in the third. Where the *DSM-II* had left it to the reader to extrapolate what could constitute masochism or sadism, the *DSM-III* offers explicit detail on its many practices, including rape fantasies, binding, bondage, blindfolding, cutting, pinning, piercing, paddling, spanking, humiliation, being defecated or urinated upon, acting like an animal, electric shocks, and self-mutilation (286). The *DSM-III* warns that sexual masochism can entail "hypoxphilia," where sexual arousal is obtained through oxygen deprivation, which can lead to unintentional death.

This scrupulous litany of masochistic acts, ranging from the "mildest" form in rape fantasies to the most "dangerous" form in asphyxiation, gives the reader a graphic picture of masochism's many possibilities. On its face, the text attempts to assist its readers in identifying masochism's variable forms. Yet Foucault reminds us that "we must conceive of discourse as a series of discontinuous segments whose tactical function is neither uniform nor stable" (1990, 100). Viewed in this light, the list also operates as a frank sexual text that not only allows for voyeuristic pleasures in gazing upon the sexual other, but also acts as an inspirational document, revealing the variety of pleasure open to someone who is willing to step outside of "reciprocal affectionate sexual activity."

At the end of the narrative description of sexual masochism, a boxed text provides the official "Diagnostic criteria for 302.83 Sexual Masochism":

A. Over a period of at least six months, recurrent intense sexual urges and sexually arousing fantasies involving the act (real, not simulated) of being humiliated, beaten, bound, or otherwise made to suffer.
B. The person has acted on these urges, or is markedly distressed by them.
(American Psychiatric Association 1981, 287)

Both A and B must be fulfilled to merit a diagnosis of sexual masochism. The diagnosis thus requires two crucial elements: the patient must have experienced recurrent sexual impulses involving her own suffering, and she must have acted on such feelings or be significantly distressed by them. On the surface, the "distress" criterion makes some sense. If a patient reports to a health professional that she is markedly distressed about her sexuality, she presumably requires assistance. But what the *DSM* does not contemplate is that she could be distressed because of social stigma, and not because there is something inherently wrong with her sexuality (Wright 2010, 1230). The other possible criterion – that the patient acted on her feelings – exemplifies the historical psychiatric privileging of mental willpower.

Recall Krafft-Ebing's construction of sexuality as a voracious force that continually tugs at "man's" willpower. To resist its harmful allure, Krafft-Ebing asserted that if he has the strength of mind, a man should be able to tame the destructive impulses and channel his sexuality towards socially acceptable expressions. Similarly, in the *DSM-III's* criteria for sexual masochism, you are still considered non-pathological – even if you have masochistic urges – so long as you have the willpower to resist these urges (and so long as there is no distress). Simply put, the non-pathological individual can assert mind over matter. The perversion thus lies in the assessment that you have allowed sexual matters to overcome your rational mind.

Similar to the section on masochism, the section on sexual sadism also includes a detailed list of activities: "Sadistic fantasies or acts may involve activities that indicate the dominance of the person over the victim (e.g., forcing the victim to crawl, or keeping the victim in a cage), or restraint, blindfolding, paddling, spanking, whipping, pinching, beating, burning, electrical shocks, rape, cutting or stabbing, strangulation, torture, mutilation, or killing" (American Psychiatric Association 1981, 287). Again, as with the section on masochism, the list fleshes out multiple instances of sadistic activity. And in its search for the truth of sadistic paraphiliac sexuality, the text allows the reader voyeuristic and perhaps vicarious pleasure in learning about all the ways one can make another suffer.

The *DSM-III* also lumps three categories of sexual sadists together: those with sadistic fantasies, those who enact sexual sadism on a consenting partner (who may "suffer" from sexual masochism), and those who inflict their sexual urges on non-consenting victims. The manual unifies these categories of sadism through the central fact that "it is the suffering of the victim that is sexually arousing" (American Psychiatric Association 1981, 287). There is no attempt to discern the different pleasures that might be engaged with a consenting as opposed to a non-consenting partner. Further, the recipient of the sadistic activity is rendered a *victim* in the assessment. This erasure of a masochist's agency in a consensual sexual encounter with a sadist will later be replicated in theoretical, pop cultural, and legal representations of s/m encounters.

The manual's conception of masochism and sadism reveals a significant difference between the two: the authors suggest that only sadism can be potentially inflicted on a non-consenting partner, and not masochism. This perception of masochism's inherently passive nature further compounds the view that masochism is, as Freud put it, a "problem." The psychiatric authorities find it inconceivable that the sexual desire to be dominated is an active impulse that can be inflicted on another.

The *DSM-III* identifies another issue peculiar to sadism, which is that "usually … the severity of the sadistic acts increases over time" (American Psychiatric Association 1981, 287). No evidence is cited to support this claim. Interestingly, the manual does not make the same claim about masochism. Sadism appears to be more susceptible to the notion of a slippery slope where, for example, the belief is that a light spanking ultimately leads to a severe beating. Embedded in this idea is the understanding of sadism as insatiable; part of its thrill is the newness of the activity. Once a particular sadistic act loses its novelty, it also loses its kick. The supposed escalating desires of sadism then pose a particular danger to consensual masochists, who may be forced into more extreme activities to keep their sadistic lovers happy. This depiction of the naive masochist who gets in over her head will also be conveyed in a variety of other discourses that contend with s/m.

Published in 1994, the *DSM-IV* marked a small victory for many sadomasochists who were attempting to de-pathologize their desires (American Psychiatric Association 1994). Though the descriptions of both sadism and masochism remained essentially unchanged, the diagnostic criteria underwent one significant modification: acting on the sadistic or masochistic urge no longer automatically signifies a mental disorder. In 2000, a "text revision" of the *DSM-IV*, entitled the *DSM-IV-TR*, was published (American Psychiatric Association 2000). I will cite from this manual, as the definitions for the *DSM-IV* and the *DSM-IV-TR* are virtually identical. The diagnostic criteria for sexual masochism states:

A. Over a period of at least 6 months, recurrent, intense sexually arousing fantasies, sexual urges, or behaviors involving the act (real, not simulated) of being humiliated, beaten, bound, or otherwise made to suffer.

> B. The fantasies, sexual urges, or behaviors cause clinically significant distress or impairment in social, occupational, or other important areas of functioning. (573)

Practising masochists who do not experience "clinically significant distress" or "impairment in important areas of functioning" are therefore not deemed to be suffering from the paraphilia of "sexual masochism."

Similarly, the diagnostic criteria for sexual sadism had also been revamped in the *DSM-IV-TR* to allow a space for non-pathological sadism. It states:

> A. Over a period of at least 6 months, recurrent, intense sexually arousing fantasies, sexual urges, or behaviors involving acts (real, not simulated) in which the psychological or physical suffering (including humiliation) of the victim is sexually exciting to the person.
>
> B. The person has acted on these sexual urges with a nonconsenting person, or the sexual urges or fantasies cause marked distress or interpersonal difficulty. (American Psychiatric Association 2000, 574)

Again, as with sexual masochism, part A remains virtually unchanged. It is part B that is altered to express a fundamentally different conception of the disorder. Whereas in the *DSM-III*, acting on the sadistic impulse alone would have qualified the individual as an official "sexual sadist," in the *DSM-IV-TR* there are only three reasons why such a label is merited: if the activity is imposed with a non-consenting person, if it causes marked distress, or if it creates interpersonal difficulty. This allows for the possibility that sexual sadism can be practised within certain confines without warranting the clinical label of "sexual sadist."

Although the diagnostic criteria for sexual sadism and sexual masochism have been changed to de-pathologize certain sadomasochistic activities, the difference between their respective Part Bs conveys different concerns about each tendency. While both sexual urges will require a diagnosis if there is "clinically significant" or "marked" distress, again only sadism is contemplated as an urge that can be forced on a non-consenting individual. Once again, masochism is categorized as inherently passive, lacking the threat or the forcefulness to be inflicted on another. At first glance, this assumption may appear reasonable: how do you force someone to force you? In fact, in a 2003 family law case that will later be discussed, *Nova Scotia (Minister of Community Services) v. A.C.*, evidence pointed to a woman being forced to sexually dominate her partner, although this was disregarded by the court on the basis of the view that one cannot impose one's own masochism on an unwilling partner.

Another notable difference in the *DSM-IV-TR* is how sadistic and masochistic tendencies can blemish other areas of life. The manual states that sexual masochism occurs if there is impairment in "social, occupational, or other important areas of functioning," while sexual sadism occurs if the feelings cause "interpersonal difficulty." Masochism emerges as a problem that is more diffused than sadism, and one that can threaten a person's overall functioning, not just in the interpersonal or sexual realm. Sadism's issue is more focused; its danger lies in how it affects relations with others. Despite masochism's purported passivity, the *DSM-IV-TR* constructs this paraphilia as a more far-reaching hazard, the meaning and significance of which is not contained within the sexual or interpersonal realm. This differentiation recalls Freud's conception of moral masochism as a pathology that can ruin an individual by causing her to seek pain and self-destruction in areas of life beyond the bedroom. In this sense, although masochism arrived after sadism in the *DSM* series, the *DSM-IV-TR* supports Freud's later view that this sexuality is potentially destructive and in need of diagnosis and treatment.

However. the most recent edition. published in May 2013, the *DSM-V*, appears to offer a more tolerant approach to those who practise s/m and are in contact with the mental health profession. This tolerance rests in the fact that the *DSM-V* allows that not all who have a paraphilia will experience paraphiliac *disorder*.[5] For example, with sexual masochism, the definitional criteria are:

Sexual Masochism Disorder [302.83]
A. Over a period of at least 6 months, recurrent and intense sexual arousal from the act of being humiliated, beaten, bound, or otherwise made to suffer, as manifested by fantasies, urges, or behaviors.
B. The fantasies, sexual urges, or behaviors cause clinically significant distress or impairment in social, occupational, or other important areas of functioning. (American Psychiatric Association 2013, 694)

If someone meets only criterion A, but not B, then according to the "Diagnostic Features" section, the individual can be said to have a paraphilic interest in masochism, but not a paraphilic disorder. If she meets both criteria A and B, then she suffers from sexual masochism disorder. Similarly, the diagnostic criteria for sexual sadism disorder state:

Sexual Sadism Disorder [302.84]
A. Over a period of at least 6 months, recurrent and intense sexual arousal
from the physical or psychological suffering of another person, as manifested by fantasies, urges, or behaviors.
B. The individual has acted on these sexual urges with a nonconsenting
person, or the sexual urges or fantasies cause clinically significant distress
or impairment in social, occupational, or other important areas of functioning. (American Psychiatric Association 2013, 695)

Again, meeting only criterion A indicates a paraphilic interest in sadism, but not a paraphilic disorder. If she meets both criteria A and B, then she suffers from sexual sadism disorder. The sub-workgroup that headed revisions of the *DSM–V*'s paraphilia section justified this approach by explaining that it "leaves intact the distinction between normative and non-normative sexual behavior, which could be important to research-ers, but without automatically labeling non-normative sexual behavior as psychopathological."[6]

While this may seem like a helpful distinction, the s/m practitioner is still halfway to a psychopathology, even if she does not meet the B crite-rion. Remember that the text is called the *Diagnostic and Statistical Manual of Mental Disorders*, suggesting that all included categories are associated with disorder. After all, the *DSM* is not a sociology text that addresses sexual variation, but rather a guidebook for medical practitioners whose labels – whether paraphilia or paraphilic disorder – can have serious ef-fects on a person's status in society. As Susan Wright suggests, despite the clinical separation, the paraphilia – even without being labelled a disorder – still carries with it a diagnostic code, which may in turn lead social service providers and legal authorities to continue to see con-sensual sadism and masochism as pathological (Wright 2010, 1230). Furthermore, in some ways, the *DSM-V*'s distinction between paraphil-ia and paraphiliac disorder can be seen as a step backwards from the *DSM-IV-TR*. Recall that in the *DSM-IV-TR*, if someone practises "mas-ochism" or "sadism" that is consensual and does not cause significant distress, impairment, or interpersonal difficulty, in theory, the labels of "sexual sadist" or "sexual masochist" would not be applied at all. In the *DSM-V*, the net has been widened, and such a person would be diag-nosed with a paraphilia, which of course can still be stigmatizing, even if it is not deemed a "disorder." Despite these concerns, the National Coalition of Sexual Freedom (NCSF), an American group that focuses on the rights of the s/m community, has taken a pragmatic approach.

Their public statement on the *DSM-V* states: "NCSF continues to urge the complete removal of these paraphilias from the DSM. However like the incremental removal of homosexuality (to egodystonic homosexuality and then finally taken out in 1987) this is an important step for the BDSM-leather-fetish community" (NCSF 2010).

Another important change to note in the *DSM-V* is that the first part of criterion B for both sexual masochism and sexual sadism has become identical: "The person has clinically significant distress or impairment in important areas of functioning." In this way, both masochism and sadism are constructed as having the same potential to cause personal problems in the individual. But, as with the *DSM-IV-TR*, only sadism is contemplated as a sexuality that can be forced upon another. The picture of masochism as inherently non-threatening to others remains intact.

Conversely, the masochist's potential to physically harm herself is underscored in one erotic practice. Sexual masochism disorder's diagnostic criteria instructs the diagnostician to specify if the disorder is accompanied with "asphyxiophilia" where "the individual engages in the practice of achieving sexual arousal related to restriction of breathing" (American Psychiatric Association 2013, 694). Later in the description of the disorder, the manual warns that "accidental death while practicing asphyxiaphilia" is a potential consequence of the disorder (695). Linking this stigmatized activity with masochism, and then constructing it as potentially fatal, helps to justify the pathologization of masochistic desire. In addition, this concern of the risks associated with what the BDSM community calls "breath play" can be also seen in feminist, pop cultural, and legal discourses, in particular, with the film *Killing Me Softly* and the case, *R. v. J.A.*, which I shall discuss later in this book.

Interestingly, commentary that accompanies the diagnostic criteria for both disorders in the *DSM-V* has some oblique, and sometimes misleading, references to the BDSM sexual subculture, something not seen in previous editions of the manual. Under the subsection "Differential Diagnosis" of sexual sadism disorder, the manual recognizes that "the majority of individuals who are active in community networks that practice sadistic or masochistic behaviours do not express any dissatisfaction with their sexual interests, and their behaviour would not meet DSM-5 criteria for sexual sadism disorder" (American Psychiatric Association 2013, 697). This sentence is a breakthrough in the DSM psychiatric discourse, as it claims that the *majority* of s/m practitioners are not, by definition, mentally disordered. Yet in another section, consensual BDSM comes to be linked with disorder and criminal behaviour.

The "Prevalence" subsection under sexual masochism disorder states, "The population prevalence of sexual masochism disorder is unknown. In Australia, it has been estimated that 2.2% of males and 1.3% of females had been involved in bondage and discipline, sadomasochism, or dominance and submission in the past 12 months" (694). The "Development and Course" subsection under sexual sadism disorder references the same study, immediately after a statement noting that sexual sadism in forensic samples is a mostly male phenomenon (697). Strangely, the *DSM-V* does not provide a citation to this Australian study. However, given the regional context and specific percentages provided, I am confident the references are to Richters, Visser, Rissel, Grulich, and Smith (2008). The study, which specifically set out to test the implicit anti-s/m assumptions found in the *DSM-IV-TR*, found that those who practise BDSM are not more likely than the general population to have had a history of being sexually coerced, or to experience psychological or sexual difficulties. While the study does contain the prevalence information cited by the *DSM–V*, the figures represent persons engaged in BDSM practice, not persons suffering from paraphilic disorders. It is therefore misleading and problematic that the *DSM–V* cites the study in its discussions of sexual masochist *disorder*, and forensic (i.e., criminal) sexual sadism. In other words, while the inclusion of terminology such as "bondage and discipline" can be seen as a step towards recognition of the s/m subculture, the fact that an empirical study that de-pathologizes sadomasochists is used in explicating their pathologization reflects not just the misuse of a reference, but perhaps more troubling, the continuing conflation of consensual s/m with mental disorder.

Another issue of concern in the commentary is found under the subsection "Associated Features Supporting Diagnosis." In this short two-line subsection, the only associated feature identified is the extensive use of pornography for both disorders. The association of pornography with practice, specifically pathological and non-consensual practice, reflects the long-standing moral panic about the effects of graphically explicit material in the socio-legal imaginary. As we shall see in chapter 4, the criminalization of BDSM pornography as obscene in Canada is built upon the assumption that the material causes harm. The *DSM-V* now provides psychiatric support to the truth-claim that consuming BDSM pornography is itself an indicator of a mental disorder and can lead to the enactment of such activities, with or without the consent of others.

The final issue I would like to point out with the *DSM-V* is, I believe, an error or oversight in the "Diagnostic Features" subsection of sexual sadism disorder. The text states, "If admitting individuals declare no distress exemplified by anxiety, obsessions, guilt, or shame, about these paraphilic impulses, and are not hampered by them in pursuing other goals, and their self-reported, psychiatric, or legal histories indicate that they do not act on them, they could be ascertained as having sadistic sexual interest but they would *not* meet criteria for sexual sadism disorder" (American Psychiatric Association 2013, 696). I believe the authors of this text forgot that, according to the diagnostic criteria, the third issue they address is not whether the sexual sadist in question has acted on her impulses, but whether she has acted on them with a non-consenting person. In other words, this part of the commentary overlooks the importance of consent in making the distinction between interest and disorder. While the official diagnostic criteria are more important than the commentary, such word choices can have serious implications for individuals. Frances Allen, chair of the *DSM-IV* Task Force and a key critic of the *DSM-V*, has warned "not to underestimate the potential mischief caused by seemingly tiny word changes." As an example, he elaborates, "My greatest regret about DSM-IV was our inadvertent substitution of an 'or' for an 'and' in the criteria set for Paraphilia. This one stupid slip contributed to the unconstitutional preventive detention of thousands of sex offenders" (Allen 2013). Similarly, one can imagine anti-s/m psy experts on the stand exploiting this part of the commentary to suggest that anyone who acts on her sadistic impulses, regardless of consent of the other, is suffering sexual sadism disorder. Indeed, my analysis in chapter 5 will demonstrate that, despite the fact that the *DSM-IV* and the *DSM-IV-TR* allow for functional, consensual non-pathological sadism and masochism in theory, psy experts frequently referred to these DSM texts to testify that s/m acts, in and of themselves, were evidence of pathology. Thus, despite the disaggregation of a paraphilia from a paraphilic disorder in the updated diagnostic criteria, the *DSM-V*'s ambivalent and sometimes misleading wording may continue to contribute to the marginalization and criminalization of s/m practitioners in legal cases.

Challenging the Pathologizing Gaze

While the official psychiatric regime continues to regard s/m desires as worthy of paraphilic labelling, as evidenced by the criteria of the *DSM-V*, other scholars have attempted to challenge this pathologizing perspective. In *Pain & Passion: A Psychoanalyst Explores the World of*

S & M (1991), Robert Stoller produces an ethnographic study of s/m practitioners that not only humanizes them, but also breaks down the barrier between perversion and normalcy. While highlighting the specific characteristics of the s/m subculture, his project effectively de-exceptionalizes s/m practitioners, such as when he observes, "My non S&M psychoanalytic patients are at least as self-destructive as my S&M informants and patients" (28). More recently, Staci Newmahr's 2011 participant observation ethnography of the Caeden SM community in England further contextualizes s/m practitioners and theorizes the meaning of this marginalized sexuality from the inside. The fact that Newmahr personally participated in s/m sessions as part of her research, and chronicled these events as part of her monograph, radically breaks down the binary between scientific observer and s/m participants as objects of knowledge, and thus continues the project of de-stigmatization. From a place of complexity and ambivalence, Margot Weiss's 2011 ethnographic study of the BDSM community in San Francisco's Bay Area tracks the circuits between sexual desire, BDSM practices, and larger social relations. Refusing to either pathologize or romanticize BDSM, Weiss interrogates BDSM sexual practices within the context of late capitalism. On a broader scale, Thomas S. Weinberg (2006) has canvassed social scientific literature from the last three decades that also demonstrates a counter-discourse. He argues that empirical studies from the social sciences have found that s/m practitioners are not characteristically deviant or unhealthy, but rather are "emotionally and psychologically well balanced, generally comfortable with their sexual orientation, and socially well adjusted" (37).

In support of these perspectives, I end this chapter by briefly considering the current oppositional work of Charles Moser, a doctor, professor, and chair of the Department of Sexual Medicine for the Institute for Advanced Study of Human Sexuality in San Francisco, and Peggy Kleinplatz, a clinical psychologist, sex therapist, and professor in the Faculty of Medicine and the School of Psychology at the University of Ottawa. Their scholarship is particularly important because both doctors specifically address and challenge the *DSM*'s criteria for identifying a paraphilia on scientific terms. They have also brought together interdisciplinary challenges to the pathologization of s/m though their co-edited anthology, *Sadomasochism: Powerful Pleasures* (2006), which seeks to interrogate the meanings of s/m, document the political resistance to hegemonic constructions, and highlight the misunderstandings and prejudices that stigmatize sadomasochists. In further challenging the clinical gaze, Moser has also teamed up with J.J. Madeson, a self-identified practitioner of s/m, to demystify and explore s/m in their book, *Bound to Be Free: The SM Experience* (1996).

For Kleinplatz and Moser, sadomasochists' experience of stigmatization can be attributed largely to the classification of sexual sadism and sexual masochism in the *DSM-IV-TR*. In their essay "Is SM Pathological" (2005) they argue that despite the *DSM-IV-TR*'s claims to objectivity and empiricism, a survey of the literature demonstrates that cultural values, and not scientific data, underscore the definitions of sadism and masochism. They conclude, "There is no evidence to demonstrate that SM, however common or uncommon, creates personal distress or dysfunction for participants, or otherwise endangers consenting individuals any more than occurs in the course of other, socially sanctioned pastimes" (259). The authors accordingly advocate the removal of sadism and masochism from future editions of the *DSM*.

In their essay "Does Heterosexuality Belong in the DSM?" (2005a), Moser and Kleinplatz de-familiarize the issue of sexual pathology and highlight the prejudices against unusual sexual activities. By carefully transposing the criteria for a paraphilia to heterosexuality, the authors propose the following definition for a new disorder:

> Diagnostic criteria for 302.1 Heterosexuality
> A. Over a period of at least six months, recurrent, intense sexually arousing fantasies, sexual urges, or behaviors involving sexual activity with an adult of the other sex.
> B. The person has acted on these sexual urges with a non-consenting person, or the fantasies, sexual urges, or behavior cause clinically significant distress or impairment in social, occupational, or other important area of functioning. (262)

The authors then outline common heterosexual behaviours (e.g., the high divorce rate, or the prevalence of sexual harassment) that demonstrate that under the *DSM-IV-TR*, heterosexuality could just as easily be classified as a mental disorder and a paraphilia as the other listed paraphilias. Their agenda, of course, is not to have heterosexuality added to future editions of the *DSM*, but rather to show the anti-kinky bias of the *DSM-IV-TR*. The authors conclude that the classification of certain unusual sexual behaviour as paraphilias is not based on any unique identifiable harm or danger engendered in the sexual practices, but rather is a means of exercising social control.

Perhaps most radically, in "*DSM-IV-TR* and the Paraphilias: An Argument for Removal" (2005b), Moser and Kleinplatz argue that the concept of a "paraphilia" as a psychopathology fails to meet the definition of a mental disorder, as defined by the *DSM*. The *DSM* claims that its diagnoses are based on objective science, but after a literature review and an examination of the factual claims put forth regarding paraphilias, the authors conclude, "The *DSM* criteria for diagnosis of unusual sexual interests as pathological rests on a series of unproven and more importantly, untested assumptions" (106). The authors further point out that the pathologizing of unusual sexual practices has led to serious social disenfranchisement for the practitioners, including loss of jobs, loss of child custody, failed security checks, and victimization of assault (107).

Although they emphasize the negative social consequences of the pathologization of paraphilias, in particular for sadomasochists, a large part of the persuasiveness of Moser and Kleinplatz's arguments lies with their credentials as doctors and scientists. They seek to demonstrate that the inclusion of the paraphilias is insupportable from a scientific perspective. While this stance, of course, attaches truth to rationality, objectivity, and empiricism, their counter-hegemonic strategy has significant epistemological force because they challenge the *DSM* on its own terms. Moser's testimony and insights will further come up in the chapters on law, as he appears in the obscenity case of *R. v. Price* and in the human rights case of *Hayes v. Vancouver Police Department* as an expert witness who testifies to the benign nature of s/m (*R. v. Price* 2004 and *Hayes v. Vancouver Police Department and Barker* 2010). In addition, in chapter 5, I cite Moser, along with his co-author, Marty Klein, on a child custody case, where an s/m practitioner lost most of her access rights to her child because of the pathologization of her s/m relationship. The work of Moser and Kleinplatz, along with their co-authors and the social science literature, thus points to recent contestation of s/m as a mental disorder.

Conclusion

Before moving onto an examination of the feminist discursive treatment of sadism and masochism, it is worth recapitulating the main themes articulated so far in the medical-psychological literature. In the works of Krafft-Ebing, Freud, and Ellis, sexuality emerges as both an epistemological and an ontological stage upon which science enacts particular truth-claims of humanity, animality, and gendered essences. Sexuality is reified as an observable and knowable thing within discourses that seek to separate human from animal, mind from body, civilized from savage, man from woman, and normal sexuality from pathological sexuality. Yet paradoxically, sadism and masochism are constructed as natural phenomena, rooted in biological impulses particular to the separate masculine and feminine roles that nature has bestowed on human and animal kind. Thus all three of these doctors understood sadism and masochism as exaggerations, not contradictions, of natural biological drives. The pathology rests with their excessiveness and their detachment from procreative activity.

The *DSM* series continues the project of discerning sexual disorders by offering precise definitions and diagnoses of sexual behaviour in need of medical intervention. From one edition to the next, there is an increase in lines, in pages, and in the details of the enumerated sexual pathologies. The definitions of sadism and masochism offer voyeuristic glimpses of these sexual disorders from a clinical distance. And despite the fact that the most recent definitions of sadism and masochism have de-pathologized certain consensual sadomasochistic activity, the labels of "sexual sadism" and "sexual masochism" remain as paraphilias and hazard zones that, in effect, are guilty until proven innocent. The *DSM-V* continues to exceptionalize sadism and masochism, but spawns even more categories by separating paraphilia from paraphilic disorder. Though the *DSM* series never articulates positively what sexual order would look like, the reader knows from the list of sexual disorders what it is *not*. The narrative indicates that sexual order becomes tainted when s/m comes into play and can be fully debased into sexual disorder if the behaviour is not held in check.

In addition to the social scientific scholarship, the writings of Moser and Kleinplatz represent an oppositional movement against the pathologization of s/m, and indeed all the "paraphilias." The doctors challenge the unsubstantiated claims of the harms and dangers of paraphilias, which reflect not objective science, but bias and an agenda of social control. Interestingly, their argument for a removal of the paraphilia section from the *DSM* points also to an opposition to the expanding discursivity of sexuality. They suggest *less* discourse about sexuality, at least in the fields of mental disorder. And although the *DSM* has not yet adopted these perspectives, the following chapters demonstrate that they can have influence in the legal regulation and construction of s/m.

2

Feminists Divided:
The Battle over S/M in the Sex Wars

In the last chapter on medico-scientific accounts of sadism and masochism, s/m theorists adopted a clinical gaze to separate the medical expert from his object of study. By contrast, when sadomasochism (s/m) began to emerge as a point of contention for Western feminists, there was no claim of impartiality: this was personal.

This chapter situates the treatment of s/m during a turbulent period in feminist history known as "the sex wars" and deconstructs the truth-claims generated amidst these acrimonious decades. While there is no precise timeline of when the wars started or ended (or indeed, whether there was ever truly a resolution), the most intense battles took place from the late 1970s to the early 1990s, with definite skirmishes occurring both before and after this time.[1]

The sex wars encompassed a range of multiple yet interconnected issues. S/m was a key area of dispute, but there were also heated disagreements about pornography, butch-femme lesbian identity, public sex, transgenderism, sex work, monogamy, heterosexuality, bisexuality, dildo use, and in fact any sort of vaginal penetration for sexual stimulation.[2] Although there was some notable criss-crossing of positions, combatants generally divided themselves into two camps: those who categorically opposed some or all of the above practices, and those who did not – either because they felt personally implicated as practitioners, or because they perceived their opponents as having oversimplified the political implications.

The "against" feminists fell into a variety of subgroups that represented distinct but overlapping analyses and agendas. They included lesbian feminists, lesbian separatists, political lesbians, anti-pornography feminists, dominance feminists, and radical feminists. The feminists in the rival camp were also a heterogeneous bunch, loosely united by their advocacy for distinct, yet again often overlapping, political agendas. They included anti-censorship feminists, sex-positive feminists, sex-radical feminists, and of course those who identified with a controversial practice, such as butches, femmes, or sadomasochists. There is one more faction that should be noted here: the "neutral" camp. These feminists, who produced a number of retrospectives after the height of the sex wars, claimed to offer a more impartial examination of the issues without taking sides.[3]

I offer no pretensions of neutrality in my analysis of these various camps. It should be obvious from my first two chapters that my sympathies favour the "sex-radical" position. That being said, however, I endeavour to interrogate the truth-claims about s/m that were put forth from *every* side of the debate. I acknowledge I devote more time to deconstructing the platforms espoused by s/m's most ardent detractors, as well as the position held by more "moderate" voices, and less time on discussing arguments from the pro-s/m side. This is because those who objected to s/m seemed compelled to offer more elaborate analyses regarding *the truth* of s/m than did those who defended the practice. In addition, lesbian sadomasochists often countered criticism indirectly by writing erotica that affirmed their desires, most of which falls outside of my analytical mandate.

A primary purpose of this chapter is to contextualize the s/m sex wars as an incitement to sexual discourse. Having a "war" allowed all participants to continually be engaged in heated sexual dialogue. There was a constant call for feminists to conduct a more rigorous self-interrogation of their sexual feelings, to share their shameful desires, and to then interpret those desires properly. Which sexual practices were to be deemed feminist? Which were to be rejected as patriarchal? Was there an acceptable transition between these two realms? And who was entitled to decide? All this and more had to be investigated, revised, settled upon, and then put into action. And all this discourse was solicited for the greater good of getting at the truths of both sex *and* feminism.

In the battle over s/m, it was specifically lesbian s/m that was contested. The notion of a "lesbian sadomasochist" crystallized into a debated identity during the sex wars in a way that "heterosexual sadomasochist" did not.[4] As such, heterosexual s/m practice did not precipitate an internal crisis within feminism, because heterosexual sadomasochists generally did not actively take up political space within the women's movement. As for the pro-s/m literature of the era, much lesbian-penned writing tended to ignore heterosexual sadomasochists, while others were eager to differentiate their brand of s/m from the – presumptively exploitive – straight variety.[5] The anti-s/m side focused almost exclusively on condemning lesbian s/m and sought to reveal how this lesbian sexuality in essence replicated patriarchal heterosexual dynamics – which were often presumed to be sadomasochistic by definition.

A few other differences between the sides should be noted. Lesbian sadomasochists were not just writing about sexual practices using an analytical framework, they were also producing erotica, poetry, personal coming-out narratives, guidebooks, and instructional manuals on s/m. Thus not all of their texts could be classified as vicarious kink; some were explicit and direct kink. For the most part, as stated above, I will not be analysing s/m erotica unless it directly informs the feminist debates. This is because my project seeks to focus on the epistemic pleasures and anxieties of s/m as an object of study, and less on the economy of desire within the dynamics of the practice itself. Of course, the claims that combatants in the wars made *about* these dynamics will be scrupulously analysed. Here the "against" side relied upon direct analytical pieces, personal accounts, and fictional stories that were meant to convey the inherent harmfulness of s/m practice and pornography. I consider all of these texts vicarious kink, and so all of these narratives are put on the operating table to be discursively dissected.

The chapter draws upon texts from the United States, England, and Canada. Each country had its own defining moments during the sex wars, but the American controversy and texts enjoyed the most visibility and had a large impact on the debates in English Canada and England. It should also be noted that the issue of lesbian s/m attracted less controversy in Canada than it did in the United States and in England. For Canadians, the sex wars were much more heavily focused on pornography and censorship.[6] As such, to the extent that s/m was an issue for Canadian feminists in the public sphere, it manifested mostly as a question about the legality or criminality of s/m or "violent" sexual representation in text, and not in practice.

The rest of this chapter proceeds in three parts. In the first part, I employ broad brushstrokes to paint a genealogy of the sex wars and locate s/m's place within them. In the second part, I examine key texts from the anti-s/m camp, noting that the pleasures and anxieties of knowledge about s/m intersect with those of abjection, disgust, and rejection. The discussion here includes some of the feminist theorists who claimed a neutral or more nuanced position towards what they described as two polarized sides, as much of this literature ended up reinforcing and perpetuating anti-s/m truth-claims, despite purporting to critique the prohibitionists for being too monolithic. These texts relied on the tactic of constructing oneself as a "moderate" intervener, untouched by the "hysteria" of the anti-s/m side or the "hedonism" of the pro-s/m side. In the third part of this chapter, I examine key writings by sadomasochist feminists and their defenders. The pleasures of writing one's own desires are evident, but I posit that this is increased when such sexuality provokes abjection anxieties, disgust, and the potential for public rejection. In other words, as Halperin notes, there is pleasure in abject rebellion (2007). In my analysis of these positions I sometimes push past the time period bracketed by the sex wars to reveal the extent to which these battles are still being waged, and ask whether the critiques and the defences have shifted or evolved since the height of the wars.

Contextualizing the S/M Debate in the Broader Sex Wars

There are two overlapping historical strands of social phenomena that wrap around the controversy of lesbian s/m: one is the historical debate within second-wave feminism concerning pornography, and the other is the notion of lesbian feminism as a political identity.

The feminist conflict over pornography implicated s/m in two ways. First, there was the question of whether s/m porn should be definitively cast as patriarchal, heterosexist, and/or violent. Second, the issue of lesbian s/m challenged notions of sexual difference perpetuated by some supporters on the anti-pornography side. The backdrop of lesbian feminism as a political and in some ways desexualized understanding of lesbianism also forms part of the landscape. Lesbian sadomasochists who foregrounded their sexuality as an expression of attraction and pleasure often rebelled against what they perceived to be a sentimentalized and sanitized version of lesbianism advanced by lesbian feminists. To complicate the picture even further, many lesbian sadomasochists were part of the anti-pornography movement and identified as lesbian feminists, insisting that lesbian s/m could be reconciled with these perspectives. These multiple identifications would ultimately challenge the stability of political categories for second-wave feminists.

The upsurge of second-wave feminism in the 1970s addressed many issues, including legal rights related to marital status, abortion, pay equity, media representations of women, pornography, and violence against women. However, it was mostly the last two concerns, often equated with one another, that would provide the contested terrain upon which a groundswell of opposition would eventually arise from s/m lesbians and other sex-radical feminists.[7]

A key moment in this history began in 1976 with the creation of the activist feminist group Women against Violence against Women (WAVAW) and Women against Violence in Pornography and the Media (WAVPM). As part of their activist work, WAVPM provided regular educational "tours" of red-light districts and presented a slide show that correlated "degrading" or "violent" images – including s/m imagery – with harmful attitudes towards women. In 1978, WAVPM organized a conference entitled "Feminist Perspectives on Pornography" that culminated in a protest that drew five thousand women to march behind a banner for the eradication of pornography.

While there had been some tentative articulations of lesbian s/m subjectivity in the 1970s,[8] the first major challenge against the prevailing anti-s/m stance of the women's movement was launched in 1979 when Samois, a lesbian s/m group, held its first public meeting and published the pamphlet *What Colour Is Your Handkerchief?* (1979). The booklet identified Samois as a group for "feminist lesbians who share a positive interest in sadomasochism" (2). This feminist self-positioning sparked outrage for many radical feminists and lesbian feminists who perceived the claim as an attack on the fundamental tenets of feminist theory. A number of bookstores refused to carry the pamphlet, and some publications would not accept advertising for it. Later that same year, Samois member Patrick Califia published "A Secret Side of Lesbian Sexuality" in the *Advocate*, in which he[9] came out as a lesbian sadomasochist and narrated his sexual interests ([1979] 1994). Califia and fellow Samois member Gayle Rubin, a founding voice in queer theory, would come to most visibly represent the pro-s/m lesbian side.

During the late 1970s, conflicts between Samois and WAVPM were on the rise as WAVPM continued to equate consensual s/m with violence, but dodged meetings with Samois members who sought to discuss their alternate perspective. In 1980, WAVPM held a forum on s/m at the University of California, Berkeley, which some members of Samois picketed bearing signs proclaiming, "This Forum Is a Lie about S/M." In the same year, the anti-porn anthology *Take Back the Night: Women on Pornography* was published, containing transcripts of many presentations from the 1978 WAVPM conference (Lederer 1980). One transcript in particular, an interview between Laura Lederer and Judith

Bat-Ada, denounces s/m as being characteristically about male sadism, where the inclusion of "masochism" in the aggregated term was cast as a ploy to justify male violence (116).

Another blow against lesbian s/m came in 1980 when the American feminist advocacy group the National Organization of Women (NOW) proclaimed its Resolution on Lesbian Rights (Blasius and Phelan 1997, 468).[10] The document took the stance that s/m and pornography, among other things, were fundamental contradictions to lesbian rights, and unequivocally condemned the practices as issues of exploitation and violence. In the concept paper that was circulated with the resolution, a recurring allegation in the anti-s/m literature was made explicit: the practice of lesbian s/m was a contamination from gay men. NOW suggests that non-feminist gay organizations have imposed s/m (along with pederasty, pornography, and public sex) onto its legislative agenda, and that feminists must resist this corrupting influence (Blasius and Phelan 1997, 468).

Adrienne Rich (1980) also dissociated lesbianism from gay male identity, situating it as a uniquely female phenomenological experience. This perspective had an oblique impact on the terms of the debate on lesbian s/m, as it continued a strand of 1970s lesbian feminist theory that conceived of lesbianism as political resistance against male domination.[11] Rich's article follows in this vein, theorizing heterosexuality not as a "choice" but as an institution "imposed, managed, organized, propagandized and maintained by force" to keep women subordinate to men and alienated from one another (248). Rich further introduces the concept of the lesbian continuum, which expanded the notion of lesbianism beyond a sexual/genital experience to include a multitude of ways in which women connect with and support one another.

Meanwhile, Califia – who, in many ways, wanted to refocus lesbianism on the sexual – published another article in *Heresies* that attempted a "rapprochement between feminism and S/M" (Califia 1994) as well as a ground-breaking book on lesbian sexuality, *Sapphistry* (Califia 1988c). The book specifically named s/m as a neutral "variation" of lesbian desire. Protests abounded, and again some bookstores refused to carry the volume, while others would sell it only under the counter.

In 1981, Samois published the first edition of *Coming to Power*, an anthology that explored lesbian s/m from a number of vantage points, including personal narratives, erotica, historical accounts, and analytical pieces (Samois 1981). Once again some bookstores refused to stock the text, and anger escalated until a few years later the book was burned outside a women's bookstore in London, England. Also in 1981, the feminist journal *Heresies* put forward a sex-radical position in its "Sex Issue," reproducing Califia's article "Feminism and Sadomasochism" and publishing Amber Hollibaugh and Cherrie Moraga's dialogic piece, "What We're Rollin Around in Bed With: Sexual Silences in Feminism, A Conversation toward Ending Them." Also included was a critique of NOW's resolution on lesbian rights and its categorical denunciation of s/m and pornography.

Samois experienced conflict again in the early 1980s with the Women's Building, a community centre in San Francisco. This feminist centre initially refused Samois rental space, an exclusion in stark contrast to the Women's Building's standard open policy, which had allowed many other groups access to the space, including men's and non-feminist organizations. After a series of meetings in which Samois members defended the organization as non-racist and non-violent, the Women's Building administrators relented, albeit with rental conditions, including one requiring that Samois members not engage in "offensive" behaviour.

While all of these events stirred up controversy and dissent, a landmark event in the American sex wars was the 1982 Barnard College Scholar and the Feminist Conference, entitled "Towards a Politics of Sexuality" ("Barnard Conference"). The conference sought to accommodate the dual theme of pleasure and danger, with the understanding that promoting pleasure, as well as reducing danger, were both necessary parts of feminist sexual politics. While it attracted more than eight hundred attendees, the conference met with tremendous opposition from certain groups of feminists, whose tactics included contacting Barnard officials to complain the conference was pro-pervert and anti-feminist, and on-site protests with leafleting and picketing. S/m, along with butch-femme identity and pornography, were specifically targeted as forms of "anti-feminist" sexuality that the conference allegedly endorsed.[12]

The early 1980s was also a fruitful time for textual objections to s/m. The 1982 anthology *Against Sadomasochism: A Radical Feminist Analysis* devotes virtually its entire contents to condemning and critiquing lesbian s/m (Linden et al. 1982). In 1982 and 1983, Catherine MacKinnon wrote two paradigm-shifting articles that catapulted dominance feminism onto the political stage. The articles adopted a neo-Marxist perspective on women's subordination. In "Feminism, Marxism, Method, and the State: An Agenda for Theory" (1982) MacKinnon locates sexuality as *the* linchpin of gender inequality. Woman is defined and delimited through and by sexuality. She suggests that a central component of feminist method is consciousness-raising, whereby women collective-ly recognize their social construction and seek to reconstitute the meaning of their experiences. In the follow-up article, "Feminism, Marxism, Method, and the State: Toward a Feminist Jurisprudence" (1983) MacKinnon continued theorizing the centrality of sexuality in the subordination of women. This article made a significant contribution to the anti-s/m side, as MacKinnon not only defines the male/female dyad through an eroticization of dominance and submission, but seeks to account for the pleasures (or lack thereof) of each party in this encounter. In this way, she challenges the line drawn between rape and intercourse, as well as the utility of the notion of consent. She states, "Women are socialized to passive receptivity; may have or perceive no alternative to acquiescence; may prefer it to the escalated risk of injury and the humiliation of a lost fight; submit to survive. Some eroticize dominance and submission; it beats feeling forced" (650). MacKinnon thus articulates a social-constructionist argument that features in much anti-s/m literature: s/m desires are beamed directly into our psyches from the patriarchy. As such, regardless of any pleasure that may be salvaged from the experience, consent to s/m is construed as a recapitulation to the patriarchal dominance/submission sexual framework, not as a moment of genuine agency or choice.

In the British context, a defining moment in the sex wars occurred in 1984 when anti-s/m lesbians sought to evict an s/m support group from the London Lesbian and Gay Centre (LLGC). According to Emma Healey, who detailed the episode in *Lesbian Sex Wars* (1996), the battle had equivalent significance to the Barnard conference controversy in the United States. A key figure in the British anti-s/m camp during this time was Sheila Jeffreys, who wrote "Sadomasochism: The Erotic Cult of Fascism" (Jeffreys 1986, reprinted Jeffreys 1993). The article linked s/m to the rise of fascism in Germany and suggested that to allow the s/m support group to have access to a meeting place in the LLGC would be to lend support to future fascist movements.

In 1984, back in the United States, an anthology stemming from the Barnard conference was published, entitled *Pleasure and Danger: Exploring Female Sexuality* (Vance 1984 reprinted 1989). Of particular note is Rubin's essay, "Thinking Sex: Notes for a Radical Theory of the Politics of Sexuality" (Rubin 1984 reprinted 1989). In this piece, Rubin challenges feminism's authority as the privileged and most insightful lens through which to analyse the politics of sexuality, arguing that certain feminist theory has in fact distorted the dynamics of sexual hierarchy. On the other side of the political fence, the Minneapolis anti-pornography ordinance, drafted by MacKinnon and Andrea Dworkin in 1983, was passed by city council before being vetoed by the mayor in early 1984 (Downs 1989, 61–2). A revised version of the ordinance was soon passed without veto in Indianapolis. The ordinance set out to define pornography as the "graphic sexually explicit subordination of women, whether in pictures or in words" that also included, among other things, women enjoying pain or humiliation, women as sexual objects for domination, and women in positions of servility or submission (MacKinnon 2001, 1517). As such, without actually specifying s/m per se, the ordinance would likely have had a censoring impact on s/m representation. However, it should be noted that the ordinance was not criminal legislation, but instead enabled a civil action by women (or men and transpeople who are treated "as women") who were harmed by pornography, as defined by the legislation. This event mobilized anti-censorship feminists in New York and Madison, Wisconsin, who formed the group Feminist Anti-Censorship Taskforce (FACT). This group joined in a coalition of media organizations to legally challenge the ordinance, and in 1985 filed an amicus brief in the U.S. Appeals Court that included the support of eighty other feminists, including noted lesbian-feminist champion Adrienne Rich. The court eventually found the ordinance unconstitutional. In Los Angeles and Boston, politicians considered whether to enact their own versions of the ordinance, a prospect that was again met by newly formed local FACT chapters. Although the politicians in these places ultimately decided not to pass the ordinances, the debates were vigorous and sometimes decided by one vote.

Although the anti-s/m contingent was prominent and vocal in the late 1970s and early 1980s, as sexuality was continually debated among feminists over the next decade, the sex-radical perspective rapidly gained ground. While prominent anti-pornography feminist texts continued to be published,[13] Rubin's call to analytically separate gender and sexuality in order to interrogate "erotic stratifications" would spur new ways of thinking about power and sexuality. In 1990, Judith Butler's *Gender Trouble* (1990) further expanded and reworked the sex-radical side, shifting the theoretical frame towards postmodern and queer theory. Butler questioned the centrality and cohesiveness of the subject "woman" in feminist politics, arguing instead that sex, as well as gender, must be interrogated as a construction and an effect of power. Furthermore, Butler argued that a parodic relationship to gender could expose and denaturalize compulsory heterosexuality and its star players, "man" and "woman."

In addition, the anti-pornography feminist side lost some support as the effects of its alignment with state actors and conservative bodies became visible. Carole Vance points out that though the Indianapolis ordinance was quashed, the censorship arguments provided right-wing groups, like the Meese Commission, with updated equality-seeking rhetoric to justify their puritanical agenda (Vance 1993). This strategy was then deployed to condemn a wide range of representation as "degrading" and therefore "obscene." The most vivid example was in 1989, when conservative politicians attacked the National Endowment for the Arts (NEA) for its support of Robert Mapplethorpe's photographs depicting homoerotic and s/m themes. This campaign culminated in the NEA's director blocking funding the following year to four performance artists who addressed gay, lesbian, and feminist themes in their work. In 1991, the U.S. Congress passed legislation requiring NEA funding applicants to sign oaths promising not to produce work that "might be considered obscene." In 1998, the U.S. Supreme Court upheld the requirement that NEA funding recipients meet "general standards of decency" in their art. In Canada, as I note below, the 1992 Supreme Court's *Butler* decision upholding the *Criminal Code*'s obscenity provisions was used disproportionately against gay and lesbian erotica. These examples highlight some of the costs of radical feminist support of non-feminist, and often downright homophobic, state bodies engaged in deciding what could be deemed "degrading" and therefore deserving censorship.

In Canada, as I have mentioned, the "sex wars" manifested mostly as "the porn wars" – that is, as debate on the regulation of pornography. One of the most important books that intervened on the anti-censorship side was the 1985 anthology *Women against Censorship* (Burstyn 1985b). All the essays took the stance that it is a feminist mistake to align with governmental campaigns to censor obscenity. In "Political Precedents and Moral Crusades, Women, Sex and the State" (1985a), Varda Burstyn contextualizes the feminist pro-censorship position within a historical trend of female alliance with social control movements. Burstyn recalls the ways women, particularly middle-class women who supported the regulation and criminalization of prostitutes, ended up victimizing poor women. She draws an analogy with the current feminist support of censorship, making the subtle but poignant indictment that anti-pornography feminism is heralded by women privileged enough to be spared the costs of such government collusion. Burstyn states, "The legacy of the first wave of feminism suggests that it is very easy for women who are relatively privileged vis-à-vis other women, who have greater access to – and confidence in – government to lose sight of the potential treachery of a male-dominated, profit-protecting state; of the way in which such a state, even when parts of it are staffed by women, can work against the interests of the majority of women" (29–30). Although Burstyn is more diplomatic than s/m feminists like Califia, the suggestion remains that those attempting to prohibit "violent" pornography are reinforcing middle-class and sexist systems of control.

On the other side of the battle in Canada, Susan G. Cole published *Pornography and the Sex Crisis* (1989a), which adopts a dominance feminist perspective on pornography as a practice of female subordination for sexual pleasure. Cole proposes a civil remedy for harms incurred because of pornography, comparable to the Dworkin-MacKinnon Minneapolis Ordinance. Also reproduced is a 1985 review of *Women against Censorship*, in which Cole criticizes the book for abstracting the issue of pornography and ignoring the "real" women who are victimized by the business (145).

Although Cole's civil remedy has never been adopted in Canada, the anti-pornography side achieved an impressive legal victory in 1992 when the Supreme Court of Canada issued its precedent-making decision, *R. v. Butler*. The truth-claims of this case will be examined in more detail in chapter 4, but suffice it to say that the court defined obscenity using a harms-based approach, adopting MacKinnon's view that certain visual representations operate as a form of sex discrimination. While the decision allowed the state to criminalize sexual depiction deemed "violent," "degrading," or "dehumanizing," the reality is that adult pornography is rarely prosecuted in Canada today. Instead, the porn wars manifest most visibly in the practices of Canada Customs, which continually targets gay and lesbian representation, usually when it overlaps with s/m content. In chapter 4, I address this struggle in the context of the ongoing legal battle between gay and lesbian bookstore Little Sisters and Canada Customs. As a result of the censorship effects wrought by border security targeting of gay and lesbian s/m text, in many ways, the "porn wars" continue in Canada.

The Anti-S/M Side

Against Sadomasochism: A Radical Feminist Analysis (1982)

As stated, the anti-s/m movement grew out of both the lesbian feminist and radical feminist positions of the 1970s and 1980s. I thus begin my analysis of key texts from the abolitionist camp by examining the polemical book representing both of these perspectives, whose no-nonsense title proclaimed its monolithic position: *Against Sadomasochism: A Radical Feminist Analysis* (Linden et al. 1982). The anthology is a useful starting point for at least two reasons. First, the collection came out three years after Samois's *Handkerchief,* and many of the essays respond directly to the issues raised in that forty-five page pro-s/m booklet. Second, many of the anthology's contributors came to be the most visible opponents to lesbian s/m, and their arguments were replicated in subsequent discursive attacks throughout the sex wars.

One central rebuttal to the self-positioning of *Handkerchief* was the argument that lesbian s/m could never be reconciled with feminism. The articles in *Against Sadomasochism* reflect the extent to which the truth of s/m became a definitional border war for feminism. The identity of "feminist" was constructed as singular and self-evidently aligned with radical feminism. As such, much of the anti-s/m analysis was coloured by indignation over the crime of *identity-theft* by lesbian sadomasochists. Anti-s/m lesbian feminists were forced to contend with women who bore a marked resemblance to themselves in identity and sexual orientation, and yet who simultaneously reminded them of what was most despised: patriarchal sexual configurations. In this way, s/m lesbians emerged as abject threats who straddled the border between feminist subject and patriarchal object. The anxiety of this "mixed category" had to be managed. The task of anti-s/m feminists was to redraw the boundaries and strengthen feminist categorical imperatives in order to drive s/m lesbians and their defenders out from this identity.

Jeanette Nichols, Darlene Pagano, and Margaret Rosoff dedicate their entire article to refuting Samois's claim to feminism, as demonstrated by the title of their contribution, "Is Sadomasochism Feminist? A Critique of the Samois Position" (1982, 137). They argue that pleasure derived from sadomasochistic activity is "a conditioned response to the sexual imagery that barrages women in this society" (139). In this view, the body is held to have anti-epistemological value. The authors' solution to s/m desires is to resist acting upon them, and instead to investigate their patriarchal roots in a supportive (anti-s/m) women's group. In other words, since lesbian s/m is derivative of patriarchal sexuality, a genuine feminist must analyse such fantasies. If she cannot reprogram her sexual responses, she must at least refrain from acting upon these induced corporeal urges. Feminist praxis seems to overlap here with Krafft-Ebing's solution to uncivilized libidinal urges: mind over matter.

The authors further suggest that feminist sexuality should be bound within an emotional and dyadic long-term commitment, complaining that society has encouraged "sex for pure physical pleasure" which is "characterized by lack of feeling, growth or intimacy [and] not often satisfying on any emotional level" (Nichols, Pagano, and Rosoff 1882, 142–3). They then contend that lesbian sadomasochists replicate this dynamic, stating, "While a mutual sexual fantasy or scenario may give a heightened sense of intimacy, like the 'trust' developed in this context, it differs greatly from the intimacy developed through the ups and downs of a relationship" (143). The assumption, of course, is that s/m is linked to casual sex, and non-s/m to long-term relationships. But more importantly, the notion that true feminist sex can happen only within an emotionally invested long-term relationship reflects an adherence to the mind-body dualism of the scientific discourse, although in many ways expressed instead as a heart-body dualism. And as in the scientific normative agenda, the mind/heart is privileged over the body. Sex for sex's sake is understood as incompatible not only with feminist sexuality, but true intimacy.

Another article in *Against Sadomasochism* further challenges the language of liberation in connection with s/m. In "Why I'm against S/M Liberation," a transcript of a speech given by Ti-Grace Atkinson to a pro s/m group, she berates the crowd, "You distort feminism unconscionably" (1982, 92). Atkinson, like Nichols, Pagano, and Rosoff, cannot abide sadomasochists' claim to feminism. Atkinson also perpetuates the dualism between physical sexual pleasure and the feminist agenda, stating, "I do not know any feminist worthy of that name who, if forced to choose between freedom and sex, would choose sex. She'd choose freedom every time" (91). What I find particularly remarkable about this statement is not that Atkinson prioritizes freedom over sex, but rather that she can conceive of freedom *without* sex. Accessing sexual pleasure is seen, at best, as trivial to the practice of feminist freedom. This explains her later statement, "By no stretch of the imagination is the Women's Movement a movement for sexual liberation" (91). Sex is to be analysed, regulated and politicized, not "liberated."

Another tactic used by anti-s/m feminists to evict s/m from the feminist terrain, as noted in connection with NOW's Resolution on Lesbian Rights, was to characterize it as a contamination from gay male culture. Robin Ruth Linden begins the *Against Sadomasochism* anthology by meditating on what she perceives to be the emotional atmosphere of her surroundings in the Castro district of San Francisco (1982, 1). She explains that the majority of pedestrians in her neighbourhood are gay men. Despite acknowledging that this demographic offers her "a freedom from the fear of being raped or murdered," she maintains that there is nonetheless "a feeling of threat: nameless, amorphous. The passion is cold, at times macabre" (1). She explains that this mood is a result of gay men sporting sadomasochistic apparel, and that recently she had also discovered the "occasional woman in similar dress" (2). Later she says that the lesbian s/m hanky code – which signals different s/m desires to potential lovers – is modelled on a similar system used by gay men. By beginning her introduction to the anthology with a sketch of gay male s/m culture, Linden definitively puts forth a truth of lesbian s/m as derivative and imitative of gay male sexual dynamics.[14]

Other articles in the collection continue this origin story. In particular, male feminist John Stoltenberg attacks gay male culture for relinquishing its "revolutionary potential" and spreading s/m into the mainstream (1982, 124). He posits that gay men, whom he insists enjoyed great influence over cultural productions such as fashion and advertising, are to blame for "the current obsession with sadomasochism ... which is now sweeping the country" (125). Stoltenberg further argues that the resulting preponderance of s/m-themed cultural productions is harmful to women, stating, "We are witnessing the convergence of what was once deemed a 'gay sensibility' with what was once deemed a 'heterosexual sensibility.' That convergence ... now reveals itself fully as thriving on female degradation" (125). His article casts s/m in gay male culture as "tantamount to spitting in the faces of women who are struggling to be free" (124). Stoltenberg addresses the lesbian practice of s/m only peripherally, stating, "There is no reason to presume that a masochistic woman is exercising more freedom of choice or acting more autonomously if her constrained will and body are subjected to the sadism of another woman" (128). In Stoltenberg's view, gay male, heterosexual, and lesbian s/m all amount to the same thing: the perpetuation of female powerlessness.

The anti-s/m literature also identifies another form of powerlessness that is trivialized by lesbian sadomasochists, namely the powerlessness and oppression of racial and ethnic minorities. Herein lies another truth of s/m espoused by anti-s/m theorists: s/m sexuality is inherently racist. In *Against Sadomasochism* this allegation can be divided into two intertwining claims. First, it is contended that the act of role playing a dominant-submissive relationship mocks the non-consensual racial hierarchies that occurred in slavery and continue to occur in social relations between white people and people of colour. The second objection is rooted in the anxieties of the abject, whereby the anti-s/m theorists believe the use of props and rhetoric from racist regimes perpetuates the values of such regimes. The later examination of Sheila Jeffreys's article "Sadomasochism: The Erotic Cult of Fascism" ([1984] 1993) demonstrates the most extreme version of this argument, where she alleges that s/m itself was partly to blame for the atrocities committed by white supremacist regimes such as Nazism.

In *Against Sadomasochism*, the article "Racism and Sadomasochism: A Conversation with Two Black Lesbians" shows how race discourse comes to be intertwined with abjection anxieties over the disrupted meaning of political identity and hierarchy. In it, co-author Rose Mason states, "To make sadomasochism an issue, a community issue, a feminist issue, a political issue … angers me; it has no place. I think it is racist for them to even call themselves an oppressed minority" (101). The conversation goes on to personalize the issue by construing s/m as a luxury that Black women cannot access. Karen Sims states, "The kinds of things that women into sadomasochism are saying that they are dealing with, like submission, and like power dynamics and control, are things that I have to deal with every day. So it seems real absurd to take this on as something to be played with or something to explore because there are things that a whole race, many races of people are trying to get out of, and that's being submissive, that's living in a society where we are totally controlled" (103). In support of this statement, Mason rebukes an imagined s/m lesbian audience: "How dare you take the privilege at my expense" (Sims, Mason, and Pagaon 1982, 103). These statements attempt to articulate the harm of lesbian s/m to people of colour. There is an "expense," and the women who are paying for it are not the lesbian sadomasochists (presumably white), but rather the lesbians of colour who are struggling for survival. While the authors do not point to any material or concrete disadvantage they experience in daily life because of lesbian sadomasochists, their claim is that it wields affective power; there is a conviction that the practice insults their struggles in a racist world.

At the end of the article, the clear-cut distinction between white lesbian sadomasochists and victimized Black women is complicated. The presence of lesbians of colour who do embrace s/m as part of their identity is acknowledged, although their acute abject status makes them virtually unintelligible in the authors' normative framework. Such women are characterized as making up only an "extremely small" number in Samois, and the authors maintain that the lesbian s/m community is "mainly white" (Sims, Mason, and Pagaon 1982, 103–4). (They do not remark that the greater feminist community is also mainly white.) Darlene Pagano addresses a television show that featured a mixed-race lesbian s/m couple where she identifies the top as white and the bottom as Black. She relates a "horrible scene" where the Black lesbian partner stated, "'But I like to be her slave'" (104). None of the participants of the *Against Sadomasochism* article can account for her identity as an s/m lesbian, nor can they bring themselves to condemn her for her statement. Instead, blame gets deflected. Pagano accuses the television station of being racist for broadcasting her statement, suggesting that it was used to justify s/m. Yet it is ironic that a feminist concerned with the equality of Black women would have preferred that a Black woman's statement be censored in a television program, leaving her to appear mute and without agency, rather than have her articulated desires complicate an analysis of the inherent racism in s/m. Or perhaps Pagano would have preferred that she not appear at all, thereby reinforcing the invisibility of Black women in the s/m lesbian community. This racialized lesbian sadomasochist figures as abject more than a white lesbian sadomasochist because, as a public sadomasochist who flaunts her sexuality, she problematizes the monolithic construction of Black woman as victim of s/m. Part of the strategy of proving the racism of s/m was to simply discount women of colour who participated in the sexual practice. They are not construed as traitors or weak-minded in the way that some anti-s/m writing generally describes women who participate in s/m. Instead, they are simply disregarded as being the exception and thus unimportant for an analysis of racism and s/m.

This strategy occurs again in Alice Walker's epistolary contribution to *Against Sadomasochism* (1982). In her fictional piece, Walker appears to be addressing the same non-fictional television show mentioned in the Sims, Mason, and Pagaon article. Walker states through her character Susan Marie that *"regardless* of the 'slave' on television, black women do not want to be slaves" (208, emphasis added). I emphasize the word *regardless* in Walker's statement because it points to the reductionist strategy of anti-s/m critics. Effectively, Walker has *no regard* for Black women who embrace a sexuality she finds politically repugnant.

Her desires and identity are deemed unnecessary and irrelevant to an indictment of s/m as racist. As such, there is no need to get at the truth of the Black lesbian submissive on television.

While the language of "master and slave" prompted outrage among many anti-s/m feminists, the appropriation of Nazi symbols and the role playing of Nazi-dom and Jewish sub-dynamics triggered equal condemnation. In "Swastikas: The Street and the University" (1982) Susan Leigh Star accuses sadomasochists of deluding themselves that Nazi symbols can be detached from the material reality of Nazism. She states, "Swastikas are not acceptable symbols to use under any conditions. They are too linked, first by my street sense and then by close historical examination, to my own death and the destruction of all Jews" (134). In this indictment, identity politics is put to work again, this time by a Jewish feminist thinker who personalizes the issue to add impact to her analysis. As with Sims and Mason, who position themselves as Black lesbians trying to survive in a racist society, Star positions herself as a Jewish street-smart lesbian whose own life is put on the line because of s/m appropriation of Nazi symbolism. In both cases, the authors use their marginalized status to demonstrate the tangible harm of s/m practice. It is maintained that s/m sexuality is not benign. It harms women from oppressed racial, ethnic, or religious backgrounds because they can experience these symbols only as a threat.

But unlike the previous authors, who did not specify a nexus between lesbian sadomasochists' use of master-slave role playing and direct harm to Black women, Star puts forward some concrete ramifications when sadomasochists publicly wear Nazi symbols. She not only argues that people like her experience the public use of Nazi symbols as "a kick in the stomach" (which is similar to the argument about the affective harm of s/m advanced by Sims, Mason, and Pagaon), but also conjectures that real Nazis will feel empowered by their use. Star propounds this hypothesis as a "material reality" ignored by lesbian sadomasochists (1982, 135). This turns out to be a recurrent thread in the anti-s/m discourse: sadomasochists defend their practices in a vacuum and don't pay enough attention to "reality."[15] It should be noted, however, that there are those who contest the "reality" that lesbian sadomasochists were indeed publicly wearing Nazi regalia. Emma Healey intimates that anti-s/m feminists perpetuated the myth of lesbian sadomasochists' public use of Nazi dress to shock and to win easy political points. She quips, "As many lesbian feminists seemed to be seeing swastikas as American tourists were seeing the Loch Ness Monster" (Healey 1996,

100). Furthermore, a critique of this public practice does not necessarily demonstrate the "material reality" of s/m in general, or of harms flowing from the private use of Nazi symbols.

Possibly the best way for anti-s/m feminists to expose the "reality" of s/m relationships was to draw on autobiographical accounts of s/m dynamics. By sharing personal experiences of s/m, some anti-s/m feminists went beyond addressing the political ramifications to address the private ramifications, seeking to reveal the individual (as opposed to societal) costs of this sexuality. The incitement to discourse required that anti-s/m feminists scrutinize and confess their own dalliances with s/m sexuality in order to derive its true meaning. As Foucault has argued, "Western societies have established the confession as one of the main rituals … for the production of truth" (1990, 58). As such, who better to indict s/m than former sadomasochists?

Against Sadomasochism contains two short s/m confessionals. In "Letter from a Former Masochist" (1982), Marissa Jonel takes the reader on a rollercoaster ride that begins with the high of sexual intensity and ends with the low of captivity and domestic violence. In "Sadomasochism: A Personal Experience" (1982) Elizabeth Harris recounts how s/m activity initially fulfilled her lifelong fantasies, but eventually left her emotionally devastated. Though both tales end with a moralistic warning that women need to abdicate this form of sexuality lest they become completely destroyed, both tease the reader with glimpses of taboo sexuality and furtive pleasure. As Ann Coughlin has argued, "Confessional discourse enhances or perhaps, even, creates in the first instance the erotic pleasure that the participants attribute to the sexual experiences confessed by the speaking subject" (1995, 1337). Through their autobiographical narration, these anti-s/m confessionals manifest as vicarious kink, where the pleasures of s/m are reproduced in conjunction with articulations of shame and regret.

One striking similarity between these two authors is that both adopt pseudonyms to cloak their real names. In this regard, both women embed themselves in a tradition of anonymous erotic confessional narratives.[16] A secret identity conveys that the author is fearful of the judgment of others and perhaps for her own safety, and piques the reader's curiosity by signalling that her story is so scandalous that the author was obliged to withhold her true name. Jonel further incites the reader's curiosity by beginning her letter with "Dear Robin, I'm just going to write this and not think about it because it makes me nervous when I envision it in a book" (1982, 16). Right from the start of Jonel's epistolary narrative, the reader is alerted to the fact that this true confession will involve some juicy bits that still make this "former masochist" nervous.

In the beginning of each narrative, Jonel and Harris disclose that before they ever entered into an official s/m relationship, they enjoyed submissive fantasies. Harris illustrates this personal tidbit with a detailed example: "My earliest fantasies and experiences began at the age of six when I would tie myself up in the bed sheets at night and imagine I was a beautiful black horse being captured and mistreated by evil men" (1982, 93). Jonel explained that with her earlier lovers, she "responded to roughness and sometimes had fantasies of being overpowered" (1982, 16). Masochism is presented as having been deeply ingrained in both authors before they had ever entered into a relationship involving explicit s/m sex. This aspect of the narrative corresponds to the anti-s/m feminist proposition that women are conditioned from childhood to respond sexually to dominance.

When both authors find partners who complement their desires, they initially describe relationships characterized by sexual excitement and emotional intensity. Jonel describes her s/m scenes as "very exciting" and "the ultimate risqué act" (Jonel in Linden 1982, 17). She exclaims later that with regard to the s/m sex, "I loved it. There was new meaning in my life!" (17). The taboo nature of the sexuality appeared to also have a positive impact on her relationship with her "sadist" lesbian partner: "My lover and I had this wonderful secret bond and sm strengthened the ties in our relationship" (17). Jonel states that after she began enjoying s/m sex with her lover, "all my fantasies of being submissive, being controlled, were being acted upon" (17).

Harris, too, experienced previously unknown pleasures when she started dabbling with s/m. In fact, she was non-orgasmic until she experimented with sex toys and rougher sex, activities she connects on a continuum with s/m. She divulged that through dildo penetration, she finally "discovered orgasm through pain" (1982, 93). With even more ambivalence, Harris tells another anecdote in which, after having a "violent" session of "fucking … my orgasm left me on the verge of hysterical tears" (94). With her next lover, a man this time, she initiated the sadomasochistic activity. She recounts, "I was aroused, near orgasm and I asked him to slap my breasts. The pain was shocking, like cold water after heat, and enjoyable" (95). Both narratives begin by portraying s/m as a vehicle to acute gratification. Sexual fantasies were being fulfilled, orgasms were now flowing freely, and new avenues of pleasure were being discovered. Even Jonel's anecdote about how "violent fuck-ing" brought her to orgasmic tears marks its own kind of cathartic plea-sure. The intensity of the release opened up the floodgates of emotion.

However, both authors quickly attempt to undermine the exhilaration they describe. Jonel analogizes her experience to one of drug addiction. After describing the pleasure, satisfaction, and emotional intimacy de-rived from s/m sex, Jonel laments, "I can see this now as the beginnings of the addiction to sm" (1982, 17). In the next paragraph Jonel details how this "addiction" manifested. "For me, and many of the women I know who were/are involved in sm, it becomes a consuming part of one's life. Scenes are planned and much time, effort and money is put into toys and devices" (17). Later in her narrative, she deploys an addic-tion model to explain her escalating masochism. "I felt myself feeling less and needing more real pain to get excited. It's like drugs – you de-velop a quick tolerance to the pain" (18). She continues, "In my rela-tionship and those of friends who were into sm, the violence or severity of sm escalated as the relationship continued" (20). Finally, after explain-ing how abusive her relationship had become, she maintains, "There was a part of me that never wanted the sm to end and after a couple of years I was totally addicted to my lover being in total control" (19).

By using the addictiveness trope, Jonel characterizes s/m as a pathol-ogy. She suggests that when sex takes up a lot of time in a relationship and involves planning, effort, role playing, and non-human objects, it has become a dependence and a disorder. Furthermore, Jonel engages the slippery slope assumptions of drug use to illustrate the escalating dangers of s/m sexuality. The assertion is that if you allow yourself the pleasure of mild submissiveness and masochism, your nerve endings will dull, and your desires will become more extreme and general-ized, until eventually you lose all autonomy and get really hurt. Her characterization of masochism conforms to Freud's notion of "moral masochism," whereby the sexual pleasure derived from being hurt or humiliated becomes detached from the erotic and bleeds into the rest of one's life. When Jonel recounts her break-up with her abusive lover, she states, "I feel that breaking my addiction to sm and the daily humilia-tion and feeling of enslavement was the hardest thing I've ever done in my life" (1982, 21). Thus Jonel was not just "addicted" to the sexual pleasure of s/m, but also to the feelings of powerlessness that she expe-rienced throughout the relationship.

Harris, too, attempts to disparage the enjoyment she gained from her sadomasochistic encounters. After describing the pleasure received when her male lover slapped her on the breasts, she quickly follows with a qualification: "It did not feel warm or loving but it complemented my arousal" (1982, 94). Later, when Harris explains that she and her boyfriend switched top and bottom roles, she expresses frustration: "I was not satisfied with the dominant role. I could not hurt him; he was always in control because of the safe-words. And when he was dominant he was bumbling, never hurting me where or how I wanted to be hurt" (94). Finally, she describes the catalytic moment that ended her engagement with s/m. After being teased with a glass of water, her lover playfully threw the entire contents in her face – an incident that Harris defines as sadomasochistic, exemplifying the elasticity of the term in her account. In response, she "burst into tears and sobbed for a long time" (94). She concludes, "Except for the accidental and cathartic water-throwing, sadomasochism never touched my real emotional needs" (95).

Although Harris's attempts to undercut the positive feelings she derived from her s/m encounters, her narrative still provides a complicated picture. First, she shows that s/m was initially enjoyable but soon became frustrating because of the incompetence of her lover and because the safe word curtailed her own topping desires. This seems to contradict the escalation theory of s/m and gives credence to the notion that having a safe word does indeed place limits on the top's behaviour. The fact that she and her male partner switched top and bottom roles also demonstrates a fluidity in s/m relationships that most anti-s/m texts refute.

However, Harris does perpetuate the assumption found in many anti-s/m texts that sex *should* be about love and emotion. By characterizing s/m as neither warm nor loving, and not meeting "real emotional needs," she supports the underlying assumption that sex *should* be about emotional fulfilment, and that sex for physical pleasure alone is problematic. Further, despite the fact that s/m is credited with providing her with her first orgasm, this is construed and demeaned as purely "physical."

Both authors conclude by defining s/m as a pernicious influence that is less about mutual pleasure and more about mutual dysfunction. Jonel correlates her experience of domestic abuse with sadomasochistic sexuality; in her narrative, her own abdication of control and autonomy, and her lover's abuse and manipulation, were expressed through a sadomasochistic framework. But she also seeks to add objectivity to her analysis by relying on anecdotal evidence. She claims that other women in her community are also being abused within the context of s/m relationships, and that a counsellor for battered lesbians had asserted that the rise of s/m has a "direct connection" to "abuse, hospitalization and abuse-related deaths among lesbians" (Jonel 1982, 19). Jonel does occasionally express some hesitancy in her condemnation of s/m, for example by suggesting that *maybe* some lesbians who practise "mild" and "limited" forms of s/m are not in abusive relationships. However, her ultimate conclusion returns to a monolithic stance: "All this bullshit about consensual sex, changing roles back and forth, safe words, etc. *ad nauseam* – is, to my mind, just a cover that encourages women to be violent. Sadomasochism is violence" (19).

In contrast, Harris does not begin her piece by essentializing s/m as inherently abusive. She does not characterize her s/m experiences within the context of domestic violence, and in fact describes the male lover with whom she had the most explicit s/m experiences as a "caring man" and a "nice person" (Harris 1982, 94). For her, s/m was "a symptom of unacknowledged pain" and "obsessive behaviour," a practice that provided an avenue for her to delay experiences of grief (she never hypothesizes what motivated her boyfriend to engage in s/m with her) (95). However, by the time she gets to her conclusion, Harris (like Jonel) has implicitly linked s/m with violent abuse, stating, "I am disturbed by the rationalization of violence against women, especially by feminists" (95). Thus both authors see s/m as, in essence, a pathological camouflage for violence.

Yet despite all these personal revelations about the dysfunctional habits of s/m, both authors confess that they continue to harbour s/m desires. Harris acknowledges, "I still have sadomasochistic fantasies" (1982, 95), and Jonel wonders if she is being hypocritical when she admits, "I still have s/m urges and fantasies" (1982, 19). S/m is thus construed as a persistent desire, one not easily amenable to intellectual persuasion. Though much of the anti-s/m literature talks about integration, these s/m confessionals reveal the way anti-s/m discourse is focused on tensions in the self, enforcing a Cartesian framework of the body. Once again, the message is that our sexual psyches, corrupted by patriarchal conditioning, must be disciplined by the mind's feminist consciousness. As Felicity Nussbaum has pointed out, "Memoirs work as moral lessons to encourage women to regulate themselves" (1989, 179), and specifically, I would add, to encourage women to regulate their libidos.

This moral packs a much bigger punch because it is put forward by "native informants" who are still plagued by their unruly s/m desires.

Unlike most of the other anti-s/m writers, who at most only allude to s/m thoughts, these writers can claim they've been there. Their autobiographical narratives attest to the "fact" that s/m is not about pleasure or love, but instead about abuse and dysfunction. And like ex-gays, they are seen as living proof that despite one's desires, one can rise above it and resist the allure of sexual dysfunction.

Yet while these confessionals clearly have a moral to their stories – that s/m will not provide healthy sexual release and could lead to abuse or even death – the accounts still portray s/m as an avenue to acute pleasure. Jonel's personal letter constructs s/m as a dangerous but exhilarating addiction. Harris's contention that s/m did not tap into her "real emotions" is belied by her revelation that the practice brought her to orgasm for the first time, and to "hysterical tears" not once, but twice. In this sense, anti-s/m confessions traffic in the thrill of *going too far* and harness the delights of shame when revealing dirty secrets.

The two confessionals also provide ambivalent accounts of the quality of experience of non-s/m or "healthy" vanilla sexuality. What is notable is that vanilla sexuality is not defined in terms of arousal or physical pleasure. Instead, other values and emotions, like love, respect, and equality, are presented as superior goals for intimate relations. Jonel exemplifies this trend when she asserts, "It's possible to go from the drama and high energy/emotion of sm back to 'vanilla' sex. 'Vanilla' sex is *not* unexciting" (1982, 22; emphasis in original). As with the negation in the title of the movie *Not a Love Story*, the defensive claim that "vanilla" sex is not unexciting, with an emphasis on the "not," reveals an anxiety about the practice of vanilla sex. Jonel can't bring herself to actually say vanilla sex *is* exciting. Instead she uses a double negative, a disavowal that betrays the fear that vanilla sex might be humdrum in comparison to the "drama and high energy/emotion" found with s/m sexuality. Indeed, her next sentence fails to make vanilla sex any more sexually appealing, as she assures the reader, "Relationships can exist with a balance of power" (22). Thus she instructs the reader to think less of sex and more of a "balanced" relationship. And even a relationship with a balance of power seems tenuous, as she merely states it can "exist" – a humble word implying the minimal level of vitality.

Harris also ends her account by urging the reader to refocus her sexual priorities. After dismissing s/m as a dysfunctional coping device, she concludes, "Our women's sexuality is a source of healing, renewal and creativity. We do not need and we cannot afford to adulterate it" (1982, 95). Here again, a woman's (true) sexuality is defined outside of the terms of carnal pleasure. And because Harris had previously described the lurid thrills and orgasmic releases she achieved through s/m, a juxtaposition is created. On one side, s/m is positioned as physically gratifying but emotionally empty, and on the other, vanilla sexuality is positioned as emotionally fulfilling without any comment about its physical pleasures. The suggestion is that physical pleasure is less important than emotional fulfilment and healing.

The last two articles in *Against Sadomasochism* that I want to discuss intensify the notion that s/m is unhealthy by casting it unequivocally as a disease. Vivienne Walker-Crawford's contribution, "The Saga of Sadie O. Massey" constructs s/m as a "cancerous growth that has taken a firm root in most wimmin" (1982, 150). As such, she does not fully blame sadomasochists for succumbing to this sickness, stating, "The proponents of sexual sadomasochism have turned themselves inside out to mirror our disease. This disease is frightening in its enormity. We immediately recoil, not wanting to recognize its vileness" (150). Cheri Lesh's contribution to the same collection, "Hunger and Thirst in the House of Distorted Mirrors" (1982) also relies upon a quasi-medical explanation of s/m as a cultural disease. Like Walker-Crawford, Lesh admonishes self-righteous anti-s/m feminists for condemning sadomasochists as "twisted and sick" while believing that the critics are "apart, safe, immune" (203). She states of sadomasochists, "They're acting out the symptoms of the illness I was exposed to. I don't look sick. I am a silent carrier" (203).

Although this may seem a sympathetic, though condescending, portrayal of sadomasochists who are victims of a patriarchal infection that affects all of us, Miller points out that disgust often presents itself in the language of sickness. He states, "We blame the ill for their sicknesses even as we paradoxically try to exculpate the guilty by defining them as sick, which in turn will subject them to blame for being so infected" (1997, 203). Sadomasochist lesbians are presented as "sick" feminists, but they are still culpable. Miller continues, "Sickness, we think, is a punishable offence" (203). Accordingly, the construction of sadomasochists as visibly sick – which draws implicitly on the purported neutrality of science and medicine – actually solidifies their disgustingness as people who failed to ward off or conceal this patriarchal disease. The message becomes: we are all sick, but lesbian sadomasochists flaunt their sickness, instead of repressing, healing, or at the very least hiding it. Lesbian sadomasochists are ultimately construed as a contaminating force that threatens feminist circles. Lesh recalls a conversation she had with lesbian sadomasochists: "While they talked of liberation and uninhibited pleasure their pain and fear and rage filled the room like invisible poison gas, squeezing my lungs narrow" (1982, 203). Though Lesh allegedly detects negative emotions hidden beneath lesbian sadomasochists' claims of enjoyment, she also holds them responsible for poisoning her environment. Sadomasochists are thus blamed for their lack of self-awareness of their sick condition, which endangers the more enlightened lesbians who are working on self-healing and consciousness-raising.

"Sadomasochism: The Erotic Cult of Fascism" (1984) and "Remember the Fire: Lesbian Sadomasochism in a Post Holocaust World" (1986)

The next two documents I consider came out in the mid-1980s and reveal a more pronounced moral panic about the influence of lesbian s/m, going so far as to blame s/m desire, in part, for Nazi fascism. As I stated above, Sheila Jeffreys wrote "Sadomasochism: The Erotic Cult of Fascism" (1984) as part of a campaign to have a sadomasochist support group evicted from the London Lesbian and Gay Centre (LLGC). As in the Barnard conference, the battle was not just over the discursive boundaries around the "feminist" label, but over feminist material resources as well. Sheila Jeffreys was part of a London group called Lesbians against Sadomasochism, which attempted to convince the members of the LLGC to ban sadomasochist groups by linking s/m to the rise of fascism in Germany. She states in her article, "There is a historical example of the connection between S/M and fascism which we ignore at our peril" (172). Relying primarily on accounts written by a British novelist who apparently visited Berlin in the 1930s, Jeffreys asserts, "Before the nazi takeover in Germany in 1933 S/M was a flourishing and growing sexual practice, particularly among gay men" (172). Here again, the connection between lesbian s/m and contamination from gay male sexuality is set up. Perhaps most disturbingly, Jeffreys seems to lay some blame for the Nazi Holocaust on gay men, a group that was targeted by that regime. Jeffreys argues that these gay s/m dynamics attracted unemployed and alienated German youth and would later be adopted by Hitler. She finally concludes in her article that, bearing this "history" in mind, "what is ritual today can be reality tomorrow" (181). Her scare tactics thus imply that to allow the s/m support group to have access to a meeting place in the LLGC would be tantamount to encouraging future fascist movements.

Written in about the same time period, Irene Reti's article "Remember the Fire: Lesbian Sadomasochism in a Post Holocaust World" (1993a) also seeks to explore links between s/m and Nazism. Reti asserts, somewhat anachronistically, that s/m was a defining factor during the Roman Empire, the medieval Inquisition, slavery, the Holocaust, and in modern-day despotic regimes in South Africa and Central America (81). However, her focus is "to document the blatant and more subtle ways in which sadomasochism fuelled the Holocaust" (81). In this regard, her first piece of "evidence" is the claim that Nazi prison guards were prompted by sexual sadism when they meted out sexual torture against the prisoners. She then compares this to current practices of s/m, stating, "Sexual punishment and discipline are also key elements of lesbian SM" (84). Reti next argues that Nazi guards used excrement as part of their strategy to humiliate prisoners, and she compares this to a short piece of lesbian s/m erotica that uses excrement as part of the scene. S/m erotica turns up again in her next point when she compares a short story by Califia to the German adulation of Nazi soldiers. In her view, both perpetuate the construction of sadists as handsome, and both are premised on a glorification of militarism (89). Reti finally concludes that s/m notions of "beautiful masochism" and "romantic suffering" have distorted history, such that Jewish victims of the Holocaust are portrayed as passively accepting their fate and even enjoying their suffering. She condemns the practice of lesbian s/m for perpetuating this myth: "To play masochist in bed is to endorse the Nazi picture of reality in which there are sadistic torturers who believe their victims enjoy being punished and humiliated" (93). Lesbian bottoms are thus indicted for rationalizing genocidal practices through their sexual enjoyment of s/m.

Reti's and Jeffreys's "proof" of the connections between s/m and Nazism reveals a reductionist and literalist interpretive perspective that ignores the context of fantasy, role playing, and s/m's strategy of appropriation. As Anne McClintock has argued, "Demonising S/M confuses the distinction between unbridled sadism and the social subculture of consensual fetishism. To argue that in consensual S/M the master has power, and the slave has not, is to read theatre for reality; it is to play the world forward ... Consensual S/M 'plays the world backwards'" (1993, 207). In other words, revealing the surface similarities between s/m and fascist props and scenes misses the entire point of s/m; it *is* a derivative form of sexuality. By "playing the world backwards," practitioners of s/m unapologetically browse from the history of oppression to create scenes of pleasure. (Of course, whether this appropriation is irresponsible or not is another question that many other anti-s/m writers have addressed.) But my point here is to reveal the way Reti and Jeffreys sidestep the issue of consent and role playing to conflate historical accounts of violence with a subculture's reinscription of those accounts for the sake of mutual pleasure.

For both Reti and Jeffreys, the economy of desire of lesbian s/m is in direct relation to the economy of desire of Nazism (as well as slavery and other racist regimes). This goes beyond the critique that sadomasochists trivialize real oppression. Although both authors stop short of labelling lesbian sadomasochists as actual fascists (although they come quite close), lesbian sadomasochists are condemned for actively seeking pleasure in the same dynamics that underpinned Nazi brutality, and for promoting the notion of willing victims. Ironically, both authors acknowledge that the erotic legacy of Nazism is that many experience sexual arousal from s/m imagery. However, both contend that instead of cultivating this pathology, lesbians who sexually respond to s/m should refrain from acting out these scripts and should instead support each other in analysing their desires. The imperative becomes, once again, mind over matter. And this again is reminiscent of Krafft-Ebing's suggestion that in Christendom, "man" must exercise willpower to overcome his baser animalistic desires. Though the anti-s/m feminists locate s/m desire in patriarchal nurture, and Krafft-Ebing in Mother Nature, both conclude that the body's urges must be disciplined by the enlightened mind.

"Upsetting an Applecart: Difference, Desire and
Lesbian Sadomasochism" (1986)

In 1986, Susan Ardill and Sue O'Sullivan, two self-identified socialist-feminist lesbians, took a middle-of-the-road position on s/m, arguing not that the mind had to necessarily discipline the body, but rather that it had to interrogate its desires. In their retrospective article "Upsetting an Applecart: Difference, Desire and Lesbian Sadomasochism" (1986) the authors seek to critically examine the struggle at the London Lesbian and Gay Centre (LLGC) from a moderate insider's perspective. Ardill and O'Sullivan were members of the Lesbian Coordinating Committee for the LLGC, and formed a subgroup, Lesbian Feminists for the Centre (LFC), which stood apart from the two polarized factions – Lesbians against Sadomasochism (LASM) and the Sexual Fringe – who were battling over the issue. Ardill and O'Sullivan explained that while they were deeply troubled by the divisional moralism of LASM, they also wanted to challenge the Sexual Fringe's uncritical embrace of s/m and sexual pleasure. Rather than seeking an absolute ban or complete acceptance of s/m groups, LFC proposed the enactment of rules that would govern how sadomasochists presented themselves. In particular, LFC suggested that all groups should be allowed to meet, but that members should be prohibited from wearing swastikas or leading one another around by a chain (LASM had claimed both practices were frequently engaged in by lesbian sadomasochists). The Sexual Fringe accepted this proposal. LASM vigorously opposed it, wanting a full ban on sadomasochist groups, and accused LFC of being "liberal" and unconcerned with the rights of minority women.

Ardill and O'Sullivan decry the inflammatory nature of LASM's tactics, which included, after failing to get a permanent ban on sadomasochist groups at the LLGC, the distribution of leaflets claiming that the centre was "rife with fascists, racists, misogynists and sadomasochists" (51, quoting LASM leaflet). Yet the authors also wanted to challenge the "libertarianism" of the Sexual Fringe. They claimed that, "by default, their position seemed to amount to one of 'uninhibited pursuit of the sexual high'" (52). The authors then equate this attributed position to "glorifying a kind of individualism" (52). Yet the authors were unable to cite any literature from the Sexual Fringe that would support its construction as libertarian, individualistic, or focused solely on sexual pleasure. In fact, the Sexual Fringe was made up not just of sadomasochists, but also included bisexuals, transsexuals, and, interestingly, celibates (48–9). The support of transsexuals – as a sex/gender identity, not a sexual orientation or practice – suggests that the Sexual Fringe's mandate extended beyond sexuality, while the support of bisexuals and celibates suggests that its focus was not individualistic, but coalitional with other sexual minorities as well as with people who were abstaining from coupled or group sexuality.

The main criticism levelled by Ardill and O'Sullivan seems to be that the members of the Sexual Fringe were not adequately self-reflective about the nature of their sexual practices. As Rubin has pointed out, "moderates" who defended sadomasochists' right to participation still condemned them for not interrogating the meaning, roots, and historical context of their sexuality (Rubin 1989, 304). This is exemplified when Ardill and O'Sullivan complain that the Sexual Fringe *"failed to acknowledge* ... that sexuality can be problematic" (1986, 52; emphasis in original) and that its members "tended to exclude any discussion about the ways sexual relations *are* related to the rest of our lives" (52). The authors imply that there is a political imperative for sadomasochists to self-scrutinize their sexuality and interrogate their desires. For sadomasochists to choose to gather in a social or affirming group at the LLGC to simply enjoy and accept their desires was construed as irresponsible. The implied suggestion was that every lesbian group should be a consciousness-raising group whose members must politically justify – or at least account for – their desires. In this sense, Ardill and O'Sullivan are fully implicated in an incitement to sexual discourse. They insist that sadomasochist sexuality must be analysed and probed, not necessarily from a moral perspective but from a rational and political one. This insistence recalls Foucault's characterization of the modern era: "this need to take sex 'into account,' to pronounce a discourse on sex that would not derive from morality alone but from rationality as well" (1990, 24). This mandate is also a variation of the mind-over-matter imperative. The mind does not necessarily have to control the body, but it should at least try to theorize its urges.

The other significant claim made by Ardill and O'Sullivan is that by validating the sexual practices of its members, the Sexual Fringe was implicitly denigrating non-sadomasochists. Again, no citations are offered in support. The authors state that the Sexual Fringe *"failed to acknowledge* that 'vanilla' sex can be exciting" (1986, 52: emphasis in original). Later they complain that the Sexual Fringe "romanticized categories of 'deviant' sexual practice, if you can't claim one of their identities, well, frankly, you're boring. Boring equals vanilla sex" (52).[17] This display of vanilla defensiveness seems to impose a normative obligation upon the sadomasochist members to not just account for their own desires, but also to reassure those who don't share them (i.e., vanilla-oriented people), that their desires were also exciting. The complaint ascribes to sadomasochist lesbians a remarkable degree of influence over the sexual self-identities and self-perception of non-sadomasochists. And when considering the anti-s/m movement, which created actual books, pamphlets, and entire groups for the sole purpose of denouncing s/m, the expectation that sadomasochists were obliged to support vanilla-oriented people in their desires seems strange. After all, there were no books called *Against Vanilla Sex*. I wonder if this vanilla defensiveness points to an underlying anxiety found in much of the anti-s/m

literature, a creeping suspicion that perhaps vanilla sex is *not* as exciting as s/m sex after all.

Unleashing Feminism: Critiquing Lesbian Sadomasochism in the Gay Nineties (1993)

Examining the controversy over s/m in the 1990s reveals the extent to which the discourse began to evolve. The anti-s/m feminists became more defensive, recognizing and lamenting the growing acceptance of s/m within lesbian and feminist communities, and yet persevering in the project of enlightening feminists and lesbians about the problematic nature of s/m. Eleven years after *Against Sadomasochism* was published, another anthology emerged that once again was entirely dedicated to the condemnation of lesbian s/m: *Unleashing Feminism: Critiquing Lesbian Sadomasochism in the Gay Nineties* (Reti 1993b).

One article in *Unleashing Feminism* provides an updated version of the allegation that s/m perpetuates systemic racism. In "Rodney King, Racism and the SM Culture of America" (1993) Jamie Lee Evans blames sadomasochistic beliefs as well as racism for the acquittal of the four policemen who were caught on camera attacking King. She states that because of the infiltration of "sm thinking," the jury believed that King was in control of the beating, such that he could determine its length and severity. Evans then likens this scenario to claims made by sado-masochists that the bottom is always in control and sets the limits dur-ing an encounter. In drawing this analogy, she seems to assert that the jury members were somehow conditioned by the s/m subculture to view scenes of police brutality as if they had taken place within the context of a consensual and negotiated kinky scene.

At the end of this article, Evans pulls out her identity politics trump card: she reveals that not only is she a woman of colour and a lesbian, but she is also a ritual abuse survivor. As a child in a "Satanic foster home," Evans recounts that she was "whipped, beaten, burned, chained, tied down, tied up, gagged, gang raped, choked, and forced to witness all of the above being done to other children" (1993, 77). She implies an analogy here to s/m, stating, "Believe me when I say there is nothing liberating about being the bottom of these types of assaults" (77). She then explains that not only did she have to endure this horrific abuse, but as a "mind-fuck" she was "forced to *ask* to be raped, beaten, burned" (77; emphasis in original). She recounts being forced to say, "'Yes, I want to lie in a coffin of snakes, yes I want the lid to be closed, yes, I want to be buried in the earth'" (77). Evans thus seeks to conflate the practice of bottoms asking the tops to dominate them in a negotiated s/m scene with her own recollections of being compelled to ask her satanic abusers for the dispensation of nightmarish abuse.

Read Evans's survivor narrative twenty years later and her allegations appear incredible, part of a moral panic over satanic child sexual abuse that swept through therapeutic, religious, and feminist circles from the mid-1980s to the mid-1990s, without supporting evidence to substantiate the hundreds of claims of "recovered" memories that detailed extreme horror movie scenarios.[18] Yet the issue here is not whether this actually happened to Evans; rather, what is striking is the way that s/m bears partial responsibility for the atrocities in her narrative. As with her conclusion that "sm ideology" supported the acquittal of the accused in the King case, Evans posits that for lesbian sadomasochists to declare their pleasure in meting out or receiving pain is to strengthen the justificatory framework used by rapists and attackers to rationalize their abuse. As such, it is irresponsible for lesbian sadomasochists to be public and unrepentant about their desires, because this provides fascists, Satanists, and the police with justification for violence. Evans's arguments reveal how, amidst the throes of a moral panic, a peripheral group is wheeled onto centre stage and marked as a major social threat, implicated in such atrocities as genocide, police brutality, and childhood abuse.

On a less inflammatory note, in another article in *Unleashing Feminism*, Kathy Miriam considers the shift in lesbian sadomasochist politics from the 1980s to the 1990s. In "From Rage to All the Rage: Lesbian-Feminism, Sadomasochism and the Politics of Memory" (1993) Miriam argues that early lesbian s/m discourse initially sought inclusion within the feminist category, but she opposed it: "Lesbian sadomasochism is about, above all else, a radical cleavage between feminism and lesbianism" (13). However, her article is not concerned with this particular scuffle in the identity wars. Instead, Miriam is concerned with the ways lesbian s/m has incorporated hetero-patriarchal dynamics and practice, while erasing the political impact of lesbian feminism. She states, "We can indeed read the emergence of sadomasochism as a 'rupture' in lesbian identity – a rupture in the political, feminist definition of lesbian as rebel against heterosexuality" (17–18). Here Miriam, following in the footsteps of Adrienne Rich, defines lesbianism not in terms of a positive sexual/genital choice, but rather as an oppositional political stance against heterosexuality. As a result, instead of challenging hetero-sexuality, Miriam contends that "lesbian sadomasochism confirms the boundaries of the 'straight mind'" (32) and perpetuates a "heterosexual social order" (33). A lesbian-feminist perspective is leveraged here to construe lesbian s/m as a pollution of political lesbianism. This view-point soundly castigates lesbian s/m both for incorporating heterosex-ual activity (dildos, fantasies that include men, fantasies of being men, sometimes even having sex with men), *and* for adopting the dynamics of heterosexuality, which Miriam, like MacKinnon, views as resting on the erotic charge of dominance and submission.

"Come to Me Baby, or What's Wrong with Lesbian SM" (1994)

A document produced in England in the early 1990s also implicitly con-demned lesbian s/m for its integration of, and alliance with, hetero-sexual norms. In "Come to Me Baby, or What's Wrong with Lesbian SM" (1994), Reina Lewis and Karen Adler conduct a literature review of lesbian erotica they label sadomasochistic. They determine that "the two key tropes associated with the increased signification of sm in les-bian erotic fiction are penetration and anonymity: A dramatic increase in fucking and violent sex, heretofore associated with heterosexual practice, is accompanied by the displacement of sex from nurturing, sisterly relationships to isolated and casual sexual encounters" (435). By using the familial tropes "nurturing" and "sisterly," the authors con-tinue in the anti-s/m feminist tradition of constructing authentic lesbi-an sexual practice as being less about physical pleasure and more about emotional connection within a long-term relationship. They challenge the suggestion that lesbian s/m sexual activities can be distinguished completely from the heterosexual variety, stating, "Lesbian sm claims holy status via its lesbianism and argues that lesbianism can incorpo-rate heterosexual fantasies and acts without the loss of previous lesbian identification" (436). Later in the article, the authors criticize lesbian s/m for normalizing dildo-use and "fucking," concluding that the emerging s/m normative framework in these texts renders non-kinky sex as the abnormal sexual practice (436). The article closes with a post-script in which the authors complain of the continual expansion of s/m visibility, and the blurring of lesbian, gay, and s/m fashions in the mainstream into the singular identity of "deviant chic" (440). Again, an abject anxiety surfaces; Lewis and Adler perceive the discrete category of lesbian erotic identity deteriorating because of its supposed absorption of heterosexual as well as gay cultures. There is a suggestion that lesbianism should remain hermetically and hermeneutically sealed from trends, practices, and theories that are connected to sexual subjectivities that include males.

Lesbian Sex Wars (1996)

The last text to consider in the anti-s/m vein is a book that constructed itself as a relatively "neutral" observer. Emma Healey's retrospective monograph, *Lesbian Sex Wars* (1996), sets out to trace the feminist conflict in Britain, considering such hotbeds of controversy as butch-femme lesbian identity, s/m, and dildos. Throughout the book, Healey alternates between condemning lesbian feminism for denying the importance of sexuality, and condemning the sex-radical position for uncritically celebrating all sexuality. In the latter project, her strategy frequently relies upon exaggerating the political claims of lesbian sadomasochists, while at the same time describing the s/m activities that would be most likely to inspire disgust in the reader.[19]

For example, Healey employs both tactics when addressing the political stakes of s/m sexual practice. Healey states, "It is, of course, rather difficult to create a meaningful political ideology around the right to give your lover an enema" (1996, 109). In this commentary, Healey does not cite any lesbian sadomasochists who claim to be endowing enemas with such political clout (although I think it *is* possible to do so). Instead, she follows this sarcasm with a quotation from a lesbian she interviewed who stated, "I face enough oppression in my life for simply being a lesbian, without wanting to go home and have my partner piss on me" (109). Again, this statement calls upon cultural disgust towards the abject fluid of urine – as the previous reference did with enema's association with faeces – to stand in for substantive analysis. On the surface, the statement simply conveys that the speaker believes having a partner urinate on her would be inherently oppressive; the unstated assumption is, however, that the reader would naturally share in her disgust.

Later in the book, Healey looks back on the contributions of lesbian sex-radicals and states, "SM, like lesbian feminism before it, is no universal panacea. It is questionable whether the lesbian world will be truly liberated just by learning to pierce our partner's labia so we can lace her cunt up" (1996, 152). In these editorializing asides, Healey sets up a straw s/m lesbian who easily crumbles under her caustic wit. Yet nowhere does Healey cite these seriously misguided sadomasochists who supposedly believe their kinky sexuality will serve as a "universal panacea." Furthermore, by using the hypothetical scenario of labia piercing and vaginal lacing in her argument, Healey invokes the racialized practice of infibulation to malign lesbian s/m. Her descriptions of s/m sexuality tend to dwell upon the more extreme, dangerous, or culturally taboo practices on the s/m continuum, thereby attempting to elicit the reader's disgust to fortify her analysis. As Miller has noted, "We perceive what disgusts and tend to imbue it with defective moral status for that reason alone" (1997, 180). Instead of calling upon the milder, less taboo s/m activities of bondage or role playing, Healey's scenarios elicit disgust to do the work of criticism, supplemented by exaggerated and unsubstantiated claims about lesbian sadomasochist political beliefs.

There is one notable exception in Healey's practice of non-citation of lesbian sadomasochists. She does cite Califia's introduction to his book of erotica, *Macho Sluts*. After two lengthy quotations in which Califia speaks of the struggles of lesbian writers with their inner censor (without any reference to s/m), Healey concludes, "Califia is right to suggest that lesbians have censored themselves about sex, but the implication that somehow all lesbians writing about sex would have written SM if they only had the courage, is really rather daft" (1996, 151). Admittedly, that would be rather daft; however, an examination of Califia's introduction shows that no such insinuation is ever made. In the same paragraph where Califia addresses the inner censor, he states, "Nobody's an expert on women's sexuality … I doubt anyone ever will be qualified to generalize about what all women want" (1988b, 14). Califia's introduction recognizes the plurality of women's desires and never states that all women are sadomasochists or would enjoy s/m erotica. Instead, he writes from the position of a sadomasochist writer who is seeking to create a space of pleasure and affirmation for those who might share his erotic proclivities.

Healey again misreads Califia's introduction when she states, "While the stories in *Macho Sluts* can be read as a courageous attempt to push the boundaries of lesbian sexuality to its absolute limits, it is odd that the introduction to the book suggests that all this has got to be good for you too" (1996, 151). Yet just one page after the passage already cited by Healey, Califia states, "I do not believe that sex has an inherent power to transform the world. I do not believe that pleasure is always an anarchic force for good. I do not believe we can fuck our way to freedom"

(Califia 1988b, 15). This statement not only contravenes Healey's exaggerated claims of Califia's beliefs; it also shows that Califia, as a major spokesperson for lesbian sadomasochists, was explicitly *not* trying to create a political ideology of erotic enemas, or any other form of s/m practice.

Although Healey claims a neutral position, her criticisms of the sex-radical position mirror many of the strategies used by explicit anti-s/m literature. Both camps relied on exaggeration and mischaracterization to describe the political and ontological claims of lesbian sadomasochists. I think Healey's hyperbolic renderings became even easier to pull off after the height of the sex wars because memories had faded, and fewer interested parties would actually have read the relevant source texts. In addition, as Rubin has observed, "It is all too easy to marginalize radicals, and to attempt to buy acceptance for a moderate position by portraying others as extremists" (1989, 303). Although Healey has done important work in chronicling the British sex wars, she capitalizes on the persuasive powers of disgust to caricature the lesbian s/m position.[20]

Abjection/Rejection/Negation: The Satisfaction of Ousting Sadomasochists

Looking back at the campaigns against s/m, it is clear that the abject status of lesbian sadomasochists called for specific expulsion strategies. Recall that beyond the theoretical debates were battles that had a direct impact on the material lives of those associated with s/m. Conferences, community centres, and bookstores were just some of the sites where sadomasochists and/or their literature were rejected. In conjunction with the desire to maintain a cohesive and totalizing definition of feminism, the expulsion strategies allowed furtive access to s/m. The constant need to negate lesbian s/m was part of the incitement to discourse, a way to access the taboo pleasures of s/m without being tainted by it.

To illustrate, I want to review and expand upon the many ways that anti-s/m feminists sought to expel or censor s/m lesbians. To begin, allow me to elaborate upon the details of the controversy at the 1982 Barnard conference. In "More Danger, More Pleasure: A Decade after the Barnard Sexuality Conference" (1993) Vance explains that the agenda of the conference was to create a space of dialogue for women to explore female sexuality from political, experiential, and artistic vantage points, with the goal of making space for diverse and conflicting accounts. The conference planners challenged the hegemony of the anti-pornography feminist position, with its privileged construction of sexuality as a site of danger and oppression. Instead, the aim was to embrace the paradoxes of sexuality as a source of both pleasure and danger.

A week before the conference, anti-pornography feminists mobilized a telephone campaign to convince Barnard College officials that the conference contradicted the feminist mandate of the series and promoted patriarchal values. While they failed to prevent the conference from taking place, Barnard officials did confiscate the *Diary of a Conference on Sexuality*, a booklet that would have provided participants with context and schedules, just two days before the conference began. The seizure was justified on the grounds that the pamphlet carried Barnard's name and could therefore be construed as an endorsement by the college of the particular views expressed in the document (Vance 1989a, 431–2).

On the day of the conference, anti-pornography protesters arrived wearing T-shirts that read "For a Feminist Sexuality" on the front, and "Against S/M" on the back. The protesters were apparently part of a conglomerate group called Coalition for a Feminist Sexuality and against Sadomasochism, which, according to its leaflet, was made up of members from other activist circles, including Women against Violence against Women, Women against Pornography, and New York Radical Feminists. This leaflet, which protestors endeavoured to distribute to conference participants, claimed that the conference gave stage to a "tiny off-shoot of the women's movement" that "support and practice pornography, that promote sex roles and sadomasochism, and that have joined the straight and gay pedophile organizations in lobbying for an end to laws that protect children from sexual abuse by adults" (Pally 1982). The leaflet then went on to name the offending participants. Some were listed directly, such as the groups No More Nice Girls, Samois, and the Lesbian Sex Mafia, and individuals such as Gayle Rubin, Dorothy Allison, and Pat Califia (although Califia was only an attendee at the conference). Others who appeared to be listed indirectly included Joan Nestle and Amber Hollibaugh, who were referred to obliquely as "several women who champion butch-femme sex roles" (ibid.). According to Vance, the leaflet inspired a "phantom" conference that was meant to redress the purported one-sidedness of the Barnard conference. Its basic agenda was to condemn s/m, pornography, and butch-femme roles among lesbians as "anti-feminist" (1993, paragraph 14).

Repercussions of the smear campaign against the conference included the Helena Rubinstein foundation's withdrawal of funding for the Scholar and the Feminist Series in the following year. While the conference did occur in subsequent years, Barnard officials were much more active in managing its agenda and controlling its contents. Some of the individuals singled out as deviant or anti-feminist by the leaflet also apparently had anonymous calls made to their employers conveying the same message. As such, they suffered professionally, including being dis-invited to speak at feminist panels and conferences (Vance 1989a, 434).

Besides this infamous battle in the sex wars, recall that a variety of other incidents occurred in which anti-s/m feminists attempted to exclude or expel s/m lesbians. In San Francisco, staff at the Women's Building refused to allow Samois to rent space for gatherings in the 1980s (Rubin 1987, 212–13). As previously discussed, this mirrored the anti-s/m feminists in Britain who, with more success, managed to evict a sadomasochist group from meeting at the LLGC for six months in the mid-1980s. Recall also that fear of the dissemination of positive accounts of s/m led feminist and progressive bookstores to engage in censorship that included restricting or banning publications associated with s/m sexuality, or even – in a McCarthyist moment in 1983 – the burning of copies of *Coming to Power* outside of a women's bookstore in London (Healey 1996, 23).

Emma Healey tells of further controversies over s/m in England in the 1980s. The film *She Must Be Seeing Things* sparked protest among anti-s/m feminists who interpreted it as promoting sadomasochistic and butch-femme themes. Activists attempted to prevent its screening in various cities throughout England, often using tactics that relied upon "direct action," which included an attempt to rip the film out of the video machine, placing a fake bomb at a theatre lavatory, storming the stage, and in one successful effort, pouring cement down the toilet in a cinema (1996, 114–16). Perhaps most shocking of all was a violent incident that Healey recounts involving a newly opened lesbian s/m club in 1987. After its launch, members from LASM showed up with crowbars, attacking the club and threatening some of the patrons (129).[21]

All of these events – the protests, smear campaigns, book bannings and burnings, evictions, violent threats, and aggressive interference with public events – demonstrate the extent to which anti-s/m feminists were caught in a moral panic over the possible influence of lesbian s/m. What heightened these fears was the fact that it was not outsiders who introduced sedition; rather, lesbian sadomasochists had emerged from within the women's movement and from lesbian feminism itself. They were thus portrayed as a fifth column, furtively injecting patriarchal ideas behind feminist lines. From this panicked perspective, a lesbian sadomasochist appears as a grotesque and abject composite of the ideal and internal sexuality (lesbian) with the unacceptable and external sexuality (sadomasochist), and as such fundamentally "disturbs identity, system, order" and transgresses "borders, positions, rules" (Kristeva 1982, 4). As Julia Kristeva elaborates in *Powers of Horror*, when an abject phenomenon threatens the subjectivity of a body politic, decontamination must be initiated (1982). Hence the extreme measures outlined above to evict sadomasochists from the ranks and suppress their discourse in the marketplace of feminist ideas.

Yet ironically, in their bid to suppress sadomasochist ideas, the protesters continually invoked them in their discursive strategies. Consider the names chosen in their purification campaigns. The group protesting outside the Barnard conference called itself a Coalition for a Feminist Sexuality and against Sadomasochism, while sporting T-shirts that proclaimed the same message. In England, the most visible protesting group designated itself Lesbians against Sadomasochism, which, unlike the coalition, did not articulate what they were supporting; their entire purpose was simply to oppose another set of sexual practices. The two collections discussed at length above – *Against Sadomasochism: A Radical Feminist Analysis*, and its follow-up a decade later, *Unleashing Feminism: Critiquing Lesbian Sadomasochism in the Gay Nineties* – also defined their purposes in oppositional terms. What is ironic is that in much of the literature of these "against" discourses, the claim is made that lesbian sadomasochists are a tiny group of women, unrepresentative of the majority of feminists or lesbians.[22] Yet the vehement and prolix response of the "antis" seems to belie the marginality of the sadomasochist presence. Furthermore, the chosen titles for their activist groups and their polemical writings constantly kept s/m in the feminist and lesbian spotlight.

There is perhaps another, more insidious purpose to these namings, and indeed to the vast bulk of the anti-s/m literature. In their condemnations of lesbian s/m, feminist activists were granted a privileged access to these sexual practices. Couched in negativity, s/m could be infinitely talked about, dissected, probed, and described in the most graphic terms. Both Freud and Foucault provide insight into how negation could be deployed for the sexual satisfaction of the anti-s/m camp.

When considering ways to discover the unacknowledged urges of his patients, Freud explains, "Negation is a way of taking cognizance of what is repressed; indeed it is already a lifting of a repression, though not of course, an acceptance of what is repressed" (Freud 1981d, 235–6). Negation then, is both a creative and a defensive mental process – creative because the subject can access and express an unconscious desire in a cloaked form, but defensive because she can protect her ego by condemning it. Through their vociferous and violent protest against the presence and the discourse of lesbian s/m, the anti-sadomasochists were allowed to imagine and outline in vivid detail what sexual horrors were being gratified. The sheer amount of energy put into their negation indicates the presence of a repressed desire, or at the very least, a repressed curiosity, a latent voyeurism.

And as Foucault has pointed out, the negation of sexuality, the condemnation of sexual practices, and the regulation of sexual identity can all be said to amount to one thing: talking about sex. The anti-s/m activists were caught up in a frenzied incitement to speak about sex, to delve into the most vile and patriarchal manifestations that they could imagine. The project of laying out what s/m *really* means, and contrasting that to what the lesbian sadomasochists claimed it meant, was a way to access knowledge-pleasure, as well as (or rather, in conjunction with) vicarious pleasure. Rather than censoring s/m through the force of their outrage, anti-s/m activists actually managed to discursively proliferate it.

The Pro-S/M Side

One consequence of this discursive proliferation was the growth of a resistance discourse, one that appropriated much of the language of the anti-sadomasochists but reversed its normative agenda. As Rubin points out, "Ironically, several acrimonious battles over the relationship of S/M and feminism enhanced the process of nascent community formation" (Stein 2003, *s.v.* "Samois" 67). Because the anti-s/m feminists were so vehement and vocal about their disapproval and disgust, lesbian sadomasochists in turn mobilized and found definition in their opposition to these hostile attitudes. They could operate under the banner of "outlaw" – marginalized by both the mainstream and lesbian feminism.

What Colour Is Your Handkerchief:
A Lesbian S/M Sexuality Reader (1979)

As stated, the first major publication to defend lesbian s/m was the booklet produced by Samois, *What Colour Is Your Handkerchief: A Lesbian*

S/M Sexuality Reader (Samois 1979). The title refers to a sexual code whereby the colour of one's handkerchief signifies a preference for certain kinds of sexual engagements. For example, wearing a grey handkerchief in your left pocket signals to potential partners that you like to instigate bondage; placed in your right pocket, it indicates that you want to be put into bondage. As the booklet explains, Samois adopted the system from gay men, incorporating slight alterations to make it more suitable for lesbian sexuality. In the title, Samois thus prioritized sexual desire and forged a link between lesbian and gay male sexuality. This approach contested the prevailing feminist tendencies to consider sexuality only in the terms of sexual danger and oppression and to define one's sexuality in opposition to men, both heterosexual and gay. Although the booklet itself contains many theoretical articles, the title boldly foregrounds sexual pleasure as inter-discursively linked to male sexuality.

The booklet begins with a "Statement" that describes Samois and its definition of s/m. As described above, Samois defined itself as a group of "feminist lesbians who share a positive interest in sadomasochism" (1979, 2). The "Statement" explains that Samois holds regular meetings that address s/m topics ranging from politics to sexual technique. The booklet describes s/m as "an eroticized exchange of power negotiated between two or more sexual partners" (2). *Handkerchief* thus defines s/m outside of the terms of pain, humiliation, violence, or top/bottom dynamics. Instead, power becomes the central focus, something that, in itself, implies neither inequality nor hierarchy. The "Statement" insists that s/m "must be consensual, mutual and safe," and that "S/M can exist as part of a healthy and positive lifestyle" (2). These assertions further attempt to pre-empt allegations of violence or abuse by emphasizing the consensual nature of s/m and its compatibility with a functional lifestyle. The "Statement" then positions Samois as developing a "lesbian-feminist perspective on s/m" that challenges hetero-sexism and male supremacy, even as it seeks to rebut the stereotyping and stigmatization of sadomasochists in feminist communities. Both feminist and mainstream cultures are constructed as holding problematic conceptions of s/m. The "Statement" concludes by explaining that the name Samois is derived from *The Story of O* and was chosen for its evocation of lesbian episodes in that novel. Again, Samois forages unapologetically into non-lesbian discourses, taking its name from an ostensibly heterosexual novel that had been heavily criticized by the women's movement because of its alleged misogyny and promotion of violence.

Embedded in this strategy are the seeds of what Judith Butler would later identify as a parodic reinvention of hegemonic scripts (1990).

The articles in the booklet also attempt to rewrite the prevailing feminist script of the body. While anti-s/m and anti-porn discourse often perpetuated the view that the body's urges could not be trusted because of patriarchal indoctrination, *Handkerchief* recuperates the body as a source of knowledge. In the essay "Cathexis: A Preliminary Investigation in the Nature of S-M," Barbara Lipschutz invokes both nature and biology to justify the practice of s/m. She asks, "Do we trust each other enough to expose and claim the "dark" sides of our nature?" (Samois 1979, 9). Later she suggests that s/m may be "written on the genetic code of all (some?) of us" (9). While Lipschutz veers towards the stolid pillars of genetic and nature essentialism in these passages, she stops short of advancing the claim that *everyone* is imbued with latent sadomasochistic tendencies. She does, however, encourage her readers to explore the possibility, stating, "Your body will tell you whether or not you are turned on by S-M. Listen to it" (10). From this vantage point, an argument follows that the body – with its urges, pleasures, and releases – holds a singular insight into the truth of s/m. A corporeal epistemology was put forth that attempted to challenge the anti-s/m side's blanket portrayal of physical desire as an overdetermined product of patriarchal conditioning.

Other articles in *Handkerchief* also took a personal approach by describing the pain that flows from being an oppressed sexual minority. A recurring theme here was to rely on the trope of the closet to express the fear and shame that many sadomasochists experience in connection with their sexuality. In "Coming Out on S&M," a short personal piece in *Handkerchief*, the author, identified as "Drivenwoman," lists three shameful sexual secrets from her childhood: she was masturbatory, lesbian, and sadomasochistic. After coming to embrace her "self-love and woman-love," she admits that she is still "in the closet on S-M" (Samois 1979, 12). This is confirmed by her use of a pseudonym.[23] Another contributor to *Handkerchief*, known by the pseudonym "Skip A.," also references the trope of the closet in "Don't Close the Closet Door Just Because There's Leather Inside" (26). Skip A. laments, "Untold individuals remain isolated in closets of shame, guilt, and frustration with their S/M fantasies." (12). The author contends that for some, the coming-out around s/m is actually more difficult and painful than coming out as gay or lesbian. From these lesbian sadomasochists, who claim to have insight into multiple forms of oppression, a possible truth-claim is shared between both the anti- and pro-s/m discourse: the notion that being identified as a current or former sadomasochist renders one vulnerable to criticism or unfair judgment from others in the feminist community. Indeed, this point is underscored by the fact that authors in both *Handkerchief* and (as described above) *Against Sadomasochism* used pseudonyms to conceal their identities.

While these personal histories provided insight into the phenomenology of lesbian s/m, Gayle Rubin's contribution to *Handkerchief*, "Sexual Politics, the New Right, and the Sexual Fringe," attempts to draw linkages between the oppression faced by s/m lesbians and others in the "sexual fringe," which also includes prostitutes, pederasts, transsexuals, and gay men interested in public sex. Rubin posits that those in the sexual fringe have borne the brunt of a societal moral panic, cataloguing myriad ways they have been silenced, marginalized, excluded, and criminalized. She holds established women's and gay organizations as well as mainstream culture accountable for neglect of and hostility towards sexual/gender minorities. She warns, "If we are not careful, we will be using feminist politics to rationalize and perpetuate harmful stereotypes [about the sexual fringe] that originate not in feminism, but in our puritanical heritage" (Samois 1979, 29). In this warning, Rubin inverts the anti-s/m truth-claim of the patriarchal origin of s/m desire. Instead, she argues that criticism against s/m and others in the sexual fringe can originate in puritanical (presumably patriarchal) conditioning, rather than being grounded in reasoned feminist analysis. Another inversion of the anti-s/m discourse concerns race. Rubin argues for tolerance by identifying s/m as "exotic," a racial cultural trope that implies s/m is a neutral sexual variation (30). This argument is further developed in her other articles, most fully in "Thinking Sex."

Besides these measured arguments that likened anti-s/m sentiment to homophobia and racism, *Handkerchief* also relied on the strategies of satirizing the criticisms launched by the anti-s/m side, and appropriating the pejorative labels as rebellious self-identification. A prime example was the name given by Samois to its publications and public information committee; in this regard, the caption on the last page of *Handkerchief* reads, "This Booklet is a Product Of: The Ministry of Truth / The Truth Often Hurts/The Ministry of Truth" (Samois 1979, 45). The literary reference, of course, invokes the fictional government in George Orwell's dystopic novel *1984*, which was in fact in the business of spreading falsehoods. Califia would later explain the reasons: "the Ministry of

Truth (MOT) … chose its name from *1984* as a joke. We had been called fascists so often that it was beginning to be predictable, so the MOT decided to rattle everybody's cage a little. Samois' propaganda arm didn't exactly self-select for reverence or circumspection" (Califia 1987, 264). The use of such a name was both provocative and strategic. It signalled to the anti-s/m feminists that their accusations of fascism were not only being disregarded, but were also being mocked to trivialize the anti-s/m perspective.

"A Secret Side of Lesbian Sexuality" (1979)
and "Feminism and Sadomasochism" (1980)

Patrick Califia was likely the most notorious activist to defend lesbian s/m and chronicle the sex wars from a sex-radical position. Califia wrote "A Secret Side of Lesbian Sexuality" in 1979, to be followed a year later by "Feminism and Sadomasochism" ([1979] 1994 and [1980] 1994). Both articles were first published in the *Advocate*. In these texts, Califia defines and defends s/m, describes his sexual interests, chronicles the mainstream harassment of sadomasochists, and criticizes segments of the women's and gay movement for "objectifying" and "degrading" sadomasochists.

Califia characterizes s/m as "a consensual activity that involves polarized roles and intense sensations" ([1980] 1994, 168). Again, when s/m is defended, the definition often avoids loaded terms like *dominance, submission*, or *pain* in favour of more neutral terminology that does not hold a pejorative valence. Califia also defends the practice of role playing, stating of sadomasochists, "We select the most frightening, disgusting, or unacceptable activities and transmute them into pleasure. We make use of all the forbidden symbols and all the disowned emotions. S/M is a deliberate, premeditated, erotic blasphemy" ([1979] 1994, 158). Later he states, "In an S/M context, the uniforms and roles and dialogue become a parody of authority, a challenge to it, a recognition of its secret sexual nature" (164). The notion that role playing oppressive relationships is a parodic attack on authority launches an epistemological challenge against the anti-s/m contention that to eroticize these scenarios is to endorse their real-life application. It also foreshadows later postmodern and queer arguments concerning the counter-hegemonic potential of mimetic practices. Califia thus attempts to neutralize the argument that s/m replicates oppressive structures, instead associating s/m with the subversive art and political savvy of parody. He later puts forward an anti-essentialist perspective on symbols of power and oppression by arguing, "No symbol has a single meaning. Meaning is derived from the context in which it is used. Not everyone who wears a swastika is a Nazi" ([1980] 1994, 169–70).[24] This contextual argument goes to the very heart of the disagreement between sadomasochists and anti-sadomasochists. Recall that in *Against Sadomasochism*, Susan Leigh Star claims that authors like Califia invest in a solipsist belief that one can control and determine the meaning of symbols or ideas despite larger socio-political contexts (Star 1982, 134). Her conclusion that Jewish people will invariably experience the use of swastikas by sadomasochists as a threat, and that neo-Nazis will view it as an affirmation, was presented as an inescapable reality. Califia counters arguments such as Star's – that sadomasochists show insensitivity to the historical and material reality of oppressed people – by emphasizing that sadomasochists themselves are an oppressed group that suffer street violence, systemic discrimination, and harassment. Califia thus argues that anti-s/m feminists themselves are in the business of decontextualizing. From his view, they decontextualize the ways lesbian sadomasochists put symbols of oppression to use in mutual pleasure and self-affirmation, and ignore the oppression that lesbian sadomasochists suffer because of homophobia and societal disgust for "perverts."

Califia further contextualizes s/m by arguing for the cathartic uses of the practice. This justification is located in the body and promotes the corporeal epistemology that was noted in *Handkerchief*. Califia states, "As a top, I find the old wounds and unappeased hunger. I nourish. I cleanse and close the wounds … A good scene doesn't end with orgasm – it ends with catharsis" ([1979] 1994, 163). This understanding of s/m goes beyond defending it as a benign sexual practice. In contradiction to both psychiatric and feminist condemnation of s/m as unhealthy or pathological, Califia asserts that s/m can be a *healing* ritual.

Unlike Rubin, Califia offers personal details about his "pervert" life to further elucidate and defend lesbian s/m. His tone is provocative, even confrontational: "I am a sadist. The polite term is 'top,' but I don't like to use it. It would dilute my image and my message. If someone wants to know about my sexuality, she can deal with me on my own terms" ([1979] 1994, 158). Califia proceeds to describe a typical s/m date that begins with an erotic information-gathering session about the bottom's preferences and any health issues that might affect what kind of activities they can do. In this description, Califia establishes himself as a vigilant "sadist," cognizant of safety and disability, and challenges the image of a self-centred and irresponsible abuser.

As the theoretical date progresses, Califia explains that he might initiate more explicit activities, which could include ordering his date to strip. He provocatively elaborates, "When I take away a woman's clothing, I am temporarily denying her humanity with all its privileges and responsibilities" ([1979] 1994, 161). This statement makes an aggressive intervention against the anti-s/m contention that s/m is dehumanizing. Califia apparently agrees with some aspects of this assessment but finds erotic emotional benefits in doing so; the bottom is relieved of the "responsibilities" of humanness. There is the suggestion that the construct of humanity can be a trapping that interferes with the sexiness of a scene.

To further establish the sexiness of s/m in opposition to vanilla, Califia goes on the offensive by using sarcasm to demean lesbian-feminist visions of sexuality. He states, "True lesbians are not sex perverts. They are high priestesses of feminism, conjuring up the wimmin's revolution. As I understand it, after the wimmin's revolution sex will consist of wimmin holding hands, taking off their shirts, and dancing in a circle. Then we will all fall asleep at exactly the same moment. If we didn't all fall asleep, something else might happen – something male-identified, objectifying, pornographic, noisy, and undignified. Something like an orgasm" ([1979] 1994, 159). Here, Califia pointedly suggests that cultural lesbian feminists are overly focused on nurturance, equality, and community at the expense of pleasure and sexual satisfaction.[25] His use of sarcasm and exaggeration shows that anti-s/m feminists were not alone in attempting to deride the other camp's position on sexuality by using such rhetorical devices. But perhaps Califia's harshest argument was his accusation that anti-s/m strategies operated in direct collusion with mainstream culture. One way to establish this was by positioning state sexual control and the oppressive behaviour of the feminist and gay and lesbian movements along a single continuum. For example, Califia equates the police harassment of leather bars in San Francisco with the Gay Freedom Day Parade Committee's proposed resolution to prevent people from wearing leather or s/m outfits in the parade. He argues, "Women and gays who are hostile to other sexual minorities are siding with fascism" ([1979] 1994, 164). This statement inverts the anti-s/m contention that s/m dynamics replicate fascistic regimes by insisting that those who seek to suppress minority sexual practices have the closer allegiance to fascism.

Califia further focuses on the ways that cultural and anti-pornography feminisms have become aligned with repressive and oppressive patriarchal structures, stating, "The women's movement has become a moralistic force contributing to the self-loathing and misery experienced by sexual minorities" ([1980] 1994, 166). Again, Califia traces the opprobrium faced by s/m practitioners back to hostility in the women's movement, seeking to hold anti-s/m feminists accountable for their role in contributing to oppression. The article concludes by reversing standard moralizing discourses through this accusation of anti-s/m feminist insensitivity: "I'd like to know when you're going to quit blaming us, the victims of sexual repression, for the oppression of women. I'd like to know when you're going to quit objectifying us" (174).

Through such exchanges, Califia and other lesbian sadomasochists attempted to challenge anti-s/m feminists' guarded monopoly on the feminist label *and* the victim label. Unlike the contributors to *Against Sadomasochism*, who argued that "feminist" sadomasochism was a contradiction in terms by its very definition, lesbian sadomasochists did not directly discredit their opponents' claim to feminism. Instead they attempted to reveal the hypocrisy of this brand of feminism, and the ways that political campaigns against lesbian s/m ended up further marginalizing already oppressed women.

Coming to Power (1982)

This indictment of liberation movements is also expressed in the introduction to the Samois anthology *Coming to Power*, which attempts to rebut many of the political claims of lesbian-feminist discourse. Katherine Davis states that s/m sex between feminist lesbians has been a "scary skeleton hidden in the corner of our otherwise cleaned up closets" (Davis in Samois 1982, 7). Again, the trope of the closet implicitly draws an analogy between gay or lesbian subjectivity and sadomasochist subjectivity. Davis recounts that when s/m lesbians came out of this closet, they were ostracized, censored, and vilified by many in the lesbian-feminist community: "We are being cast out, denied. We become heretics" (8). This self-construction as "heretic" is, to a certain extent, another way of portraying oneself as *heroic*. In Halperin's conceptualization of such vilification and rejection, the pariah becomes analogous to the saint: "The pariah, like the saint, is no longer subject to all the usual rules, no longer governed by the regime of the normal. He has escaped, slipped the bonds of conventional sociality, through the very extremity of his degradation and misfortune" (2007, 73). A romantic picture is drawn of lesbian sadomasochists as radical dissident pariahs, rejected because of feminist dogma. There is a pleasure in standing in opposition to established feminist principles and understanding oneself as an outcast and an outlaw. Foucault reminds us that the power-pleasure in regulating and condemning sexual anomalies is mirrored by the power-pleasure in defying and thwarting authority: "The pleasure that comes of exercising a power that questions, monitors, watches, spies, searches out, palpates, brings to light; and on the other hand, the pleasure that kindles at having to evade this power, flee from it, fool it, or travesty it. The power that lets itself be invaded by the pleasure it is pursuing; and opposite it, power asserting itself in the pleasure of showing off, scandalizing, or resisting" (1990, 45). This does not deny the pain of exclusion, but rather demonstrates that in describing such pain, lesbian sadomasochists had recourse to narrative satisfaction, exhibiting power and pleasure by constructing themselves as an oppressed and hounded sexual minority that nonetheless continued to flaunt its brazen desires. Their stories did not just report their experiences of being subjected to feminist bigotry, but also recounted how lesbian sadomasochists were courageously fighting against it.

Rubin elaborates on the history of anti-s/m feminist intolerance in her contribution to *Coming to Power*, entitled "The Leather Menace: Comments on Politics and S/M." It should be noted that the title itself already invokes the history of feminist and mainstream hostility to sexual minorities. "Leather Menace" is a play on the term "Lavender Menace" – a pejorative label used by Betty Freidan to describe the influence of lesbians in NOW and the women's movement (Freeman 1975, 232–3). Rubin's intertextual title references the historical moment when lesbians embraced Freidan's negative term and appropriated it to describe their oppositional politics against the exclusionary practices of the women's hetero-normative movement at the time. This strategy of turning insults into badges of honour recalls Halperin's account – through Jean-Paul Sartre and Jean Genet – of the positive power of abjection, where people spitting on you in contempt can be reimagined into people showering you with roses (Halperin 2007, 75).

Rubin begins her history by outlining incidents involving the criminalization of consensual s/m under the guise of various bawdy-house, anti-prostitution, and assault laws in both the United States and Canada. Sadomasochists who had been charged were severely punished, with some obliged to serve multiple-year prison terms for their consensual sexual practices. She further reports on media stories that capitalized on the shock value of s/m and its association with gay sexuality to both undermine gay liberation movements and demonize sadomasochists. In this way, Rubin emphasizes the ways the media prevaricated about the dangerousness of s/m, for example by circulating a false statistic that alleged 10 per cent of San Francisco's homicides were related to s/m (1987, 204).[26]

In the second part of her article, Rubin turns her critical attention to feminism's response to this moral panic. She explains that while this relentless campaign of hostility and criminalization was underway, the women's movement was "conducting a purge against its own rather tiny S/M population" through multiple strategies to marginalize and exclude sadomasochists (1987, 210). These incidents, some of which are described above, included bookstores refusing to carry s/m-positive material, feminist publications refusing to print pro-s/m articles, the eviction of Samois from the Women's Building in San Francisco, and NOW's 1980 resolution on "lesbian rights" that condemned s/m and other minority sexual practices. These examples of censorship and expulsion give evidence to the claim that certain forces within the women's movement were seized by a moral panic, eschewing dialogue and debate in favour of the total excommunication of lesbian sadomasochists from feminist spaces.

Rubin also relies on a cultural analogy to strengthen the notion that s/m is a benign sexual difference. She states that laws targeting s/m material will have the effect of "scapegoat[ing] a bunch of people whose only crime is exotic sexual tastes" (1987, 210). Again, the use of the term "exotic" endows s/m with a cultural otherness, even as it simultaneously extends a tantalizing eroticism. Rubin more explicitly invokes the trope of culture later in her essay when she critiques anti-s/m feminists for "passing judgment on what are essentially cultural differences in sexual behaviour" (215). Further into her argument, Rubin laments, "Sex is one of the few areas where cultural imperialism is taken as a radical stance" (226). In advocating for tolerance of s/m "culture" she concludes, "Cultural relativism is not the same thing as liberalism" (226). Rubin's anthropological background thus assists her in critiquing her critics, turning the tables on their accusations of cultural insensitivity.

Califia also canvasses the history of feminist and mainstream oppression of lesbian sadomasochists, most notably in his contribution to *Coming to Power* entitled "A Personal View of the History of the Lesbian

S/M Community and Movement in San Francisco" (1987). In this piece, Califia, like Rubin, traces both feminist and mainstream hostility to the emergence of Samois and lesbian s/m identity. He fleshes out many of the same incidents addressed by Rubin and also recounts being personally harassed by feminists as he tried to get information on s/m (246), the vandalism of s/m support-group posters in women's bars (250), experiences of rejection and harassment when s/m groups attempted to join gay freedom parades (261), and the particulars of the conflict between Samois and Women against Violence in Pornography and the Media (WAVPM). Califia characterizes this last struggle as typifying the kinds of hostility Samois encountered from other feminist groups. He reports that WAVPM excluded him and Rubin from attending a conference, refused to show its anti-pornography slideshow to Samois, refused to meet with Samois to discuss the use of s/m imagery in its campaign, and made only token efforts to be inclusive of diverse opinions at a forum it was organizing on the topic of s/m in the lesbian community. By cataloguing these specific instances of exclusion, censorship, and harassment in feminist and mainstream contexts, Califia attempts to establish the oppressed status of lesbian sadomasochists.[27]

Besides narrating the histories of marginalization and criminalization of s/m, *Coming to Power* also has more personal articles. "If I Ask You to Tie Me Up, Will You Still Want to Love Me?" returns to corporeal epistemology, as author Juicy Lucy attests to the healing powers of s/m via the currency of identity politics (1987, 29). In response to anti-s/m feminists who accuse her of being a "rapist/brutalizer/male-identified oppressor of battered womyn," she states, "*I* was a battered womyn for years & claim the right to release & transform the pain & fear of those experiences" (30; emphasis in the original). She later states that through s/m, "the terror & powerlessness of the rapes & beatings were being defused" (34). From Lucy's perspective, past trauma can be alleviated by consciously engaging in role playing and power dynamics. She closes the article by confessing that before she began participating in s/m practices, she felt "invaded" by fantasies of "rape & mutilation & death." Since embracing s/m, however, those fantasies have faded and been replaced by "sensual erotic fantasies about lesbians, myself, this earth, anything I want" (35–6).[28] Thus from Lucy's perspective, s/m has the effect on her psyche that is precisely the opposite of the one claimed by its detractors, both feminists and sexologists. Instead of habituating her to sexual violence, Lucy's fantasy life has been purged of violent imagery. Thus while some sadomasochist lesbians propounded a "naturalness" to sadomasochistic tendencies, others construed sadomasochistic practice as a therapeutic tool to overcome past trauma. What united these positions was a challenge to political analysis divorced from bodily experience.

Susan Farr expresses a similar investment in corporeal knowledge in her personal contribution to *Coming to Power*, stating, "I am a person who trusts her body and its sensations more than her mind and its thoughts" (1987, 184). In this construction of subjectivity, "the body" is detached from the mind as an independent and meta-discursive source of information and truth.[29] By this logic, the body is given the ability to speak and give guidance to action. Thus while the anti-sadomasochists counselled the virtues of an enlightened mind over corrupted matter, some supporters of s/m insisted upon reversing this hierarchy, positing that matter (i.e., the body) should rise up against the repressive mind. As with the anti-s/m arguments, this perspective is premised on a distinction between mind and body. However, a fundamental difference from the pro-s/m viewpoint is that patriarchy and anti-sex feminism have been forged together to engender guilt and shame in the minds of sexual minorities, and it is the mind that is therefore considered suspect.

"Thinking Sex" (1984)

Ultimately, I believe the most important and influential text to theorize the position of sexual minorities from a sex-radical view was Rubin's Barnard conference article, published in 1984 in the anthology *Pleasure and Danger*. The article, entitled "Thinking Sex," does not focus exclusively on s/m; rather, s/m is placed within the larger political context as one of many sexual-minority practices that suffer injustice (Rubin 1984). I will not attempt to summarize the entire article, which covers a range of issues and conflicts relating to sexual inequality, but instead will highlight the ways Rubin challenges anti-s/m truth-claims and puts forward her own framework for understanding the political place of s/m within society.

The article begins by giving an overview of sexual injustice from the nineteenth century, examining how social mores – often in partnership with the law and psychiatry – focused on regulating non-normative sexual practices. Rubin documents the ways in which things like masturbation, obscene literature, erotic art, abortion, birth control information, prostitution, and (later in the twentieth century) homosexuality coalesced as epicentres of sex panics, provoking harshly punitive responses. She argues that while many of these sex panics have subsided, they remain part of our moral heritage, perpetuating a sexual order that hierarchizes people on the basis of their erotic preferences.

Rubin conceptualizes this hierarchy in two diagrams that chart the people and behaviours that are deemed acceptable, and those that are marginalized, pathologized, and/or criminalized. In the first illustration (reproduced as figure 2.1), she maps the "charmed circle" of sexual behaviours that are celebrated if they adhere to certain hegemonic strictures (1981, 281). Notably for our purposes, "vanilla" sexuality is placed within the circle in juxtaposition to s/m, which is relegated to the "outer limits." The second illustration (reproduced as figure 2.2) presents a continuum of sexual behaviours from the "best" to the "worst" (282). Here s/m falls under the label of "bad sex," and stable lesbian and gay relationships are considered a "major area of contest," while of course married monogamous heterosexuality is deemed "good sex." Significantly, Rubin posits that vanilla lesbian sexuality accrues more acceptability and privilege than s/m sexuality of any orientation. This assertion stands in direct contrast to the anti-s/m feminist truth-claim that s/m sex is not merely acceptable within mainstream culture, but embodies the prevailing order by which sexuality is constructed under patriarchy.

Rubin does not directly challenge anti-s/m truth-claims with a set of her own counter-claims of the essential meaning of s/m. Indeed, Rubin pinpoints such varieties of "sexual essentialism" as an "ideological formation" that contributes to reinforcing the sexual hierarchy (1981, 275). Drawing upon Foucault, Rubin proposes a constructivist framework for the analysis of sexual oppression. She challenges pro-s/m discourse that relies on the repressive hypothesis – that is, on the idea of a "natural" libido repressed by societal constraints – arguing that these corporeal epistemologies forwarded by certain lesbian s/m writers rely too heavily on essentialism to defend s/m practice. Instead, she argues that a radical approach to sex will focus on the political stakes of sexual oppression and the ways certain behaviours are deemed natural or unnatural, and are accordingly allocated privileges or denied affirmation. She suggests that instead of ranking sexualities in terms of good/ natural or bad/unnatural, we need to work towards the idea of benign sexual diversity, whatever its origin or aetiology.

The charmed circle:
Good, Normal, Natural, Blessed Sexuality

Heterosexual
Married
Monogamous
Procreative
Non-commercial
In pairs
In a relationship
Same generation
In private
No pornography
Bodies only
Vanilla

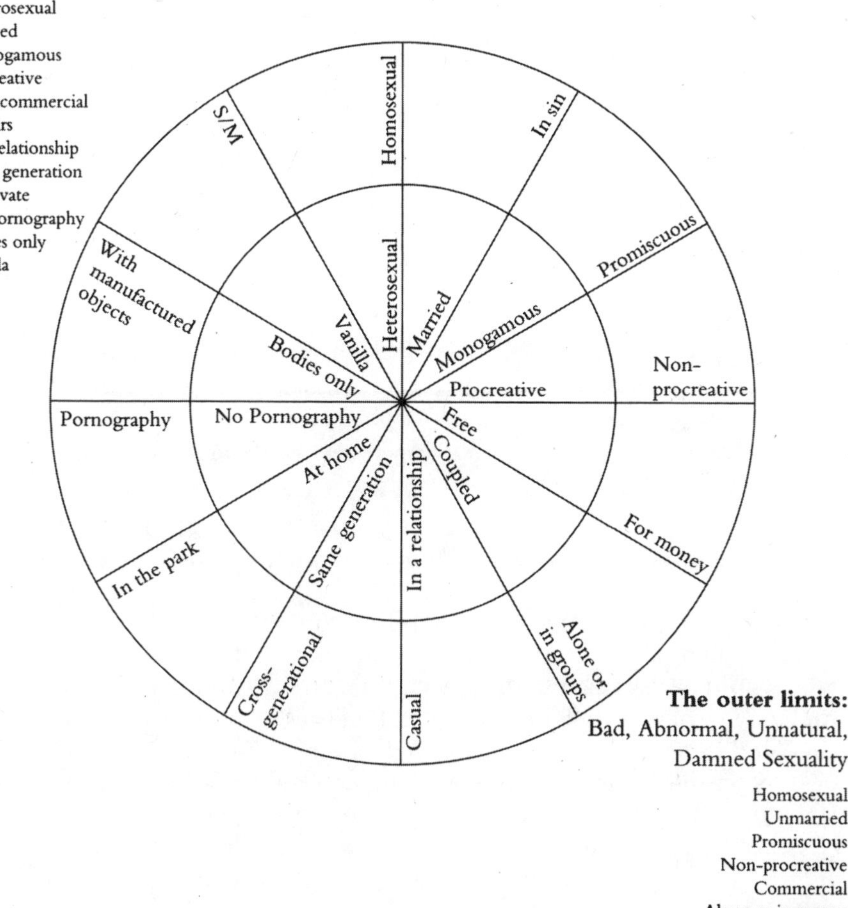

The outer limits:
Bad, Abnormal, Unnatural,
Damned Sexuality

Homosexual
Unmarried
Promiscuous
Non-procreative
Commercial
Alone or in groups
Casual
Cross-generational
In public
Pornography
With manufactured objects
Sadomasochistic

Figure 2.1: The Sex Hierarchy: The Charmed Circle vs the Outer Limits

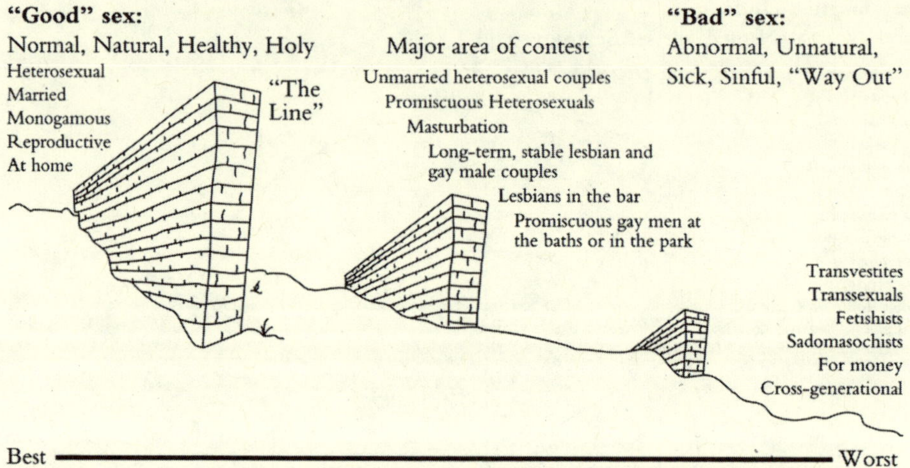

Figure 2.2: The Sex Hierarchy: The Struggle over Where to Draw the Line

Rubin returns to the race and culture analogy to illustrate that a sexual orientation or preference need not be biological to deserve respect. Again drawing upon her background in cultural anthropology, she makes a point about cultural relativism and sexuality: "Progressives who would be ashamed to display cultural chauvinism in other areas routinely exhibit it towards sexual differences. We have learned to cherish different cultures as unique expressions of human inventiveness rather than as inferior or disgusting habits of savages. We need a similarly anthropological understanding of different sexual cultures" (1981, 283–4). Rubin thus counters the anti-s/m feminist position that s/m is embedded in patriarchal mainstream culture by maintaining that s/m is actually its own distinct and marginalized culture. The trope of culture in the defence of s/m operates here both literally and as metaphor. S/m is construed as a sexual subculture with its own characteristics and tendencies, but Rubin also draws upon the metaphor of ethnic culture, attempting in a sense to play her own race card.[30] This is made explicit when Rubin states that the "sexual morality" that condemns s/m "has more in common with ideologies of racism than with true ethics" (1989, 283). Thus, while the anti-s/m feminists were condemning s/m for appropriating racist garb, replicating white supremacist roles, and legitimating oppressive racial hierarchies, the defenders of s/m were launching their own attack using "like race" arguments.[31]

Perhaps Rubin's most provocative challenge to the anti-s/m perspective was her suggestion that feminism itself was an inadequate theory to address sexual oppression. Rubin contended that the dominant feminist framework of the day grew out of the anti-pornography movement, which had managed to promulgate its own sexual order. While lesbianism had replaced heterosexuality as the most enlightened model for intimate relations, those sexualities that continued to be demonized remained consistent with the exclusions articulated by the dominant order. Notably, s/m was ranked among the most objectionable sexual pursuits within both normative frameworks. Rubin argued that this feminist perspective scapegoated "non-routine acts of love rather than routine acts of oppression, exploitation, or violence" (1989, 301). Yet while Rubin defended these "non-routine acts," she was careful not to idealize the sex industry or sexual minorities, acknowledging that they are just as likely to be sexist as any other segment of society. What Rubin emphasized is that it should not be assumed that unusual sexual communities are more so.

Rubin concludes that anti-pornography feminist analysis merely replicates conservative sexual morality, which, instead of relying on a notion of sin or vice, explains minority sexual practices (particularly if engaged in by women) with theories of brainwashing or psychological damage. While she acknowledges that sexual choice is influenced by outside forces, Rubin's contention is that structural constraints push people towards normality, not perversity. Ultimately, she maintains that biases in the prevailing feminist theory reflect the need to conceptually decouple sexuality and gender, arguing that while feminism might be the best theory to understand gender oppression, it is not necessarily an effective tool for the analysis of sexual oppression. She states, "The criteria of relevance in feminist thought do not allow it to see or assess critical power relations in the area of sexuality" (1989, 309). This argument refutes the anti-s/m feminist perspective that construed feminism (i.e., radical feminism or lesbian-feminism) as the most powerful tool to unlock the meaning of s/m and sexual oppression in general.

Rubin's "Thinking Sex" article can be considered a germinating seed for what would eventually come to be called queer theory. Relying on

Foucauldian insight to posit the social construction and historical contingency of sexual identity, Rubin foreshadowed later queer theorists like Judith Butler and Eve Kosofsky Sedgwick who, by the early 1990s, were denaturalizing the categories of gender, sex, and sexuality through discursive and historical analysis.[32] Furthermore, Rubin's inclusion of transpeople, cross-generational intimacies, sex workers, and sadomasochists of any orientation into her analysis anticipated the restlessness of queer theory's analytical frame, which moved beyond the homo/hetero binary. Rubin, like the queer theorists who would follow, interrogated the ways that discourses of deviance have played out upon multiple sex, gender, and sexual axes.

Macho Sluts (1988)

In a literary way, Patrick Califia continued this project in his 1988 book of erotica entitled *Macho Sluts* (1988b). The collection includes not just lesbian s/m scenarios, but also heterosexual s/m encounters and a gay male s/m story. Califia insists that lesbians are entitled to appropriate sexual props outside of lesbianism for their fantasy life without compromising their identities, and in this way he (like Rubin) attempts to push the boundaries that demarcate hegemonic sex, gender, and sexual scripts.

While this approach seems to challenge sex essentialism, interestingly, Califia also propounds a corporeal epistemology in his introduction. He declares of his s/m erotica, "It is a visible act of love, written for any reader who is not a traitor to her own cunt" (1988b, 10). Again, the earnest belief that the body can and should be trusted to guide behaviour and sexual decisions, that it should be listened to instead of betrayed, flies in the face of urgings from the anti-s/m camp to be suspicious of purely physical desires. As Julia Creet argues, these kinds of arguments in defence of lesbian s/m create a dichotomy between "honest sexual fantasy and hypocritical or repressive feminist politics" (1991, 141). The anti-s/m feminists are set up as the repressive force, traitors to their bodies in their relentless pursuit of politically correct praxis.

This feminist repression is exaggerated in one of Califia's short stories, "The Hustler," which imagines a dystopic future where a tyrannical form of moralistic feminism has taken over the world. This fantasy is worth analysing, as it not only seeks to turn on the reader, but also makes an intervention into the sex wars through erotic parody.

The story begins after a violent "women's revolution" gives rise to an American society run by women who enforce strict gender and sexual norms. The protagonist, Noh, finds herself at odds with the new moral order because of her "rebellious streak" and "exotic sexual preferences" (there's that "exotic" cultural descriptor again for s/m) (1988a, 182). She makes a living as a sadomasochist sex worker who will dominate for money.

In the opening scene, Noh finds herself having to account to a potential employer for her latest arrest. During the interview, she explains that her conviction included prostitution (although they only charged her client, the "jane," who had "paid for objectification" (1988a, 201), misogyny (because she hit the client as part of their s/m scene), sexual harassment (because of her use of sexist epithets during the scene), and public assumption of sex roles (because of her short boyish haircut). Noh also keeps contraband products in her house, in particular dildos, which, according to the law, "are 'a device that demeans women'" (191). In this world view, anti-s/m feminist "truths" and institutional law have merged.

Noh reveals that during her teenage years she attempted to hide her sexual deviance by joining a watchdog student group with a mandate to police those in their school who demonstrated "regressive tendencies," described as "holdovers from exploitive, male-dominated, consumer-capitalist sexualities" (1988a, 196). The jig is up for Noh, however, when her accusations against a male professor incite him to grab her and discover she has placed pins in her bra for masochistic pleasure. While no serious contact ensues, the reader learns that the professor was prosecuted for rape because of his grabbing, with Noh brought up on charges as an "accessory to violence against women" – the woman in question being herself.[33] The unfairness of both charges makes a clear ideological statement: Califia dramatizes the fanaticism he perceives in real-world feminist campaigns to weed sadomasochists out from feminist space. And there is also a not-so-subtle suggestion that those who so violently protest against lesbian s/m may in fact be latent perverts who are hiding their sexual desires and confusion in repressive zealotry.

The language of this repression is later replicated in sarcastic dialogue. Noh has just met a timid woman who is seeking to purchase dominance services. Noh says mockingly to her potential client, "What did we have a revolution for if women are going to wallow in this reactionary masochism? Hmm? It's decadent, diseased, self-indulgent,

immature, parasitical" (1988a, 206). Califia mimics the accusations of
the anti-s/m feminists in this speech, and in the process not only paro-
dies their perceived high-minded rhetoric, but audaciously appropriates that rhetoric to heighten the eroticism of his story. Again the
transformative power of abjection, as Halperin understands it, manifests: "its antisocial splendor: its filthiness, its disgracefulness, its thrills,
its delirious risks and dangers, its defiance – its surprising strength as a
source of instinctive, unconquerable pride and resistance" (2007, 81).
In his quote, Halperin is describing the rebellious force of abjection in
relation to gay sex, but I believe his triumphant account is just as applicable to the lesbian s/m sex in Califia's story.

It should be remembered that, for some, sadomasochist desire is premised on role playing shameful scenes, on the eroticism of telling or
being told how *bad* someone is, especially how *bad* someone's sexuality
is. The unwitting effect of anti-s/m feminist rhetoric on such s/m practitioners was that it in fact offered erotic fodder through its shaming
tactics and political denunciations. McClintock argues, "One of S/M's
characteristics is the eroticizing of scenes, symbols, contexts and contradictions which society does not typically recognize as sexual"
(1993, 224). Not only did anti-s/m feminists effectively endow lesbian
sadomasochists with sexy outlaw status, but they actually came to figure as characters in sadomasochistic fantasy. In the sexual economy of
Califia's story, it is *sexy* when Noh demeans her client, showering her in
disgust-laden words that could have come directly from the pages of
Against Sadomasochism. The reader knows that the client is craving this
kind of sexual attention, for as Creet argues, the eroticism in the narrative is "dependent on the hypocrisy of the established order" (1991,
153). Lesbian sadomasochists not only appropriate patriarchal structures for role playing, they also appropriate feminist hierarchies, which
privilege vanilla over s/m sexuality in order to create material for
sadomasochist fantasy. The outlaw status of s/m dykes featured in this
story thereby harvested not just emotive satisfaction, but also sexual
pleasure from feminist condemnation.

Unfortunately for Califia, the outlaw status prominent in his story
was not only metaphorical. In chapter 4, I will note the history of repeated censorship that *Macho Sluts* faced at the Canadian border. But
notwithstanding this legal issue, as the 1990s progressed, sadomasochists would gain ground both in their occupancy of feminist terrain and
in winning mainstream acceptability and access to material resources.

The Second Coming: A Leatherdyke Reader (1996)

Eight years after *Macho Sluts*, a sequel to *Coming to Power* was published called *The Second Coming: A Leatherdyke Reader*, which chronicled the evolving discourse around s/m, and the activist gains that had been achieved (Califia and Sweeney 1996). And while the tenor of the debate still retained its heritage of rebelliousness, it also began to incorporate more queer understandings of identity.

Like its predecessor, *The Second Coming* incorporates erotica, poetry, graphics, historical accounts, and academic and political analyses. But an important difference should be noted in the subtitles of the two anthologies. *Coming to Power* was subtitled *Writings and Graphics of Lesbian S/M*, and its cover identified Samois as a "lesbian/feminist S/M organization." In *The Second Coming*, however, the term *lesbian s/m* is supplanted by the term *leatherdyke*, and there is no reference to feminism. The lack of an explicit feminist association indicates that the debate over the meaning of the label had begun to lose significance, at least for sadomasochists. Furthermore, none of the material attempts a "rapprochement" of feminism and s/m in the way that earlier pro-s/m articles had done. While some authors clearly still identified with feminism, none seemed invested in having to prove or legitimate this claim. This battle had now given way to new controversies over identity, as indicated by the term *leatherdyke* – said in the anthology's introduction to encompass bisexual and transwomen who have an interest in s/m between women (Califia and Sweeney 1996, xvi). Thus the mandate of this pro-s/m "lesbian" community had expanded to include identities that were, and continue to be (particularly in regards to transpeople), under siege within certain feminist circles.

The articles also reflect a commitment to diversity. Two parts are dedicated to the issue of inclusiveness and the problems of marginalization. In part 2, "Who Is My Sister? Challenging the Boundaries of the Leatherdyke Community," s/m is theorized by transpeople, a bisexual woman, and a professional dom. In part 4, "We Are Here Too: The Diversity of Perversity," the reader learns about the struggles of women of colour and women with disabilities within the s/m community. Indeed the whole anthology reflects women from diverse backgrounds, distinguishing it from *Coming to Power*, which had ruefully acknowledged the lack of contributions by clearly identified women of colour or women with disabilities. The diversity of the contributors indicates a broadening of the community, better outreach work by editors, and the expanded presence of s/m lesbians/dykes feeling empowered to take up space. It also implicitly challenges the anti-s/m contention that s/m is practised primarily by privileged white women.

The anthology also addresses problems within s/m practice. In "S/M Symbols, Fascist Icons, and Systems of Empowerment," Linda Wayne applies a deconstructionist and historical analysis to s/m's use of imagery from oppressive systems, in particular Nazi regalia (Wayne 1996, 242). She argues that a conflation of s/m practice and "heteropatriarchal neoimperialist culture" relies on visual self-evidence to reify evil, making it easily recognizable through the use of particular imagery and symbols. In addition, the conflation de-historicizes the subgroup's (as in sadomasochists') ongoing struggles as an oppressed and marginalized sexual minority. Having said that, Wayne does contend that those who "adopt a historically accurate symbol such as the swastika are representing themselves in a way that is continuous with the dominant imagery and state-level ideological interests of Third Reich Nazism ... [and are] choosing a 'plaything' that has been recuperated within the living symbolism of current Neo-Nazi subgroups" (249). This analysis does not land far from the claims advanced by Star in *Against Sadomasochism*, where she maintained that the appropriation of Nazi symbolism may affirm neo-Nazis (1982, 131). Thus Wayne does not proffer an all-out defence of the use of imagery culled from oppressive orders. Instead, she calls for a more nuanced and historical understanding, of both the oppressed status of s/m practitioners and of the ways reified symbols of evil may resonate with current systems of oppression.

Another problematization of s/m occurs in Califia's "A House Divided: Violence in the Lesbian S/M Community" (Califia and Sweeney 1996, 264). In this piece, Califia names domestic violence in the community as both a "dirty secret" and a long-standing problem. He recognizes that because s/m lesbians have struggled so hard to convince the outside world that s/m does not equal violence, it is difficult to admit when violence does occur. In tackling the silence around this issue, Califia does not simply explain away domestic violence among s/m lesbians by taking recourse in the truism that domestic violence hits every community. In fact, he acknowledges that certain kinds of violence may be facilitated by the facade of a consensual s/m interaction. Califia devotes the remainder of his article to helping the reader identify domestic violence, suggesting strategies for dealing with it – including contacting the police – and outlining "A Code of Honor for Leatherdykes."

The articles in *The Second Coming* thus demonstrate a certain confidence in s/m identity. No longer compelled to constantly defend themselves and their sexuality, leatherdykes could begin to explore the diversity of their backgrounds and desires and address challenges in the community. I want to note one interesting moment, however, where corporeal epistemology recurs. A line in the dedication reads, "This book is also dedicated to any woman who is brave enough to look inside her own heart and cunt for the truth about her sexuality." Once again, the body, particularly the traditional centre of a woman's libido, her "cunt," is endowed with the truth of one's sexuality. The fact that the cunt is here linked to the heart perhaps gestures towards a reconciliation or even an imbrication of the emotional and physical self. Accordingly, with the conspicuous elision of any reference to "the mind," the suggestion is conveyed that sexual truth is not to be found in rational thought, but in rather more visceral processes.

Jane Sexes It Up (2002)

It is interesting to note that sex-radical feminism in the new millennium also relies on the truth of visceral reactions to defend s/m. In the 2002 "Gen-X" feminist anthology *Jane Sexes It Up*, editor Merri Lisa Johnson credits Dorothy Allison's book *Bastard out of Carolina* for creating a space where feminists could re-imagine and re-create experiences of abuse within a context of fantasy and self-empowerment (Johnson 2002b). Johnson aligns herself with this project, stating, "We press forward with this improper feminism in the spirit of Bone [the protagonist in *Bastard out of Carolina*], the fictionalized but familiar girl-child inside us all who combats the abuse heaped on her body with stories of her own desire" (9). This statement recalls earlier pro-s/m arguments that attest to the therapeutic value of the sexual practice, particularly in exorcising experiences of abuse. In another contribution to the anthology addressing the politics and pleasures of sexual spanking, Chris Daley similarly maintains, "We have the ability to transform practices developed in patriarchal cultures into turn-ons, sexing up what would have otherwise tied us down" (2002, 128). Arguments justifying s/m on account of its transformative power have continued from the heyday of the sex wars to the current wave of feminism. Such texts posit that oppressive roles and acts do not have to be utterly rejected, but instead can be transformed to serve the goals of feminist sexual empowerment. This claim ultimately connects both the corporeal epistemology that locates truth in our bodily urges and postmodern insights on the subversive potential of appropriating and re-signifying hegemonic scripts.

Conclusion

I hesitate to conclude this chapter here because my investigation of the anti-s/m side is over twice as long as the pro-s/m material. While my research found that the anti-s/m literature made many more truth-claims about s/m, and therefore took much longer to canvass, I cannot help but be aware that this rather lopsided survey constitutes its own intervention in the sex wars. And yet I do not want to fall into the seductive self-construction of "moderate," whereby I purport to demonstrate how both sides were equally problematic, in order to prove my own objectivity. I hope that in my historical and discursive examination of the "moderate" positions (i.e., Ardill and O'Sullivan and Healey) I have shown how these authors purchased their supposed neutrality, and sought to characterize themselves as more reasonable, by exaggerating and distorting the claims made by lesbian sadomasochists.

In attempting to stamp out s/m, the anti-s/m movement challenged the claims of consent and mutuality made by lesbian s/m practitioners, seeking to essentialize s/m as oppressive, violent, patriarchal, heterosexual, gay-male identified, racist, fascistic, and anti-feminist. In these discourses, anti-s/m feminists accessed vicarious pleasure in their detailed descriptions of patriarchal s/m dynamics. Their strategies of expulsion also allowed them to manage the threat of the abject s/m figure, while simultaneously inciting more discourse on s/m. On the other side, s/m was defended as a therapeutic tool, a parody of oppressive orders, and a separate (sexual) subculture with customs and behaviours that have been misinterpreted by both mainstream and feminist society. The pleasures of audacity and proud identification with outlaw status allowed these authors to harness an emotive satisfaction in rebellion, even as the anti-s/m discourse generated scenes of sexual shame that could be parodied in fantasy material. However, the major defence strategy of the pro-s/m supporters was to characterize the anti-s/m side as exclusionary, mean-spirited, and anti-dialogic, and to emphasize that lesbian sadomasochists experienced significant oppression as a result.

Today, the predominance of postmodernism in academia, as supplemented by the critique of essentialism, has strengthened the account of s/m as transgressing against – and not collaborating with – hetero-normativity. While the topic is still addressed from a variety of academic vantage points, the rightness or wrongness of s/m sexuality, and its feminist or anti-feminist status, are questions that have receded into the background of the feminist stage.[34] Instead, what has grabbed centre stage – in my experience – are the debates between feminist scholars on the status and meaning of sex work and trans-subjectivity.

There has also been a willingness among some scholars to heed Rubin's sex-radical recommendation to de-privilege feminism when theorizing sexuality. Most notably, in *Split Decisions: How and Why to Take a Break from Feminism*, Janet Halley argues – as the subtitle suggests – that putting feminism on hold, particularly when it comes to sex, is a good idea (2006). This theoretical hiatus, in Halley's view, allows one to "see around corners" of feminist construction and to notice, maybe even take seriously, the harm happening to others that not only is flying below the feminist radar but is actuated by feminist praxis. Throughout her book, Halley references s/m dynamics by addressing identifiable s/m practitioners, but also by detecting s/m in everyday interactions. For example, in rereading a sexual harassment case between men, Halley provides four alternative scenarios that convey complex and pleasurable sexual interactions that, she suggests, should not fall within sexual harassment law. In describing the proposed hypotheticals, Halley draws on s/m lingo: "willingness to be mastered," "dominance/submission sexual interaction," "play the bottom," and "power/submission relay" (297–9).[35] She later insists, "It's not exclusively the perverts who engage in scenes like those I've just affirmed as good who seek incoherent experiences in sex: I think most of us experience sex (when it's not routinized) as an alarming mix of desire and fear, delight and disgust, power and surrender, surrender and power, attachment and alienation, ecstasy in the root sense of the word and enmired embodiedness" (302). This attempt to de-exceptionalize s/m – in Eve Sedgwick's terms, a universalizing (as opposed to minoritizing) move – takes a break from feminism to defend and even celebrate the pervasiveness of s/m erotics.

Law, however, has not adopted Halley's celebratory account of s/m. Instead, the truth-claims of the anti-s/m feminist movement have gained prominence in legal discourse. The conflation of s/m with violence, and the characterization of its dynamics as inherently degrading, even when consent is explicit, seem to have been internalized by much of the socio-legal imaginary, particularly in Canada. In this sense, the anti-s/m feminist perspective continues to hold impressive sway over the debate. It may be out of vogue in certain academic circles, but this feminist viewpoint has managed to offer a new justificatory framework for the law to criminalize, regulate, and control sadomasochistic sexuality, all in the name of anti-oppression.

I develop this argument in more detail in chapters 4 and 5, which investigate the multiple discursive threads that weave into law's truth-claims regarding s/m sexuality in pornography and practice. But before this analysis, there is one more arena of cultural production on s/m that should be considered: cinematic portrayals. The following chapter turns to this popular affective arena where the vicarious pleasure of s/m representation is at its most blatant.

3

S/M in Showbiz

There is an obvious but significant difference between cinematic stories and the psychiatric and feminist representations that have been examined: while the latter two make overt truth-claims about the nature of s/m sexuality, mainstream movies are ostensibly about *make-believe*. Indeed, the credits of many fictional films contain some version of a disclaimer: "Characters, places, and incidents in this film are fictitious. Any resemblance to actual events, locales, or persons, living or dead, is entirely coincidental." While these disclaimers locate films in the imaginative realm, they also signal the emotive and convincing impact of cinematic narrative and the corresponding need for directors to manage their liability. Movies can feel very real.

Popular culture's cinematic representation of s/m as an object of entertainment could thus be said to allow for the most direct vicarious interaction with s/m sexuality. As a visual and aural medium, popular films capture and communicate s/m pleasures viscerally. One way to justify this resemblance is to contextualize the represented s/m within a plot structure (as flimsy as it may be) that culminates, inevitably, with a moral at the end of the story. As such, fictional stories on s/m contribute to popular knowledge, that is, popular conceptions of right and wrong, truth and falsity, and perhaps most importantly, deserving and undeserving fates. In other words, poetic justice is political. The popular film industry, like psychiatry and feminism, is a truth-machine, an apparatus that articulates and forms ideology.[1] As such, film is in a dynamic relationship with the social construction of reality that both reflects and produces popular notions of sexual order.[2]

But unlike sexological or feminist theory, in film, the truth-value of the s/m narrative hinges not upon convincing empirical studies or

analytical critiques, but rather upon convincing characters whose actions and fates make sense within the plot, and thus support larger ideological orders. In this chapter, I demonstrate that when s/m features as a
theme or plot device in popular culture, the dialectic between fascination and repulsion comes into play. On the one hand, films about s/m
indulge voyeuristic pleasure in witnessing s/m's blatant violation of
sexual norms. But ultimately, this voyeurism must be purged by containing s/m sexuality within hegemonic strictures, most notably upon
gender, but also often with respect to class, race, and sexual orientation.

The chapter is divided into three sections, roughly separated by the
gender and sexual orientation of the depicted s/m practitioners, each
of which has its own moral framework. In the first section, I examine
movies that portray s/m featuring the woman as the top and the man
as the bottom. This section is further subdivided between two types of
topping women: the sexually dominant woman and the professional
dominatrix. The second section turns to movies that dramatize the in-
verse gender configuration, where the man is sexually dominant and
the woman submissive. Of course, this dynamic could be said to feature
in a host of films, from *Gone with the Wind* to *Twilight*, but here I focus
exclusively on movies that make intentional reference to recognizable
s/m dynamics that go beyond the preponderant male-active/female-
passive sexual script typical of many films about heterosexual protagonists. In the last and shortest section, I consider the depiction of
gay male s/m in popular film. I look briefly at the controversial movie
Cruising, the art-house movie *Frisk*, and the depiction of the gay s/m
rapists in *Pulp Fiction*. There is no separate section on lesbian sadomasochists because, in my research I have found there are no popular films
that look exclusively at lesbian s/m dynamics. However, the first two
sections, while primarily heterosexual in scope, do have a few depictions of female same-sex desire, most notably in *Basic Instinct*.[3]

Boys on the Bottom, Babes on the Top

Dominating Woman as a Femme Fatale

The dyad between women who get off on sexual dominance and the
submissive men who worship them, while titillating, creates a social
disruption that must be managed. By reversing the male-active/female-
passive sexual dynamic, and by explicitly displaying kinky sexuality,
sexual and gender normativity is undermined. In s/m films, sexually

aggressive women often invoke the femme fatale motif, as they lure the male protagonists into more and more danger. Yet in the representations of this sexual arrangement, the female partner usually must bottom to a man at some point in the narrative. In the next section, I show how this is in contrast to the sexually dominant man in film, who can remain consistently on top throughout.

The 1986 film *Something Wild* offered a relatively positive view of female dominant behaviour. In this movie, Charles Driggs (Jeff Daniels), a middle-class man and "closet rebel," crosses paths with the unemployed and free-spirited Lulu (Melanie Griffith). After catching Charles walking out of a New York City diner without paying his bill, Lulu takes a shine to this latent non-conformist and offers him a ride back to his downtown office. But once Lulu gets Charles in the car, she veers off course. She drives him to New Jersey, tosses his beeper out of the window, convinces him to join her for a drink in the car, surreptitiously steals from a cash register (unbeknownst to Charles), and winds up leading him to a sleazy motel. In their room, she throws him on the bed, while he – clearly excited – explains that he would prefer to keep his T-shirt on because, he states, "I don't feel comfortable yet." She straddles him, dangles a pair of handcuffs, and asks, "You game?" Intrigued, he allows her to handcuff his wrists to the bedpost. She rips off his T-shirt – in defiance of his earlier request – rips off her own top, and then – always keeping him guessing – calls his office. To his (initial) horror, Charles must explain his absence at the office while manacled to the bed – as Lulu fellates him. Throughout this first encounter, Charles continually responds to Lulu's advances with protest and hesitation. But each time he surrenders, he derives exquisite satisfaction in following Lulu's lead.

In this first sequence, Lulu's handcuffs signal multiple themes (see figure 3.1). First and most obviously, she clearly enjoys being dominant in bed. With Charles restrained, she is free to push past his boundaries, for example by stripping him naked despite his expressed decision to keep his shirt on. But the handcuffs also invoke criminality and risk. The audience has already witnessed Charles slyly leaving a café without paying his bill, Lulu drinking and driving, and Lulu robbing a liquor store. The appearance of handcuffs in the bedroom reinforces the notion that there is something illicit about this couple. And though Charles is clearly smitten, the audience (who knows that she has stolen money) may believe that Lulu is simply hustling him. Audience members might wonder if she is a femme fatale using her sexuality to

Figure 3.1: Lulu: Femme fatale

lure him into a vulnerable position so that she can rob him once she has him helplessly handcuffed to the bed.[4]

However, in the subsequent scene after their lovemaking, Lulu has not disappeared with Charles's wallet. Instead, she invites him to join her on a trip to her hometown in Pennsylvania. Charles agrees – happily sporting the handcuffs, which are still attached to one wrist. The audience gets a sense of how much Charles enjoys being Lulu's submissive when she unlocks the handcuffs outside of her mother's house. She explains, "I'm setting you free." He counters, "Maybe I don't want to be free." But after this moment, the erotic dynamics of the film seem to shift. Lulu explains to Charles that he should address her as "Audrey," and this new name (her real name) coincides with a new character trope: she goes from being a femme fatale to a damsel in distress (see figure 3.2).

In the next sequence, the couple arrives at Audrey's high school reunion, where they meet up with Ray, Audrey's husband, who has just been released from jail. Soon thereafter, the film shifts generic gears from off-beat romantic comedy to on-beat dramatic thriller. Ray kidnaps the couple, involves Charles in an armed robbery, breaks Charles's nose and then dismisses him, believing that he and Audrey can reunite – while he keeps her under constant surveillance. Charles eventually rescues Audrey from her violent ex during two different incidents, outsmarting Ray the first time, and stabbing him to death the second time. At the end of the movie, Charles and Audrey find each other outside the same coffee shop where they had first met. Audrey, who has forsaken her exotic clothing to appropriately assume an *Audrey* Hepburn look, offers him a ride, just as she did at the beginning. Charles accepts without hesitation, but their dynamic has notably shifted from the first

Figure 3.2: Audrey: Damsel in distress

scene. As they walk towards the car, Charles indicates that Audrey should stay on the passenger side, while he gallantly opens the door. She acquiesces. The last shot of the couple shows Charles walking around the car towards the driver's seat.

The second half of the movie seems to back away from some of the transgressive inroads of the first half. When the couple arrives in Lulu/Audrey's hometown and she assumes her Audrey persona, she ceases to be a source of danger and instead becomes the one *in* danger. Charles takes masculine control and becomes Audrey's proverbial knight in shining armour, proving himself to be not just a nicer guy than her husband, but also the superior rival. At the end, his status as the one in control is symbolically clinched when he takes the driver's seat. As for Lulu/Audrey, she continues to answer to the name Audrey, so the audience is also alerted that the female protagonist has left Lulu behind and has come to embrace her "real" self by answering to her "real" name. It seems that Audrey, unlike Lulu, is happy to be in the passenger seat.

Though *Something Wild* does not demonize a sexually dominant woman, it does need to attenuate her wildness. In the first half, Lulu is the pursuer and Charles is the object of her desire. In the second half, Lulu/Audrey becomes the object of desire, being fought over by two men. As Cameron Bailey argues, "At that point Ray takes over the function of social disruption from Lulu, and Audrey becomes merely the prize in a conventional love triangle" (Bailey 1988, 31). As for the representation of a sexually submissive man, the movie does not make Charles an object of disgust or ridicule; however, it does require him in the second half to recuperate his masculinity by saving the damsel in distress and winning her heart. Gendered order is restored.

The racial and class dynamics of the story should also be mentioned for their role in representing s/m as other. While all of the main characters register as white, racialized working-class bodies make up a conspicuous presence in the background of the narrative. The first close shot of a person in the movie is a young African-American man holding up a radio cassette player on his shoulder and listening to the salsa fusion song that has been accompanying the opening credits (see figure 3.3).[5] At the end of the film, the diner waitress, Sister Carol (a reggae dancehall singer in real life) sings a remake of "Wild Thing" in a doorway while the credits roll beside her (see figure 3.4). African-American bodies further marked as working class and "ghetto" (the stereo, for example, has been referred to as a "ghetto blaster") sandwich the plot, lending a racialized ambience and an inner-city chic to the narrative.

In between these two scenes, there are also numerous shots of working-class African-American people who play minor parts as, for example, a gas attendant, hitchhikers, and street rappers.

These African-American, "ghetto hip" characters – few of whom have speaking parts – come to the service of the protagonists as symbolic accoutrement, but not as subjects. Their presence signals sexuality and wildness. This is particularly demonstrated by Lulu's literal accoutrements in the first sequence, where she is wearing what appear to be African jewellery and a necklace with a pendant bearing a picture of the continent of Africa. When she straddles Charles in the motel room, she presents what again looks to be an African doll, then a gourd, and finally the handcuffs. Lulu's daring sexuality is thus coded as African/ Black; "she is imaged (before she reverts to Audrey) as a white idea of an exotic, black woman, a wild thing, an unpredictable cipher" (Bailey 1988, 33). As Lola Young argues, *Something Wild* capitalizes on the association of Black femininity to deviance by appropriating Black iconography (Young 1996, 195). And as Norma Manatu has argued, Black female subjectivity in cinema has been overdetermined as hypersexual and aggressive (Manatu 2003).

The class status of the racialized characters, as well as Lulu's unemployment and streetwise ethos, position the film within the category of what Keith Gandal calls "classploitation" films: "stories about the poor that are exploitive in the sense that they seem to come out of middle-class fantasies" (2007, 6). Under Gandal's taxonomy of classploitation subgenres, the particular fantasy at play in *Something Wild* would be identified as a "slumming drama": "The poor and lowlifes have it better because they are free of status and money concerns and live for

Figure 3.3: Racialized figure to open the film

enjoyment, love, and art and music in primitive social harmony. They have to teach the upper classes, and thus the plots in this genre involve happy downward mobility and liberating liaisons across classes" (6). Lulu represents this bohemian "low life," whose spontaneity, kinkiness, and harmonious affinity with African-American street culture teaches Charlie to liberate himself from the constraints of white middle-class identity. At the end of the film, Charlie quits his job, dons a funky tie, and joins Lulu/Audrey in sexual and occupational freedom. In this way, "downwardly mobile" fantasies depoliticize poverty. The message is that the ones who really need "saving" under a capitalist order are the economically privileged and their repressed libidos, not the unfettered poor with their licentious sexuality.

In addition, recall how in the early psychiatric literature, out-of-control s/m sexuality was attributed to "savage" and working-class cultures. White middle-class civilized Christians were also susceptible to these urges, but when they capitulated, it was understood as giving in to their animalistic atavistic selves. In *Something Wild*, it seems that s/m dynamics involving conscious power play and the reversal of expected gender roles are also understood in racialized and classed terms. *Something Wild* thus marks s/m as sexually other, in part by marking it as working-class and racially other. But again, in the end, not only does gender order get restored, but so does racial order. Audrey forsakes her racialized Lulu identity, along with her penchant for dominance, to assume the role of a gender-normative white woman. And in terms of class, while it appears that both Audrey and Charlie are unemployed, she still manages to dress like an upper-class woman, and he seems entirely unconcerned with finances. The couple can partake in the joie de vivre of the happy poor, without the harshness of actual poverty intruding on this fairy tale ending.

Figure 3.4: Racialized figure to close the film

Fast forward to some twenty years later, and another movie features a wild girl with a knack for getting the object of her desire into bondage. In *Wedding Crashers*, Gloria (Isla Fisher), a seemingly sweet and virginal bridesmaid, becomes the sexual prey of Jeremy (Vince Vaughn), an unrelenting womanizer. Jeremy and his partner-in-crime John (Owen Wilson) sneak into weddings pretending to be guests so that they can, in Jeremy's words, "meet gorgeous ladies that are so aroused by the thought of marriage that they'll throw their inhibitions to the wind." The first plot point begins after Jeremy has discovered that his latest conquest, Gloria, is a "five-stage clinger," that is, a woman who has just confessed her love after losing her virginity to him. Jeremy wants to escape, however he and John wind up as guests at the family's estate for the weekend.

Gloria turns out not to be a sweet and shy girl, but a sex-crazed aggressor. She relentlessly pursues Jeremy, lap dancing on him despite his protests, and masturbating him to ejaculation under the dinner table. Later that night, Jeremy wakes up to find himself tied up and spreadeagled to his bed with a naked Gloria straddling him. She explains that she's worried she's not "adventurous enough" for him, and that she wants to "make all [his] fantasies come true." As Jeremy protests, his words are cut off as she duct tapes a sweaty sock into his mouth. The scene fades out as the audience hears Jeremy's muffled scream.

Later that night, Jeremy wakes up to find himself still tied up, with Gloria's gay brother Todd (Keir O'Donnell) on top of him. Todd believes that he and Jeremy had earlier shared "a moment" and is anxious to consummate this connection. A horrified Jeremy denies this, but in response, Todd presents a painting of Jeremy, which he describes as "sexual and violent." Todd then asks if Jeremy wants to play "tummy sticks," which of course Jeremy refuses, all the while struggling against the ropes that continue to bind him. Eventually Jeremy convinces Todd that they will talk the next day if only he will leave. Todd reluctantly leaves, but not before he kisses his own finger and then places it on Jeremy's clearly unhappy lips.

The scenes with Gloria and with Todd are comical, but for different reasons. With Gloria, although Jeremy expresses consternation at his restrained predicament, a number of factors lead the audience to believe he will enjoy the encounter. Jeremy has already had sex with Gloria and clearly still desires her. The audience also knows that Jeremy is a heterosexual character whose personality is in part drawn from the star-image of Vince Vaughn as a hyper-heterosexual man. Gloria is presented as a conventionally beautiful and nubile woman. The editing techniques also establish the situation as non-threatening. The scene begins with Gloria's perky breasts grazing Jeremy's face, an image that could easily be drawn from a conventional pornographic film. Their conversation is filmed in a shot-reverse-shot sequence, such that Gloria and Jeremy are framed in medium close-up during virtually all the moments of their respective dialogue. In this way, the audience can occupy the listener's point of view as it switches between the two characters, thus relating to them both. And although Jeremy's facial expressions convey dismay and exasperation, an examination of figure 3.5 shows he does not express disgust. As such, various factors combine to render the reversal of gender norms, with Gloria literally and figuratively on top, humorous. Despite Jeremy's protests, the scene does not suggest a literal assault is taking place.

While the first scene of non-consensual bondage appears funny, with a cocky womanizer under the control of a petite and gorgeous woman, the scene with Todd banks on homophobic discomfort to draw laughs. Todd's description of his painting of Jeremy as "sexual and violent" intimates that he is interested in something hard core. Jeremy now appears to be vulnerable to a genuine sexual assault, and when Todd places his kissed finger onto Jeremy's lips, Jeremy seems to experience this as a violation. It is still meant to be a funny scene, but the humour comes from the fact that Jeremy is disgusted by Todd, can't physically push him away because he is restrained, and must instead appease him by promising to talk the next day. As Miller has observed, "The comic and the disgusting … share significant points of contact" (1997, ix).

The editing also contributes to the discomfort and humour of the scene. Their conversation is filmed in a two-shot close-up sequence,

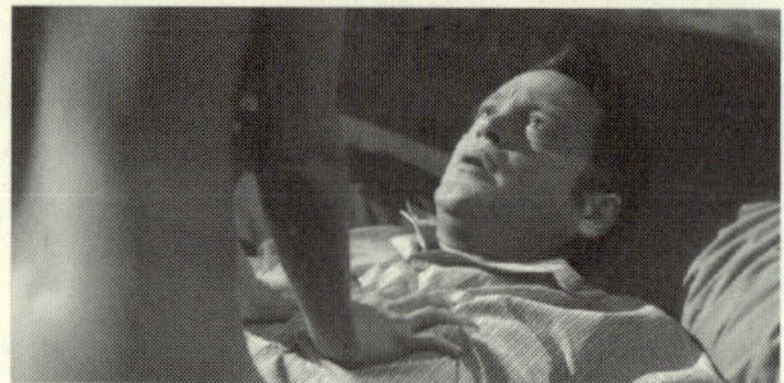

Figure 3.5: Jeremy's look of dismay with Gloria

and as a result there is an unsettling proximity between the two men, emphasized by Jeremy constantly trying to pull away as far as possible from Todd. Jeremy's expression also conveys disgust, not dismay (see figure 3.6). In Charles Darwin's study of facial expressions, he observes that extreme disgust is conveyed when "the mouth is opened widely, with the upper lip strongly retracted, which wrinkles the sides of the nose, and with the lower lip protruded and everted as much as possible. This latter movement requires the contraction of the muscles which draw downwards the corners of the mouth" ([1872] 2001, 123). In the movie still (figure 3.6), notice how this description accurately reflects Jeremy's facial expression. Thus while both encounters are presented as non-consensual, the heterosexual s/m with a feminine woman topping a macho man is cute and funny, and the gay s/m with a man on top of another man is disgusting and funny.

The next scene takes place in the morning where Jeremy insists to John that they must leave. In a comic diatribe, Jeremy explains that he didn't get much sleep because of the "midnight rape" and the "nude gay art show" that took place in his room. He later states that he can't discuss the details, except to say that he "felt like Jodie Foster in *The Accused*." The references to sexual assault are meant to be facetious. Again, s/m with the woman on top is portrayed as funny, not threatening, even when Jeremy recounts the experience in the language of rape. If the genders were reversed, i.e., if a woman had recounted a "midnight rape" to her friend, the anecdote would likely not have been funny at all. And Jeremy's reference to his encounter with Todd as a "nude gay art show" defuses and desexualizes what actually could have been seen as another moment of sexual assault.

Jeremy soon has a change of heart towards Gloria. As the movie progresses, he realizes that he has fallen for Gloria's wanton ways and so decides to forsake his philandering, after which they start dating

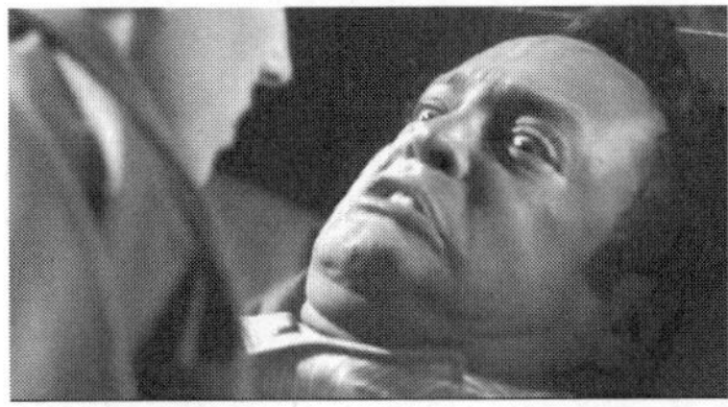

Figure 3.6: Jeremy's look of disgust with Todd

exclusively. After a few months, he proposes, and she enthusiastically screams, "I do."

In this film, the bondage is a very small part of the narrative. It signifies not so much Gloria's sexual dominance as her sexual assertiveness and adventurousness. Unlike in *Something Wild*, the bondage scene is more funny than sexy, particularly because it is followed by Gloria's brother coming into the room with his own plans of seduction. And in the end, Gloria's wildness and sexual excess come to be contained in marriage.

Something Wild and *Wedding Crashers* both portray free-spirited women with a penchant for putting men in bondage but restore gendered order at the end by putting the man back in control: Charles will drive (i.e., he will decide where they will go), and Jeremy proposes to Gloria (i.e., he ultimately decides in what direction the relationship will go). The films *Basic Instinct* (1992) and *Body of Evidence* (1993) also feature sexually dominant women, but this time in the genre of murder mystery rather than comedy. The female protagonists, Catherine Tramell (Sharon Stone) and Rebecca Carlson (Madonna), more coherently embody the femme fatale as someone who is, as Doane maintains, "the figure of a certain discursive unease, a potential epistemological trauma … she never really is what she seems to be" (1991, 1). Note that the initial riddle and threat of Lulu and Gloria as independent and sexually assertive women was resolved within the bounds of hetero-normativity, not at the end of the films, but in the middle. But with Catherine and Rebecca, the narratives keep you guessing right till the end (and afterwards). What is the nature of these femmes fatales? Is death the only way to restore order?

The first and more famous of these two s/m femme fatale films, *Basic Instinct,* opens with a sex scene: a beautiful white woman, whose face is hidden by the veil of her blond hair, has sat up to straddle her white male lover. She pulls out a scarf and ties his hands to the bedpost without any protest. As she gyrates back and forth, she reaches behind her, and when it sounds like the man has just reached the beginning of an orgasm, she stabs him repeatedly in the neck with an ice pick. The prime suspect for the murder is the superlatively wealthy Catherine Tramell, the deceased's girlfriend, who was the last person to be seen with him. Because the victim was found tied up and semen was detected on the sheet, the police figure something kinky was happening before the murder. In the interrogation room, Catherine is asked by one police officer whether she has ever "engaged in any sadomasochistic activity?" She denies having ever tied up her late lover but intimates that she has tied up others.

Detective Nick Curran (Michael Douglas) is assigned to the investigation of Catherine, and the audience learns that Nick himself is no angel. Internal Affairs has investigated Nick for four shootings in the last five years, he has a history of abusing alcohol and cocaine, and he used to be a smoker. While Nick had begun to move away from this dysfunctional behaviour, things start to unravel after he meets Catherine. And the more time Nick spends with Catherine as the plot unfolds, the more he exhibits destructive behaviour. After Catherine's interrogation, Nick starts to drink heavily again. He later has sex with his ex-girlfriend, Beth, in an aggressive way that could reasonably be categorized as date rape (she says "no" and "stop," right before he penetrates her from behind). He starts smoking again after this, in what symbolically appears to be a re-appropriation of phallic power. Later in the movie, he attacks an Internal Affairs officer, believing his personal file had been sold to Catherine. That night he gets extremely drunk.

The inevitable sexual consummation between Nick and Catherine begins when he sees Catherine inhale cocaine and then kiss her part-time girlfriend, Roxy, at a club. Later, Catherine moves towards him and they begin to kiss, and a sex scene follows at her house. During this encounter, they switch top and bottom positions, and at one point Catherine in apparent ecstasy digs her nails into Nick's back, causing lines of blood to flow. The scene culminates with Catherine climbing on top of him and tying his arms with a white silk scarf, identical to the one used during the opening murder scene. However, their simultaneous orgasms do not lead to murder, but rather to a loving embrace. Near the end of the movie, the mystery of the first murder, as well as the subsequent murders of the Internal Affairs officer and Nick's "only friend," Gus, seem to be resolved, as the evidence points strongly (through convoluted plot twists) at Beth, who herself had been a former lover of Catherine's. Nick kills Beth in apparent self-defence, then returns to his apartment to a tearful Catherine, who is displaying none of the self-assurance and nonchalance that has characterized her throughout most of the movie. The last shot of the couple features the two making love with Nick on top. The camera then pans down, and the last shot of the film reveals an ice pick under the bed. Most people, including the director, interpret this shot as establishing Catherine, not Beth, as the murderer ("Basic Instinct, Trivia").

In many ways, Catherine figures perfectly as a femme fatale, marked by ambiguity. Is she the murderer, or the victim of a devious frame-up? Is she straight or lesbian (bisexuality itself being a transgression of the hegemonic hetero/homo binary)? Is she just using Nick (whether to thwart the investigation or as material for her new book), or is she falling in love with him, her toughness just a facade to hide her true feminine vulnerability? And, most pertinent to this analysis, is she a consensual sadomasochist or a pathological sadist? Catherine is an enigma that disrupts established knowledge systems and categories, most notably with regard to sexual difference. If she is a murderer, a manipulator, and a lover of women, she has appropriated masculine characteristics of aggression and cunning and has taken a male object of desire for herself, i.e., a woman. Regardless of whether she is a sadomasochist or a sadist, she takes control in bed and thereby usurps the traditional masculine role.

Her s/m bent, along with her bisexuality and her unsentimental enthusiasm for "fucking," all signal her sexual excess, another marker of the femme fatale. Doane maintains that the femme fatale's sexuality is the antithesis of the nurturing maternal sexuality; she has a high sex drive and enjoys non-reproductive intercourse (1991, 1). Indeed, at the end of the movie Nick suggests that they can settle down, have children, and live happily ever after, and Catherine counters with "I hate rug rats." She has no desire to put her kinky sexuality to procreative use.

George Ross Ridge's study of the femme fatale figure in French decadent literature maintains that s/m is a constant theme in the narratives, with the women usually taking on the dominant role (1961, 354). S/m is itself a source of definitional instability, as it aggregates concepts that are normally thought of as antithetical, like pleasure and pain, or consent and bondage. Gender roles are troubled, not just because the woman has taken sexual control, but because, as in *Basic Instinct*, Catherine's use of bondage is a means to overcome sex difference. The man's presumed superior strength is suppressed and the woman can now take charge. She can penetrate/rape him, a prerogative that is understood to be open only to a man in a heterosexual encounter. In *Basic Instinct*, Catherine uses this advantage to kill her lover with an ice pick, a phallic symbol if ever there was one.[6] Indeed, Catherine's weapon of choice makes an intertextual linkage to a classic film noir, *Scarlet Street*, in which the emasculated protagonist realizes he's been duped and kills the femme fatale in a sudden paroxysm of masculine rage – with an ice pick. *Basic Instinct* can be understood as a retelling of the film noir narrative in which Catherine avenges the murder of *Scarlet Street*'s femme fatale figure, appropriating the phallic ice pick, and killing the man who so willingly fell into her bondage trap. As such, Catherine's s/m contributes to the overall picture of her as a threat to sex/gender coherence, as well as to sexual order.

Yet in comparison to what happens in *Something Wild*, s/m is not signified as African-American in *Basic Instinct*. Instead, whiteness comes to the forefront of the narrative. Robert Wood (1993) argues that *Basic Instinct* can be read as "white noir," where the classic narrative elements of film noir are present, yet the colour scheme of the movie is its antithesis. Surprisingly, Wood's article does not reflect on the racial semiotics of this "white noir," but Chris Holmlund's article on "Hollywood's Deadly (Lesbian) Dolls" does provide a cogent argument that whiteness as a racial category is a central theme in the plot of *Basic Instinct* (1994, 39). Holmlund notes the obsessive recurrence of whiteness in the film. Catherine is blonde. The scarf that she uses for sexual bondage is white. Catherine puts on a white dress to go to the police station. During perhaps the most infamous moment in the film, Catherine flashes the police officers a quick shot of her blonde pubic hair while she uncrosses and crosses her legs. Catherine's house is white, with imposing white pillars, and the exterior walls of her beach house are white. And there are numerous references throughout the film to cocaine, a drug that goes by the name of "white lady" in slang. Nick used to abuse cocaine, the police find cocaine at the first murder site, and during the night-club scene, Nick observes Catherine snorting the drug with her girlfriend, Roxy.

A notable aspect of these signifiers of whiteness is that they are directly or indirectly associated with wealth. Catherine is a platinum blonde, not just down to her roots, but to her pubic hair as well. As

Dyer argues, "Blondeness, especially platinum (peroxide) blondeness, is the ultimate sign of whiteness. Blonde hair is frequently associated with wealth" (1986, 42–3). Furthermore, as Dyer has pointed out, a white subject with blonde hair registers as "whiter" than non-blonde white subjects (1997, 44). The white scarves used during the murder and the bondage scene with Nick are expensive Hermès designer brand. Catherine's white home is a mansion complete with a uniformed maid, and her beach house is huge and luxurious. And cocaine is an expensive drug, generally associated with the wealthier class. Dyer argues that white people's whiteness is differentiated by class; the richer the white person, the whiter they register (57). Catherine's racial and symbolic whiteness is indisputable, almost hyperbolic. But there is an interesting paradox to her heightened whiteness. Dyer notes that one characteristic of whiteness is its invisibility and, as such, its ability to pass itself off as "the norm, the ordinary, the standard" (3). But in Catherine's case, her affluent whiteness is so patent that it effectively gets converted into an otherized category because of its blatant visibility. Its sheer opulence makes her conspicuously white. In other words, while the representation of white people in film generally does not call attention to the whiteness of the characters, in *Basic Instinct*, Catherine's whiteness is brought to the forefront of the narrative. I posit that not only can working-class white people become racialized (as in the pejorative terms *redneck* and *white trash*), but superlatively wealthy white people can as well. The audience learns that Catherine's estate is worth $110 million. Her class status sets her apart from the norm. It also disrupts gender norms, as her independent wealth means that she does not need a man's support, and indeed is much richer than any man with whom she comes into contact in the movie.

The representation of Catherine's whiteness is hypersexual and menacing. When she exposes her blonde pubic hair to the police officers while tangentially telling Nick that "fucking on cocaine" is "nice," she is intimidating the men and making *them* sweat during *her* interrogation. She is white femininity gone awry; the money has corrupted her maternal instincts. Not only does she hate children, not only does she tie men up for sexual thrills, but she kills just to see if she can outsmart the authorities. As such, her wealth is tied to her whiteness as well as to her sexual and moral depravity. As with other movies that feature menacing s/m subjects, such desires are often associated with the decadence of the rich.

If Catherine is the sadist, it seems that Nick is both her mirror and her complement. He exhibits aggression and violence towards persons other than Catherine, sexually assaulting Beth, attacking the Internal Investigations officer, and later stating to two psychologists, "Go fuck yourselves." But with Catherine he cedes control in bed, allowing her to call the shots much of the time. Towards himself he exhibits masochism; under Catherine's influence, it seems that some of his aggression has turned inwards. He starts smoking again and drinking to excess. He sabotages his job through his belligerent and cocky behaviour. Perhaps most self-destructively, he pursues Catherine as a lover while remaining convinced she is the murderer, allowing her to put him into precisely the same restrained and vulnerable position as the first victim. He seems to exhibit all three stages of masochism that Freud articulated in "The Economic Problem of Masochism" (1981b). His sexual arousal at bottoming for Catherine indicates "erotogenic masochism," that is, pleasure in pain, particularly when she scratches him to the point of bleeding. His enthusiasm for assuming a passive role in bed indicates "feminine masochism." And his excessive drinking and smoking, his self-sabotaging behaviour at work, and his courtship of a key suspect of sexual murder all make him a prime candidate for "moral masochism." Recall that Freud theorized that erotogenic and feminine masochism can lead to moral masochism, which he describes in non-sexual terms: "The [moral] masochist must do what is inexpedient, must act against his own interests, must ruin the prospects that open out to him in the real world and must, perhaps, destroy his own real existence" (169–70). If wanting to top in bed is an indicator of a pathological, even homicidal, personality, then wanting to bottom in bed comes to be linked in the narrative to a self-destructive, even suicidal, personality.[7]

And yet the conclusion does not deliver the usual cathartic ending to a classic film noir, in which the man casts off the femme fatale's spell and realizes her duplicitous nature, and she is killed or at least imprisoned, often because of this very man. Here, Nick mistakenly believes (or chooses to believe) that Beth was the killer, and Catherine is alive and well at the close of the film. As previously mentioned, the final scene begins with Nick returning to his house to find a terrified and tearful Catherine. The last time he had seen her, Catherine had unceremoniously ended their affair, implying that she had been using him. But during this final encounter, she confesses in a choked voice, "I can't allow myself to care about you … I lose everybody." This is an interesting twist on the conventions of the film noir genre, where the final scenes routinely have the femme fatale reveal her true mercenary intentions, often explaining how she had fooled the man all along for selfish purposes. Indeed, it is during such a scene in *Scarlet Street* that the protagonist is provoked to stab the femme fatale to death. In contrast, in *Basic Instinct*, Catherine has been posing as a blatant femme fatale from the beginning of the narrative, courting suspicion by appearing cold, self-centred, and hyper-sexual. In the final scene, she implies that this was a defence strategy and for the first time displays feminine emotionality and tenderness. Nick takes her in his arms and they make love. Although Catherine does straddle him again during the final moments of intercourse, there is no bondage this time. They climax simultaneously and then embrace. Just when the audience is lulled into believing her innocence all along, Catherine reaches for something under the bed. The "shock" ending reveals that she was reaching for the ice pick, but perhaps what is more shocking is that she apparently decides not to use it on Nick.

One interpretation of this ending is that under Nick's influence, Catherine becomes a redeemed femme fatale. After Nick kills Roxy (by forcing her car off a bridge, admittedly following Roxy's earlier attempt to run Nick over), Catherine's heterosexuality is apparently clinched when she informs Nick in a post-coital moment that she has "no luck with women." At the end of the film, it seems that Catherine and Nick are going to remain lovers, and the final shot of the couple with Nick on top implies that Catherine's sexual dominance has been attenuated. In addition, Catherine's perverse urge to kill has also seemingly been abated. Earlier in the film, she states in reference to Roxy (who had killed her two brothers when she was a minor) that killing is *not* like smoking, you *can* stop. Perhaps true love prevented her from grabbing the ice pick and killing Nick.[8]

After all, Nick could be her soul mate. He too is a killer (he "accidentally" shot two tourists dead, he caused Roxy to plunge to her death, and he shot an unarmed Beth). Further, he displays aggressiveness towards authority figures and clearly enjoyed his moment of sexual dominance over Beth during the ambiguous rape scene. The final sexual scene – when Catherine allows Nick to take the top position – signifies a partial restoration of gendered order (see figure 3.7). Catherine has ceded control to Nick at the denouement of the narrative, which perhaps has circumvented the generic film noir imperative that the femme fatale must die or at least be punished. But the threat of otherness, Catherine's phallic weapon, still lurks under the bed, ready to strike at any moment.

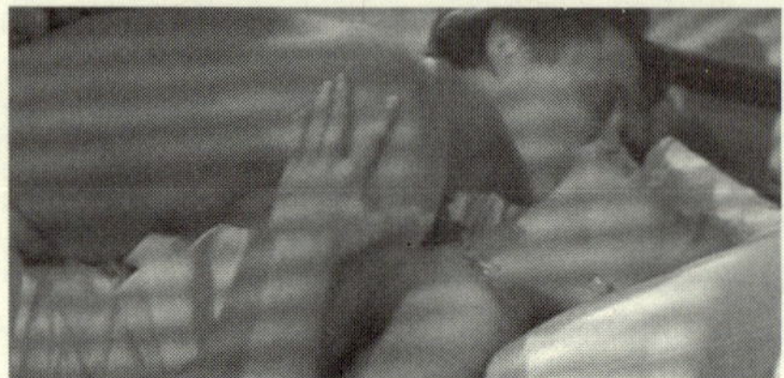

Figure 3.7: Nick on top at the end of the narrative

Many critics lambasted the 1993 film *Body of Evidence* as a cheap imitation of *Basic Instinct*. But for our purposes, it is an important film because it makes explicit what *Basic Instinct* only implied: s/m gets literally put on trial in the narrative for being a corrupt and deadly practice. And while the femme fatale is acquitted of murder, the verdict of the film is unambiguous: s/m is guilty.

The first scene begins in the bedroom of a luxurious mansion. Again s/m desire is associated with extreme wealth. The camera focuses on a pair of nipple clamps on the night table, as a television set in the background plays a home video showing an older man handcuffed to a bed while a young blonde woman straddles him during intercourse. The camera pans to the bed and the same man is shown lying dead, his eyes open but unseeing in front of the television. The woman in the video is Rebecca Carlson, who stands to inherit eight million dollars from the death of her lover, Andrew Marsh (Michael Forest). She gets charged with murder under the theory that she slipped her lover cocaine, knowing that he suffered from major heart disease, and then proceeded to have rigorous s/m sex to induce a heart attack. Rebecca hires Frank Dulaney (William Dafoe) to represent her, and the two soon begin an s/m affair that continues throughout the trial.

The narrative unfolds as a courtroom drama and erotic thriller, throughout which s/m is the subject of accusations and defences that draw heavily on the language of disgust. At trial, although the main criminal act would have been slipping the cocaine to an older man with a weak heart, Frank accurately prophesizes that the prosecutor Robert Garrett (Joe Mantegna) "is going to build his case on [Rebecca's] sex life." Accordingly, Robert attempts to buttress the prosecution's shaky and circumstantial case by casting Rebecca as a perverted femme fatale and capitalizing on the "communalizing capacities" of disgust (Miller 1997, 194). In his opening remarks, Robert claims that Rebecca is a

"ruthless calculating woman … who disguised herself as a loving partner." At trial, the prosecution casts s/m activities within the terms of
a "pattern of abuse." Robert further attempts to objectify Rebecca by
stating that her body "is the murder weapon itself." A key prosecutorial
witness, Joanne Braslow (Amy Archer) also represents the voice of disgust. She refers to Rebecca as a "cokehead slut" and proclaims that
Rebecca and Andrew "didn't have normal sex." Joanne herself was a
former lover of Andrew and was confident he would return to her because "men don't marry women like her [Rebecca]."

In their defence of s/m, Rebecca and Frank attempt to reckon with
other people's disgust. In his opening remarks, Frank states to the jury,
"You may find it [s/m sex] offensive. You may even be disgusted by
what you hear." By acknowledging their possible disgust, Frank attempts to make the jury members cognizant of this possible bias in determining Rebecca's culpability. Rebecca nonetheless worries that the
jury members' disgust will ultimately determine their verdict, but she
insists that the people who condemn s/m have "taken something good
between two people in love and made it dirty." She sets herself up as a
romantic outlaw challenging the hypocrisies of the general public. This
recalls, to a degree, the s/m lesbian self-construction as a sexual outlaw
during the sex wars, which challenged the alleged repressive hypocrisies of both feminist and mainstream culture.

In contrast to this emotional account of her s/m affair with Andrew,
Rebecca also invokes the animal world to defend s/m. She asks her
lawyer, "Have you ever seen animals make love Frank? It's intense. It's
violent. But they never really hurt each other." When Frank protests,
"We're not animals," Rebecca rebuts definitively, "Yes we are."

While this assertion recalls the early psychiatric discourse that turned
to animal behaviour for confirmation of the naturalness of s/m, it also
directly confronts the disgust associations of s/m to animalism. Though
Nussbaum and other disgust theorists have posited that disgust is
bound up with a human disavowal of our animality, there can also be
transgressive pleasure in blurring the distinction between human and
animal. As Halperin suggests, such an abject pleasure can be extracted
from other people's disgust (2007, 93). Rebecca delights in the discomfort she causes Frank when she asserts that humans are also animals. At
the same time, it is a seductive line; it implies that animals may be delving in pleasures that human pretensions have prevented for most people. As Miller states, "For all the concern to claim ourselves superior
to animals and our horror that we are assimilable to them, there is a

countervailing admiration and envy of them, a desire to live *up* to them" (1997, 49). Our disgust with animals carries with it a desire for animal subjectivity, the allure of fully embracing the physicality of sex.

On trial, Rebecca offers more psychological explanations for s/m. Aside from insisting that she and Andrew were deeply in love, she also provides a standard account of male submissiveness. Her lover was always in charge in his public life, she explains, and so in bed he wanted to cede control. At the same time, she insists that Andrew "picked the [s/m] games" that they engaged in, to counter the suggestion that she led him into perversity.

The sexual component of the movie is provided by the erotic tension and subsequent affair that occur between Rebecca and Frank. Their first sexual encounter is distinctly sadomasochistic. Frank allows Rebecca to restrain him with a belt and to pour hot candle wax on his body (see figure 3.8). But later, Frank appropriates sexual control. During an argument in which Frank blames Rebecca for tipping his wife off about the affair, he angrily grabs her and throws her on the ground. Afterward, he handcuffs her face down and penetrates her from behind, while she resists (figure 3.9). It is an ambiguous rape/sex scene reminiscent of Nick's assault on Beth in *Basic Instinct*, where the woman seems to protest the activity initially, but soon appears to enjoy it. This is a significant moment in which Frank regains masculine control of the affair, again similar to when Nick takes the top position at the end of *Basic Instinct*. However, Rebecca still has a few tricks up her sleeve.[9]

After a convincing show of innocence on the stand, the jury finds Rebecca not guilty. However, before she leaves the courtroom, Rebecca insinuates to Frank that she was guilty all along. Because the film editing techniques establish identification with Rebecca, the audience, as well as Frank, is meant to experience a jarring wake-up call that this *femme* is truly fatal. That night Frank goes to confront Rebecca at her home, where he hears her arguing with a witness, Doctor Alan Paley (Jürgen Prochnow). Frank learns that Rebecca and Alan were lovers who had planned the murder and concocted a scheme in which their coordinated and perjured testimony would bathe her in innocent light. However, Alan is furious when he discovers that Rebecca slept with her lawyer. In classic femme fatale style, she shows her true colours at the end of the story, mocking Alan's jealousy by stating, "I fucked you. I fucked Andrew. I fucked Frank. That's what I do, I fuck. And it made me eight million dollars." The camera is now looking up at her; she appears intimidating and has indeed turned out to be a "ruthless

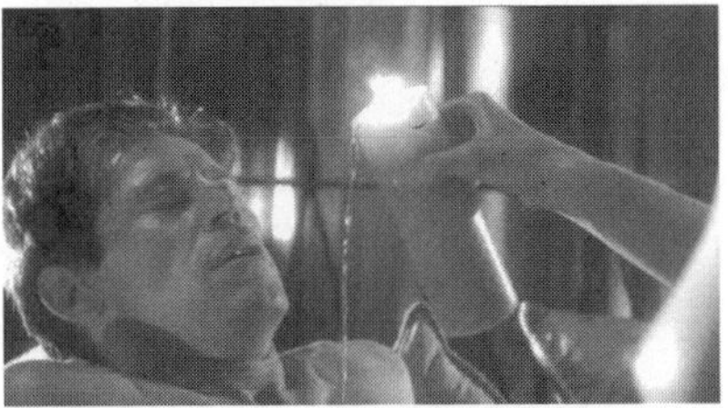

Figure 3.8: Frank submits to Rebecca

calculating woman," as Robert had claimed in his opening statement. And the narrative remains consistent with the film noir genre when Alan, the duped man, becomes enraged and kills her. In case the audience has not grasped the patently obvious moral of the story, the prosecutor shows up at the end to smugly pronounce that "people get what they deserve." In this moment, Robert has become the unambiguous voice of the moral community, which implicitly includes the audience members. Robert's unwavering disgust for Rebecca has been vindicated, and Frank has now fully converted to the disgust side. Frank leaves the scene a redeemed man, and his wife welcomes him back with open arms.

Body of Evidence, like *Basic Instinct*, trades on Madonna's hyperwhiteness as a menacing signifier, links s/m to the decadence of the rich, and places cocaine, "the white lady," at the murder scene. But the most important and striking parallel to *Basic Instinct* is the moral message regarding sexually dominant women, who are portrayed as dangerous, self-centred, and pathological. However, unlike *Basic Instinct*'s unsettling ending, which reveals that the killer has likely gotten away with murder, *Body of Evidence* bluntly restores all sexual order. The femme fatale is killed by her co-conspirator, and her other dupe (her lawyer and the protagonist of the story) returns to the fold of marital normativity.

Body of Evidence could be said to be both acutely voyeuristic and exhibitionistic. The film's release came hot on the heels of the publication of Madonna's graphic coffee-table book *Sex*, in which she exhibits her body in a variety of kinky and taboo postures, including sadomasochistic (Madonna 1992). Any audience member who has read the book knows that Madonna has confessed she is drawn to s/m; as she states in her book, "There is something comforting about being tied up" (18).

Figure 3.9: Frank aggressively takes the top position

Madonna is also a defender of s/m; as she states later in the book, "I talked to a dominatrix once and she said the definition of S & M was that you let someone hurt you who you know would never hurt you. It's always a mutual choice" (21). Madonna, the performer, who is already discursively enmeshed with s/m culture, becomes the palimpsest upon which Rebecca, the character, is drawn. As such, the scenes in which "Rebecca" performs s/m acts register as particularly real and authentic because of Madonna's notorious star-image. Madonna is brazenly exhibiting her sexuality, and the audience is voyeuristically consuming it. But while the movie traffics in the pleasures of voyeurism, it also gratifies disgust and expulsion pleasures.

During the sex scenes, disgust with s/m can work as a mental barrier to unconscious desires – what Freud called a reaction formation (1975, 44). As Miller has noted, this perspective of disgust suggests that "foul is fair"; s/m registers as "foul" in one's consciousness in order to cloak an unconscious determination that it might be experienced as "fair" (1997, 110). But Miller goes further to suggest that disgust might not just be a veneer over our desires, and instead it might be that "the disgusting itself has the power to allure" (111). In this sense, Rebecca's sexual excess and dominance incites voyeurism, not just because it might be sexually pleasurable, but also because it might be disgustingly pleasurable.

But by the end of the film, Rebecca has become morally repugnant, and the audience is aligned with a more comfortable narrative of disgust, as articulated by Robert. As Miller has argued, "Disgust and indignation unite the world of impartial spectators into a moral community, as co-sharers of the same sentiments, as guardians of propriety and purity" (1997, 195). This communal disgust is also implicated in a shared pleasure in erecting the line between clean and dirty, implicitly endowing all the disgust-bearers with the status of normal, untainted, and morally healthy.

The pleasures of disgust are also intertwined with the cathartic satisfaction in the death of Rebecca. The term *catharsis*, derived from the Greek word "to purify," conveys the need to wash away the previous emotions generated by a narrative. In the case of *Body of Evidence*, the audience can be exonerated for having been implicated in the pleasures of s/m and voyeurism through the cathartic pleasure of expulsion. Recall that Julia Kristeva locates the pleasure of expulsion in Freud's theory of the anal-sadistic phase, where the child derives pleasure both from expelling waste and in destroying. This psychoanalytic construction provides some insight into the economy of pleasure in *Body of Evidence.* In the normative order of the film, Rebecca has been deemed to be a kind of social waste, not just because she is a murderer, but also because of her sexual excess and gender-transgressive dominance. At the end of the film, she is shot twice, crashes through a window, and falls into the ocean; her influence and her power have been literally and symbolically washed away. There is poetic justice – an aesthetic pleasure – in seeing her murdered by the very man whose perjured testimony had secured her murder acquittal. Later, when Robert shows up at the crime scene, he begins to smoke a cigarette: a classic post-coital activity that suggests a libidinal satisfaction with the murder of Rebecca. He then pronounces to Frank that what happened to Rebecca was "karma." Rebecca is put in her place, not just by her duped ex-lover, but also by the defeated prosecutorial attorney. In the end, Robert claims victory while her corpse is rolled away. The audience is thus invited to partake in the satisfaction that justice prevailed, even though the justice system had failed.

A subsequent femme fatale/male submissive tale worth considering for its notions of justice and perversion is the 2001 comedy *One Night at McCool's*. In this pastiche narrative, three different men relate conflicting stories about how a temptress named Jewel (Liv Tyler) turned their lives upside down for better, or more accurately, for worse. Significantly, Carl Harding (Paul Reiser), an egotistical lawyer, falls under Jewel's spell because she caters to his sexual submissive desires. In a humorous seduction scene, Jewel whips Carl while she cajoles him into agreeing to provide her free legal representation.

Unlike in *Basic Instinct* or *Body of Evidence*, there is never a moment where Carl tops Jewel, and in terms of femme fatale narrative imperatives, he pays dearly. At the end of the film, Carl, clad in a leather submissive outfit with his hands tied behind his back, is portrayed as feeble and cowardly. A gunfight has broken out between rival men, and Carl, without a gun – phallus-less in a sense – is praying that his body not be found wearing the fetish outfit. Carl manages to flee the scene, and he is running down the street elated for having escaped unscathed. In the final moment of the film, however, a large metal storage box randomly drops from a crane and kills him. This is meant to be a funny and unexpected way to close the story. But I posit that it is funny only because the narrative has worked hard to objectify and distance the audience from Carl. As a male submissive, he is unmanly and unsympathetic and becomes the object of a normalizing gaze, "not just to-be-looked-at but to-be-laughed-at" (Gray 1994, 9).[10] He dies a cartoon death.

In contrast another suitor, Randy – played by the conventionally attractive Matt Dillon – is the male protagonist with whom the audience is encouraged to sympathize. If such a tragic thing had befallen Randy, it would not have registered as humorous. Carl is the butt of the final joke of the film because as a male submissive, he inverts gender expectations in an explicit and self-conscious way. As such, he gets ruthlessly killed off, experiencing a fate that makes sense in the narrative because of his emasculated sexual position.[11]

The expulsion pleasure at work here is premised on the destruction of a kinky subject being funny, while in *Body of Evidence* it is premised on the satisfaction of retribution. Yet in both pleasures is the shared satisfaction that gender transgression has been punished. The male submissives in *Body of Evidence* are also punished in different ways. Recall that Rebecca easily killed her lover, Andrew, because he allowed himself to get into a bondaged and helpless situation. Her duped lover, Alan, becomes both the instrument of retribution and an object of punishment, as in the end he will go to jail not just because he killed Rebecca, but also because he fell under her seductive spell when he agreed to help her murder Andrew. Only Frank gets to walk away, in part because he assumed the dominant position when he forced Rebecca to take a submissive sexual position during the quasi-rape scene. He restores his masculinity in that moment. And in the end, the narrative bestows grace on Frank, as he is allowed to reconcile with his wife and resume a "normal" life.

Dominatrix with a Soft Centre

One might think that professional dominatrices, whose work involves taking the top position and meting out harsh treatment to submissive clients, would be represented as even more dangerous in cinema. But interestingly, most of the movies that fall under this category are not about femme fatales, but rather about women who, for one reason or another, have become emotionally hardened – and who need the love of a man to help them cede control and get in touch with their true femininity.

Exit to Eden exemplifies this genre. In this 1994 comedy, Sheila Kingston (Rosie O'Donnell) and Fred Lavery (Dan Aykroyd) are cops who go undercover to an s/m resort island to catch a suspected killer. Although the s/m component provides many opportunities for humour, the film proffers salient and standard defences of the sexual practice. While Fred voices the opinion of the social conservative, pronouncing that s/m is "so disgusting," Sheila counters that "it's just an alternative lifestyle." The owner of the resort, a doctor, maintains that supporting s/m is consistent with supporting "freedom of choice."

The movie also makes specific references to s/m safe practices. For example, the clients of the resort are instructed that "all pairings are consensual." Indeed, this film stands out for its informed portrayal of the s/m subculture, and certainly it is more educational than *Basic Instinct* or *Body of Evidence* about conventions that ensure mutuality and safety. In those two femme fatale narratives, s/m happens spontaneously, without negotiation or verbal consent, whereas in *Exit to Eden*, the s/m encounters are carefully contrived, and consent has been explicitly articulated. However, even here the portrayal of the erotic dynamic between a dominant woman and a submissive man reveals an anxiety about sex roles and the need to visually restore gendered order, much as *Basic Instinct* and *Body of Evidence* did when their male protagonists reasserted sexual control.

The s/m eroticism in the narrative revolves around a love story between "Mistress Lisa" (Dana Delaney), a dominatrix who runs the resort, and Elliott Slater (Paul Mercurio), a first-time visitor to the island and a closeted male submissive. Through s/m training sessions, Lisa teaches Elliott to succumb to his submissive side and admit his enjoyment. After Elliott accepts his submissiveness, however, there is barely any more expression of it. Instead, their relationship shifts into a more conventional love story. While Lisa tries to keep a professional distance from her submissive client, Elliott doggedly pursues her, trying to persuade her to give in to her obvious attraction to and affection for Elliott. The audience gets insight into Lisa's resistance when she explains to Sheila that she became a dominatrix because she used to be a victim, and now she wants to "be in control" because it feels "safe." Lisa later admits to Sheila, "It would be nice not to be in control and still feel safe." As such, dominating for Lisa is not described as a sexual turn-on, but as a defence mechanism. This is in contrast to the racialized character of Nina Blackstone (Iman), one of the "bad guys" in the film, who is portrayed as inherently dominant and even sadistic.

But Elliott finally pushes past Lisa's emotional walls and she agrees to go on a romantic getaway with him. After a night of cuddling, Elliott initiates intimacy "with no party tricks," which is shown to mean non-kinky missionary-position sex (see figure 3.10).

At first, Lisa informs Elliott that she finds this sexual position "awkward." But after he tells her to "just relax" she ends up enjoying the bottom position. By the end of the film, Lisa is fully in touch with her feminine side, and she gladly accepts Elliott's marriage proposal.

The denouement both reinforces sexual normativity and makes small inroads towards normalizing perversity. Though they will likely still incorporate female dominance and male submission into their sex life, the last sex scene portrays Lisa and Elliott engaging in vaginal intercourse with Elliott on top. As such, non-kinky sex has gained the primary position in the narrative. It is as if all of the s/m activities previously shown were mere lead-up or foreplay to an inevitable culmination in normative heterosexual intercourse.

But the narrative subverts hetero-normativity when Lisa decides not to forsake her work as a dominatrix, nor cease running the resort, after the marriage. In addition, Lisa and Elliott discuss having children, which both reinforces hetero-normativity and destabilizes it. On the one hand, the fact that they are arranging their relationship within a standard nuclear framework promotes *family values*. On the other hand, the suggestion that "bondage and babies" are not mutually exclusive increases acceptance for kinky subjectivity in the social imaginary. As chapter 5 will show, parents who are kinky may have their parental competence challenged in custody battles for their non-normative sexual practices, even if there is no evidence to suggest that such practices have had any impact on their children. Furthermore, getting married and having children are central components to sexual citizenship, and in this way, Lisa and Elliott establish their right to belong in society.[12]

Interestingly, a side-plot involving Sheila's love life also reinforces hetero-normativity. During her investigation on the resort, Sheila went undercover as a dominant client who was paired with a male submissive, Tommy Miller (Sean O'Bryan). Throughout her time at the resort, Tommy, clad only in kinky underwear, attempts to entice Sheila into

Figure 3.10: Elliott and Lisa engaging in missionary-position sex

engaging in s/m encounters, but she cleverly eludes his advances. After the investigation, Sheila meets Tommy as they are leaving the resort. Tommy is now sporting an impressive suit and Sheila learns that he is not a full-time pervert, but a CEO who simply comes to the resort "to relax." Sheila's interest is piqued. In a voice-over, Sheila divulges that once they left the resort, she began to date the wealthy Tommy. Tommy's prestigious job, his class status, and his manly attire at the end of the film mitigate his previous submissive behaviour and thus render him a more eligible bachelor from a hetero-gender normative perspective.

Another movie that straddles the ideological realm between creating acceptance for perversity and solidifying gender and sexual norms is the 1998 British film *Preaching to the Perverted*. In this comedic romantic drama, a socially conservative member of Parliament, Henry Harding (Tom Bell), is on a crusade to shut down a fetish event that occurs regularly in London. Henry represents the adamant voice of disgust with s/m and its practitioners through his use of the language of contagion. Complaining to a media representative, he bemoans that "perversion is out of the closet" and "their beliefs are infecting the media." As Miller has observed, disgust often relies upon pathologizing tropes, as is evidenced by the way anti-s/m feminists often label s/m lesbians as "sick." But this does not exculpate the diseased pervert. As Miller further comments, "Sickness, we think, is a punishable offense" (1997, 203). Henry's criminalization and condemnation of s/m is also exposed as hypocrisy. In his opening scene, he reads a newspaper article about Tanya Cheex (Guinevere Turner), a professional dominatrix and a performance artist. He complains, "When will porno sickos like Tanya Cheex be bound and gagged?" This ironic statement conveys a double standard towards "degrading" treatment. Henry is disgusted with the "sick" pleasures of s/m, but his imagined punishment for sadomasochists fits within an s/m framework. Later, Henry makes reference to an actual 1993 British case, *R. v. Brown* (a case that I examine in chapter 5 on the legal regulation of s/m practice). He states of the House of Lords decision, "Not long ago, a number of perverts were jailed for nailing their penises to planks, and even sicker acts. If it had been up to me, I would have cut the penises off!" Again, the film demonstrates the sadism and hypocrisy of the disgust position. Violence and degradation are not being condemned; rather, the consensual extraction of pleasure from "violence" and "degradation" is being condemned.

While Henry embodies the voice of disgust, the male lead in the movie, Peter Emery (Christien Anholt), also negotiates disgust when he finds himself falling in love with a dominatrix. Henry hires Peter, an obedient young man, to infiltrate the s/m scene, convincing him that it is a "Christian cause" to stop these perverts. Peter enters the secret world of underground fetishism as a beginner, covertly gathering evidence of "physical harm," that is, skin breaking or bruising, which would support a conviction of assault under British law, despite the consent of the players. In the course of his investigation, Peter falls in love with Tanya.

At the start of the film, Tanya is presented as fiercely independent, instructing an announcer not to refer to her as a "woman" but as a "*womon*" because she "woo[s] no man." The audience learns that when she's not onstage, Tanya lives in an elaborately kinkified loft that is home to numerous fetishists, dominants, and submissives who – quite literally – worship the ground she walks on. Most notably, there is Tanya's loyal assistant and part-time lover, Eugenie (Julie Graham), who appears to be seeking a more serious relationship with Tanya. And there is Lunk (Enzo), a racialized male submissive who takes pleasure in servicing his mistress's every whim.

While Tanya enjoys sexual encounters with her two devotees, she spurns all emotional entanglements and is most adamant that she does not want to be vaginally penetrated or do any other "straight" activities. Indeed, after Lunk tries to initiate heterosexual intercourse with Tanya, she furiously screams, "No penetration, ever … I get more pleasure from my clit ring in a few seconds than I could get from that thing [his penis] in a million years!" Lunk is banned from the loft forever.

When Peter enters this scene, he and Tanya slowly negotiate a sexual relationship that centres on oral stimulation, thereby respecting Peter's wish to retain his virginity and Tanya's preference for kinky sexuality. However, like Mistress Lisa in *Exit to Eden*, Tanya initially resists getting too personal with her boy toy. One morning Tanya wakes up to find Peter cuddling her and she aggressively pushes him away, stating, "This is vanilla, this does not happen." She clearly has issues, not just about certain sexual practices, but about emotional intimacy.

And yet one day, Tanya confesses to Peter that her "darkest fantasy" involves role playing as a newlywed and having heterosexual intercourse. On a whim, the two decide to enact the fantasy and check into a motel, with Tanya dressed in a white bridal outfit and Peter in a tux. In the morning, Tanya wakes up furious, despite the fact that it was her fantasy. She screams at Peter, "You fucked me! Don't ever come near me in your miserable life again!," and storms out of the room. She is evidently confused and scared by her deep feelings for Peter, and her willingness to allow him to figuratively and literally *penetrate* her.

Despite Tanya's harsh words of rejection, Peter remains loyal to her by retracting his commitment to his employer at Parliament. Peter spends nine months in jail for perjury after he changes his testimony regarding the s/m activities he witnessed. This sacrifice wins Tanya over. When Peter is released from jail, he is greeted by Tanya, who is nine months pregnant with their child, conceived on the night they enacted her "straight" fantasy. They reconcile, working out a mutually agreeable arrangement for intimacy. Peter moves into the loft and becomes Tanya's manager, stating clearly to one client that he is *not* a slave. In the final conversation that establishes their intimate bond, Tanya jokes, "One day I'm going to give you such a spanking." Peter replies, "Not in my life you won't," to which Tanya retorts, "Then don't get any ideas about regular vanilla sex with me." They have both drawn their personal lines around what they are willing to do in bed. But notice that Peter's rejection of spanking is definitive and consistent with his stated desires throughout the film. In contrast, Tanya tells him not to get any ideas about "regular vanilla sex," but the audience knows that she already confessed this to be her "darkest" fantasy. As such, Tanya's statement is less convincing; she might want to play out her fantasy again. In addition, her decision to enter into a monogamous relationship, at least offstage, further aligns her with normality. Tanya, like Lisa in *Exit to Eden*, has been softened by the love of a man. Her previous rejection of penetration and relationships has been abdicated.

In addition, at the end of the film, Eugenie is no longer Tanya's part-time lover, but has instead become a nursemaid for Tanya's baby. As in *Basic Instinct*, same-sex desire is evacuated. But while the lesbian rival gets killed in *Basic Instinct*, Eugenie's threat is neutralized though maternalization. As Adrienne Rich has commented, "A woman's status as childbearer has been the test of her womanhood" (1979, 261). Tanya proves her maturity and her normalcy by bearing a child, and Eugenie by nursing the baby.[13] Furthermore, Tanya's bisexuality has veered towards heterosexual monogamy, at least in practice. The film thus fits within a classic sexual conversion narrative where bisexuality is understood as a temporary phase that one outgrows (Garber 1995, 346–7). Peter is cast as a kind of Prince Charming whose kiss rescues Tanya from her emotional frigidity, and from the perversion of same-sex desire.

The 1984 film *Crimes of Passion* is another rescue narrative in which the love and support of a man helps an emotionally detached sex worker to renounce her cold-hearted ways. According to Roger Ebert, the ostensible goal of this risqué film was to "explore the further shores of sexual behaviour" (1984), yet by the end of the film, a more apt description for its moral register might be to "shore up the boundaries around sexual normativity." While the film dramatizes a host of sexual kinks, the plot concludes by positioning monogamous vanilla sex as the apex of emotional fulfilment and sexual satisfaction.

This romantic thriller involves a woman (Kathleen Turner) who lives a double life. By day, she is Joanna Crane (see figure 3.11), a middle-class fashion designer, described by her boss as a "mystery" who turns to "ice" if a man attempts to speak with her. By night, she assumes the persona of China Blue (see figure 3.12), a blasé fifty-dollar-per-trick sex worker who specializes in fulfilling men's kinky fantasies, which includes role playing rape scenarios and putting men in bondage. Notice that her sexworker name is racialized (China) and coloured (Blue), semiotically linking perverse and commercial sexuality with non-whiteness. Apparently, this double life was actuated by Joanna's history as a victim of sexual violence and physical assaults perpetrated by her ex-husband and her father.

Joanna meets Bobby Grady (John Laughlin), initially as a client for her sexual services. He pays for a non-specified sexual encounter, but before they begin Bobby attempts to coax her into disclosing her identity, asking, "Who are you?" She retorts, "I'm a hooker, you're a trick, why ruin a perfect relationship?" While she maintains strict emotional distance before they have intercourse, afterwards she appears both deeply moved and vulnerable.

Soon after her night with Bobby, Joanna's light-hearted attitude towards her sex work shifts and she begins to find it degrading. After a

Figure 3.11: Joanna

wealthy couple picks up China Blue in a limousine, they proceed to insult her. The wife states, "Arthur, don't stick your tongue in her ear. You have to be careful with these people. You don't know what kind of germs they could be carrying." In this instance, Joanna is both objectified when she is spoken about as if she were not there and/or had no feelings, and construed as diseased, a germ carrier whose sexual services need to be consumed with caution. The next date is experienced as even more dehumanizing. Catering to the submissive desires of the client, China Blue handcuffs the man and penetrates him with a police baton.

But after the session is over, China Blue is in tears, while the client responds to her distress by spitting in her face. The scornful gesture, while re-establishing the client's dominant position, also expresses his disgust towards himself and the "hooker" who indulged his desires. *She* becomes the one humiliated by her performance, as if the inversion of the male top/female bottom gendered order tainted her femininity. This is expressed when China Blue, after splashing her face, tries to recover her dignity by engaging in the feminine ritual of makeup application. The eyeliner and lipstick become smudged and grotesque; in this moment she is unable to put on the accoutrement of femininity. The audience sees her across the distance of two mirrors, further emphasizing the growing detachment between China Blue, the female dom, and Joanna, the real woman (see figure 3.13).

Meanwhile, Bobby tracks Joanna down at her apartment in an effort to convince her to abandon the China Blue persona and begin a mutual relationship with him. Joanna confesses to Bobby, "No man has ever given me that kind of faith, that kind of respect." Her sex-worker alter ego is represented as a dissociation from Joanna's *true* self: "It's not

Figure 3.12: China Blue

me," she says of China Blue, so it feels "safe." As with Lisa in *Exit to Eden*, being sexually dominant is not represented as an inherent part of her sexual orientation, but rather as a coping method. And as with the climax in *Exit to Eden*, the male suitor convinces his beloved to risk intimacy without any disguises, and they make tender love, with the man on top (see figure 3.14).

The narrative also incorporates a parallel thriller plot in which a psychopathic street preacher (Anthony Perkins) has become obsessed with "saving" China Blue from her sinful ways. In the end, the preacher has completely internalized the identity of China Blue and is dressed in her signature "hooker" outfit (a trans-phobic echo from Anthony Perkins's role in *Psycho*), embodying a kind of verisimilitude of the sex worker's identity. Joanna kills him, and in that ultimate act of destruction, she kills her deviant alter ego. The preacher's dying words signal the end of Joanna's second life: "Good-bye China Blue," he says, before collapsing dead.

This theme of a second personality in crisis recalls *Something Wild's* female protagonist Lulu/Audrey. And much as Melanie Griffith's character abandoned her Lulu identity at the end of the film in favour of the softened and compliant Audrey, Kathleen Turner's character renounces her China Blue identity and resigns from sex work to fully and exclusively embody Joanna, a monogamous, unambiguously white, non-kinky woman. In the last scene, the audience learns that Bobby and Joanna have begun a bona fide relationship that incorporates trust and sexual intimacy. As such, the concluding moral of the film further suggests that Bobby's romantic persistence saved Joanna from both her stunted emotional state and the purported degradation of sex work.

Figure 3.13: China Blue distorted through the looking glass

Crimes of Passion, like *Exit to Eden* and *Preaching to the Perverted*, represents a male fantasy of the kinky sex worker as a modern damsel in distress. These damsels do not need to be rescued only from outside threats, but also from themselves. This narrative is not unique to kinky sex worker narratives but could be said to characterize a number of Hollywood movies that position a female sex worker in the starring role. *Pretty Woman* is the quintessential "hooker with a heart of gold" fairy tale, complete with a rich bachelor who not only saves the sex worker from poverty but whisks her into monogamous hetero-normativity (Campbell 2006).[14] Nonetheless, the kinkiness factor in the examined films heightens the emotional stakes. Sex workers who perform sexual dominance are represented as damaged women who have retreated into their sexual persona to elide their feminine vulnerability; they seem to suffer from a phobia of getting hurt physically or emotionally by a man. As such, female sexual dominance in these films is not represented as an orientation, but as a defence strategy. However, true love has the power to save these women and teach them to give up control.

In contrast to these narratives, the non-professional and (sometimes) sexually dominant women Lulu and Gloria in *Something Wild* and *Wedding Crashers* do not hesitate to fall in love. They are not represented as emotionally damaged, nor is their penchant for taking control in bed represented as a defence strategy. Instead their sexual dominance is rolled into a general attitude of sexy adventurousness. However, in the end, they too succumb to gender imperatives by allowing the beloved man to take the lead by the end of the story.

In the femme fatale narratives, female sexual dominance is seen as an orientation and thus more menacing. The psychopathic Catherine

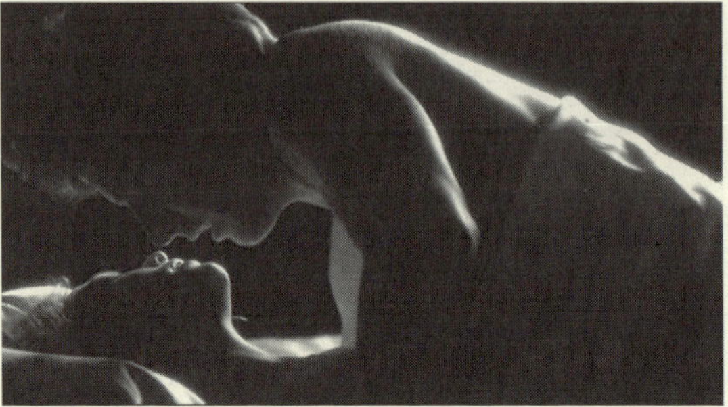

Figure 3.14: Bobby and Joanna engage in vanilla missionary-position sex

in *Basic Instinct* clearly derives sexual pleasure from putting her lovers into bondage. And by the end of the narrative, she is a confirmed killer. However, there is a suggestion that she may have been rehabilitated from her pattern of serial murder because of the love and compatibility she has found with Nick, and the fact that she allows him to assume the top position in their final sexual encounter. In *Body of Evidence*, karma strikes when true love fails to touch the heart of the sexually dominant woman. Like Catherine, Rebecca clearly enjoys sexual dominance, and this appears to coincide with her devious murder plans. But her alpha-femaleness never wavers. Even when Frank takes sexual charge, her temporary submissiveness seems to have been all part of her manipulative plan to lure Frank into a sense of control. As such, she must die a violent death, succumbing to the generic imperatives of a classic femme fatale narrative.

Before moving onto the next section, it is worth mentioning one recent Canadian film that resists most of the Hollywood conventions in its portrayal of female sexual dominance and male sexual submission. The 2007 indie film *Walk All Over Me*, portrays such kinky characters as holistic and complex – protagonists for whom the audience can cheer. The plot centres on Alberta (Leelee Sobieski), a hapless young woman who flees hometown trouble to seek refuge in Vancouver with Celene (Tricia Helfer), her former babysitter now turned dominatrix. Celene's profession inspires and intrigues Alberta. When she finds herself strapped for cash, Alberta decides to try her hand at sexual dominance, despite her self-deprecating and tentative personality. The audience adopts the point of view of Alberta, the newcomer to s/m territory, as she peruses Celene's client interview tapes, skipping through more hardcore submissives and cringing in disgust when one apparently lights his body hair on fire.

But one hopeful catches her fancy. Paul (Jacob Tierney), also an s/m newbie, states in his interview, "I'm not sure how this is supposed to work, but I'd like to try giving up control, for once." Alberta arranges a rendezvous with Paul, picking the preposterous venue of a food court to enact their first "scene." Paul is enchanted by his awkward dominatrix, whose "dominating" goes only to the extent of ordering Paul to don a dog collar and get extra chocolate sauce for her sundae. Alberta's tenuous authority is then pushed beyond the breaking point when Paul insists on another date by getting on his knees and begging like a dog. Alberta, embarrassed by the onlookers, acquiesces. At his place, they begin to get more comfortable with their s/m roles but are rudely interrupted by bad guys from Paul's past who believe – wrongly – that he stole money from his boss. In the end, Alberta solves the mystery of the missing money and rescues both Paul and Celene, who had been kidnapped. The narrative arch thus dramatizes the transformation of Alberta from a victim on the run to a hero who saves the day. What is particularly counter-hegemonic is that Alberta actuates her inner strength by adopting both the costume and the attitude of a dominatrix in full control of the situation. This reverses the character trajectory of the heroines in *Exit to Eden*, *Preaching to the Perverted*, and *Crimes of Passion*, where the abdication of their sexually dominant persona signalled their maturity and strengthening sense of self.

But while *Walk All Over Me* stands out as a counter-example to the Hollywood norm of dominatrix characters, its s/m love story is still on the tame side. Recall that Alberta expressed disgust as she assessed videos of the more intensely submissive applicants. Alberta clearly feels judgmental towards men with extreme kinks, as during her first meeting with Paul, she asks her new client, "You're not a freak, are you Paul?," to which he replies, "No, I'm disappointingly normal." At the end of the movie, Paul asks Alberta for another date, but when she hesitates, he again pulls his begging-dog tactic to convince her. Although his method may resemble an s/m posture, in other ways, he is in no way different from a classic hetero-normative male suitor who refuses to take no as an answer. To further undermine their dom/sub relationship, Alberta crouches down to meet him on the floor, thereby equalizing their positions, and agrees to the date (see figure 3.15).

Figure 3.15: Alberta crouching down to meet her suitor eye-to-eye

Thus *Walk All Over Me* still relies on certain hetero-normative codes to draw the audience into the unusual love story, while displacing abjection onto more hardcore kinky practices.

Swaying between Danger and Pleasure: Male Doms and Female Subs

The Danger Zone: Passion out of Control

The 1986 film *Nine and a Half Weeks* garnered both criticism and praise for its head-on depiction of an s/m relationship. In his favourable review, Roger Ebert claims that the film is "notorious as being the most explicitly sexual big-budget film since *Last Tango in Paris*" (1986). Indeed, the director of *Nine and a Half Weeks*, Adrian Lyne, apparently likened his movie to *Last Tango in Paris*, as both films feature the erotic dynamics of male dominance and female masochism (Mills 1986, 46–7). However, *Nine and a Half Weeks* may differentiate itself from its predecessor by explicitly portraying unambiguous scenes of s/m practices. Nonetheless, what remains entrenched is the normative logic of *Last Tango in Paris*, which deems such a love affair unsustainable.

In *Nine and a Half Weeks*, Elizabeth (Kim Basinger), an art gallery employee, falls under the seductive spell of an exceedingly wealthy commodities broker, John (Mickey Rourke). As the relationship develops, a distinct pattern of control and submission is established, as Elizabeth's independence slowly drains away after each encounter with her lover. John not only orchestrates s/m sexual activities, he chooses what Elizabeth will wear, enjoys feeding her by hand, insists on brushing her hair, and unilaterally decides when they will be together and when apart. At the end of the movie, Elizabeth finally decides that the pleasure of sexual submissiveness has been outweighed by the degradation she experiences. In the final scene, Elizabeth is softly crying as she walks away from John, and his controlling ways, for good.

In addition to representing s/m as an all-pervasive dynamic of male control and female passivity, the film also perpetuates the truth-claim that s/m sexual practice is inherently escalating, which we have seen in both the psychiatric literature and the feminist literature. Recall that the *DSM-IV-TR* states that one aspect of sexual sadism is that "usually ... the severity of the sadistic acts increases over time" (American Psychiatric Association 2000, 574). In the anti-s/m feminist literature, the claim was also made that s/m was a slippery slope towards more extreme acts. For example, Jonel draws on anecdotal experience in claiming, "The violence or severity of sm escalated as the relationship continued" (1982, 20). In *Nine and a Half Weeks*, Jonel's description manifests as the couple's relationship unfolds. Their activities start off relatively mild, with John asking Elizabeth if he can blindfold her. But soon thereafter, John demands that Elizabeth do things she finds degrading, like lift up her skirt for a spanking. Her refusal brings about an ambiguous rape/sex scene similar to the forceful sex scenes between Nick and Beth in *Basic Instinct*, and between Frank and Rebecca in *Body of Evidence*.[15] Towards the end of the film, John attempts to convince her to participate in a role-playing session where she is meant to crawl on the ground, picking money off the floor that John flings at her. Although Elizabeth initially participates in this sexual scenario, she ultimately finds the game degrading and refuses to continue. At the climax of the movie, John orchestrates a threesome with a sex worker to which Elizabeth acquiesces, allowing the sex worker to caress her as she is blind-folded. But when Elizabeth sees John receiving caresses from this woman, she physically attacks them both and then flees the scene in humiliation.

The film also correlates s/m with criminality, both sexual and nonsexual. Towards the beginning of the movie, John and Elizabeth engage in public sex at the top of a clock tower. The inherent thrill in the risk of getting caught is also implicated when Elizabeth shoplifts a necklace on John's instruction. On the cusp of illegality, John provides Elizabeth with male attire so that she can pass as a man and accompany him to a private men's club. But later that night, they get into a street brawl with homophobic men who have read them as gay lovers. The climax of the movie, when John has arranged a threesome with a sex worker, dramatizes the most taboo activity by implicating the couple in the criminality of prostitution. Thus the inherent risk-taking of the criminal behaviour operates as a kind of aphrodisiac that feeds the couple's passion. But more importantly, breaking the law becomes conceptually linked to s/m in the narrative and signals the couple's descent into immorality.

This spiral into illegality also coincides with an increase in disgust-markers and moments. When John orders Elizabeth to lift up her skirt for a spanking, she appears disgusted by the idea. She makes to leave, but at the door, reverses course and comes after him with fists flying, screaming, "Who the fuck do you think you are!" The fight then segues into a quasi-rape scene, where John forces Elizabeth onto the dining room table and rips off her underwear while she struggles to get free. But soon it appears that Elizabeth is deriving pleasure from the encounter. This is an interesting moment where Elizabeth's disgust at the thought of receiving a spanking seems to operate as a reaction formation. If the thought were truly and unambiguously repugnant to her, she would likely have simply stormed out of the apartment as planned. But if spanking secretly or unconsciously turns her on, she would not want to leave. Her pent-up sexual repression comes out as a violent attack on John, which brings about a forceful sexual encounter and ultimately, orgasmic satisfaction.

When Elizabeth role plays as a man, abjection as well as disgust are engaged. She disrupts gender categories by dressing in drag, and sexual norms as she and John pass as a gay couple. At a restaurant, John starts to kiss her while people look on in disgust. After they fight off the homophobic men who have chased them into an alley, they make passionate love in a filthy passageway, while water from a broken pipe soaks their bodies. The nastiness of the scene is heightened when a quick shot reveals a stray cat with a dead mouse in its mouth. The dirty background and the disgust evoked in others complements the eroticism of the moment. As Miller has stated, "Sexuality is constructed around the desire to indulge disgust, to roll in the mud so to speak" (1997, 127).[16] And much like the pro-s/m feminists during the sex wars, the disapproval of others feeds into their passion as they revel in their outlaw status.[17]

Disgust and abjection are most viscerally expressed in the climax of the movie. Recall that Elizabeth's realization that John has taken the s/m too far is triggered when he introduces a third party into their relationship by hiring a sex worker. While being touched by a woman seems to turn her on, witnessing this sex worker touching John humiliates Elizabeth and she flees the scene. Later that night, Elizabeth vomits in a sink, clearly revolted by the sexual scenarios in which she has participated. It appears that she has suddenly recognized her sexual desires and submissiveness as an abject phenomenon, an "otherness" contained within her that she is now seeking to expel (Makarushka 1995, 147–8).[18] Vomit is an acute abject substance, not just because it is an excretion, but also because it emits out of the wrong orifice; food is normally supposed to go in the mouth and exit out of the anus. Yet vomiting is also a form of purgation. Elizabeth is cleansing her body of its desires that have suddenly come to disgust her. Miller identifies this type of disgust as surfeit disgust: a disgust that is not a cloak to protect oneself from acknowledging problematic desires, but rather a disgust that comes from overindulgence in food, drink, or sex (1997, 110). Elizabeth is vomiting out her surfeit submissive sexuality, much the way she would vomit after over-eating or over-drinking.[19]

As earlier representations have evidenced, disgust can signal a reaction formation to conceal desire, or be a consequence of excessive pleasure. In much the same way, the racialization of s/m can signal both an alluring savagery and an unsettling otherness. Accordingly, *Nine and a Half Weeks* capitalizes on the racialization of sexual perversity in an oblique way to underscore the "darkness" of the couple's desires. Just as *Something Wild* made use of racialized minor characters strewn in the background of the film, *Nine and a Half Weeks* makes semiotic use of the racialized body as background to foreshadow the "exotic" sexuality that will soon be portrayed. The geographic locale of the relationship, New York City, provides a gritty urban backdrop for the narrative. As Hirschman argues, the film makes use of the urban versus rural semiotic code, whereby the city represents a site of degradation, and the countryside a space of sanctity (1991, 24). But one important aspect of this urban setting that Hirschman does not comment upon is the inclusion of many shots, most notably in the opening scene, of Elizabeth passing racialized people as she navigates the busy sidewalks of Manhattan. For example, the film provides shots of African-American joggers, an African-American woman with her dog, and two different shots of African-American men cleaning the window or mirror of a car. Later that night, John and Elizabeth meet for the first time at an Asian butcher shop, where the owner is seen spiritedly arguing with another

Asian man in their native tongue. The next chance encounter happens at a street fair where a Caribbean band creates an exotic mood with their uplifting reggae song.

These racialized background characters in *Nine and a Half Weeks* are used as semiotic props to dramatize the non-normative sexuality upon which Elizabeth and John have embarked. As Gwendolyn Foster states, "Blackness in cinema is often associated with bad conduct, hypersexuality, monstrous behaviour, and the threat of otherness" (2003, 68).[20] Similarly, Lola Young argues, "In film, 'dirty' or transgressive sexuality may be displaced onto the racial Other" (1996, 53). These racial "others" signal a narrative space for sexual diversity and carnality. John and Elizabeth's whiteness becomes tainted by the racialized-sexualized-animalized others, who reside at the edges of the film and create an ambience of taboo sexuality.

The association between people of colour and depraved white sexuality thus creates a fissure in the white subjectivity of the leading characters. Foster argues that cinematic performances of whiteness often feature "whiteness as its own other" (2003, 3). She argues that the "bad white" signifies "out-of control sexuality" (73), and that in such films "the monster-other is not only white but in struggle with his own body … [Such subjects] are cultural relics, examples of 'bad' whites often at war with their own (sometimes) 'good' selves" (68). Under John's influence, in the midst of the multicultural diversity of the city, Elizabeth comes to embody the good-white/bad-white woman, struggling with her emerging carnal (read racialized) sexuality.

This use of the racialized body to signify sexual depravity is particularly conspicuous during their final sexual tryst. The sex worker whom John has hired is Latina and speaks only Spanish throughout the encounter. She is therefore racially marked as "other," both visually and verbally. It is this direct confrontation with the racialized (as Latina) and sexualized (as a sex worker) "other" that throws Elizabeth's status as white into crisis. To be clear, I am not arguing here that the film is consciously promoting this message. Rather, the defining moment when Elizabeth finally recognizes her own degradation relies upon the logic of whiteness as the *unmarked* signifier of sexual purity, and the underlying cultural associations of Latina subjectivity to hyper-sexuality, dangerousness, and depravity (Foster 2003, 142).

What helps Elizabeth re-embrace her good white self is the presence of an unambiguously good white character: Matthew Farnsworth (Dwight Weist), a painter with whom Elizabeth is working. In the one scene that takes place outside of New York City, Elizabeth meets Farnsworth at his cottage in the countryside. And as Hirschman argues, "The countryside symbolizes the mutual sanctity which she [Elizabeth] and Farnsworth share and makes their ultimate degradation in the city all the more poignant" (1991, 24). Again, while Hirschman does an insightful semiotic reading of the pastoral setting, I would extend this analysis to consider its racial dynamics. Farnsworth lives away from the multicultural urbanity of the city. He comes to embody the good white, an identity that Elizabeth has slowly abdicated as she has allowed John to take her on a deviant sexual journey. After Elizabeth flees from her encounter with John and the sex worker, she sees Farnsworth at the art gallery where they are launching his exhibit. Her eyes meet Farnsworth's over a loud, drunken, and debauched crowd of people, and in that look she recognizes not just their mutual degradation, but also a place of goodness in his face that is signified as white – i.e., a whiteness that has not been tainted by urban (read racialized) depravity. Thus despite the fact that *Nine and a Half Weeks* ostensibly portrays a relationship between two white people, the narrative relies heavily on racial tropes that signify sexual immorality and whiteness as the unmarked space of purity (though clearly open to pollution). In other words, the film in some ways is about managing cultural pleasure and anxiety about the (dis)integrity of white identity. In the end, the lines get redrawn, and there is no longer an internal struggle between the bad-white and the good-white in one body. Elizabeth recovers her former good-white status by forsaking her s/m relationship, and John remains unwaveringly a bad-white subject.

Sixteen years after the release of the box office hit *Nine and a Half Weeks*, the 2002 erotic s/m thriller *Killing Me Softly* went straight to DVD in North America (Nix 2002). Though the film is little known and was panned by the few critics who bothered to watch it, it is worth a brief analysis because of its normative vision of s/m relationships. In particular, the narrative makes a truth-claim about the unsustainability of such an intense passion, even as it testifies to its inherent superior pleasures.

The love story involves Alice (Heather Graham), a "flatlander" from Indiana, who falls passionately and nonsensically in love with Adam (Joseph Fiennes), a daredevil mountaineer. And just as a climber will scale tall mountains, Adam's rough lovemaking also escalates in severity during the narrative. And just as the storybook Alice falls down a spooky rabbit hole, Alice in this movie falls down the slippery slope of s/m.

The plot begins with Alice living a humdrum life in London with her *nice* boyfriend when she chances upon Adam on a busy sidewalk. Their eyes lock, their fingers accidentally touch, and a few hours later their limbs are entangled in passionate, if a bit forceful, sexual intercourse. Afterwards, Alice tries to transfer the erotic charge of her infidelity to her boyfriend by taking the top position during sexual intercourse. It does not work. Alice soon realizes that her safe boyfriend was not going to satisfy her anymore. She leaves him for Adam, and after a short amount of time, Alice and Adam are engaged.

Adam's need to control Alice both sexually and non-sexually follows an escalation. Their first few intimate encounters are not explicitly kinky, but involve rough sex, so rough that Alice explicitly informs Adam in one instance, "You're hurting me" because of his tight embrace. Later, Adam manifests his brutality when he interrupts a mugging and violently beats upon the crook. The narrative thus links Adam's violent streak with his sexually passionate nature. In addition, Adam, like John in *Nine and a Half Weeks*, also takes control of non-sexual decisions. For example, much to Alice's chagrin, Adam forces her to undergo an arduous hike on her wedding day. That night, their first, and really only, explicitly kinky encounter happens. Adam ties a scarf around Alice's throat and during sexual intercourse, alternately pulls and releases the two ends of the scarf to restrict her breath. She states in a voice-over, "I gave up all control and let him decide when I could breathe and when I couldn't. I loved it." But later, when Adam suspects that Alice is cheating on him, he non-consensually ties her up on their kitchen table while she struggles to get free. This is a non-sexual moment that establishes the slippery slope between consensual erotic s/m and abusive behaviour. During his interrogation, Adam states to Alice, "I could break your neck, I love you so much." Alice is terrified and thus brings us to the thriller part of this erotic thriller.

After they get married, Alice begins to suspect that her husband might have killed his two previous lovers. Although the plot piles on clues that point to him, this turns out to be a red herring. The climax of the movie reveals that Adam's sister was the killer, who, because of one incestuous fling when they were kids, has been obsessively in love with her brother ever since. And this revelation helps to establish Adam, to a degree, as an object of disgust since, as Miller has pointed out, "Incest prohibitions ... are generally maintained by disgust" (1997, 15). Further, the narrative overlaps the perversion of s/m with the perversion of incest. After the shock disclosure, and after Adam's sister has been killed, Alice reaches out to her husband – whom she had previously accused of murder at a police station. However, trust between the couple has been broken. They split up.

Two years after the break-up, Alice admits in a voice-over, "Not a day goes by without at least one thought about the passion." In the final scene, Alice and Adam coincidentally pass each other on a set of escalators, his going up and hers going down. The camera gives the audience two point-of-view shots, allowing the viewer to access the perspective of each character watching the other on the escalator (see figures 3.16 and 3.17). The camera viewpoint segues into a shot-reverse-shot sequence, visually encouraging the audience to identify with both positions. In her last rumination of the affair, Alice articulates the visual escalator metaphor: "Maybe a flatlander like me can't live at that altitude. Maybe it would never have been possible to sustain what we had. Maybe. Well, that's what I tell myself." The finale of the film positions Alice as a haunted sexual subject, one susceptible to daily visits by the ghosts of her s/m past. Such desires persist, whether they are acted upon or not.

Recall that this claim was made by the former sadomasochists in their confessional accounts in *Against Sadomasochism*. Marissa Jonel wonders if she is being hypocritical in her condemnation of lesbian s/m because she "still [has] sm urges and fantasies" (1982, 19). Similarly, Elizabeth Harris confides, "I still have sadomasochistic fantasies but I have no desire to follow them" (1982, 95). The idea that tasting s/m pleasure corrupts your libido is given vivid description in the autobiographical novella, *Nine and a Half Weeks*, upon which the movie of the same name was based. In the last paragraph of the narrative, McNeill explains that she ended the s/m affair and has since attempted to resume a normal love life. The final sentence, however, attests to the persistent and incurable effect of s/m: "What remains is that my sensation thermostat has been thrown out of whack: it's been years [since the s/m affair] and sometimes I wonder whether my body will ever again register above lukewarm" (117). And this closes the account. There is a paradox embedded in such narratives. On the one hand, s/m passion is presented as acutely pleasurable and exquisitely arousing, unattainable in the non-kinky world. On the other hand, it also creates instant addicts. One ride on this sexual-emotional rollercoaster and the submissive partner will never be able to fully enjoy non-kinky sex again; the

Figure 3.16: Point-of-view shot as Alice descends

passion will forever pale in comparison to the memories of the s/m high. Nonetheless, the moral of such stories is that female submissives must exercise mind over matter, lest they lose their identities and possibly their lives in the vortex of such violent pleasure.

This imperative of exerting willpower over the unwieldy libido is reminiscent of Krafft-Ebing's warnings that "love unbridled" will create havoc and destruction (1965, 2). It is interesting to note that Krafft-Ebing generally identified men as the ones susceptible to becoming enslaved to a rapacious sexual appetite, while women were seen as less libidinous and more emotional. Yet in these modern s/m narratives, women's love comes to be subsumed in their lust for their dominant lover and their enjoyment of submissive satisfaction. In this way, though male dominant-female-submissive narratives warn women to resist the allure of s/m sex, at the very least they tacitly acknowledge the existence of a strong female sexual drive.

The next film to consider, David Cronenberg's 1983 film *Videodrome*, also features a woman with a powerful libido grounded in submissive sexuality. But while I include this film in my cinematic analysis, it should be noted that – as is the case with many of Cronenberg's films – *Videodrome* is marked by a magic realist ambivalence that defies easy interpretation. Nonetheless, its use of s/m sexuality as a signifier within the larger narrative is instructive of its broader cultural construction. And despite its status as art-house cinema, the message about s/m does not effectively deviate from the normative view of *Nine and a Half Weeks* or *Killing Me Softly*, but rather manifests as a more extreme indictment. In *Videodrome*, the lovers do not survive their foray into s/m; instead, their sexual proclivities are linked to homicide and self-destruction.

The story focuses on Max Renn (James Woods), the president of a Canadian independent television station that specializes in pornography

Figure 3.17: Point-of-view shot as Adam ascends

and violence. In an early scene that foreshadows Max's journey into sexual depravity, the viewer witnesses his negative assessment of a pornographic preview tape. An unimpressed Max condemns the show as "not tacky enough" to turn him on and much too "soft." But soon his technician hacks into *Videodrome*, a show that is anything but soft. The encrypted series features graphic sexual torture and murder without any plot or context – what a colleague of his will later label as genuine "snuff TV." Max – whose name personifies the desire to *maximize* sensational experience – is enthralled. As he investigates the origins of this show and the allegation that the violence is authentic, he begins dating Nicki Brand (Deborah Harry), an alluring Siren who beckons him into the world of sadomasochism. On their first date, they watch a pirated *Videodrome* tape together, and to Max's surprise, Nicki is instantly turned on. Max learns that Nicki's kinky sexuality is not confined to voyeurism, and she initiates him into a sadomasochistic sexual encounter that includes Max piercing her ears with a needle while they embrace – with *Videodrome*'s sexualized torture sequences playing in the background.

Nicki later declares to Max that she wants to audition for *Videodrome*, confidently stating, "I was *made* for that show." Max tries to warn her that the "mondo" producers play too "rough," but in response, she burns her breast with a lit cigarette to prove that she's up for it (see figure 3.18).

Max is horrified, but he still accepts the lit cigarette when Nicki offers it back to him, suggesting that he too shares in (or at least is being further infected by) her extreme desires. The film takes a surreal turn soon afterward, when Max learns that the *Videodrome* show that has so captivated him brings on intensely real and disturbing hallucinations. While it is ambiguous what *really happened*, there is a suggestion that Nicki's pursuit of masochistic pleasure ultimately gets her killed, as Max later watches a tape of her being strangled to death on *Videodrome*.

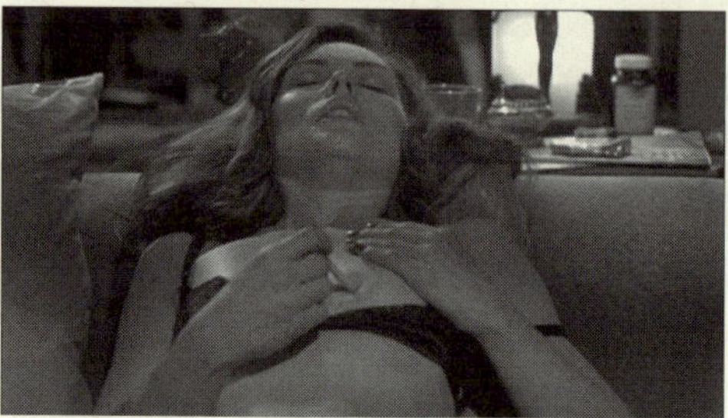

Figure 3.18: Nicki burning herself with the end of a lit cigarette

By the end of the film, a confused and deranged Max, under the influence of *Videodrome* and ideologues, goes on a killing spree. The last scene finds him beckoned again by the figure of Nicki, who has reincarnated on television and explains to Max that "death is not the end" and that he should join her in the "next phase." She demonstrates how he can achieve "total transformation" by playing a televised scene featuring Max putting a bullet through his brain. A transfixed and obedient Max mimics the scene he has just observed on the screen, and the last shot of the film reveals Max shooting himself to death. Max has apparently *maxed* out his craving for sensation.

The homicides and suicide that conclude the film dramatize the slippery slope from representation to reality, and from consensual sadomasochism to sadism and self-destruction. This is in direct opposition to Max's earlier claim that his hardcore television station is not just benign, but good for society: "[I] give my viewers a harmless outlet for their fantasies and their frustrations. As far as I'm concerned, that's a socially positive act." Here Max offers the catharsis hypothesis that posits that the representation of taboo sexuality and violence provides a vicarious avenue that satiates perverse cravings – without any real harm to others. But the narrative belies this justification. Max's visual consumption of *Videodrome* is soon followed by his desire to act out sadomasochistic practices, which in turn leads to straightforward sadistic acts, and then suicide. The film further advances s/m's nefarious power on the psyche, as the producer of *Videodrome* explains that exposure to "s/m" and "violence" on television opens up receptors in the viewer's brain, allowing them to be controlled. The film thus establishes the tangible harms that flow from hardcore sexual texts, dramatizing the radical feminist claim that pornographic representation perpetuates attitudinal harm.

I end this section with a nod to the cult classic horror movie *Hellraiser*, which hyperbolizes the message that s/m sex will become all-consuming and catastrophic. The working title for this 1987 film was *Sadomasochists from Beyond the Grave*, and its moral message coincides with the persistent truth-claim that s/m is an escalating and deadly desire ("Hellraiser, Trivia," 1987). The film centres on a playboy named Frank who had tried to satiate his relentless desires through s/m and "exotic" sexual practices. However, as he explains to a former lover, "It's never enough." His voracious hunger for s/m sensation leads him to invoke the Cenobites, a group of demons who offered him "an experience beyond limits. Pain and pleasure … indivisible." However, when Frank finally has enough, he attempts to escape the Cenobites' realm. But to return to full human form again, he needs his former masochistic lover, Julia, to kill men so that he can feed on their blood. In the end, the Cenobites catch up to Frank – because once invoked, these monsters hold your soul forever. Contextualizing the Cenobites within the framework of sexology, these metaphoric creatures stand in for the irrevocable destructive influence s/m can have, not just on its practitioners, but also on those in their surroundings. They embody Krafft-Ebing's view of unrestrained sexuality as "a volcano that burns down and lays waste all around it; it is an abyss that devours all" (1965, 2). For Frank and Julia, there is no turning back to their normal selves. In *Hellraiser*, s/m is literally a one-way ticket to hell, as the Cenobites suck the couple back into their demonic dimension in the climax of the film.[21]

The Pleasure Zone: Passion in Matrimony's Embrace

In 2002, a popular and critically acclaimed film defied the cinematic convention of s/m unsustainability involving male dominance and female submission. In the romantic comedy *Secretary*, the couple finally gets to live happily ever after.

The plot centres on the awkward and fragile Lee (Maggie Gyllenhaal) who begins her first job as a secretary in the law office of Mr Grey (James Spader). Soon thereafter it becomes apparent to both of them that while Grey likes to dominate Lee, she also likes to submit to her boss. They work these erotic dynamics into their office life, such that, for example, a typo by Lee will result in a sound spanking from her employer. However, Grey decides that such a perverse affair cannot continue, and he fires Lee, thereby terminating their affair. Had the movie ended at this point, it would have imparted a moral message comparable to that of films such as *Nine and a Half Weeks* or *Killing Me Softly*. Instead, Lee refuses to accept Grey's reasoning. She holds a sit-in vigil at his office to prove her submissive love to him, and comes out to her community as a sadomasochist. Grey is convinced and they reconcile. Lee leaves her job as legal secretary and becomes his lawful wife, and this closes the film.

The editing techniques, the set design, and the overwhelming interiority of the romance draw the audience into this unusual love story and help stave off disgust reactions. Initially, the interactions between Lee and Grey are shown in shot-reverse-shot sequences, but as their romance blossoms, they begin to share the frame, often as a symmetrical dyad. Many of the film's scenes are framed head-on and symmetrically, imparting a reassuring ambiance, particularly when combined with the slow editing (see figure 3.19). To add to the comfortable feel of the mise en scène, the couple is seen mostly in shallow focus, so that only their faces or bodies are distinct while the background is blurry and dim. This personalized technique allows the audience to share the intimacy of the couple. The setting of the film further personalizes their romance. Up until the end, their romance takes place exclusively in the law office; there is a sense that they are in their own special world – that the normal rules of romance and sexuality do not apply to them (see figure 3.19). Grey also maintains an elaborate horticultural oasis in his ornate office, and the audience sees him fussing over the care of his orchids. The embellished surroundings and the elaborate indoor garden, to an extent, feminize him and soften his sexual dominance. He appears to be a much less threatening character than the male dominants in films such as *Killing me Softly* or *Nine and a Half Weeks*.

Indeed, in many ways, *Secretary* can be read as a rebuttal to the truth-claims generated in *Nine and a Half Weeks* about the degrading, dangerous, and unsustainable nature of s/m relationships and the dysfunctional behaviour of the couple.

For instance, while *Nine and a Half Weeks* dramatized an independent woman's loss of identity and dignity, *Secretary* features a troubled young woman who finds her strength and a sense of self through her initiation into s/m. *Secretary*'s plot commences with Lee having just completed in-patient treatment at a mental institution following her history of self-inflicted harm. In moments of acute distress, she physically injures herself, usually through cutting. After her discharge from the hospital, Lee moves back in with her parents in the suburbs. She demonstrates none of the urban sophistication or independence that Elizabeth

Figure 3.19: Lee and Grey in their own world

commanded at the beginning of *Nine and a Half Weeks*; instead, Lee is child-like and awkward. When her alcoholic father resumes his drinking, Lee again resorts to self-induced pain to cope with her feelings. But when she begins working for Grey, things start to change. Under his stern guidance, she starts to dress more attractively and speak with more confidence, and stops cutting herself, for good this time. When Grey instigates the s/m affair, Lee fully embraces her submissive sexuality, often taking the initiative to entice her boss into performing more s/m acts with her. Towards the end, she stands up to those in her community who would condemn her submissive sexuality and convinces Grey that they can, indeed, sustain a loving s/m relationship. By partaking in s/m, Lee not only finds true love and hot sex, but also her self-respect and mental health. She gains a sense of subjectivity by channelling her masochistic tendencies towards a sexual aim. Her body ceases to be an object for self-abuse and instead becomes a self-directed vehicle for pleasure.

Secretary's male protagonist, Grey, also stands in stark contrast to John in *Nine and a Half Weeks*. While John is aggressively dominant and self-assured, Grey appears more accessible, more human. Grey's class status, though privileged, is unremarkable. His sole practice affords him a comfortable upper-middle-class life, but nothing approaching the luxury that John enjoys. And as opposed to John's arrogance, Grey appears a desperate, even pathetic man struggling with his inner demons. One scene evokes the visual trope of being closeted about one's sexuality, as Grey fearfully hides in a wardrobe because an ex-girlfriend has unexpectedly shown up at his office (see figure 3.20).

Unlike John, Grey suffers from self-loathing, convinced that there is something perverse about his sexual tendencies. At one point, he writes a letter to Lee beginning with "Dear Lee, This is disgusting. I'm sorry. I don't know why I'm like this." Here the sadomasochist himself takes

Figure 3.20: Grey in the closet

on the voice of disgust. And yet at this point in the story, because of the editing techniques as well as the plot line, the audience is already invested in the romance. As such, the audience is not likely to partake in a shared moment of disgust with Grey; instead the letter arouses pathos. The self-disgust is seen as a barrier that needs to be overcome for the couple to get together. And in the end, Grey does indeed transcend this disgust because of Lee's unwavering belief in their kinky couplehood. Because of Lee's perseverance, Grey finally comes to accept that his dominant sexuality can be a vital part of a healthy relationship.

In this way, *Secretary* attempts to disaggregate the role of being dominant in bed from being a domineering person. Similarly, in the case of Lee, the film disaggregates the role of being submissive in bed from being a subordinated person.

Another remarkable difference between *Nine and a Half Weeks* and *Secretary* is how the presence of the law frames each narrative. Recall that in *Nine and a Half Weeks*, the more Elizabeth succumbs to John's depraved scenarios, the more she descends into criminal behaviour. In *Secretary*, the lovers not only abide by the law, they both work in a law office. Grey is a lawyer, a symbol and an upholder of the law. Of course, the film flirts with the idea of sexual harassment, as Grey's probing personal questions, dominant style, and sexual advances would be contrary to criminal and civil law if the actions were not welcomed. Yet it is clear from Lee's reactions that Grey's behaviour is positively the most welcome thing that has ever happened to her. And at the end of the film, she ceases to be his secretary and becomes his wife. The law of marriage comes to sanctify their relationship and dispel any possible lingering illicit associations to the s/m. In contrast to *Nine and a Half Weeks*, where criminality frames the couple's sexual conduct, in *Secretary* the law folds them into normativity and an idealized heterosexual order.

Ultimately, the most conspicuous way that *Secretary* challenges the normative vision of previous s/m love stories is by portraying the sexuality as sustainable and steady. In *Secretary*, there is no escalation in the severity of their sexual practices. Grey and Lee's first explicitly s/m encounter, when he spanks her over his desk, is probably the most hardcore s/m activity represented in the film. Subsequent activities include role playing and bondage, but the lovers never engage in dangerous or criminal conduct. And after Grey finally accepts that they can integrate s/m into a "normal" loving relationship, they have tender non-kinky intercourse. As Brenda Cossman has argued, "Sexual excess is, at this moment, contained within romantic love" (2004, 870). This is further expressed in the soundtrack that accompanies their reconciliation, where Lizzie West sings, "What grace have I, to fall so in love?" Interestingly, in Barrett's survey of responses to this movie from individuals in the BDSM community (2007), she found that many resented the normalizing intentions of the movie. Yet I would maintain that an important counter-hegemonic message of the film is that a relationship built on s/m desire does not have to escalate in severity, and can go back and forth from tender kisses to harsh spankings.

Secretary thus attempts to make room for female-submissive and male-dominant subjectivity within the terms and constraints of sexual citizenship. The woman is not a victim, but rather an agent of desire. The man is not a control freak, but rather a closeted victim of self-repression. And the portrayal of s/m as not a slippery slope that ends in crime, degradation, or destruction, but rather an avenue leading to mutuality, respect, and true love, breaks from Hollywood conventions concerning this kinky practice. Yet the film is also fraught with other hegemonic relations and assumptions about what must be embodied by an acceptable sexual couple.

One thing such a couple must apparently embody is whiteness. Recall how in *Something Wild* and *Nine and a Half Weeks*, racialized persons and objects were used as semiotic props to dramatize the non-normative sexuality upon which the protagonists embark. In *Secretary*, the couple is never associated with racialized persons, as there are virtually no people of colour in the film.[22] But the fact that there are no representations of people of colour does not mean the story is racially neutral. As Dyer has argued, if whiteness is to be analysed only when there are racial "others" as a point of reference, this will "reinforce the notion that whiteness is only racial when it is 'marked' by the presence of the truly raced, that is, non-white subject" (1997, 14). Thus the exclusively white cast of *Secretary* has semiotic significance on its own terms, as well as in contrast to *Nine and a Half Weeks*.

Although both the main leads are white, because of their gender roles, their whiteness is played differently on the screen. The character of Grey occupies the non-particularity of "being "just" human."[23] Because his race does not register in the popular imagination as being a race, he is simply a man with unusual tastes in the bedroom. If he was marked as Black or Latino, his s/m proclivities would most likely resonate with cultural associations of such men to animality. But as a white man, Grey has the privilege of invisibility and generality. His middle-class status as a sole practitioner lawyer further neutralizes and makes invisible his race as white.

Lee, as a white person, also enjoys this hegemonic position of being non-raced, but because she is a woman, her body's whiteness is particularly displayed (and objectified) for symbolic value (Dyer 1997, 71). In a number of shots, the film trades on her whiteness in order to convey her innocence. In one scene, she is sitting with her mother, her sister, and her sister's friends by her parents' pool. While Lee is covered from head to toe to avoid any sun exposure, the others are apparently getting a tan. Although all of the women are white, Lee's determination to keep her skin as white as possible heightens her symbolic whiteness, that is her "purity, cleanliness [and] virginity" (70). These characteristics become evident at the end of the film in a most ironic fashion. After sitting for days at Grey's desk in a white wedding dress, after urinating through that dress and onto the floor, Lee is still represented as a pure white bride when her lover comes to rescue her. He carries her to an upstairs room and lays her down on a bed made literally of grass, capitalizing on the link between a pastoral setting and acceptable, clean sexuality. Next, Grey bathes Lee, further emphasizing her emerging purity within their new hetero-normative relationship. Afterwards, the camera luxuriates in Lee's thin, naked, white body, while Grey remains fully clothed. And when they make love the next day, she is clad in little-girl white socks and white panties. Though the audience is aware that she has had vaginal intercourse with another man earlier in the film, the symbolic value of her white and infantilized clothing seems to restore her virginity. In these shots, Lee's whiteness and her bridal and virginal clothes operate synergistically to convey innocence, moral purity, and beauty (see figures 3.21, 3.22).

Despite the movie's celebration of literal and symbolic whiteness, the racial other does creep into the narrative in one oblique way. *Secretary*

Figure 3.21: Lee's heightened whiteness

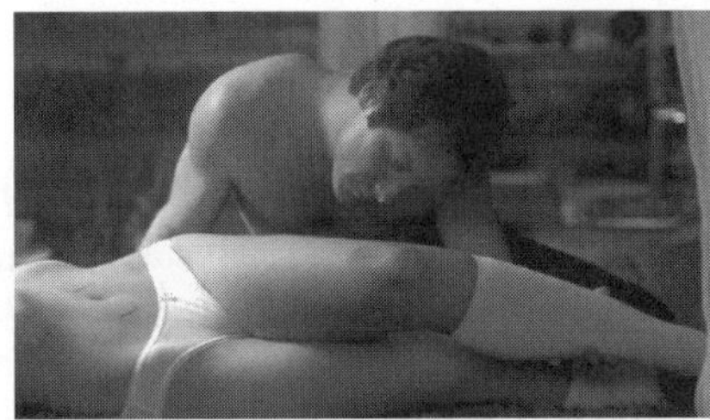

Figure 3.22: Lee's heightened whiteness

Figure 3.23: Racialized fetish object 1

Figure 3.24: Racialized fetish object 2

trades on the sexualization of the racial other through the use of fetishized art objects. During one music montage that occurs after Lee and Grey begin their s/m affair, the camera focuses on two consecutive shots of wooden statues that Grey keeps outside of his office (see figures 3.23 and 3.24). The figures appear to be of Asian origin and invoke hegemonic cultural associations of such imagery with mysterious sensuality. Layered over these images is the sumptuous voice of Leonard Cohen crooning the love song "I'm Your Man." In the off-space, the audience can glean that our two main characters are gratifying their s/m desires, as the sounds of spanking and Lee's moans of pleasure meld with Cohen's throaty voice.

This use of "exotic" objects to stand in for the white bodies of Lee and Grey reveals the extent to which, as Dyer has noted, "endemic to the representation of white heterosexuality [is the construction] of sexual desire as itself dark" (1997, 13). Yet unlike *Nine and a Half Weeks*, which uses actual racialized human bodies to represent the danger and "darkness" of the couple's perverse sexual desires, *Secretary* manages the threat of the other by employing racialized objects, not persons, to convey the kinkiness of the couple's sexuality. As Dyer has noted, "Projection of sexuality on to dark races was a means for whites to represent yet dissociate themselves from their own desires" (28). As such, projecting the white couple's sexuality onto a totemic representation of a "dark" culture exploits the racialization of "exotic" sexual practice without putting the whiteness of the two leads into crisis.

In contrast to the multicultural setting of New York City in *Nine and a Half Weeks*, the geographic locale of *Secretary* is the suburbs of Florida. Instead of seeing multiple shots of garbage and pollution, there are multiple shots of parks, grass, and water that symbolize the purity and the wholesomeness of the couple's sexuality. Notably, while in *Nine and a Half Weeks* there is a night-time alley shot of a stray cat with a dead mouse in its mouth, which suggests the dark, dirty, and destructive nature of the couple's sexuality, in *Secretary*, a brief daytime shot featuring Grey releasing a mouse from a humane trap onto an attractive sidewalk symbolizes the life-affirming quality of their sexuality (see figures 3.25 and 3.26).

And as with the scene in *Nine and a Half Weeks* that features Farnsworth in the countryside, good whiteness is associated with rural or suburban spaces marked, in part, by the absence of people of colour. The difference is that while *Nine and a Half Weeks* associates the rural space with civilized (read non-kinky) sexuality, *Secretary* is attempting to purify

Figure 3.25: Cat with dead mouse from *Nine and a Half Weeks*

and sanctify s/m sexuality by associating it with the goodness of nature. In this sense, it contradicts the sexual logic of *Nine and a Half Weeks* by relying on the same racial logic. Ultimately, Lee and Grey both embody good whites, and their love story falls under the category of what Foster names "white heterotopian fantasy narratives which perform and celebrate whiteness" (2003, 95). Part of their acceptability is contingent on their status as unambiguously unracialized good white lovers.

Besides their whiteness, another currency that Lee and Grey have is their attractiveness. This is not a comparison I draw between *Secretary* and *Nine and a Half Weeks*, since *Nine and a Half Weeks* cast the conventionally beautiful Kim Basinger and Mickey Rourke to draw the audience into their love story. Instead, it is a comparison within the narrative of *Secretary* itself. The story provides representations not just of acceptable and sympathetic s/m subjects (Grey and Lee), but also of disgusting and abject ones. After Grey breaks up with Lee, she initially attempts to meet other men who share her kinky desires. The first man is revealed to be short and bald. Besides being conventionally unattractive, he apparently has poor manners, as the audience learns from a voice-over that he tries to pinch Lee's nipples before they get into his car. The next man has a shaggy beard, wears a full moustache, and registers as working-class. This man wants Lee to urinate for his sexual pleasure. The last man is rendered unsympathetic because of his absurd desires. Lee explains that his kink is to be tied to a gas stove with the burners on full blast while she throws tomatoes at him. In other words, he is a masochist who is aroused by humiliation. The film purchases sympathy for our two leads, in part by differentiating them from these sadomasochists who are not conventionally attractive, who lack standard social skills, who are not middle-class, whose kinks are too extreme, or who fail to adhere to the male-top/female-bottom dynamic. In this sense,

Figure 3.26: Grey releasing a mouse from a humane trap in *Secretary*

the project of rescuing sadomasochism from the realm of abjection appears inextricably tied to relegating others to the status of abject, upon whom disgust can be displaced.[24] Juxtaposed to these abject sadomasochist subjects, Lee and Grey access acceptability. They are white, attractive, middle-class, kinky but not too kinky, and they adhere to the gender imperative of a male-top/female-bottom configuration.

All that being said, what ultimately binds these characteristics into normalcy is the couple entering into marriage. As Brenda Cossman's queer feminist reading of the movie aptly notes, "Lee's masochism, and the couple's desires were reigned in through the tropes of heterosexual domestication: romantic love, marriage, and suburban domesticity" (2004, 869). In Lee's words, "We looked like any other couple you'd see." Marriage and monogamy bestow on them a normalizing privacy shield. Before this, they were conducting their affair at the office; to an extent, they were violating the public/private dichotomy by bringing sex into the workplace. But as Mason Stokes has argued, in narrative formulations that provide nuptial closure to a story, "marriage successfully com[es] to the rescue of whiteness – whiteness and heterosexuality become normative copartners, both invested in buttressing and feeding off of the cultural normativity of the other" (2001, 20). Lee and Grey's marriage reinforces their whiteness, their class status, and their proper gender roles, even as it assimilates their non-normative sexual practices. As such, at the end, order seems to be restored. Lee ceases to be Grey's secretary and becomes his housewife, and their sexual practices are absolved of any wrongdoing.

Monogamy is further entrenched as part of the normative package in *Secretary*. At the end of the film, Lee definitively breaks off any romantic and sexual connection she had with a young man, Peter, with whom she had previously been involved. Regarding Edward's commitment to monogamy, in the original screenplay Lee says in a voice-over at the end of the film, "Edward hired a new secretary. I insisted it be a man, and Edward complied" (Wilson 2003, 142–3). The director of *Secretary*, Steven Shainberg, explained that they put that line into the screenplay to allay any fears that Grey might resume his s/m antics with the new secretary (obviously assuming that Edward is heterosexual and not bi-sexual). Shainberg later explains that he ended up cutting that line out of the film because he "felt their relationship had gone far enough that hopefully we believed in some way he [Grey] had been healed, too, that he didn't need to be doing at the office with the next secretary what he did with Lee" (143). The director's normative view clearly envisions a commitment to monogamy as a positive step in the characters' devel-opment. As such, it was not just marriage, but monogamy, that marked the couple's maturity and sexual well-being.

In addition, recall that in *Nine and a Half Weeks* it was the breach of monogamy that finally signalled to Elizabeth that the affair had gone too far. It was not the ambiguous rape on the dining room table, or John's violent threats with his belt. Rather, Elizabeth is pushed over the brink when she sees the sex worker stroking John. In fact, she physi-cally attacks both John and the sex worker in a rage before fleeing the scene. It seems then that both *Nine and a Half Weeks* and *Secretary* share a normative perspective that a successful and sustainable relationship requires monogamy.

Secretary reveals the ways a film can simultaneously be mainstream and counter-hegemonic. Lee and Grey are both portrayed as sympa-thetic characters who must overcome internal and external prejudice against their sexual preferences. Yet a discursive analysis of *Secretary* reveals that the depicted s/m is rendered acceptable only within par-ticular hetero-normative strictures. In order to package s/m to a main-stream audience, the movie had to rely on other hegemonies: the couple's whiteness, their middle-class status, their attractiveness, their male-top/female-bottom heterosexuality, and their domestication into marriage and monogamy.

Decadence and Carnality: Gay Male Sadomasochists

While most of the narratives on heterosexual s/m involve stories of love and romance, the representation of gay s/m locates these desires almost entirely in the carnal casual-sex realm. Director William Friedkin's noto-rious 1980 film *Cruising* is a prime example of this trend.

The urban murder mystery set in the s/m leather bars of Greenwich Village provoked outrage among gay rights protestors who were convinced the movie would perpetuate homophobic stereotypes (Wilson 1981). But unlike *Basic Instinct*, which evidently benefited from the curiosity provoked by protests, *Cruising* was not a success. More recently, however, it has undergone a renaissance and earned fans from both the gay community and cinema aficionados, being screened in the last few years in the Castro district and at the Cannes Film Festival (Van Iquity 2007).

The film concerns a police officer, Steve Burns (Al Pacino), who is sent undercover into the gay s/m leather scene to catch a serial killer. The murderer's modus operandi is to prey on men who are into "heavy leather, s/m," which is, in the words of Police Captain Edelson, "a world unto itself." The first murder occurs when a leather-clad man in a police-fetish outfit (the killer) picks up another man. Post coitus, the killer pulls out a knife and opens up a box of fetish gear from which he extracts some leather ropes. Using his knife as a threat, the killer ties up his recent fling and then stabs him to death, linking the previous kinky consensual scene to the vicious homicide.

Steve is chosen for the job because he fits the profile of the previous victims in age and physical appearance. Embracing this opportunity, which will considerably advance his career, Steve moves into a gay part of town. He begins socializing with his neighbour Ted (Don Scardino), a more mainstream gay man who stands in contradistinction to s/m gay subjects and the leather scene. But Steve does more than simply befriend a gay man. As part of his undercover work, Steve cruises a suspect and allows himself to get tied up in the exact vulnerable position as the first victim. This man turns out to be a false lead, but the police violently interrogate him nonetheless.

The homophobia and violent tactics of the police bother Steve tremendously, and the work slowly begins to take its toll on him. He becomes alienated from his girlfriend, Nancy (Karen Allen) and starts to develop a violent temper, randomly attacking Ted's boyfriend, who had accused him of flirting with Ted. At one point, Steve attempts to quit the assignment, explaining to the captain that "things are happening to me" and "I can't handle it." But the captain convinces him to stay on the assignment and Steve eventually tracks down the killer. The suspect is placed within police custody and it seems as if the case is closed. Or has it? Later that night, the audience learns that Ted has been stabbed to death. The narrative suggests that Steve himself may now have become a killer, assuming the identity of his previous nemesis. The last scene furthers this ambiguity. While the movie shows Steve reconciling with his girlfriend, Nancy, and resuming his previous sexually normative identity, he also has brought home props from his undercover work. Nancy finds a bag of fetish gear in Steve's apartment, which includes a leather jacket, police hat, and sunglasses, all signature paraphernalia worn by the killer. During the last few moments of the film, Nancy tries on these fetish items in front of a mirror and surveys her appearance with pleasure.

In response to the protests against *Cruising*,[25] the film begins with a disclaimer: "This film is not intended as an indictment of the homosexual world. It is set in one small segment of that world which is not meant to be representational of the whole." In its attempt to distinguish mainstream gay men from the s/m-gay men, the disclaimer implies that there is something unsavoury about the gay leather scene. One can assume that the film *is* intended as an indictment of that "small segment" of gay life. And the graphic portrayal of life in the s/m bars at least indulges voyeurism and may elicit discomfort from many audience members. The film features men clad in leather and other fetish gear engaging in anonymous sex, group sex, oral sex, fisting, role playing, bondage, and whipping. The atmosphere is dark, and many patrons wear cold or hostile expressions. As Steve enters the bar for the first time, the camera provides point-of-view shots that put us in his shoes as he gazes at this unfamiliar and menacing scene. But after a few visits to the bars, it seems that Steve comes to enjoy the ambience. He dances vigorously amidst his leather-clad companions, relishing the various s/m scenes that surround the dance floor. In this sense, there is an ambivalence about the way disgust operates in the film, as the audience witnesses the protagonist overcome his disgust to derive pleasure from the gay s/m scene.

In the link between s/m and violence, there also seems to be complexity and ambivalence. There is a killer stalking the scene, but this does not necessarily imply that all sadomasochists are violent. For example, in the first murder scene, the victim appears gentle and likable. But what the movie does suggest is that the s/m scene is dangerous, in particular because of its association with anonymous sex. By allowing oneself to be tied up by a stranger, one becomes particularly vulnerable to violent attacks. Yet in many ways, this message is only on the extreme end of the same continuum as heterosexual morality tales in horror movies, which regularly portray teenagers getting murdered when they indulge in sexual activity at make-out points. In both cases, the truth-claim is that sexuality is dangerous, in particular when practised casually and conducted in public spaces.

The more complex message of *Cruising* is that there is something contagious about the s/m desire. One interpretation of the movie is that during his undercover investigation, Steve uncovers his own latent homosexuality. This explains, in part, why he viciously attacks Ted's boyfriend; he does indeed have a crush on Ted but, unable to cope, sublimates it into rage against his rival. There is also the suggestion that when Ted shows up murdered, Steve is responsible. In this theory, Steve has assumed the identity of the killer who murdered his male lovers, in part because of internalized homophobia. But it is not just same-sex desire that may have been sparked by his assignment. When Steve goes to a hotel room with a suspect, he *asks* the suspect to tie him up. After the cops bust in to find him hog-tied and face down on the bed, he keeps complaining that that the police "came too soon." This could mean that they prevented him from gathering evidence, but could also mean that they prevented Steve from consummating his s/m pick-up. In the end of the film, when his girlfriend appropriates the fetish gear and gazes at herself in a mirror, there is the suggestion that she too has been or will be affected by s/m, that it has now irrevocably altered her identity. *Cruising*, in many ways like the typical heterosexual s/m narratives, constructs s/m as enticing and contaminating. Once you get a taste of its pleasures, its hold on you can never be fully exorcised.

The 1995 film *Frisk* also suggests that s/m holds both contaminating power and erotic appeal. If not for the fact that it clearly positions itself as an art-house film, its moral message would seem to coincide with Catherine MacKinnon's account of the corrupting impact of pornography consumption. The epistolary narrative traces the progression of a gay man, Dennis (Michael Gunther), who recounts to his friend how he came to be a serial murderer. It began when he first got his hands on some pornography at the age of thirteen from a permissive bookstore owner. Soon his tastes could no longer be satisfied with representations of mere "fucking," and he started to seek out s/m pornography. Later, the bookstore owner exposed him to snuff pictures, which Dennis later learns – much to his disappointment – were posed. When he gets older, Dennis begins to participate in sadistic and sadomasochistic practice with his lovers. When one lover passes out from drug use, Dennis smashes a bottle on his head. Another lover, Henry, is an insecure masochist who likes to be cut by glass and ends each of his sexual encounters with a question: "If you could change one thing about me, what would it be?" Later, the audience learns that another sadist has killed Henry during their first meeting. When Dennis hears about this, he is frustrated that he had not gone further with Henry, and soon thereafter he kills his first victim, a young male sex worker. Dennis eventually joins forces with two other sexual killers, and the three of them hire young male hustlers, whom they torture and kill. In the end, it is ambiguous whether Dennis has merely fantasized all this violence and gore. The last scene shows him taking pictures of what looks to be a pornographic snuff scenario, but again it is ambiguous whether this is also a fake.

In some ways, it feels a bit unfair to interpret the storyline literally, as this indie film could be easily read as a prototype to the social satire film *American Psycho*. The movie could be a comment on the modern-day habituation to violence, the pervasiveness of nihilism, or a Sadean attack on the hypocrisies of the age. Nonetheless, its message also perpetuates the escalation theory applied to both s/m and pornography. As Barry Walters observes in his scathing review of the film, the only meaning he derived from the story was that "consuming porn during those impressionable teen years could later turn you into a cold-blooded killer" (Walters 1996). I would add that another truth-claim fostered by the movie is that s/m practice is addictive, and that sadistic desires inevitably become increasingly violent and deadly. Even when an s/m encounter does not involve obvious non-consensual violence, the movie suggests that the sadist/top partners are not interested in mutual and complementary pleasure, but in finding convenient victims they can abuse. In other words, the pleasures derived from sociopathic sadism and consensual topping are conflated. The bottom/masochists are presented as suffering from pathologically low self-esteem. Needless to say, the film never shows the s/m partners negotiating their boundaries or implementing safety mechanisms into their play to ensure that all partners are consenting to the activities. In this way, read literally, *Frisk* imagines s/m in a way similarly to how the anti-s/m feminists conceived of it as a slippery slope, where masochists are playing out a pathological need for self-destruction or self-punishment, and top players exploit them to derive sadistic thrills. This also correlates with some of the psychiatric conceptions of the dangers of sadism and masochism, in particular Freud's theory of moral masochism, which conflated sexual masochism with self-destructive tendencies. And as with movies like *Nine and a Half Weeks* and *Killing Me Softly*, *Frisk* perpetuates the truth-claim found in the *DSM-IV-TR* that for those suffering from sexual sadism, "usually the severity of the sadistic acts increases over time" (American Psychiatric Association 2000, 530).[26]

The last movie I will discuss in this section, *Pulp Fiction*, is both the least and the most important to consider for its representation of gay sadomasochists. It is the least important because its portrayal of sadomasochists is fleeting; in a huge cast of lurid characters, it barely merits a mention. Yet at the same time, it is the most important because its enormous box office success means it was viewed by millions of people, while *Cruising* and *Frisk* were flops that few people have even heard of, let alone seen.

Pulp Fiction is made up of interlocking story threads of gangsters, hitmen, drug dealers, and other seedy characters in their daily illicit lives. The relevant scene begins with a brutal struggle involving Marsellus Wallace (Ving Rhames), a mob leader, who has just been double-crossed by Butch Coolidge (Bruce Willis), a boxer. Their tussle brings them into a pawnshop where Butch, who has gotten the upper hand, is about to shoot Marsellus dead. However, he is prevented from doing so by the storeowner, Maynard (Duane Whitaker), who has a gun himself. Maynard knocks Butch unconscious and Marsellus passes out as well. Butch and Marsellus then wake to find themselves tied to a chair and ball-gagged, staring at Maynard, who has just been joined by his friend Zed. Upon Zed's instruction to "get the Gimp,"[27] Maynard unlocks a trunk and pulls out a man who is clad completely in fetish leather gear. His head is encapsulated in a leather hood, and a zipper is closed where his mouth would be (see figure 3.27 below).

The Gimp is attached by a leash to a hook and instructed to keep an eye on Butch while Zed and Maynard take Marsellus in the back room in order to rape him. While the audience hears the rape occurring in the off-space, Butch manages to untie himself and kill the Gimp, who is unable to escape because he is constrained by his leash and cannot alert his masters because his mouth is muffled by the leather hood. Butch ends up defeating Zed and Maynard and reaching a truce with Marsellus.

In his four-out-of-four-star review of this film, Roger Ebert describes *Pulp Fiction* as a "comedy about blood, guts, violence, strange sex, drugs, fixed fights, dead body disposal, leather freaks, and a wristwatch that makes a dark journey down through the generations" (1994). It is significant, I believe, that the Gimp is referenced as a "leather freak" among a list of unsavoury actions and objects (including the wristwatch, which, the audience learns, was hidden at one point in a

Figure 3.27: The Gimp

man's anus). The Gimp is denied any subjectivity, operating more as a prop to dramatize the grotesque vileness of the gay male rapists, who like to keep a sexual submissive on hand. And in the characters of Maynard and Zed, the familiar conflation between s/m tops and genuine sadistic men is perpetuated, as is the familiar conflation between homosexuality and perversity. In addition, the name "Gimp" is used as a derogatory epithet to refer to the sexual submissive character who is retributively killed, further demeaning s/m through disablist language.[28] All this being said, I initially hesitated to impose a literal reading of the narrative, as the director, Quentin Tarantino, was clearly attempting to create a story premised on the stock characters found in pulp fiction. The movie is built upon irony, postmodernism, self-referentiality, and genre-deconstruction. Nonetheless, it also contributes to the social imaginary, and because there are virtually no representations of gay sadomasochists and precious few of heterosexual sadomasochists in mainstream film, *Pulp Fiction*'s truth-claims become even more influential. Though absurd events pepper the plot, the dialogue carries the film, fleshing these two-dimensional stock characters out into real people. For example, the naturalistic dialogue between hitmen at the beginning of the movie regarding whether a foot massage and cunnilingus are in the "same ball park," normalizes them, making them subjects to whom the audience can relate. But the "Gimp" and his sadistic masters are nothing more than evil and repulsive. Unlike the hitmen, the mobsters, and the crooked boxer, whose nuanced personalities develop in each new scene, these gay men appear only once and, like most gay subjects in mainstream film, act as mere appendage characters to the main heterosexual characters. Their s/m bent makes them all the more easily objectified. After the Gimp is killed and the audience learns that Zed and Maynard will be tortured and killed, the audience can rejoice that these perverted men will get their just deserts. The expulsion pleasure here is as straightforward as the formula, an eye for an eye. Deviants who were going to rape and murder two men are themselves going to be tortured and murdered by their intended victims.

Conclusion

A survey of films that feature s/m demonstrates the ways that s/m and its practitioners are constituted in the popular imaginary. While each section of this analysis focused on different gender configurations or sexual orientations within the represented dominant/submissive dyad, most of the films attested to the escalating nature of s/m, its danger, and/or its unsustainability. *Secretary* and *Walk All Over Me*, along with *Exit to Eden* and *Preaching to the Perverted*, stand out as exceptions, which attempt to plead a case for s/m normalcy if contained within other hegemonic strictures, such as in gender roles, sexual orientation, or marital status. Nonetheless, the bulk of the films operate as a warning against s/m practice.

Conversely, most of the films also seem to advertise the superior pleasures that one could derive from s/m, and in the heterosexual films this was true whether the woman or the man was on top. In the films that featured gay s/m, the perversity of same-sex desire and dominant-submissive dynamics were conflated to an extent, and generally not portrayed in an enticing way. But even *Cruising* suggests that there is something tempting and corruptive about s/m, something that could lure a heterosexual cop away from his beautiful girlfriend and towards the deliciously seedy gay leather scene.

The pleasures of female masochism in the cinema are often conflated with a tendency to self-destruction or pathology. In *Nine and a Half Weeks*, Elizabeth allows her submissive pleasure to overtake her self-respect and identity. In *Videodrome*, masochistic Nicki volunteers for a sexually violent cable show and later appears to have become a victim of a pornographic snuff murder. In *Killing Me Softly*, Alice suggests that she was "blinded" by the s/m passion, which led her into a dangerous confrontation with her husband's incestuous sister. Even *Secretary*, which offers the most sympathetic portrayal of s/m, perpetuates the truth-claim that s/m is linked to mental instability. At the start of the film, Lee is a pathologized subject; her repetitive tendency to self-harm is shown as a neurotic method of coping with family trauma. The fact that she sublimates this neurosis into a functional sexual practice does not neutralize sexual masochism's narrative imbrication with pathology and mental disorder. When men are portrayed as sexual submissives, gender is troubled, and the narratives tend to either reposition the man as the one in control by the end of the film (as in *Something Wild* or *Wedding Crashers*), or to objectify the man as a source of humour who will ultimately be destroyed (as in *One Night at McCool's*).

The portrayal of sexual dominants can also be usefully divided by gender, and with the females, further subdivided between those who are paid to dominate and those who are not. With the exception of James Spader's character in *Secretary*, male sexual dominants, whether gay or straight, tend to be portrayed as hyper-alpha males who lead their partners into danger and/or degradation. Female non-commercial dominants are also hyper-alpha, but they tend to suffer a worse fate than their male counterparts. Construed as femmes fatales, they usually must either submit to their male partner in the end or suffer karmic destruction. Professional female dominants, on the other hand, are typically represented within the conventions of a patriarchal rescue narrative. These are emotionally damaged women who need the love of a man – one who can take sexual control – in order to get in touch with their true femininity, i.e., their sexual receptivity to non-kinky intercourse, and their emotive receptivity to a committed relationship. An imperative to the representation of both professional and non-professional female dominants in these narratives is the notion that their sexuality must be subdued to an extent, in order for them to survive. Yet the Canadian indie film *Walk All Over Me* resists this ideological imperative, by having a troubled and insecure woman gain strength and confidence through her adoption of a dominatrix persona.

Virtually all of the movies involve a criminal element, even if s/m is not linked directly to illegal conduct. In mild forms, such as in *Nine and a Half Weeks* and *Something Wild*, the thrill of risk-taking and transgression implicated in minor criminal conduct overlaps with the pleasures of s/m. In erotic thrillers and crime dramas like *Basic Instinct, Body of Evidence, Killing Me Softly, Hellraiser, Frisk*, and *Pulp Fiction*, having a sexually dominant bent suggests a pathological and sometimes homicidal personality. Even in movies that are ostensibly sympathetic to s/m, like *Preaching to the Perverted, Exit to Eden*, and *Walk All Over Me*, the plots revolve around criminality, the law, and the justice system. *Secretary*, a movie that is indubitably about sadomasochists, is the exception to this trend, where no one breaks the law or is accused of doing so. Furthermore, the fact that the male lead is a lawyer and that most of the action takes place in the law office indicates a narrative rebuttal to the cinematic convention of associating s/m with illicitness. Yet this means the film is still in conversation with the concepts of legality and criminality.

Connected to the notion of s/m as criminal is the urban backdrop to a number of the films. Most notably, in *Cruising*, *Nine and a Half Weeks*, and *Something Wild*, s/m desire is associated with a city's dirtiness, dangers, decadence, and diversity. In *Cruising*, s/m is linked to sexual orientation diversity, construed as a characteristically gay sexual mode. In the heterosexual films, racial diversity creates a narrative space for "exotic" and "savage" sexuality. These mostly non-speaking racialized characters are strewn in the background of the cinematic images and act as props upon which the white leads project their sexual excess and adventurousness. In *Nine and a Half Weeks*, s/m as a racialized practice is ultimately condemned as a corrupting and degrading sexuality. In *Something Wild*, the coding of Lulu's sexuality as African-American and lower class signals her hipness and her wildness, but ultimately, she too must recover her white identity as Audrey to justify the happy ending. Paradoxically, in *Basic Instinct*, whiteness itself, through its association with excessive wealth and gender reversals, comes to take on the characteristics of a racialized subject. It is interesting to note that the depiction of s/m in its relation to class can thus vary. If we read *Something Wild* as a "slumming" classploitation fantasy, the free-spirited poor, who are not tied down by bourgeois sensibility, can indoctrinate the uptight middle class into s/m pleasure. In contrast, the films *Nine and a Half Weeks*, *Basic Instinct*, *Body of Evidence*, and to look at another medium, the novel trilogy *Fifty Shades*, associate s/m with the decadence of the filthy rich. *Secretary* takes exception to the racialization of s/m and its association with either wild, lower-class carnality or wealthy debauchery. By providing a white cast with a middle-class background in a clean suburban location, the film seeks to normalize the practice. Sadomasochists access symbolic sexual citizenship, in part, through the hegemony of middle-class whiteness.

While I have focused, for the most part, on Hollywood mainstream films in my analysis, when researching for this chapter I also reviewed indie films within and outside of the United States that depict s/m. In terms of truth-claims, I found that nothing was fundamentally different. Allow me to list four critically acclaimed films that exemplify how art-house cinema also conforms to the pop cultural imaginary when it comes to kinksters. In the Italian film *The Night Porter* (1974), s/m is linked to Nazism, past trauma, Stockholm syndrome, sexual dysfunction, and mutual destruction. Roman Polanski's *Bitter Moon* (1992) both sells s/m as a titillating practice and presents consensual s/m as the gateway to non-consensual abuse, humiliation, aggravated assault, and finally murder-suicide. The Austrian-French film *The Piano Teacher* (2001) is probably the most anti-s/m fictional narrative I have dealt with.[29] The story features a disturbed piano teacher who is both a sexual masochist and a perpetrator of non-consensual humiliation and violence. She pursues an s/m relationship with a student that culminates in assault, rape, and self-mutilation. Even the 2006 American indie film *Shortbus*, with its queer utopian counter-hegemonic celebration of sexual alterity – including same-sex and bisexual desire, polyamory, and group sex – still perpetuates the stereotype of a professional dominatrix terrified of true intimacy. The character of Severin (notably, also the name of the male submissive in Masoch's novel *Venus in Furs*, indicating, perhaps, that the mistress is a secret submissive), is a professional dominant who confesses that she needs help to "have a real human interaction with someone." She is portrayed as emotionally constipated, and her sexual dominance is construed as a defence mechanism. And in the end, as with the more mainstream films that depict professional dominatrices, it is a heterosexual man who delivers emotional catharsis.[30]

A number of the pejorative truth-claims about s/m in cinema reflect those made in anti-s/m feminism and psychiatry. Most notably, one of the core claims of anti-s/m feminists was the notion of s/m as an escalating and addictive form of sexuality. Another common theme found in both the anti-s/m feminist literature and a number of films is the portrayal of tops as opportunistic sadists who take advantage of bottoms, who are construed as mentally unstable and vulnerable to exploitation. Similarly, the most obvious overlap between cinematic and psychiatric truth-claims involves the belief in the inherent self-destructiveness of the masochist partner, and the perpetuation of sado-masochist desire as a savage practice. The next two chapters consider how these psychiatric, feminist, and pop cultural perspectives and normative visions are implicated in legal representation and regulation of s/m pornography and practice.

4

The Legal Fondling of S/M Pornography

This chapter examines the law's adjudication of obscenity where s/m desire is at issue, either explicitly or implicitly. It begins with the Women's Legal Education and Action Fund's (LEAF) factum (1991) for the Supreme Court of Canada's precedent-setting obscenity case *R. v. Butler* (1992), and then turns to the decision itself to find that, while the descriptor *sadomasochism* is not used in either text, the pleasures of this sexuality are clearly indicted using an anti-s/m feminist lens. I then turn to case law, where the judicial gaze constructs gay and lesbian s/m pornography as violent, degrading, or dehumanizing. The next section demonstrates how heterosexual s/m representation – although less likely to catch the attention of police or custom officers than the gay, lesbian, or bisexual variety – can nonetheless also be deemed obscene. The last section considers two recent cases dealing with heterosexual s/m representation where judges exonerated the accused, heralding perhaps a more tolerant era in judicial dealings with heterosexual adult s/m pornography.

Sex Equality as the New Justificatory Framework for Censorship

The LEAF Factum

By beginning with a deconstruction of the gender and sexual truth-claims embedded in LEAF's *Butler* factum, I identify the overlapping sensibilities of anti-s/m feminism and anti-pornography feminism. Both are premised on sexual negativity (sex is represented as a source of danger and oppression for women) and on sexual literalism (representations and role playing endorse a literal application of the enacted scenes into a non-play and non-mutual context). An examination of the *Butler* decision itself demonstrates that LEAF's factum laid the foundation for the Supreme Court of Canada to construct s/m sexuality as inhuman and beyond the tolerance of the national community. As will become evident, the Canadian obscenity jurisprudence has adopted many anti-s/m feminist perspectives.

As the anti-s/m feminists had done during the sex wars, LEAF argued in its factum that its critique of pornography and justification for censorship was not generated by moralism, but rather by the struggle for sex equality. LEAF catalogues many different types of kinky, non-procreative, and particularly s/m-flavoured sexuality and denounces them as "hate propaganda against women" that "lies about women and their sexuality" (1991). LEAF thus endeavoured to set the record straight about *the* truth of female sexuality. This truth, however, is couched in negative terms. Not interested in directly tackling Freud's famous question – "What do women want?" – the factum offers a series of sexual practices that represent what women do *not* want.[1]

One rhetorical strategy that LEAF employed to negate the desirability of certain sexual representations with an s/m quality was to intersperse descriptions of kinky sexuality with those of sexual assault. The factum claims that in pornographic material, "women are presented as being raped. Sometimes they act as if they are enjoying it; sometimes they scream, resist, and try to run" (1991). This description brings up a basic semantic distinction between sex and assault that LEAF had to override in order to validate its determination that s/m sexuality leads unambiguously to harm. In LEAF's world, representations of "rape" can include women enjoying a sexual encounter, as well as women resisting it. How did LEAF determine that the woman in their example was "presented as being raped" if she is acting as if she enjoys the activity? Did it involve stranger-sex, multiple-partner sex, or some kind of initial force? The reader has no idea. By linguistically sandwiching the scene involving enjoyable sex between a "rape" and the image of a woman protesting and resisting the onslaught, the woman's enjoyment is contaminated on both sides with the stench of violence and non-consent.

Other descriptions that more explicitly invoke s/m practice are also presented outside of their context: "Women are bound with rings through their nipples and hung handcuffed from the ceiling" (LEAF 1991). In describing harmful and analogous gay male pornography, LEAF states that in these materials "men are slapped with belts" (1991). In both of these descriptions, there is no information to assist the reader to determine whether the women or men are presented as enjoying the scenes. LEAF portrays these sexual acts as if it is self-evident that they convey dangerous misrepresentations of human sexuality. The suggestion is that bondage and slapping should be understood as strict liability offences. Such s/m acts are overdetermined as intrinsically harmful practices; the mental state of the participants, i.e., whether the actors themselves feel harmed, is irrelevant.

LEAF was concerned not only with sexual text that explicitly combined sex with "violence," but also with a class of materials deemed "degrading and dehumanizing." In these sexual representations, women (and some gay men) are portrayed as enjoying sexual activities that LEAF concludes must necessarily detract from their status as a person. Yet encoded in the accusation that a text is "degrading" or "dehumanizing" is the essentialization of what will count as human sexuality. And, as with the "violent" pornography, any depicted enjoyment of "degrading" and "dehumanizing" sexuality is presupposed as false.

One example of "degrading" pornography was the erotic staging of hierarchal social relations. "Sex acts are presented being performed on subordinates by superiors or caretakers, including employer on employee, priest on penitent, doctor on nurse, and nurse on patient" (LEAF 1991). Again, although LEAF does not name these sexual representations as s/m, they are classic s/m pairings in role-playing scenarios. Later in the factum, LEAF cites *R. v. Wagner* (1985) to further indict pornography for exploiting professional roles as erotic fodder, stating that "in such films professional women, such as nurses and secretaries, are hired solely for the purpose of sexual gratification, without regard for their professional qualifications and abilities." In these images, LEAF does not elaborate on what harm flows from fictional eroticized encounters between people in professional or social relations that involve hierarchy. Instead, there is an implicit assumption that sexual representations should portray sexual situations that would be acceptable only if they occurred in the real world. As Gotell argues, "LEAF … embraces the view that pornography/obscenity is open to literal interpretation" (1997, 96). One important truth-claim that LEAF perpetuates is that such sexual representations are prescriptive. If the scenario would be exploitive in real life, then it is obscene to depict it as pornography.[2]

In addition, s/m's theatrical use of unequal power relationships seems to trigger (unacknowledged) abjection anxiety for LEAF. Kristeva states, "The abject is perverse because it neither gives up nor assumes a prohibition, a rule, or a law; but turns them aside, misleads, corrupts; uses them, takes advantage of them, the better to deny them" (1982, 15). S/m pornography perverts hierarchy, takes advantage of hierarchy's sexual residue, and prioritizes pleasure at the expense of order and coherence. LEAF seeks to purify this abject practice by calling in arguably the most hierarchal and coercive practice, the criminal law, to punish these perverts and to re-establish order. In other words, legal hierarchy is called in to protect the sanctity of social hierarchy and to disavow its sexual leakages.

Another violated hierarchy that troubles LEAF is the one that separates and privileges human over animal. In describing "harmful" pornography that utilizes men as the victims, the factum reports that in some images, "They are in dog collars and in chains" (1991). Later in the factum LEAF cites *R. v. Wagner* (1985), where porn is censured for portraying men and women "as having animal characteristics" (1991). In both contexts, LEAF does not elaborate on the particular harm perpetuated when men and women don dog collars or embody animal characteristics. Instead, it is assumed that any sexual act that reinforces our animality necessarily must simultaneously erode our humanity. It becomes a zero-sum game. The more animalistic the person, the less human she becomes. As Rozin's psychological studies demonstrate, "anything that reminds us that we are animals elicits disgust" (Rozin, Haidt, and McCauley 2000, 642). Nussbaum further develops this argument, stating, "Disgust embodies a shrinking from contamination that is associated with the human desire to be nonanimal" (2004, 74). LEAF capitalizes on the disgust-provoking power evoked by the imagery of animalized humans to demonstrate the harmfulness of pornography in these bestial images. Their argument also recalls the early psychiatric writings that warned of the destructiveness of succumbing to our animal urges.

Other non-violent pornographic images deemed by LEAF to be degrading and justifiably censored are representations of women with (supposedly) exaggerated sex drives. LEAF's construction of women's libido as essentially moderate and monogamous recalls anti-s/m discourse that lamented lesbian s/m's celebration of sexual gratification outside the terms of emotional intimacy and commitment. LEAF states, "Women are presented as being sexually insatiable. Women are simultaneously or serially penetrated in every orifice by penises or objects" (1991). Implied in the first sentence is that women should not be presented as so lustful; theirs is a temperate sexuality. Despite LEAF's contention that they have rejected traditional understandings of obscenity, their condemnation of the insatiable woman bears an uncanny resemblance to societal condemnation of promiscuous women who transgress the feminine imperative of sexual modesty. Of course, the important difference is that while society condemns "sluts," LEAF disavows their existence, or at the very least, denies them agency. The next sentence about penetration strengthens this account. According to LEAF, no woman desires multiple or diverse forms of penetration. Presumably all women should be "satiated" with a single penetration, and it is degrading to suggest otherwise.

Other sexual activities considered "degrading" by LEAF are those connected with orifices and bodily fluids involved in non-procreative and kinky sexual play. For example, LEAF condemns the image of a woman orally stimulating a man's anus, the "money shot" (men visibly ejaculating on women's and gay men's bodies or in their mouths), and men urinating on other men. LEAF argued that social science research has found that such "degrading" material, even though it does not depict violence or non-consent, increases and normalizes male sexual aggression and discrimination against women. Yet as Gotell points out, "the concept of degradation has no inherent meaning" (1997, 97). Perhaps the reason LEAF saw degradation in such imagery is tied to conventional disgust-reactions to a dis/ordered body. Much of the imagery that LEAF denounces as harmful to women and a few gay men denotes a fear of contamination of cultural boundaries that divide the upper sphere of the body from the lower. LEAF perpetuates the hegemonic separation of the privileged head and mouth (as sites where our humanity and rationality reside) from the naughty parts of the genitals and anus (as sites where our animality and irrationality reside).

To understand why this would evoke disgust, it is helpful to turn to literary theorists Peter Stallybrass and Allon White, who argued, "The body cannot be thought separately from the social formation, symbolic topography and the constitution of the subject" (1986, 192). They investigate how the literary image of the grotesque body challenged the hegemony of the classical body as a seamless construct without openings or leakages (22). In contrast, the grotesque body conveys "an image of the impure corporal bulk with its orifices (mouth, flared nostrils, anus) yawning wide and its lower regions (belly, legs, feet, buttocks and genitals) given priority over its upper regions (head, 'spirit,' reason)" (9). LEAF objects to the grotesque pornographic body, which vandalizes the morally stratified body. First, the indicted images reverse the established hierarchy by prioritizing and foregrounding the genitals and excrement, while the head, i.e., the mind, is suppressed. Second, regions of the body that are supposed to be kept far apart are brought together: the tongue and the anus; urine and the face; the genitals and the lips; and semen and the mouth. These pairings are coded as disgusting, particularly because of the significance of the mouth as an "especially charged border" (Nussbaum 2004, 88), both privileged for its associations with verbal rationality and vulnerable as an orifice for its ability to incorporate. Rozin and Fallon argued that a central component of disgust is "revulsion at the prospect of (oral) incorporation of an offensive object. The offensive objects are contaminants" (1987, 23). As such, the mouth on the anus, for example, is an image that can evoke acute disgust, because it signifies the possible incorporation of an unquestionably abject substance, faecal matter.

As has been stated, most of the sexual representations condemned by LEAF do not involve non-consensual activity. Consent is dealt with in a contradictory way, much as it was in the anti-s/m feminist discourse. On the one hand, LEAF cites a passage from the *Report of the Standing Committee on Justice and Legal Affairs* (that Justice Sopinka would later reproduce in *Butler*) that states, "Consensualism and mutuality are basic to any human interaction" (MacGuigan Report 1978). On the other hand, LEAF indicts as violent, degrading, or dehumanizing any consensual and mutual non-procreative activity that sexualizes power, role playing, a high libido, abject body parts, or our animal selves. Consensualism thus emerges as a contingent value. The representation of a lack of consent establishes that the text is obscene. But the representation of consent and enjoyment does not establish it as non-obscene. Like anti-s/m feminism during the sex wars, anti-pornography feminism is suspicious or downright dismissive of the viability of a woman's consent to certain kinky sexual practices.

R. v. Butler (1992)

In the landmark *Butler* decision that upheld the obscenity provisions of the *Criminal Code* in Canada, s/m pornography is never addressed as such. Yet I would argue that, as with the LEAF factum, the aesthetics and the erotics of s/m haunt the text. As Hoople suggests, "The wording of *Butler* is likely to predispose any judge who followed its precedents to see all but the most innocuous forms of SM imagery as obscene" (1996, 186). In justifying the infringement of the right to free speech in the case of obscenity, the judgment utilizes vocabulary that is central to s/m eroticism. The court characterizes images of domination, submission, bondage, humiliation, and, ironically, consent in particular cases, as material that carries with it a significant risk of harm. Such images were castigated as perpetuating the undue exploitation of sex. Meanwhile, explicit sexual images that were free from violence, degradation, and dehumanization (as interpreted by the judiciary) were understood as less likely to cause harm and thus less likely to be justifiably censored.

Feminists and progressive scholars were divided on whether this new attempt to distinguish between harmful and benign sexual texts was a valid one. For example, Karen Busby, who had helped to draft LEAF's factum for the case, supported the ruling at the time, asserting that LEAF could "count the Court's decision in *Butler* as a feminist breakthrough" (1994, 176). No longer mired in subjective notions of morality and decency, it was contended that the decision instead properly focused on the harm perpetuated by certain pornographies. The court adopted the feminist approach of LEAF, whose mandate was to protect and promote sex equality, not sexual morality.

Other scholars, particularly those concerned with the targeting of sexual minorities for censorship, were not so celebratory. Les Green, in considering the specificity of gay pornography, suggested that the Supreme Court of Canada in effect "fashioned the silk purse of harm-prevention out of the sow's ear of moralism" (2000, 29). In *Bad Attitude/s on Trial*, Cossman, Bell, Gotell and Ross argued that the decision effectively criminalized the bad attitudes of sexual others (1997, 4). In contrast to Busby's enthusiastic endorsement of the *Butler* decision as an "extraordinary shift in the traditional rationale for obscenity laws" (Busby 1994, 176), Cossman describes the court's reasoning and its legacy as "sexual morality in drag" (Cossman et al. 1997, 107). Although the rhetoric in *Butler* ostensibly shrugs off the precedence of sexual conservatism in previous judicial decisions on obscenity, the subtext belies this aspiration.

In her chapter in *Bad Attitude/s*, Cossman offers a close textual analysis of the underlying justification for the obscenity legislation in *Butler*. She argues, "When we scratch the surface, we find a conservative sexual morality that sees sex as bad, physical, shameful, dangerous, base, guilty until proven innocent, and redeemable only if it transcends its base nature" (1997, 107). I wish to build on Cossman's deconstruction of the sexual essentialism and sex negativity of the *Butler* decision and analyse its specific applicability to s/m sexuality and representation. In particular, I focus on two ideological linchpins to the judgment: the reification of humanness, and the homogenization of the national community. The court's strategies of rationalizing who gets to count as part of the national community, and allowing that imaginary community to then discursively police the borders around humanness, worked synergistically to evict sadomasochists from sexual citizenship and human subjectivity. Before elaborating on these two key elements of the decision, I will briefly summarize the findings of the court as presented by Justice Sopinka and the separate opinion of Justice Gonthier, who concurred in result with the general reasoning of the court, but wished to add a different gloss to the judicial justification for obscenity legislation.

In *Butler*, the Supreme Court of Canada was called upon to determine the constitutionality of the obscenity provisions in section 163 of the *Criminal Code* of Canada. The decision focuses on the definitional subsection that constructs obscenity as "any publication a dominant characteristic of which is the undue exploitation of sex, or of sex and any one or more of the following subjects, namely, crime, horror, cruelty and violence" (*Criminal Code* 1985, s. 163(8)). At issue was whether the obscenity definition violates the *Canadian Charter of Rights and Freedoms*, which protects everyone's fundamental freedom of "thought, belief, opinion and expression" (1982, s. 2(b)). If the obscenity provision was found to violate this fundamental freedom, the question would then turn to whether such violation could be justified as a reasonable limit prescribed by law (s. 1). If so, then the legislation would be "saved" and rendered constitutional.

In its analysis of the case, the Supreme Court of Canada reviews and clarifies three interconnected judicial tests to determine whether a document constitutes obscenity. The first test invokes an adjudicating national community that decides whether it will tolerate other Canadians being exposed to the material. The second test determines whether the material exploits sex in a degrading or dehumanizing manner; if so, it will presumptively fail the community standards test. The final test, dubbed the internal necessities test, allows for an artistic defence of the work. Again, community standards are invoked to determine whether material, even if parts of it would otherwise be deemed obscene, could be tolerated because it advances a serious artistic or intellectual purpose. The Supreme Court of Canada concludes that though the obscenity legislation does violate freedom of expression, such violation is constitutionally justified.

Justice Gonthier, who was joined by Justice L'Heureux-Dubé in his concurring opinion, agreed with the overall reasoning of the majority, but modified certain assumptions regarding harm and morality that had been expressed in the main judgment. For example, Justice Gonthier objected to Justice Sopinka's assessment that the community will generally tolerate representations of explicit sex that do not involve violence, degradation, or dehumanization. While Justice Gonthier conceded that this type of material is generally more tolerated because it holds less risk of harm, he wished to emphasize that it could still be classified as obscene. He asserted that an explicit sexual text, if represented in a manner that "distorts" human sexuality, can be obscene even without violence, degradation, or dehumanization.

Justice Gonthier also deviates from the main judgment because of his emphasis on morality. Though Justice Sopinka acknowledges that a "fundamental conception of morality" (*R. v. Butler* 1992, 493) supports the obscenity legislation, he foregrounds the prevention of harm as the pressing and substantial objective that upholds the constitutionality of the statute. Justice Gonthier, on the other hand, cites both early *Charter* cases and international law to establish morality as a legitimate justification for limiting freedom of expression in democratic societies. Though Justice Gonthier and Justice Sopinka both affirm that morality has a place in the analysis of obscenity legislation, Justice Sopinka makes modest claims as to its importance, while Justice Gonthier is adamant about its centrality.

Although they treat morality differently, both judgments indict the practice and representation of s/m by reifying humanness through a series of binary oppositions: mind and body; human and animal; pleasure and pain; and community and porn-consumer. Some of these essentialized dualisms reflect the construction of humanity in the early medical and psychological literature, in which Krafft-Ebing, Ellis, and Freud had asserted that "man" must control his bodily urges with his mind, and tame his animal nature with his reason. Even though the semantics have altered, *Butler*'s articulation of the division between the community and the porn-consumer can be mapped onto the division between the normal individual and the deviant, as expressed by the doctors. However, despite these similarities in approach, the modern-day legal judgment has a completely different take on the purported connection between pleasure and pain. While the earlier scientific literature spun an evolutionary tale to link pain and pleasure, the *Butler* decision dismisses any overlap of these emotive fields as unfounded.

The judgment thus constructs humanness in such a way that s/m desire becomes not perverse or atavistic, but rather unthinkable. It is inhuman to extract pleasure from pain, and any such representation must be fallacious and dangerous.

This negation of s/m desire points to an irony in the text: despite the judges' incessant reiteration in *Butler* that they are concerned with preventing dehumanization in pornography, the judicial text in fact aggressively polices who will count as human. As Judith Butler has argued, "On the level of discourse, certain lives are not considered lives at all, they cannot be humanized; they fit no dominant frame for the human, and their dehumanization occurs first, at this level" (2004, 25). In *Butler*, the people who eroticize hierarchy, who revel in the physicality of sexuality, or who choose to pay or be paid for pornographic material are discursively dehumanized. They do not fit into the judicial framework of human sexuality, which seeks to repudiate the physicality and the animality of human sexual subjectivity.

A close reading of the judgment reveals an anxious investment in the borders that separate the mind from the body, and the human from the animal. Justice Sopinka cites the Manitoba Court of Appeal decision for the case at bar, which dismissed the constitutional challenge because the obscene material did not convey meaning, but was rather depicting "purely physical activity" (*R. v. Butler* 1990, 466). Although Justice Sopinka later rejects the conclusion that obscenity lacks meaning, he does build on the Court of Appeal's disparagement of material that revels in the physical aspects of human existence. He cites with approval Justice Wilson in *Towne Cinema*, who posited that "the public has concluded that exposure to material that degrades the human dimensions of life to a subhuman or merely physical dimension and thereby contributes to a process of moral desensitization must be harmful in some way" (*Towne Cinema* (1985) cited in *R. v. Butler* 1990, 481). In this account, the physical is seen as suspect; it harbours the ability to contaminate moral sensibilities and inflict harm in some amorphous fashion. According to Cossman, it is implicit in the *Butler* decision that "bad sex is subhuman sex. Bad sex is sex that emphasizes the merely physical dimension of sex" (Cossman et al. 1997, 112). And those who participate in or seek out "bad sex," either as porn stars or porn consumers, are engaged in subhuman activity.

In addition, notice the way Justice Wilson repeats the descriptor of "human." She states that material that "degrades the *human* dimensions of life to a sub*human* or merely physical dimension ... must be harmful in some way" (emphasis added). This tautological strategy of repeating two images of comprised humanness, first through a degrading of its dimensions, and then through the prefix "sub-" to imply a diminishment of full human status, helps Justice Wilson arrive at the inescapable conclusion that the physical part of human subjectivity is the inferior part. By employing the connector "or" between "subhuman" and "merely physical," she assumes that the physical part of being human is actually less than human. It is the part shared with animals and objects. Pornography is condemned because it transgresses the line between human and other, by de-emphasizing what has been thought to separate us (the mental sphere) and over-emphasizing what is shared (the physical sphere). The pornographic image of a "human" excised from a rational or spiritual context, who appears to be all body and no mind, is quintessentially abject. As Kristeva states in the first line of her treatise on the abject, "ni sujet, ni objet" – the abject is horrifying because it does not safely reside in either the subject position or the object position. A crisis of human identity occurs when the human subject begins to resemble the non-human object.

Justice Gonthier's concurring opinion in *Butler* continues this reliance upon the abject border separating human from animal to convey the harms of pornography. He cites with approval D.A. Downs (1989), who, he maintains, "aptly describes how these materials do not reflect the richness of human sexuality, but rather turn it into pure animality" (*R. v. Butler* 1992, 513). This statement does not disavow animality as being an inherent aspect of human existence, but it strongly demeans it. As with the earlier scientific literature, our animality is seen as an inferior but dangerous force in human subjectivity that must always be filtered through our rationality. Justice Gonthier elaborates on this construction through a direct quote from Downs, who states, "The deeper objection to sheer pornography or obscenity … is that it represents a retreat from the human dilemma and the responsibility of acknowledging the tensions in our nature. Sheer pornography also reduces us to the lower aspects of our natures by stripping away the modesty that arises from our encounter with our animality" (513). Again our "animality" is subordinated because it exists in the "lower aspects of our nature." Interestingly, the use of the word *encounter* to describe one's relationship to one's animality fractures human identity. The *Oxford English Dictionary* defines *encounter* as "a meeting face to face; a meeting (of adversaries or opposing forces) in conflict, hence a battle, skirmish, duel etc." The image conjured up by the phrase "our encounter with our animality" separates our animality, makes it something we confront and see outside of ourselves. As the dictionary attests, the definition of the word suggests a potentially hostile meeting, not a friendly one. What normally protects us from our animality is a sense of modesty. Pornography strips this away (notice the sexual undertones to this image) and we become vulnerable in the encounter. Modesty operates not just as a cloak, but as a shield to ward off our animality. In addition, this also recalls LEAF's objection to obscenity that portrays people in animalistic ways and shows women with insatiable, i.e., with immodest, sexual desires.

Justice Gonthier's investment in modesty as a crucial human characteristic leads him to expound an essentialist conception of human sexuality: "Obscene materials ... convey a distorted image of human sexuality, by making public and open elements of the human nature which are usually hidden behind a veil of modesty and privacy" (*R. v. Butler* 1992, 513). Justice Gonthier holds fast to a singular image of human sexuality, and this precludes any public and brazen expressions of sexuality. People who work in the pornography industry or enjoy pornographic material are being immodest and retreating from their true humanity. The last line of the paragraph by Downs expresses this abject fear that pornography fuels our animality, tersely declaring, "Modesty humanizes desire" (1989, 183). Though Justice Gonthier did not reproduce this statement in his judgment, its sentiment infuses his assessment of the relationship between humanness and sexuality. As with the early sexologists' account, sexual desire is overdetermined as an animalistic force that must be rendered human through the use of modesty.

When examining the specific narratives of obscenity, the court also utilizes a narrow vision of humanness to indict certain erotic dynamics as being "degrading and dehumanizing." The images the court offers can easily be positioned within an s/m framework. For example, Justice Sopinka quotes Justice Ferg in *R. v. Ramsingh*, who described "in graphic terms" what constitutes obscenity: "They are exploited, portrayed as desiring pleasure from pain, by being humiliated and treated only as an object of male domination sexually, or in cruel or violent bondage. Women are portrayed in these films as pining away their lives waiting for a huge male penis to come along ... supposedly to transport them into complete sexual ecstasy. Or even more false and degrading one is led to believe their raison d'être is to savour semen as a life elixir, or that they secretly desire to be forcefully taken by a male" (*R. v. Ramsingh* 1984, 479). The first image conjured up by the court in essence describes women who apparently enjoy submissive sexual practices. Unlike in the LEAF factum, the account does not convey women who are being violated or raped. Rather, the women are portrayed as desiring subjects. Yet the Supreme Court of Canada finds it unthinkable that such s/m representations involving humiliation or bondage could possibly be a positive experience for women. Before the court has even begun to describe the scene, it is a foregone conclusion that the material is exploitive.

The next image to which the court objects is that of women who are yearning for a "huge male penis," presumably in order to participate in penetrative intercourse. It is not clear what the court objects to in this scenario. Is it that women should not be so sex-focused? Is it that they shouldn't care about the size of the penis? Or is it that the judge rejects the possibility that some women can be transported "into complete sexual ecstasy" by anonymous and unsentimental sexual relations? Whatever the case, this is a clear negation of heterosexual and bisexual women who lust after penises.

The image the court finds "even more false and degrading" involves oral sex. But instead of providing an explanation of why the imagery of fellatio is objectionable, the court sarcastically dismisses the possibility that women will desire to "savour semen as a life elixir." As with the LEAF factum, the judgment cannot abide the notion that some women may be aroused by fellatio and swallowing, and as such the court cannot believe a woman would consent to such activities.[3] Another possibility is that the court objects to semen being ejaculated into a nonprocreative orifice.

The final notion rejected by the court is that some women enjoy force as part of their sexual activity. Throughout the description, the court flatly rejects the erotic appeal of s/m desire: pleasure wrought from pain, active desire for sexual submissiveness, or an emphasis on role playing and fantasy. Unlike the earlier scientific literature that gave credence to a certain female masochism through an evolutionary narrative, the court accuses all such images as "degrading," "dehumanizing," and "false." The effect of this assessment, however, is to dehumanize s/m practitioners. In particular, active lustful female submissives are seen as fictional, as inhuman, and as a male fantasy that real women would necessarily find degrading.

In another description of what Justice Sopinka describes as "the realities of the pornography industry," the image of promiscuous, highly responsive women, even without any hint of force or violence, is rejected as dehumanizing. Justice Sopinka quotes Justice Shannon in *R. v.*

Wagner (1985, 331), who says of pornography, "Women, particularly, are deprived of unique human character or identity and are depicted as sexual playthings, hysterically and instantly responsive to male sexual demands" (*R. v. Butler* 1992, 500). But notice that while the judicial gaze objectifies the women as "sexual play*things*" (emphasis added), the next part of the phrase – regarding the depicted women's "hysterical" and "instant" sexual responsiveness – belies the women's inert status. In other words, the women themselves are being aroused and deriving sexual pleasure from the activity. Yet the court cannot accept that women could be so easily stimulated and so aggressively desirous. Working backwards then, such women cannot be *human*. Their oversexed personality has robbed them of what the court will count as human identity. Real women apparently are not so licentious or orgasmic, or if they are, at least are not so demonstrative of their arousal.

The court continues its erasure of female masochistic subjectivity in its analysis of consent. In deciding whether something is obscene, Justice Sopinka states, "Among other things, degrading or dehumanizing materials place women (and sometimes men) in positions of subordination, servile submission or humiliation. They run against the principles of equality and dignity of all human beings. In the appreciation of whether material is degrading or dehumanizing, the appearance of consent is not necessarily determinative. Consent cannot save materials that otherwise contain degrading or dehumanizing scenes. Sometimes the very appearance of consent makes the depicted acts even more degrading or dehumanizing" (*R. v. Butler* 1992, 479). Here consent is not only rejected as an exculpatory factor in connection with images of sexualized hierarchies, but is held to be an aggravating factor in the determination of its degrading and dehumanizing qualities. Because the images have already been deemed to violate human dignity and equality, the consent is construed as necessarily fallacious. The image of a human consenting to being "dehumanized" throws into question how the court has drawn the boundaries around who will register as human. And since the court is devoted to a singular vision of what constitutes human sexuality, it must deny the persuasiveness of that consent. This recalls LEAF's factum that drew no distinction between women enjoying a sexual encounter and women resisting; the issue becomes not the subjective state of the participants, but a determination of whether the legal gaze deems the act to be degrading or dehumanizing.

Replicating LEAF's hypocrisy on the issue of consent, Justice Sopinka also quotes the *Report on Pornography by the Standing Committee on Justice and Legal Affairs*: "A society which holds that egalitarianism, non-violence, consensualism, and mutuality are basic to any human interaction, whether sexual or other, is clearly justified in controlling and prohibiting any medium of depiction, description or advocacy which violates these principles" (MacGuigan Report 1978, 493–4). Overlay this analysis and the previous discussion of consent, and a contradictory form of paternalism is evidenced: in order to protect the principle of consensualism, the legislature is justified in censoring images of consenting sexual activity because the material does not subscribe to a predetermined vision of *human* conduct. In other words, the notion of consensualism the court purports to respect is contingent upon a hegemonic formulation of sexuality. As with the LEAF factum, the citation of consensualism as a societal value comes off as mere lip service.

Justice Gonthier also adds another qualification to the issue of consent. He begins his discussion by foregrounding the liberality of Canadian laws: "It is indeed important to emphasize that the *Criminal Code* is grounded on the principles of sexual freedom between consenting adults" (*R. v. Butler* 1992, 512). Later in this discussion, however, he states that the legislature has cast a wider criminal net around what sexual activity is permissibly represented. He states, "The type of scenes vividly described in *R. v. Wagner* or *R. v. Ramsingh* might perhaps be legal if done between consenting adults, but they become obscene when they are represented" (512–13). In other words, if people consent to s/m activities as described in the previous decisions, then they are foreclosed from representing themselves in images or pictures. They should be ashamed, or at least modest, about their sexual predilections and should keep all mention of it strictly private.

This notion that the representation of a sexual activity may be criminal while the act itself would not is reminiscent of the ways anti-s/m feminists condemned not just the practice of lesbian s/m, but objected particularly to its brazen public displays. Recall that during the sex wars some feminist bookstores refused to carry s/m positive books, some women-only or feminist spaces evicted s/m support groups, and there were book burnings of s/m literature. In both the law and the feminist anti-s/m tactics, there is a sense that the dissemination of information about s/m sexuality will have a corrosive effect on society, be it the larger society or feminist community. But what these stances ultimately do is tacitly credit s/m sexuality with allure.

As such, embedded in this distinction between the activity of sexual perversion and its representation is a fear of contagion. Since the court has found that such activities violate a predetermined vision of distinctly human sexuality, then such dehumanized humans must be forbidden to circulate images or stories that affirm or promote their desires. In the words of Mary Douglas, these dehumanized s/m practitioners have been endowed with "polluting" power: "A polluting person is always in the wrong. He has developed some wrong condition or simply crossed some line which should not have been crossed and this displacement unleashes danger for someone" (2003, 140). Sadomasochists have developed the wrong desires and have crossed – or perhaps criss-crossed – the lines between mind and body, human and animal, and pain and pleasure. If s/m material is allowed to disseminate, others might be enticed to similarly disrupt these essentialized binaries.

This fear of contagion is couched in the goal of harm prevention. In citing with approval the MacGuigan Report, the court asserts, "While a direct link between obscenity and harm to society may be difficult, if not impossible, to establish, it is reasonable to presume that exposure to images bears a causal relationship to changes in attitudes and beliefs" (*R. v. Butler* 1992, 502). Yet what the court never addresses is why it is not "reasonable" to assume that sexual images showcasing consenting lustful women engaged in s/m sexuality would enforce the attitude that consent is a key component to any sexual relationship. For reasons never explained, the court is convinced that the simulated power imbalance depicted in s/m images will translate as advocacy for literal power imbalances in real-life encounters, and that the consent offered by the parties in the sexual representations will have absolutely no effect, or worse, translate as giving licence to override lack of consent.

The illogic in this formulation betrays a fear of the corrosive influence of perversity. Douglas argues that there are "pollution powers which inhere in the structure of ideas itself and which punish a symbolic breaking of that which should be joined or joining that which should be separate" (2003, 140). The sadomasochist representation symbolically breaks the hallowed linkage between modesty and humanness and perversely joins animalistic sexuality to human activity. Though the court reiterates over and over that its primary concern is the prevention of abuse against women, it conveniently ignores the conflicting social scientific evidence like the Fraser Report, which Justice Sopinka admits, "could not postulate any causal relationship between pornography and the commission of violent crimes, the sexual abuse of children, or the disintegration of communities and society" (*R. v. Butler* 1992, 501). The court, unmoved by this lack of evidence, simply prefers reports that support its pro-censorship position that images of power imbalances will lead to harm, because the conclusion seems "reasonable." Perhaps it seems "reasonable" because it coincides with an agenda of shoring up the boundaries between human and other. It also invokes the historical legacy of psychiatric writings and the assumptions of radical feminist theory, and reflects the cinematic narratives that warned of the corrosive power of sexual perversion.

Though the body is dismissed in much of the judgment as being "lower" and "animalistic," it is worth noting that in one instance the body becomes a bearer of truth. The court cites with approval the 1948 judgment in *R. v. Close*: "There does exist in any community at all times – however the standard may vary from time to time – a general *instinctive* sense of what is decent and what is indecent, of what is clean and what is dirty" (*R. v. Butler* 1992, 476; emphasis added). This description conspicuously stands out in the judgment for its faith in the body's epistemological capacity: the human "instinct" is trusted to determine where to draw the line around obscenity. Observe the way the more abstract notion of indecency is followed in this assertion by the more concrete metaphor of dirt. In this composite sentence, indecency is reified through its paralleling with dirt. Though the judge admits that there are no itemized guidelines to decide what will classify as obscene, he places his faith in an instinctual disgust reaction that the community will experience when confronted with indecency, the way anyone would react to dirt. The body's ability to distinguish dirt from non-dirt is assumed. As Miller has pointed out, "[Disgust] argues for the visibility, the palpability, the concreteness, the sheer obviousness of the claim" (1997, 194). The body can thus be trusted when it feels disgust for an image, but not when it feels arousal.

This is also part of the storyline around s/m in the anti-s/m feminist and cinematic accounts. Pleasure experienced by s/m enthusiasts is dismissed as perversion, as deviancy, or as a product of brainwashing. Pleasure in non-normative sexual practices has anti-epistemological force: it is the body misleading the mind towards violence or self-destruction. Meanwhile, the disgust that outsiders or even practitioners themselves might feel towards the sexual practice is validated. Recall how the anti-s/m feminist rhetoric deployed the language of sickness and disease to express disgust at the prevalence of s/m desire in the lesbian community. Recall also how in the end of *Nine and a Half Weeks*, Elizabeth runs away from John and ends up vomiting in the sink; she is disgusted with herself for having participated in s/m sexuality. In legal, feminist, and cinematic narratives, disgust with the sexual other has epistemological force: encoded in the body is the knowledge of how to protect itself from harm. This investment in disgust's protective powers resonates with Rozin's delineation of disgust, which he originates as "a rejection response to bad tastes, in the service of protecting the body" (Rozin, Haidt, and McCauley 2000, 637). He further argues that disgust can conflate this biological purpose with the cultural purpose of a rejection of certain sexual behaviours "in the service of protecting the soul" (637). While the court never speaks of the human soul, its belief that censorship will protect women from violence and abuse, formed without supporting empirical evidence, shows a similar muddling between the protection of the body and protection of the soul.

One way that the court validated its stance on the protective powers of censorship was to appeal to "a community standards test of tolerance" to guide its determinations. The "national community" is the final arbiter of what sexually explicit material is so extreme that "the community" would not abide other Canadians being exposed to it. This test is meant to escape the idiosyncrasy of personal taste of the judges and of the community. The question is not what pornographic material Canadians would shun for themselves, but what they would not tolerate "other" Canadians consuming. This essential Canadian "community" is discussed as if it had one single clear voice that the judges were privy to hearing.

The court does admit that there is some diversity of opinion on what material causes harm and what is innocuous. Justice Sopinka concedes that "there is a range of opinion as to what is degrading or dehumanizing" (*R. v. Butler* 1992, 484). To overcome this issue of diverse opinions, the court must conclude what the "community as a whole" would or would not tolerate. Justice Gonthier claims that "the community" is more than a simple majority, but rather must include segments of society who hold divergent conceptions of the good (524). However, despite the acknowledged pluralism of Canadian society, the court claims the ability to glean the perspective of an overriding national community. The decision, then, is not simply drawing the line between who will count as human and non-human in an abstract sense, it is also drawing kinship lines that exclude the sexual other from the national identity. When the court speaks of what "Canadians" would or would not tolerate, sadomasochists, porn stars, and consumers are literally and politically otherized as alien to the Canadian community; the judicial formulation refers to them as "other Canadians." Though the court recognizes them as Canadian, they are erased from the "imagined community" of Canadians.

In his oft-cited book, Benedict Anderson defines the nation as an "imagined political community – and imagined as both inherently limited and sovereign" (1991, 6). In the *Butler* decision, both prongs of this imaginary project are engaged. The judgment limits who will count as "the community" by excluding those who engage in sexual practices that it has deemed inhuman. And the judgment claims that the community is sovereign through its entitlement to determine what expression is permissible and what must be censored. This community sovereign power is exemplified by Justice Sopinka's statement, "The community is the arbiter as to what is harmful to it" (*R. v. Butler* 1992, 481). In this sentence, the community is reduced to a single and cohesive entity that has the right to exercise self-defence to protect against porn's influence. *Butler* reveals the extent to which censorship policies are also national strategies of identity. The borders that divide Canadians from non-Canadians are formed not only around geographical lines, but also around sexual normative lines. To put it another way, the ways in which the law imagines some Canadians belonging to the adjudicating Canadian community, and others not belonging, reflects the sexualization of citizenship.[4]

There is a faint whiff of familiarity to the early medico-scientific literature. While Krafft-Ebing was aggressively dividing civilized man from savage man through a discourse of spiritual evolution, the *Butler* decision divides Canadian from "other" Canadian through a discourse of human dignity. In both instances, a national hierarchy is being formulated that positions those whose sexual practices are deemed most human and evolved as superior to those deemed inhuman and animalistic. The judgment is an eviction of the abject from the national community in order to recreate its discursive borders around proper sexual attitudes.

It is also interesting to consider this otherization of the s/m subject in relation to the cinematic representation of s/m as racialized and exotic. Recall that in the examined films, s/m desire was often coded as foreign. For example, the sexually dominant Lulu in *Something Wild* wore Africanized clothing and listened to reggae while she seduced the handcuffed Charlie. The sex worker at the climax of *Nine and a Half Weeks* was Latina and spoke only Spanish throughout her encounter with the main couple. In both the cinematic and the legal imagination, s/m desire is rendered alien. And this construction of s/m desire as alien, animalistic, degrading, or inhuman set the stage for subsequent obscenity-related cases to vilify s/m text, no matter how much enjoyment was shown or how explicitly the consent was expressed.

Butler's Censoring Impact on Gay and Lesbian S/M Representation

R. v. Scythes (1993)

Six weeks after the *Butler* decision was released, Toronto Police successfully charged Glad Day Bookshop, a gay and lesbian bookstore, for selling obscenity. At issue was Trish Thomas's "Wunna My Fantasies," published in *Bad Attitude/s*. It is interesting to note in this case that, unlike in the *Butler* decision, Judge Paris did refer directly to s/m when setting out the background of the case, thereby linking the depicted erotic scenes with a sexual subculture. He described the magazine as "a series of articles where the writers fantasize about lesbian sexual encounters with a sadomasochistic theme" (*R. v. Scythes* 1993, para. 2). Yet when it came to assessing the content of the crucial story, he reduced the erotic dynamics to the descriptor "combining sex with violence."

This made it easier to translate the *Butler* decision's condemnation of "violent" or "degrading" pornography as applicable to the short story. Adopting the language of *Butler*, the trial court alleged that the story was obscene because it harboured a "potential for harm." The nature of the harm that might flow from those written words was never articulated. Instead the court provided a summary of the story that was meant to convey the self-evidence of its danger: "This material flashes every light and blows every whistle of obscenity. Enjoyable sex after subordination by bondage and physical abuse at the hands of a total stranger" (*R. v. Scythes* 1993, para. 9).[5] Implicit in this description is a condemnation of the fantasy of sexual pleasure derived from power play, props, pain, and/or stranger-sex.

This denouncement further reflects the anti-s/m feminist truth-claim that erotic fantasy is (selectively) prescriptive. Justice Paris is convinced that the fantasy of power play sexuality with a stranger will somehow license the reader to enact this scene in real life. Yet again, the inconsistency in this literalist interpretation is that the consent and enjoyment of the submissive player portrayed in the s/m short story apparently is not treated as similarly prescriptive. Justice Paris does not contemplate that the text might prevail upon the reader to ensure mutual pleasure when replicating the pornographic scene with a partner.

However, unlike LEAF and the *Butler* decision, Justice Paris cannot claim that female s/m sexual desires are inherently "false," as a woman had written the impugned story for a female audience. At issue here was not that the pornographic representation had distorted female sexuality, but that this form of female sexuality was inherently dangerous and harmful. As Cossman and Bell pointed out, what was put on trial were "'Bad Attitudes': the attitudes of the sexual others" (1997, 4). Lesbian sadomasochists have a bad attitude towards sexuality and must not be encouraged to fantasize about their desires. This of course reflects the stance taken during the sex wars by the anti-s/m feminist side, which grudgingly acknowledged the existence of lesbian s/m desire, but vehemently condemned its expression. Hence Justice Paris's finding of obscenity seems to reflect MacKinnon's understanding of female masochism as an unfortunate and unhealthy effect of social conditioning that should be legally suppressed.

Glad Day Bookshop v. Canada (1992)

Another case that dealt with obscenity charges in relation to sexual minorities and s/m came out shortly after the *Butler* decision and again involved Glad Day Bookshop, this time in the context of customs control. In *Glad Day Bookshop v. Canada*, Glad Day appealed a decision of the deputy minister of national revenue for customs and excise that labelled as obscene certain gay male erotic books and magazines headed to the store (*Glad Day Bookshop v. Deputy Minister of National Revenue* 1992). The appeal was dismissed. In the decision, the court again used *Butler*'s essentialist view of human sexuality, and accordingly the assumptions of anti-pornography feminism, to portray s/m sexuality as inherently harmful in the gay male context.

At the end of his reasoning, Justice Hayes provides a terse description of each confiscated text and decrees that all are "harmful" and legitimately classified as obscene. The sexuality depicted covered a wide array of sexual acts. Of the s/m variety, Justice Hayes found that depictions of "bondage, sex with pain and forced violent sexual activity" should be stopped at the border (*Glad Day Bookshop v. Deputy Minister of National Revenue* 1992, para. 83). He explains, "The material does not have any real human dimension. Harm is depicted and clearly harm would flow from the release of the material" (para. 83). In this analysis, human sexuality is again essentialized such that it precludes s/m desire. And, as in LEAF's descriptions of pornography, the reader is not informed if the "forced violent sexual activity" is portrayed as enjoyable, consensual, or within the context of a negotiated s/m scene. From the perspective of the court, the activity is self-evidently harmful, and the representation of the subjective experience of the participants in the magazines is tacitly deemed irrelevant.

Justice Hayes also deploys the labels of "degrading" and "dehumanizing" to condemn non-normative sexual practices as harmful. He states, "Explicit descriptions of consensual oral and anal sex" are degrading and thereby legally obscene, despite conceding that in the indicted magazine "there is no description of violence" (*Glad Day Bookshop v. Deputy Minister of National Revenue* 1992, para. 74). He further states that the depiction of "urination for sexual arousal" and "ejaculation on the face" lead to a "strong inference of harm" that the community would not tolerate (para. 97). As with the feminist anti-pornography censure of fellatio, anal play, and urine play, there is no elaboration of what harm flows from these activities. The judgment relies on an implicit disgust with the scenes. Furthermore, Justice Hayes assumes that the partner who receives another's urine or semen should feel degraded and that this degradation is necessarily bad and unwanted. Agency and the taboo pleasure of bathing in abject fluid are accordingly denied to the submissive partner in such sexual scenarios.

The defence attempted to complicate the literalist and essentialist interpretation of the depicted sexual scenes by calling on Barry Adams, a professor of sociology. Adams's expert opinion was that s/m text is a form of "sexual theatre" (*Glad Day Bookshop v. Deputy Minister of National Revenue* 1992, para. 50). He further testified that in the sadomasochist text on trial, it was clear that the story catered to consumers who enjoyed and sympathized with the "subordinate" position in the sadomasochist coupling. Adams's attempt to draw a distinction between misogynist pornography that calls for identification with a male aggressor, and gay s/m pornography that calls for identification with a male submissive, was, however, completely unintelligible to the court and thus discounted.

R. v. Erotica Video Exchange Ltd (1994)

Two years after this decision, same-sex s/m erotica was again put on trial in *R. v. Erotica Video Exchange Ltd* (1994). In this decision, the judiciary was confronted with the fact that the consent was not just implied but explicitly articulated. Nonetheless, the court ignored the subjective experience of the characters in the pornographic film to reach a finding of obscenity: "The overall theme is that the housekeeper or servant is acting according to the instructions or orders from her master, thus according to Dr Check [a Crown witness], colouring or negating any apparent aura of consent to the sexual activity ... While the housekeeper is asked whether she likes these things [s/m activities] and responds in the affirmative, Check says that this must be viewed in light of the master/servant theme of the movie. Check's opinion is that this scene falls clearly within the category of the sexually violent" (para. 10). Here the court relied upon an "expert witness" who had no expertise in the semiotics of lesbian text, let alone the semiotics of lesbian s/m text. Instead, the witness was an associate professor in the Department of Psychology at York University who had testified for the prosecution in cases of obscenity. His gaze clearly mirrored that of anti-s/m feminism, since he regarded the stated intentions of the characters in s/m scenes as insignificant. From his perspective, the "housekeeper's" consent and demonstrated enjoyment are unpersuasive because the "master/servant" fictional roles would compromise any meaningful consent. He reads *against* the grain of the lesbian s/m film by imposing a literalist lens to interpret the erotica. The fantasy of a "master/servant" relationship is grafted onto a literal master/servant relationship with all of the accompanying dynamics of unequal power.

And the court was persuaded. Justice James states, "With respect to 'Lesbians Bondage and Black Jack,' I am also satisfied beyond a reasonable doubt that the visitation of various sado-masochistic practices upon the servant constitutes the combination of sex and cruelty or violence, and is obscene within the meaning of Section 163(8)" (*R. v. Erotica Video Exchange Ltd* 1994, para. 36). Notice that the court interprets "sado-masochistic practices" as something that is imposed *upon* the "servant." Like anti-s/m feminism, the court sees the masochism in sadomasochism as an empty signifier. By ignoring the mutual and complementary fulfilment depicted in the s/m scene, the court refuses to acknowledge the pleasure or agency of the submissive partner.

Little Sisters Book & Art Emporium v. Canada (1996; 2000; 2007)

The three cases discussed above (*Scythes*, *Glad Day*, and *Erotica*) all took place in the early 1990s. But the saga of gay and lesbian bookstore Little

Sisters and its struggle against the censorship effects of the *Canada Customs Act*, which continues well into the twenty-first century, indicates that the intersection of homophobia and s/m aversion in freedom of expression cases is still a live issue. Interestingly, in the first *Little Sisters* trial decision, s/m representation was regarded as complex and worthy of protection, while the two Supreme Court of Canada decisions on Little Sisters' struggle against censorship have either conflated s/m with degradation or dismissed the freedom of expression interests at stake.

Let us begin with the positive inroads that were made in the trial decision, particularly in the artistic merit of s/m texts. At the court of first instance, Justice Smith found that a sadomasochist writer, as well as experts in the fields of literary interpretation, semiotics, and queer culture, offered valuable insights that assisted the court in understanding s/m representation as a cultural, creative, and political project (*Little Sisters v. Canada* 1996).

The court cited Bart Testa, an expert in semiotics and signs, who explained that a proper determination of obscenity would be compromised without an understanding of the "mixed messages" and "mixed codes" in s/m text (*Little Sisters v. Canada* 1996, para. 161). The court also heard from Becki Ross, a notable sociologist who specialized in women's studies and who had co-authored *Bad Attitude/s*, which, as mentioned above, was critical of *Butler*'s essentialization of pornographic meaning. Ross's testimony strengthened Testa's assertion of the need to understand the context of the subcultures producing and representing s/m text (para. 230). She testified that lesbian sadomasochist material catered to lesbians familiar with its codes and conventions, and that such erotica validated lesbian sexuality.

In further identifying the complex task of applying the internal necessities test, which determines if the text has artistic merit, the court cited Nino Ricci, a prominent writer and professor of creative writing. Ricci testified that the evaluator should consider multiple criteria, including plot, character, structure, uses of language, themes, authorial intent, and context. The court tacitly agreed with Ricci's sophisticated hermeneutic approach to sexual representation and found that "the proper application of that [internal necessities] test, even to sadomasochistic representations, may redeem works that might seem obscene on first impression" (*Little Sisters v. Canada* 1996, para. 228).

Yet perhaps the most radical departure from previous judicial constructions of s/m was evidence taken from the autobiographical introduction to Patrick Califia's s/m book, *Macho Sluts* (1988b). Canada Customs had repeatedly prohibited this lesbian book of erotica, even after it was re-determined upon appeal to be admissible. The court cited a lengthy portion of the introduction in order to convey the importance of a nuanced application of the internal necessities test:

> "Liberty is the right not to lie." – Albert Camus
>
> The things that seem beautiful, inspiring, and life-affirming to me seem ugly, hateful, and ludicrous to most other people. This may be the most painful part of being a sadomasochist: this experience of radical difference, separation at the root of perception. Our culture insists on sexual uniformity and does not acknowledge any neutral differences – only crimes, sins, diseases, and mistakes ...
>
> What, then, are my choices, as a writer and a sadomasochist? I could keep my sexuality private, write about other issues, other sorts of people, and tell myself that these are more important themes, more universal characters, more valid as literature. That involves telling a lie by omission – becoming invisible as a pervert, assuming an undeserved mantle of normalcy and legitimacy. (*Little Sisters v. Canada* 1996, para. 229)

By allowing the s/m text to speak for itself, the Court *humanized* a sexual identity, in defiance of previous judicial constructions that could see the commingling of pleasure and pain as only a *dehumanizing* path to sexual fulfilment. And while the court shied away from considering pleasure or arousal as an interest that the law should protect, it did elaborate on the importance of Califia's words in light of freedom of expression: "Califia here expresses the importance of homosexual sado-masochist literature in furthering the principles and values that underlie freedom of expression as outlined in *Irwin Toy, supra*. She further expresses a dominant theme prevalent in homosexual art and literature, and one that was attested to by many of the plaintiffs' witnesses, that is, the need for self-affirmation and empowerment through expression" (para. 229). The court thus recognized the competence of sadomasochists to define the significance of their representations and desires.

Taking into account these interpretive approaches, the court found that "a society committed to the values underlying freedom of expression, as our society is, cannot defend the automatic prohibition of descriptions and depictions of homosexual sado-masochism" (*Little Sisters v. Canada* 1996, para. 231). The court thus acknowledged that in obscenity cases, there may be a need for witnesses with some competency in decoding the semiotics of a particular sexual subculture. This perspective directly conflicts with earlier judgments, such as the judgment in *Glad Day* (1992), where insider knowledge was deemed to be a distortion of the "true" meaning of the texts. The trial Court in *Little Sisters*, by allowing for a polysemic reading of the s/m text that privileged insider knowledge over majoritarian sensibilities, endeavoured to boldly go where no judge had gone before.

Unfortunately, the appellate decision of this case at the Supreme Court of Canada wiped out many of these epistemological gains. Without regard to the trial judge's affirmation that an s/m text can be coded in such a way that an uninformed reader can misinterpret its meaning and its merits, Justice Binnie stated, "Portrayal of a dominatrix engaged in the non-violent degradation of an ostensibly willing sex slave is no less dehumanizing if the victim happens to be of the same sex, and no less (and no more) harmful in its reassurance to the viewer that the victim finds such conduct both normal and pleasurable. Parliament's concern was with behavioural changes in the voyeur that are potentially harmful in ways or to an extent that the community is not prepared to tolerate" (*Little Sisters v. Canada* 2000, para. 60). In this account, the Supreme Court of Canada firmly placed the supposed community (i.e., what *the judges* determine to be the essential Canadian "community"), with its patent ignorance of s/m and queer culture, as the most qualified interpreter of the semiotics and effects of all sexual representation.

Hence, the Supreme Court of Canada vitiated two important interventions made by the trial decision. First, there was a disavowal of the possibility that insider knowledge or expertise might be needed to understand the internal semiotics of distinctively gay or lesbian s/m representation. As far as Justice Binnie was concerned, if the community viewed the sexual depiction as degrading, then it was inherently degrading. Second, there was a rejection of the notion that the consent and pleasure experienced by the "slave" in an s/m encounter should, at the very least, complicate one's assessment of the dynamics of the scene. Again, the law placed s/m within a sadistic paradigm where the emotional life of the masochist partner was rendered simply irrelevant or completely refuted. As Hoople has pointed out, "Critics of SM practice invariably direct their criticisms toward the SM tops, generally presuming that SM relations are inherently unequal because the top is perceived to have all of the power in the relationship ... and that this power is corruptive and tops are inevitably led (by the powerful sexual instinct or what have you) to abuse their partners" (1996, 203–4). Justice Binnie subtly erased the agency of the "slave" by characterizing her as being an "*ostensibly* willing" recipient to "degradation" (emphasis added). And as for the submissive partner's experience of s/m as "normal" and "pleasurable," this view is undercut by the belief that it is others who are attempting to "reassure" the justices, not the "slave" herself. Justice Binnie does not contemplate that the targeted audience of the pornographic text might be those who enjoy submissive sexual practices, who would then receive both pleasure and affirmation regarding their s/m proclivities. Instead, the consumer of the s/m pornography is overdetermined as sadistic or potentially sadistic. Again, the law adopts the perspective of anti-s/m feminism to construct the masochism in sadomasochism as an empty signifier at best, a red herring at worst. And by characterizing a scene between a dominatrix and her "slave" – a classic SM erotic role play – as "degrading" and "dehumanizing," the law once again engages in the dehumanization of a sexual other.

It should be noted that LEAF acted again as an intervener, but this time it offered a much more sex-positive feminist analysis of the *Customs Tariff* and the community standards test. LEAF submitted that the Canada Customs regime was inadequate to make proper determinations of obscenity, and that this had a discriminatory impact on sexual minorities (LEAF Factum *Little Sisters v. Canada* 2000). The factum specifically addresses the targeting of gay and lesbian s/m material by Canada Customs who, it was contended, misconstrued the internal necessities test by determining much of it obscene. Though LEAF seemed to approve the spirit of the *Butler* decision, it challenged its test for obscenity: "LEAF submits that the national community standard of tolerance test should be rejected. This test obscures the two inquiries required for an obscenity analysis, that is, whether the materials pose a substantial risk of harm and whether they have merit" (15–16). LEAF suggested that a community standards test of perceived harm unwittingly invoked morality-based considerations and was premised on a "majoritarian analysis," which was detrimental to sexual minorities and their cultural expressions.

The Supreme Court of Canada rejected this critique. Justice Binnie complained that such arguments "underestimate Butler" (*Little Sisters v. Canada* 2000, para. 56). He insisted that *Butler* properly put the focus on harm, and that the test "cannot reasonably be interpreted as seeking to suppress sexual expression in the gay and lesbian community in a discriminatory way" (para. 58). Such a claim has persuasive value on the abstract level. As Aleardo Zanghellini argues in his analysis of the relationship between *Butler* and *Little Sisters*, the censorship of queer pornography, particularly if it involves dominance and submission, can be justified on the grounds that it entrenches sexism, homophobia, and female or feminine subordination, and as a result can be cast as harmful in a comparable fashion to heterosexual pornography (2004). Yet from a legal realist perspective, the application of *Butler* seems to show that queer pornography registers as particularly harmful – and therefore obscene – to the censor's eye. Considering the evidence put forward by Little Sisters to demonstrate systemic bias by both Canada Customs and judicial decisions against gay and lesbian material, it may be the Supreme Court of Canada that underestimates (and underplays) the ways in which *Butler* has been used to justify homophobia and artistic oblivion when it comes to gay, lesbian, and queer s/m text.

Of course, as noted above, while the Supreme Court of Canada gave lip service to a concern of discrimination against gay and lesbian text, s/m was beyond the pale. Justice Binnie's final thoughts regarding the contention that s/m was not exploitive but emancipatory in the gay and lesbian context was met with more platitudes about "harm." He asserts that the test is "gender-neutral," and this feature apparently eradicates the significance of the context of both gay and lesbian sado-masochist codes and their unique meaning in a sexual minority culture. If the (imagined) "community" cannot decipher the code, but instead sees only violence when there is encoded mutuality and consent, and sees only "dirt" when there is unusual aesthetic purpose and craft, then the judges and Canada Customs officers are meant to follow this majoritarian misreading.

The Supreme Court of Canada did acknowledge that Canada Customs had wrongfully targeted gay and lesbian material and infringed upon the constitutional rights of Little Sisters and gays and lesbians. However, the majority determined that the problem did not lie with the wording of the Canada Customs legislation but with its application. As such, it upheld the *Customs Act* (with the exception of a reverse onus provision in s. 152(3)). The majority hesitatingly accepted that, during the course of the litigation, Canada Customs had revised its practices and procedures to ameliorate the systemic problems with the discriminatory application of the *Customs Act*.

Six years later, the Supreme Court of Canada was confronted with evidence that Canada Customs had continued targeting gay and lesbian material and Little Sisters Bookstore. In this second series of cases, the bookstore sought advance awards of legal costs to fund two proceedings: an appeal on a Canada Customs determination that four books were obscene, and a systemic review of Canada Customs" practices (*Little Sisters v. Canada* 2007). Little Sisters was successful in the court of first instance, but both the British Columbia Court of Appeal and a majority of the Supreme Court of Canada found that advance costs were not merited in the circumstances of the two proceedings. Justice Binnie, who had written the majority decision in *Little Sisters 1*, wrote an impassioned dissent.

In dismissing the public importance of the issues, the Supreme Court of Canada marginalized the liberty interests at stake. The majority judgment declared that "the Four Books Appeal concerns no interest beyond that of the appellant itself." Chief Justice McLachlin, who was joined by Justice Charron, wrote a concurring opinion which stated, "Is this one of those rare cases where justice demands that the questions raised be litigated? ... At stake is the prospect of not learning how Customs proceeded on the Four Books Appeal and, in the event it proceeded wrongly, not having a remedial order. In my view, the possible insight that may be gained into Customs' practices through the prosecution of this case and the limited remedy, while of interest to Little Sisters, do not rise to the level of compelling public importance or demonstrate systemic injustice" (*Little Sisters v. Canada* 2007, para. 109).

Why is it that the possible violation of a fundamental *Charter* right could be so narrowly construed and so easily dismissed? Freedom of expression is generally considered a core democratic value. I suggest that it was the nature of the four books that compelled the majority to belittle the alleged violation of freedom of expression and to reduce the interests at stake as belonging only to Little Sisters and not to sexual minorities, the broader public, or democratic values. The four books – made up of drawings and written stories – revolved around gay s/m themes: *Meatmen*, volume 18: Special SM Comics Edition; *Meatmen*, volume 24: Special SM Comics Edition; *Of Men, Ropes and Remembrance – The Stories from Bound & Gagged Magazine*; and *Of Slaves & Ropes & Lovers*. Perhaps the court was unsympathetic because the representation of s/m sexuality does not seem to be redeemed by evidence of artistic or literary merit from a conventional standpoint – comics are not considered high art, and pornographic writings are not considered literary. As such, the majority opinion and Chief Justice McLachlin have little interest in gaining "insight" into why Canada Customs branded these books obscene; they already register as obscene because of their form and s/m subject matter. By denying Little Sisters' application for advance costs, the Supreme Court of Canada effectively destroyed Little Sisters' ability to launch a systemic review of Canada Customs practices and required that it further strain its financial resources if it wanted to have the four books re-evaluated.

Yet today there are very few criminal cases that deem gay and lesbian s/m representation as obscene. For the most part, adult s/m sexuality – whether gay, lesbian, bisexual, or heterosexual – is generally not targeted by police or prosecutors. Where censorship does occur is in the bureaucratic realm of customs control. This is facilitated by the fact that customs officers are not required to set out reasons for their decisions to confiscate books, or to render any form of public judgment. Usually, the only people aware of this effective censorship are those working at bookstores, who figure it out when a particular shipment does not arrive. Challenging a determination of obscenity by a custom's officer is slow and costly. And the evidence that Little Sisters has provided (again and again) is that those who are disproportionately targeted are the gay and lesbian bookstores, who must bear the cost of the bureaucratic censorship that occurs at the intersection of homophobia and disgust with s/m.[6]

Too Nasty for the Law: Heterosexual S/M Gets Its Day in Court

While there does not appear to be equal opportunity censorship in the law – gay and lesbian s/m pornography is clearly targeted, particularly through the *Canada Customs Act* – it would be wrong to maintain that heterosexual s/m text has completely escaped scrutiny or punishment under the law. The following cases demonstrate that, on occasion, heterosexual s/m representation will also be interpreted as harmful to society and thus justifiably censored.

R. v. Emery (1991)

In the early 1990s Ontario case *R. v. Emery*, trial Justice Menzies found that rap music could be deemed obscene text (*R. v. Emery* 1991). At issue was a cassette tape, *As Nasty as They Wanna Be* by 2 Live Crew, which was judged obscene, not just because of s/m references, but also because of non-procreative sexual practices. Justice Menzies states that "a goodly portion, of the several songs on the cassette tape are replete

with references to female and male genitalia, human sexual excretions, oral-anal contact, fellatio, cunnilingus, group sex, specific sexual
positions, sadomasochism, the turgid state of the male sexual organ,
masturbation, forceful sexual intercourse and the sounds of moaning"
(para. 35). In finding that the songs are not redeemed by artistic merit,
Justice Menzies states, "The lyrics overall on the recording do not, in
any way, rise to the level of serious sociological or cultural comment.
Nor, in my view, can it reasonably be found that the violence, perversion, abuse of women, graphic depiction of the sexual acts and the mi-
croscopic description of human genitalia and its excretions rise, in any
way, to the form of comedy art. The '2 Live Crew' production of 'Nasty'
has one clear message: dirty sex for the sake of dirty sex" (para. 36).

This catalogue of "dirty sex" that the court denounces reveals the
extent to which the judge conflates violence and degradation with "perverse" sexuality where women are overdetermined as the victims. The
view that natural female sexuality is necessarily antithetical to "perversion" or s/m is revealed when the court states, "There is nothing of love
and tenderness on the Nasty tape but only a message of violent sex and
denigration of women" (*R. v. Emery* 1991, para. 35). Yet the court's
description of the lyrical content mostly does not reference force, but
merely non-procreative or kinky sexuality. As such, the court reflects
LEAF's investment in the hegemonic separation of the upper parts of
the body from the lower, condemning oral sex (even when the woman
is the recipient), urine play, and anal rimming as denigrating or violent.
The judgment also reinforces the hegemony of couple-centric sexuality,
as the representation of both group sex and masturbation are castigated
as obscene. Further, the mere explicitness of references to genitalia and
sexual positions apparently harbours some insidious danger to wom-
en. It is implied that female sexuality requires "love" and "tenderness,"
and the suggestion by the lyrics that women might enjoy "dirty sex"
is not just unthinkable, it is threatening to women. This notion that
women necessarily prefer an emotional connection recalls the ways
that anti-s/m feminism condemned lesbian s/m text because it replaced imagery of "nurturing and sisterly" relations between lesbians
with representations of "fucking," "violent sex," and "isolated and casual sexual encounters" (Lewis and Adler 1994, 435). Again the perspectives of law and anti-s/m feminism converge in the gendering of
women who should be interested in sexuality only in the context of
love and long-term relationships; any other portrayal is dehumanizing
to the woman. With this truth-claim embedded in the judicial gaze, or

more accurately, in the judicial ear, Justice Menzies had no trouble hearing obscenity in the rap music.

As in *Glad Day* (1992), the defence tried to offer an alternate account
of the meaning of the lyrics, calling upon Robert Bowman, a professor
of fine arts with expertise in ethnomusicology and in particular rap
music. Bowman situated rap music within the African-American historical context as a form of folk expression. Bowman testified that the
music at issue employed exaggerated and comical rhetorical devices
such as parody or caricature to express braggadocio or sexual boast-
ing that "no reasonable person would take at face value" (*R. v. Emery*
1991, para. 33). Unfortunately, the law did exactly that. Justice Menzies
rejected Bowman's expert opinion that attempted to outline a difference between parodic sexual exploits and literal sexual exploitation.
Instead, Justice Menzies presumed himself qualified to interpret the
meaning of the lyrics, which he understood to unilaterally promote
the dehumanization of women. The court thus took the position that
a community's own semantic codes and artistic culture would be disregarded if they came into conflict with the law's literalist (and hu-
mourless and quite possibly racist) interpretive lens. Although this
trial level decision came out a year before the Supreme Court of
Canada's decision in *Butler*, it was upheld on appeal using *Butler* as a
precedent (*R. v. Emery* 1992).

Loyalist College of Applied Arts & Technology
v. O.P.S.E.U., Local 420 (2004)

While expert witnesses who complicated the law's monolithic characterization of s/m as harmful were often disregarded, defendants who
attempted to portray their desires as benign were even more forcefully
rejected. A close examination of an arbitration case demonstrates this
point. In 2004, an Ontario Arbitration Board upheld the dismissal of a
college professor, in part because of his unapologetic stance on s/m
(*Loyalist v. O.P.S.E.U.* 2004). The professor (who remained anonymous)
had apparently visited and downloaded pornographic sites featuring
bondage, discipline, and s/m (BDSM) onto two computers provided
by the school. He had also downloaded a number of other non-work-
related sites and non-BDSM pornographic sites. The Board made it
clear, however, that "the only sites that are relevant to this decision are
the numerous videos and still images taken from College computers
assigned to the grievor that all fall within the category that the grievor

himself defines as BDSM" (para. 67). As such, the issue was not simple misuse of college equipment, but the misuse of college equipment for the purposes of visiting non-normative sexual sites. The college alleged that the imagery constituted obscenity and warranted disciplinary treatment.

In response, the professor attempted to outline his own interpretation of the BDSM imagery. He asserted that BDSM was a "lifestyle" and "that people participate voluntarily in the production of these [BDSM] sites" (*Loyalist v. O.P.S.E.U.* 2004, para. 25). In its majority judgment, the Board rejected the professor's portrayal of BDSM as a harmless sexual practice. Using the *Butler* precedent as its guide, the Board found that the images constituted obscenity because they combined "violence" and sex, and were "degrading" and "dehumanizing" to women. Not surprisingly, the Board flat-out rejected the professor's attempt to foreground consent as a mitigating or exculpatory factor in the assessment of harm. Citing Justice Sopinka's comments in *Butler* that the appearance of consent can be an aggravating, not a mitigating factor, the Board stated, "If the images are of consenting adults as the grievor tried to suggest, then the depicted acts are even more degrading and dehumanizing for all the participants" (para. 69).

Reinforcing the professor's culpability was the perception that he failed to share the Board's normative understanding of BDSM as harmful to society. The Board decried, "The grievor showed no appreciation for the impact of the nature of the images. There was no recognition of the violence or degradation that could be involved in the production and the dissemination of these images. Nor did he express any understanding that degrading and dehumanizing sexual treatment results in harm to society as a whole" (*Loyalist v. O.P.S.E.U.* 2004, para. 74).

The professor was censured for having the audacity to present an alternate perspective of BDSM sexuality. It did not matter that these sites had never been deemed obscene by a criminal court. It did not matter that the college had not instituted an "acceptable technology usage" policy. It did not matter that the professor had accessed these sites only in private. It did not matter that there was no evidence of a student accusing the professor of improper behaviour. What mattered was his association with and apologetics for BDSM, which rendered him an "inappropriate role model" to students. He became a "polluting person" (Douglas 2003, 140). The professor's sexual interest was deemed a danger to women, and his disavowal of this danger was a danger to students and to society as a whole.

The fact that this was not a criminal case about obscenity, but a labour grievance, demonstrates the wide influence that feminist anti-s/m truth-claims have had upon the judicial imaginary in Canada. The professor's own accounts of BDSM were dismissed as insidiously wrong. From the law's perspective, sadomasochists are not proper cartographers of their own desires. As Terry Hoople has pointed out, "The argument goes, SM practitioners' self-representations are not adequate because they are either under the control of a perverted and depraved desire, or they have internalized and thus merely express or 'replicate' patriarchal values; in either case their self-representations betray a sort of 'false consciousness,' or are symptomatic and thus do not represent the 'truth' about SM" (1996, 179). For the law, the people who are entitled to ascertain the inherent meanings and effects of s/m pornography are those in whom it elicits disgust, not desire.

S/M Subjectivity Slowly Coming into Focus
(at Least for Heterosexuals)

R. v. Price (2004)

Other recent cases, however, have shown a certain judicial tolerance towards s/m text, particularly if it is heterosexual. In the British Columbia case *R. v. Price*, the Canadian community is conceived as more tolerant than the dominant judicial construction of s/m would have us believe (*R. v. Price* 2004). The accused was criminally charged with producing and publishing a series of obscene videos featuring graphic BDSM imagery, collectively referred to as the Eleven Videos. Price conceded that the videos contained s/m images but argued that they were not obscene. To establish s/m as an accepted form of sexuality in the Canadian community, the defence presented as evidence BDSM images available on the Internet and fictional materials that portray sexualized violence available to the Canadian consumer. The defence further called upon two medical doctors, one consumer of Price's pornographic products, and one former police officer.

Charles Moser was a key witness whom the court recognized as an expert in BDSM. Recall that in chapter 1, I identified Moser as an oppositional voice in the medical field who, along with his colleague Peggy Kleinplatz, has advocated for the de-pathologization of s/m. In his testimony in *Price*, the doctor had an opportunity to convey his scientific perspective, explaining, "Pain and pleasure are closely associated factors

in the human sexual experience. Pain giving rise to sexual pleasure is a
normal sexual experience and is the basis of BDSM" (*R. v. Price* 2004,
para. 32). Moser delineates pain and pleasure as two roads that run close
together in the human psyche and says that for some people, the roads
converge. Most importantly, he qualifies this convergence as *normal*.

Moser's account of s/m recalls the earlier sexology texts, in particular Krafft-Ebing, Freud, and Havelock Ellis's understanding of the
spectrum of s/m pleasure. Krafft-Ebing, Freud, and Ellis all situated
"love bites," "wrestling," and "horseplay" as normal and mild forms of
s/m or algolagnic activity. Similarly, "Doctor Moser testified there are
many different levels of BDSM. For example, a person biting another
person on the neck during love play is an example of a low level of
s/m" (*R. v. Price* 2004, para. 33). The difference between the early sexologists and Moser is how they characterize the more "extreme" expressions of s/m desire. Krafft-Ebing understood such impulses as a
sign that the sexual instinct had trampled over the civilizing influences
of society. Freud made sense of sadism and masochism as exaggerations where the normal goal of procreative sexuality is supplanted by
the desire to inflict or receive pain. And Ellis's account of algolagnia, his
preferred terminology, understood such desires as a symptom of a hy-
po-sexual drive that taps into the raw energy of aggression and pain to
stimulate the libido. All three doctors therefore constructed the more
extreme manifestations of s/m activity as pathological behaviour. This
is where Moser differs. According to him, the extreme examples of
BDSM in the indicted Eleven Videos – that included images of whip-
pings on naked flesh, the application of hot wax on sensitive body
parts, electric shocks to genital areas, and skin piercings on classic erogenous zones – were all part of the same continuum of s/m desire, and
were "normal and appropriate sexual behaviour," providing that all
parties involved had given their consent (para. 34). Moser thus normal-
ized these hardcore examples by positioning consent as the crux to any
healthy sexual encounter.

This privileging of consent challenges both *Butler* and the anti-s/m
feminist dismissal of consent's normative significance in s/m encounters. In Moser's expert opinion, BDSM practitioners, particularly the
submissive partners, are endowed with human agency and the ability
to choose their sexuality. Further, his explanation that BDSM practitioners would not enjoy a scene if they understood the submissive sexual partner to be sincerely protesting the activity charts a completely

different trajectory of pleasure for the consumer of BDSM pornography. Moser detaches and distinguishes s/m from literal sadism.[7] From Moser's perspective, true sadism is not compatible with BDSM because sadism is premised on the violation of another's will, while the BDSM subculture is based on a *shared* fantasy of dominance and submission.

Another medical expert witness, Dr Fisher, also assisted the defence in taking the position that BDSM pornography was not inherently harmful. Fisher testified that there was substantial scientific evidence that watching violent pornography, which included portrayals of unwilling victims, was not associated with rising rates of sexual crime. He explained that one indication was that while the Internet has provided complete access to every type of sexual material, including violent pornography, neither Statistics Canada nor the FBI had disclosed any increase in reported sexual assaults since the advent of pornographic websites. In his conclusion, Fisher systematically refuted every "common sense" claim made by the *Butler* decision on the effects of violent or degrading and dehumanizing pornography. In his expert opinion, "Exposure to diverse forms of pornography does not a) cause attitudinal harm; b) cause anti-social attitudes towards men and women; c) cause harm to Canadian Society in that it does not cause sexual aggression; d) cause people to act in an anti-social manner; e) cause the mental or physical mistreatment of women or men" (*R. v. Price* 2004, para. 51). Although Justice Low concluded that Fisher's evidence did not help him to dispose of the charges at issue, he did find his opinion reliable. In this sense, Justice Low appears to have rejected the "reasonable" suppositions of *R. v. Butler* (1992), upon which the constitutional validity of the *Criminal Code*'s section on obscenity is ostensibly premised.[8]

While Moser and Fisher provided scientific alibis for the innocuousness of the Eleven Videos, Mr MacDonald, a private detective and thirty-year veteran police officer, provided street-credibility to the project of normalizing s/m. On the instructions of defence counsel, MacDonald attended a number of BDSM events in Vancouver and Victoria, British Columbia. According to the detective's testimony, the patrons of these events demonstrated "exemplary" behaviour (ibid., para. 29). Furthermore, in attendance at these gatherings were "a significant number of people from a wide cross section of society involved in BDSM." After his investigation, the detective concluded that BDSM "was now socially acceptable" (*R. v. Price* 2004, para. 37). Though the court did not technically recognize MacDonald as an expert witness,

Justice Low gave a "reasonable amount of weight to his opinion" because of his law enforcement background (para. 38). Hence, MacDonald's testimony also helped to resignify s/m by demystifying sadomasochists; no longer regarded as a sexual outlaw, the sadomasochist subject was firmly placed within the constituency of society.

Perhaps the most humanizing evidence came from Sylvia Schneider, a self-identified practitioner of BDSM. In the decision, she is described as a "thirty-year-old hobby farmer from the lower mainland of B.C." (*R. v. Price* 2004, para. 30). The court also noted that she had a teenage daughter who apparently was aware of her mother's involvement in the BDSM community. According to her testimony, Schneider enthusiastically participated in BDSM activities, including ones similar to those depicted in the Eleven Videos. Though Justice Low never fully articulated what impact Schneider's testimony had on his decision, he did observe, "Ms Schneider impressed me as an intelligent, well-spoken and thoughtful person" (para. 30). This simple statement effectively rewrote the hegemonic script of the female sexual subject. In *Butler* and in the LEAF factum for *Butler*, a woman who enjoyed kinky sexuality that involved power play sexuality simply did not exist. Yet according to Justice Low, she was not a figment of the patriarchy's imagination. Indeed, he recast her within the hegemonic terms of citizenship by identifying her as a parent with a job.

Layered upon these expert opinions that attempt to discern the truth of BDSM, the court itself explicitly speaks sex when describing the content of the videos. Over one thousand words of the decision are dedicated to graphically describing the sexual activities portrayed in the videos, allowing for vicarious access to the kinky pornography. An interesting detail that the court returns to again and again is the explicitness of the genitalia. The court finds that in ten of the indicted videos, "the subservient party is totally naked for the majority of the video. The genitalia, anus and all other private areas of the subservient parties' bodies are closely, fully, and graphically displayed. The genitalia are either clean or nearly clean shaven" (*R. v. Price* 2004, para. 60). The explicitness of the genitalia was apparently a point the Crown attempted to emphasize in differentiating the indicted videos from other BDSM images available on the Internet and from fictional materials that portray sexualized violence. From the Crown's perspective, this explicitness rendered the indicted videos obscene.

The Crown's assertion that the truth of the status of the videos can be found in the conspicuous depiction of genitals ironically reflects a pornographic epistemology. In *Hard Core: Power, Pleasure, and the "Frenzy of the Visible,"* Williams notes that a central component to the pornographic project is "to register the previously invisible hard-core 'truth' of bodies and pleasures in a direct and unmediated fashion" (1999, 30). The Crown too is focused on probing the sexual truth of the videos, and, as with pornography, the truth lies in the explicitness and the exposure of the genitalia. It is a call to return to the pre-*Butler* days, when explicitness itself was an indication of the obscenity of an image. The Crown's investment in this position is revealed when the court notes that the fictional materials that the defence adduced as evidence were more violent but less sexually explicit. In the formula that the *Butler* decision laid down, that sex plus violence will usually equal obscenity, the Crown seems to take the position that the explicitness of the sex carries more weight than the violence when measuring the obscenity of a text.

Another difference presented by the Crown between the fictional materials and the Eleven Videos was that the former supposedly had a plot, while the latter did not. An interesting contradiction occurs in the judgment when the court adjudicates the issue of plot in the indicted videos. When describing the contents of one of the videos, the court states, "*The plot* of Rage is simple and brutal" (*R. v. Price* 2004, para. 58). Yet later, the court states, "I agree with the Crown that the Eleven Videos are devoid of any artistic or literary purpose. There is *no plot*" (para. 84). Finally, the court seems to arrive at a halfway point between plot or no plot, stating, when comparing violent fictional films to the indicted videos, "I accept that the films I Spit On Your Grave, Rape Me, Irreversible, American Psycho and Henry Portrait of a Serial Killer (the Fictional Material) have *a more sophisticated plot* than the Eleven Videos" (para. 95; emphasis added). These three somewhat conflicting assessments of the indicted videos demonstrate the indeterminacy and subjectivity involved in attempting to decide whether something does or does not portray an authentic plot.

E.M. Forster's definition of plot and its differentiation from story provides a clue to why the court struggled with the narratives contained in the Eleven Videos. Forster dissects the novel into its component parts: "We have defined a story as a narrative of events arranged in their time-sequence. A plot is also a narrative of events, the emphasis falling on causality ... a plot demands intelligence and memory" (1927, 130–1). Taking this definition as a starting point, it seems that when recognizing a "plot" in a pornographic text, there is an implication that "intelligence" must have been involved in the creation. But in the socio-legal imaginary, plots stimulate the mind, while pornography "appeals only to the most base aspect of individual fulfilment" (*R. v. Butler* 1992, para. 125), "that of physical arousal" (para. 100). The court's final conclusion in *Price* that the fictional materials have "a more sophisticated plot" than the Eleven Videos still implies acknowledgment that the indicted videos have some kind of plot, as flimsy as it may be. There is a slight move towards reconciling the splits of mind/body and plot/pornography that have dominated the socio-legal imaginary.

Ultimately, Justice Low acquitted Price of all counts, based on the opinions of Moser and MacDonald, evidence concerning the wide availability of BDSM material on the Internet, and a comparison of sexual violence contained in the Eleven Videos and the sexual violence contained in readily available fictional material. He found that, taken together, this information gave rise to a reasonable doubt as to whether the Canadian community would not tolerate other Canadians viewing the Eleven Videos on the basis that harm would ensue. This case was not appealed.

The decision stands out not only because s/m is conceived of as normal human sexual behaviour, but also because of the ways BDSM practitioners are folded into Canadian society. MacDonald attests to the diverse make-up of BDSM practitioners. Schneider is situated geographically as a citizen of British Columbia. And even the modest finding that the community might tolerate BDSM pornography subtly brings BDSM practitioners closer to being embedded in that space of belonging. This is a radical reordering of the territorial boundaries that have characterized judicial mappings of sexuality. Instead of the immutable boundary set up between sadomasochist and normative terrain, the court blurs these two landscapes, creating a more inclusive environment for diverse sexualities to become intelligible and acceptable.

R. c. Latreille (2004; 2006; 2007)

Another more recent decision, from Quebec, reflects a tolerant judicial stance towards s/m imagery. In the 2004 case *R. c. Latreille*, the accused was initially convicted for producing obscenity because of five personal pictures he had attempted to develop that depicted s/m activities including bondage, the pinching of nipples and the vagina, and marks on the body that suggested the model had been whipped. At trial, the court rejected the testimony of the defence expert witnesses, Marc Ravor, a doctor of psychology with a master's degree in sexology, and

Yves Bédard, the coordinator of film classification for the Régie du cinéma du Québec, who both maintained that the Canadian community would tolerate the images. The decision declared that the photographs "montrent une femme d'une façon dégradante et déshumanisante et en ce sens, elles constituent un matériel nocif pour la société, notamment pour les femmes" (*R. c. Latreille* 2006, para. 136).[9] The decision was upheld in Superior Court (*R. c. Latreille* 2006). The accused appealed again and was successful in the Quebec Court of Appeal (*R. c. Latreille* 2007). In finding for the appellant, it is interesting to note that the court chose not to delve into whether the s/m imagery was dehumanizing or degrading. Instead, the short written judgment found that the photographs depicted nothing more than consensual s/m activity, which the court maintained was not criminal in and of itself. As such, the images did not go beyond the tolerance of the Canadian community nor interfere with the proper functioning of society.

This case reflects the gains for sexual liberation made when the Supreme Court of Canada released its indecency decisions of *R. v. Labeye* (2005) and *R. v. Kouri* (2005), which were mentioned in the *Latreille* judgment quashing the conviction. In *Labeye*, the Supreme Court of Canada subtly and unofficially overrode *Butler*'s community standards test, replacing it with a more objective harms-based test when suspect sexual practices are at issue. The Supreme Court of Canada stated that the alleged harm must "[threaten] the basic functioning of our society" (*R. v. Labeye* 2005, para. 56), which requires a much higher standard of proof than a judge's perception of what the "Canadian community" would tolerate. *R. v. Kouri* (2005) affirmed this approach. The Quebec Court of Appeal's use of the *Labeye* and *Kouri* cases thereby indicates that s/m representation might be given a more lenient treatment in future obscenity cases.

Conclusion

A survey of the obscenity cases in Canada when s/m imagery is on trial reveals that *Butler* and the cases that came soon after adopted a feminist anti-s/m perspective, where s/m was conflated with violence and dehumanization, and women were overdetermined as the victims. These constructed female victims, consisting both of the porn stars involved in the representation and/or hypothetical women who would be abused by men inspired by the s/m pornography, were construed as inherently non-kinky and sexually moderate creatures, interested primarily in "meaningful" sexual contact (i.e., sex in the context of a relationship). Consent was given short shrift on this gendered approach, as judges seemed unable or unwilling to believe that a woman would consent to and enjoy certain forms of sexuality that included not just force and bondage, but fellatio, anal-oral contact, and multiple-partner or multiple-orifice sex.

Perhaps not surprisingly, gay and lesbian s/m representation was deemed particularly objectionable to the legal and border-control gaze. And while the recent Supreme Court of Canada decisions on indecency seem to have provided some reprieve for heterosexual s/m representation, its decision in the *Little Sisters 2* advance costs litigation shows that the freedom of expression for gays and lesbians interested in s/m has not yet attained the status of a pressing public interest.

There are many reasons why censorship by Canada Customs of gay and lesbian s/m representation might be tolerated. The process is administrative and so may appear less punitive. Or the Supreme Court of Canada may be concerned about the cost of the conflict on the public purse, hoping that any issues of discrimination will eventually peter out as gays and lesbians gain further acceptability in Canadian society. This "tolerated residuum"[10] of censorship can be attributed, at least in part, to the double-abjection of same-sex s/m sexuality. As with cinematic representations of s/m, only heterosexual s/m sexuality has gained some increasing acceptability when positioned within a marital/monogamous framework. The few representations of gay s/m in the mainstream portray dangerous sexual excess that not only breaches the boundaries of compulsory coupledom, but ultimately leads to homicidal tendencies. Perhaps the inroads gays and lesbians have made within Canadian society, such as accessing the right to marry, have been contingent upon containing their sexuality within a recognizable relationship (i.e., dyadic, monogamous, and long-term). As Judith Butler writes, "Those who live outside the conjugal frame or maintain modes of social organization for sexuality that are neither monogamous nor quasi-marital are more and more considered unreal, and their loves and losses less than 'true' loves and 'true' losses" (2004, 26–7). The Supreme Court's trivialization of the rights and dignity at stake in both *Little Sisters* decisions perpetuates the violence Butler describes, as the loss of freedom of expression for gay and lesbians is rendered untrue and unreal.

5

The Legal Fondling of S/M Practice

This chapter continues focusing on the law to analyse the legal discourse of s/m practice in a variety of contexts. S/m practice on its own, of course, is not illegal in Canada, but it is criminalized or stigmatized in a variety of legal forums. It tends to come in front of the court when something goes wrong, when there is a complaint, or when it is attached to other stigmatized or unlawful behaviour, such as prostitution, or other legal matters, such as child custody. While the case law often condemns s/m as violent, pathological, and/or harmful, there is also a small amount of case law that takes a more tolerant stance.

The first section takes a brief journey to England to examine a trilogy of cases where the criminality of s/m seemed to hinge, in part, on the sexual orientation and marital status of those accused. The second section returns to Canadian case law, beginning with cases where medical experts provide clinical assessments to determine whether the erotic tastes of the accused stray into the realm of s/m. The third section examines criminal proceedings where an accused charged with assault claims consensual s/m activity as a defence or mitigating factor, as recently occurred in the 2011 Supreme Court of Canada case, *R. v. J.A.* The fourth section focuses exclusively on the "bondage-bungalow" case, where a professional female dominant in Toronto was convicted using the bawdy-house laws of the *Criminal Code*. The final section considers the regulation of s/m beyond the criminal context. Addressing the impact of s/m practice on child custody, I examine one Canadian and one American case where a woman's access to her children was denied or curtailed, in part because of her s/m interests and practices. The final three cases I analyse reverse course and dramatize s/m practitioners appropriating the law for their own interests, instead of being subjected to legal prosecution.

A Trilogy of British Cases on S/M

Before I examine how s/m practice fares in Canadian courts, it is worth exploring three British cases on s/m, the most important being the House of Lords decision, *R. v. Brown* (1993). This internationally known case has been cited with approval in Canada and sets up a discursive terrain that lays out many recurrent truth-claims and strategies used by anti-s/m jurisprudence. Notably, *Brown* showcases the explicit use of disgust in legal argument to condemn s/m. An examination of two subsequent British cases, *R. v. Wilson* (1996) and *R. v. Emmett* (1999), which respectively distinguished and followed *Brown*, reveals the extent to which sexual orientation and marital status can have an impact on judicial tolerance of s/m practices.

R. v. Brown (1993)

In *Brown*, five House of Lords judges were called upon to review the indictment of fifteen men convicted of assault occasioning actual bodily harm, and three convicted of wounding. The incidents that gave rise to these prosecutions were in the context of consensual same-sex s/m activity. None of the participants ever complained to the police. In order to justify a prosecution, the rhetoric focused on a purported harm to a reified "public interest" (much like the reified Canadian community in *Butler*), and a presumed corruption harm to the submissives who, it was implied, were too naive to recognize their own exploitation.

The case started in 1987 when the Obscene Publications Squad, a special unit in the British police, came upon a homemade video that portrayed same-sex s/m activities. The police claimed later – after a protracted and costly investigation – that they believed the submissives were not consenting, and that they had not merely seized evidence of violent assault, but had in their possession genuine *snuff* films. A murder investigation was initiated, which was dubbed "Operation Spanner." After interviewing hundreds of people, after digging up a private garden in search of corpses, after months and millions of pounds spent, the police learned that none of the men in the video had been murdered, none of them had suffered injuries requiring medical attention, and all had been willing participants.

This did not deter the police from eventually laying charges against sixteen men with various assault-related offences.[1] In 1990, the trial Judge concluded that consent was not an eligible defence to the crimes before him. Under direction from their counsel, the sixteen defendants pleaded guilty with mitigating pleas (*R. v. Brown* 1990). Their sentences ranged from fines to full imprisonment for four years and six months. Six defendants appealed both the convictions and the sentencing. Two years later, Lord Lane of the High Court upheld the convictions but reduced the sentences, so that the prison terms ranged from three months to three years (*R. v. Brown* 1992). However, he ended his decision with a firm caveat that if the accused were ever indicted for s/m activity again, they would suffer much harsher sentences (as if a three-year sentence were lenient!) (560). In 1993, the case was appealed to the House of Lords. The convictions and the sentences were upheld in a three-to-two decision (*R. v. Brown* 1993). Four years later, the European Court of Human Rights affirmed this British decision, stating that a state is entitled to regulate private activity when issues of health, safety, and morality are involved (*Laskey, Jaggard and Brown v. United Kingdom* 1997).

My analysis will focus upon the House of Lords decision to showcase tensions in the rhetoric that constitute s/m as an ambivalent and contradictory site that is both abhorrent and attractive. The surface current that runs throughout the majority and dissenting judgments assumes a consensus that s/m, and in particular homosexual s/m, is repulsive. Yet tugging against this judgment is a rhetorical undercurrent where s/m is revealed to be dangerously enticing; beneath the disgust simmers a discernible concern that if the practice went unregulated, then people, in particular younger men, would be tempted by its implied pleasures. This concern reflects the cinematic gaze that views s/m as both thrilling and destructive. And as with the *Butler* decision and the LEAF factum, s/m comes to represent sexuality run rampant. In *Brown*, the threat embedded in s/m revolves around a series of invested, overdetermined, and hierarchal dichotomies: the perverse versus the normal, the pervert (the dominant) versus the victim (the submissive), civilized versus depraved, homosexual versus heterosexual, corrupt man versus innocent boy, and the manly versus the unmanly.[2] In the judgment, s/m constitutes a threat to the boundaries separating these polarities, and as such, s/m is *abjectified*. It tampers with categorical separations, polluting the exalted with the base. As Douglas explains, "Our pollution behaviour is the reaction which condemns any object or idea likely to confuse or contradict cherished classifications" (2003, 45). The judgment then is a form of pollution management, which attempts to repair the cherished cultural dichotomies by articulating disgust and expelling the transgressors, justified through an essentialization of human sexuality, and a purported concern over public health and safety.

In the three-to-two split decision, there is one thing that all of the judges agreed upon: that the s/m practitioners are bad (though not necessarily criminal) and should evoke disgust in the observer. For the majority, Lord Templeman decries, "Pleasure derived from the infliction of pain is an evil thing. Cruelty is uncivilized" (*R. v. Brown* 1993, 52). This indictment recalls Krafft-Ebing's conception of European society as "civilized" and thus less prone to sadistic or masochistic desires as those "other" savage nations. Lord Jauncey joined his colleague's condemnation by declaring that the pleasure derived by the dominant partner amounts to "the gratification of … perverted desires" (67). Lord Lowry, the third judge who dismissed the appeal, returns to the inflammatory, almost biblical language: "For one person to inflict any injury on another without good reason is evil in itself" (63). Later in the judgment, he pathologizes s/m as reflecting "a perverted and depraved sexual desire" (67). The majority thus determines that such "evil," "uncivilized," and "perverted" activities do not attract legal rights.

In contrast to this interpretation, the dissent does indeed find that the appellants' activities engage legal rights, although they define the triggered right as one of privacy. Yet the dissenting judges are just as invested, if not even more so, in construing the s/m practitioners as morally and aesthetically objectionable. Their dissent is based upon the legality, but not the acceptability, of s/m activity. Lord Mustill states, "Fortunately for the reader my Lords have not gone on to describe other aspects of the appellants' behaviour of a similar but more extreme kind … It is sufficient to say that whatever the outsider might feel about the subject-matter of the prosecutions – perhaps horror, amazement or incomprehension, perhaps sadness – very few could read even a summary of the other activities without disgust" (*R. v. Brown* 1993, 68). In the first sentence, Lord Mustill has already hailed the reader as a nonsadomasochist, who has "fortunately" been spared details of the extreme activities. In the next sentence the reader is again presumptively an "outsider" to the world of s/m who necessarily must view the scene pejoratively, and most likely with disgust. Throughout the rest of the judgment, he imagines the public as a monolithic community that would find the activities "worthy of censure" (69) and "repulsively wrong" (82). The second dissenting judge, Lord Slynn, also feels compelled to erect the boundary between the normal individual and the pervert. He reiterates Lord Mustill's sentiments in stating that further details of the activities of those accused must add to "one's feeling of revulsion and bewilderment" (84). Employing that universalizing pronoun "one," Lord Slynn simultaneously constitutes sadomasochists as no/one.

Towards the end of his judgment, Lord Mustill attempts to separate what is disgust-worthy from what is crime-worthy: "Leaving aside repugnance and moral objection, both of which are entirely natural but neither of which are in my opinion grounds upon which the court could properly create a new crime" (*R. v. Brown* 1993, 82). Lord Mustill appears compelled to naturalize visceral feelings of aversion and moral condemnation as a prelude to his legal stance that the activities are not criminal. Throughout his disgust rhetoric, he includes himself as part of the community of normal people who would naturally be revolted by same-sex s/m activities. It is as if, having dissented from the majority's view to criminalize the sexual behaviour, he risks becoming tainted by these sexual anomalies and cast into a suspicious shadow, unless he reassures the reader that he too feels repulsion at the thought of such predilections. Similarly, Lord Slynn wishes to clarify that exculpating the accused "in no way means that the acts done are approved or encouraged" (88). Lord Slynn and Lord Mustill thus display a heightened need to engage in pollution management because of the potential slippage between exonerating and endorsing the accused sadomasochists. As Miller has noted, "Disgust must be accompanied by ideas of a particular kind of danger, the danger inherent in pollution and contamination, the danger of defilement" (1997, 8). Sexual pollution appears especially powerful and can affix itself to anyone who allows a little moral leeway. Hence there is a need to reiterate how normal, how natural, and how justifiable it is to feel disgust when confronted with s/m activities. Though Lord Mustill and Lord Slynn stop short of outlawing the accuseds' behaviour, they morally outcast them from the public community. The lives, the humanity, the desires, and the feelings of gay sadomasochists do not fit within the hegemonic public framework. They become intelligible only as objects of disgust against which the community must define itself.

This expurgation of the sadomasochist from the public community generally focuses on the dominant player in the s/m encounter. Yet in the majority decision, the submissive too is erased as a person with active or acceptable sexual desires. The paradox of pleasure in pain is transformed into a straightforward contradiction that can be explained only through narratives of coercion, corruption, and deception. For example, two out of three majority judges insist on labelling the submissives as "victim."

Though the consent of the submissives was never disputed at the trial, Lord Templeman dismisses the submissives' consent as "dubious or worthless" (*R. v. Brown* 1993, 51). He later asserts, "The evidence disclosed that drink and drugs were employed to obtain consent and increase enthusiasm" (51). Lord Templeman accordingly stigmatizes s/m with an association to substance abuse, ignoring a consideration of how heterosexual and/or non-s/m courtship and seduction also often involves drinking or drugs.

The majority also dwells on the age differences between the dominants and the submissives, as if the younger age of the submissives would rationalize and at the same time cast doubt on their purported consent. Lord Templeman writes, "The appellants are middle-aged men. The victims were youths, some of whom were introduced to sadomasochism before they attained the age of 21" (*R. v. Brown* 1993, 51). By characterizing the submissives as victims and youth, despite the fact that they had passed the age of majority, Lord Templeman undermines their agency and their desires. By claiming that some may have dabbled in s/m before twenty-one, their current adult status is put into question. He insinuates that since some were corrupted as adolescents, their current decisions cannot hold legitimacy. Lord Lowry is also concerned with a supposed vulnerability of younger men: "As the evidence in the present case has shown, there is a risk that strangers (and especially young strangers) may be drawn into these activities at an early age and will then become established in them for life" (83). These hypothetical "young strangers" are constructed as "normal," i.e., non-kinky, men who get irrevocably corrupted by s/m through some form of sexual chicanery. This erasure and negation of consent recalls the anti-s/m feminist treatment of consent among lesbian sadomasochists, where a submissive's consent was construed as essentially meaningless, not because of drinking or age, but because of the context of patriarchal indoctrination. In both cases, the pleasure and agency of the submissive is disavowed.

In *Brown*, homophobia intersects with the erasure of submissive agency when both Lord Templeman and Lord Jauncey cite the same passage from Lord Lane of the Court of Appeal, who gave thanks that not all the young submissives had become irrevocably perverse. Lord Lane states that the appellants Cadman and Laskey "were responsible in part for the corruption of a youth 'K.' It is some comfort at least to be told, as we were, that 'K' now seems to be settled into a normal heterosexual relationship" (*R. v. Brown* 1993, 51). In this statement, not only does K's agency as a submissive become inconceivable, so does K's potentially multivalent sexuality. In other words, the notion that he could straddle the abject border between homosexual and heterosexual as a bisexual man is unthinkable. The judges apply a linear paradigm that fixates exclusively on K's current heterosexual practices and take comfort in the fact that he escaped the allure of perversity. The submissives are thus construed as passive, naive, duped, and potentially warped by their contact with older gay men. The judges refuse to see them as desiring subjects; instead they are infantilized. The law is cast as defender of this weak and easily corrupted bunch. The paternalism recalls the foundational British precedent on obscenity in *R. v. Hicklin* (1868) where Lord Cockburn stated, "The test of obscenity is … whether the tendency of the matter charged as obscenity is to deprave and corrupt those whose minds are open to such immoral influences" (*R. v. Hicklin* 1868, 371). Though the cases are separated by well over a century, the primary concern remains the same: protect the weak-minded from succumbing to an "evil" and "uncivilized" sexuality, i.e., one that defies the hetero-normative, monogamous, procreative paradigm.

Yet the very susceptibility of young men to become corrupted by others points to a tension in the judgment. Despite the judges' reiterative claim that s/m is unnatural and disgusting, the rhetoric conveys an underlying anxiety that s/m has an insidious allure. Lord Templeman states, "The victim was usually manacled so that the sadist could enjoy the thrill of power and the victim could enjoy the thrill of helplessness" (*R. v. Brown* 1993, 51). Here he concedes that the sexual act is thrilling for both the dominant and the submissive, yet insists on branding the submissive a "victim" in an effort to render the submissive's sexual pleasure legally irrelevant. Lord Jauncey warns, "The possibility of proselytisation and corruption of young men is a real danger" (59). The judge is particularly concerned about this possibility because the appellants filmed some of their sexual acts. Yet if the sexual acts are so disgusting and so unnatural, why are the judges concerned that young men will succumb to an s/m orientation simply because of a video? Bubbling under the surface of the disgust rhetoric is the belief that if exposed to s/m, more and more young men would abandon their girlfriends in search of kinky sex with older men. As Lord Lowry warns, "A relaxation of the prohibitions in sections 20 and 47 [of the *Offences against the Person Act*] can only encourage the practice of homosexual sado-masochism and the physical cruelty it must involve" (67). Lord Lowry thus inadvertently demonstrates an anxiety about the fragility of heterosexuality, and the mundaneness of non-kinky sex. As Stychin argues in his analysis of the lords' fear of homosexual s/m contagion, "The dangers of seduction of vulnerable and innocent youth into a degenerate (and all too appealing) lifestyle is a rationale for criminalizing the consensual sado-masochistic sexual encounter" (1994, 527). The presupposed innateness of heterosexuality, and the naturalness of disgust towards s/m, is belied by the judges' insistence on using the criminal law to defend the borders around non-kinky heterosexuality.

Layered upon and informed by the distinction between heterosexual and homosexual are gendered regulations on the notion of manliness. In considering what kinds of physical interferences the law will tolerate, Lord Mustill states under a heading of "rough horseplay,"

> The law recognises that community life (and particularly male community life), such as exists in the school playground, in the barrack-room and on the factory floor, may involve a mutual risk of deliberate physical contact in which a particular recipient (or even an outsider, as in *Reg. v. Bruce* (1847) 2 Cox C.C. 262) may come off worst, and that the criminal law cannot be too tender about the susceptibilities of those involved. I think it hopeless to attempt any explanation in terms of consent. This is well illustrated by *Reg. v. Terence Jones* (1986) 83 Cr.App.R. 375. The injured children did not consent to being thrown in the air at all, nor to the risk that they might be thrown so high as to cause serious injury. They had no choice. (*R. v. Brown* 1993, 77)

Male community life is thus understood to entail a certain amount of risk of personal injury. Despite the facts that consent may be absent in certain cases, and that bullying is imposed on non-consenting children, the law refuses to be "too tender" and will not interfere if the behaviour remains within certain bounds.[3] This judicial tolerance is part of a performative utterance that accepts the gendered conception of aggression within masculine social circles. Lord Templeman concedes that "violent sports including boxing are lawful activities" (47). However, when the judicial gaze is turned upon gay s/m, the activities are not recognizable as forming a part of "male community life." Lord Lowry parenthetically sneers of s/m that "it can scarcely be regarded as a manly diversion" (67). But consider what exactly separates professional boxing from s/m, in terms of the gendered nature of the activity. It seems that s/m is punished because it explicitly and audaciously sexualizes "male community life." It reveals the underlying eroticism of homo-social spaces in the playground, the barracks, and the factory floor. It also involves a feminization of the submissives. Boxing and "rough horse-play" involve chemistry between two types of "dominants" – all the male players remain, or are attempting to remain, impenetrable. Gay s/m involves men who have abdicated the gendered imperative of impenetrability, both figuratively and literally. The submissives not only wish to submit to their male dominants, but they also enjoy explicit penetration, whether through anal sex, or with erotic cutting and piercing. The law cannot abide this because, as Stychin argues in the context of gay s/m, "it is the giving of consent voluntarily and fully informed which undermines the manliness both of the victim and the aggressor" (1994, 516). Gay s/m is punished because it chisels at the homo/hetero binary, puts into crisis the heterosexuality of homo-social environments, and corrupts the accepted tautology of "boys will be boys." Boys, it seems, will sometimes be "girls," in the ways that submissives are feminized as penetrable subjects.

In order to buttress the moral conclusion that s/m is "evil" and "uncivilized," the majority judges also turn to medical utilitarian arguments to bolster their claims of objectivity. This rhetorical move is reminiscent of Krafft-Ebing, Freud, and Havelock Ellis's theories on sexuality – grounded in the discourse of science – which legitimate the identification of certain sexual behaviour as degenerate, perverse, or atavistic. In *Brown*, the majority deploys the risk of contracting HIV as an empirical fact upon which to hang the convictions. Lord Templeman remarks, "Although the appellants had not contracted AIDS, two members of the group had died from AIDS and one other had contracted an HIV infection although not necessarily from the practices of the group" (*R. v. Brown* 1993, 51). The appellants are thus construed as polluted and polluters – carriers of a disease that is already taboo for its ideational ties to gay sexuality. The fact that the activities at issue were conducted using sterilized equipment, and that the appellants employed safer sex tactics, becomes proof that they were engaging in suspect activities, not evidence of their vigilance in protecting public health and safety. Lord Templeman states, "The assertion that care was taken demonstrates the possibility of infection" (51). And this "possibility of infection" was put forward as a (decontextualized) fact that proves the appellants were up to something devious.

Lord Tullichettle also warns, "Wounds can easily become septic if not properly treated, the free flow of blood from a person who is H.I.V. positive or who has Aids can infect another" (*R. v. Brown* 1993, 59). Here

Lord Tullichettle merely points out the possible risks of infection, without addressing the specific practices of the appellants. It becomes irrelevant that the appellants were conscious of the above risks and took precautionary measures. The fact that the activities *could* bring about infection if conducted with less care is what gets put on trial. As Douglas has argued, "Naming a risk amounts to an accusation" (2003, xix). The appellants were thus forced to take on the guilt of hypothetical risky sadomasochists.

Lord Lowry further adds, "Some activity will involve a danger of infection ... When considering the danger of infection, with its inevitable threat of AIDS, I am not impressed by the argument that this threat can be discounted on the ground that, as long ago as 1967, Parliament, subject to conditions, legalised buggery, now a well-known vehicle for the transmission of AIDS" (*R. v. Brown* 1993, 67). As with the other majority judges, Lord Lowry invokes an amorphous danger of infection without considering the specificity of the appellants' activities. Although he concedes that Parliament has decriminalized "buggery," which also carries a risk of infection, he insists on the judicial entitlement to prohibit s/m in the name of public health. As Stychin argues, "The threat of AIDS becomes *the* logical outcome of sado-masochistic (or perhaps homosexual) sex" (1994, 512). While the lords are prevented from criminalizing gay sex, they can at least criminalize s/m gay sex.

Perhaps the most glaring issue, though, in all of the majority's discourse on risks and dangers of s/m sex, is their wilful disregard of the risks involved in heterosexual sexuality. Lord Lowry points an accusing finger at "buggery," which he cites as an accepted "vehicle" for infection, yet ignores the fact that penile-vaginal intercourse is also an accepted vehicle for HIV transmission. The absence of a consideration of heterosexual intercourse in their discussions of infectious risks constructs such behaviour as safe, untouched by the taboo of AIDS. The fact that condoms are necessary for both anal sex and vaginal sex in order to minimize the risk of transmission is ignored. Again, part of this regime of truth on the nature of perverse sexuality rests on ignoring the risks involved in heterosexual sexuality.

In the same paragraph that discusses the risk of AIDS inherent in s/m activities, Lord Lowry juxtaposes "sadomasochistic homosexual activity" in opposition to "family life" and the "welfare of society" (*R. v. Brown* 1993, 67). Family is coded as heterosexual and non-kinky. Sadomasochists are thus denied inclusion into the familial terms of sexual citizenship, and consequently expelled as social waste. Their kinships do not count. Their welfare is not society's. And this discursive excommunication justifies their incarceration.

R. v. Brown also exemplifies the juridical desire to speak of sex within the framework of investigating its perversions. In consolidating juridical truth on s/m sexuality, that it is illegal and contrary to the *Offences against the Person Act*, the lords had to make it an object of possible knowledge, an area that needs parsing, dissection, and labelling. Despite the judges' reiterative claim that they will spare the reader the "disgusting" details, the rhetoric reflects a voyeuristic incitement to speak of s/m sex, to articulate the most extreme details in all of their shocking glory. Lord Templeman recounts, "The charges against the appellants were based on genital torture and violence to the buttocks, anus, penis, testicles and nipples. The victims were degraded and humiliated sometimes beaten, sometimes wounded with instruments and sometimes branded. Bloodletting and the smearing of human blood produced excitement … Some activities involved excrement" (*R. v. Brown* 1993, 51). In the first sentence of this quote, Lord Templeman provides explicit and graphic details of the body parts and activities. It is as if naming these particular body parts – buttocks, anus, penis, testicles, and nipples – evidences the illicit nature of the activity. Yet the pleasure derived from the so-called torture of these parts is ignored. As Eve Sedgwick has pointed out, ignorances "are produced and correspond to particular knowledges and circulate as part of particular regimes of truth" (1990, 8). The judge's wilful ignorance of the subjective experience of the "torture" corresponds to an invested knowledge of human sexuality that purposefully excludes the desires of gay sadomasochists.

In the next sentence, Lord Templeman has already concluded – before he describes the beatings and brandings – that the submissives were "degraded and humiliated," again erasing their phenomenological experience of the encounter and assuming degradation and humiliation are always unwanted. The lord ends off his list of horribles by invoking the abject substances of blood and excrement. The first image, that of bloodletting, may have legal significance based on his interpretation of the legislation, because it would involve the puncturing of skin. Yet the second tidbit – that the appellants and their "victims" appropriated excrement in their sexual activity – is not legally relevant to the *Offences against the Person Act*. As with the LEAF factum, there is no attempt to explicate what harm flows from anal/excrement play. The taboo nature of excrement is used to illustrate the illicitness of the activity and link it to violence.

Lord Jauncey also provides enticing clues to the accuseds' activities. While he claims that he can express his decision "without going into details of all the rather curious activities in which the appellants engaged," he nonetheless betrays his desire to indulge his and his reader's curiosity about the sexual activities on trial (*R. v. Brown* 1993, 59). On the very next page, he states somewhat tongue-in-cheek, "If it is to be decided that such activities as the nailing by A of B's foreskin or scrotum to a board or the insertion of hot wax into C's urethra followed by the burning of his penis with a candle or the incising of D's scrotum with a scalpel to the effusion of blood are injurious neither to B, C and D nor to the public interest then it is for Parliament with its accumulated wisdom and sources of information to declare them to be lawful" (60). Lord Jauncey appears unable to resist articulating the most extreme examples of s/m with clinical precision: foreskin, scrotum, urethra, incisions, and effusions. And as with Lord Templeman, he excludes from this picture the negotiations involved in enacting the scene, the consent and enthusiasm of the hypothetical persons of A, B, C, and D, and the pleasures they extract from the activity. The truth of s/m sexuality in *Brown* is achieved by a blending of decontextualized "facts," clinical language, the iteration of taboo bodily parts and excretions, and wilful ignorances.

The *Brown* decision reflects many of the truth-claims articulated in the three previously examined movies that address gay s/m: *Cruising*, *Frisk*, and *Pulp Fiction*. In these texts, the intersection of two maligned sexual identities, homosexual and sadomasochist, proliferates anxieties and pleasures in the socio-legal imaginary. First and most obviously, both the lords in *Brown* and the films see gay s/m as intrinsically dangerous. The majority lords were convinced that criminalization was justified to prevent the risks of injury (unintended or otherwise) and HIV transmission. In *Frisk* and *Pulp Fiction*, gay dominants are portrayed as sadistic rapist-killers, and in *Cruising*, the gay s/m scene is constructed as a breeding ground for sexual violence. Furthermore, in *Brown*, while gay s/m is castigated as disgusting, the majority lords feared that its pleasures were contagious and corruptive, with young men particularly vulnerable to falling prey to its appeal. Similarly, in *Cruising* the young heterosexual protagonist is drawn to gay s/m, and in *Frisk*, the protagonist explains that his interest in s/m, and then sadistic killing, was sparked by his introduction to gay s/m porn at a young age. Finally, the *Brown* decision and the films are working within the economy of vicarious s/m: both the filmic and the judicial texts offer up vivid details of gay s/m activities so that the audience can voyeuristically consume the sexual other, while at the same time achieving closure and catharsis with the killing or incarceration of a gay s/m subject.

R. v. Wilson (1996)

Three years after the House of Lords' *Brown* decision, the English judiciary was confronted again with the question of consent to injury. The accused, Wilson, had branded his initials on his wife's buttocks with a hot knife. During a medical examination, a doctor observed the branding and contacted the police. Wilson was charged under section 47 of the *Offences against the Person Act*, the same legislation that was used to indict the accused in *R. v. Brown*. At trial, the judge cited the *Brown* decision and reluctantly directed the jury to convict (*R. v. Wilson* 1995). The Court of Appeal distinguished the two cases and quashed the conviction (*R. v. Wilson* 1996). Lord Russell gave four interconnected reasons why *R. v. Brown* did not apply to the case before him. The wife was considered a competent adult, capable of consenting to the activity. The branding was analogized to tattooing, a lawful activity when performed with consent. There was no aggressive or sexual intent on the part of the husband. Finally, it was not in the public interest to interfere with private marital relations. An examination of the assumptions under each of these reasons reveals an exigent need to protect heterosexuality, marriage, and monogamy from the taint of perversion.

In contrast to the submissives in *Brown*, whose agency, choices, and experiential truth were denied, Mrs Wilson is described as an adult making free choices. She is referred to as a woman of "mature years" (*R. v. Wilson* 1996, para. 3) who "not only consented to that which the appellant did, she instigated it" (para. 11). Her "maturity" is apparently meant to convey her ability to consent to injury, which stands in contrast to the "youths" who were so described in *Brown* to erode their agency and construct them as misled and corrupted. What is ignored is that Mrs Wilson and the submissives in *Brown* were all legal adults. An even more blatant parallel is the fact that the submissives in *Brown* also instigated many of the s/m activities; indeed, some self-inflicted pain as well. Yet their sexual choices were overlooked by the lords' use of infantilizing discourse.

Lord Russell further attempts to distinguish the facts in front of him from s/m cases by considering the disparate intentions and pleasures involved in the activities. In order to separate the issues, Lord Russell contends that "the question certified for their Lordships in Brown related only to a sadomasochistic encounter" (*R. v. Wilson* 1996, para. 12). He ignores the underlying eroticism of having initials branded on one's buttocks. Indeed, Mrs Wilson initially desired her husband's initials on her breasts, but her husband refused to brand her there. Buttocks and breasts are classic erogenous zones, yet Lord Russell attempts to discount this implication by stating, "The appellant's desire was to assist her in what she regarded as the acquisition of a desirable piece of personal adornment, perhaps in this day and age no less understandable than the piercing of nostrils or even tongues for the purposes of inserting decorative jewellery" (para. 11). In addition, Lord Russell cites testimony of the accused who said of the branding, "It was done for love" (para. 5). And later, Wilson paraphrases his wife who allegedly stated, "'I'm not scared of anybody knowing that I love you enough to have your name on my body'" (para. 11). In contrast, Lord Russell asserts that s/m is done for "the purposes of sexual gratification" (para. 10). Such a distinction implies, as Weait suggests, that "the law will acknowledge the validity of consent, where the injury is not one in which pleasure is taken" (Weait in Langdridge and Barker 2007, 73). Furthermore, the notion that branding does not fall under the rubric of s/m is contradicted by Pat Califia's how-to s/m book *Sensuous Magic* (1993b, 134), Thomas Murray's explanatory monograph, *The Language of Sadomasochism: A Glossary and Linguistic Analysis* (1989, 44), and Pauline Réage's famous s/m novel *The Story of O* (1965), all of which contemplate branding as a characteristically sadomasochistic activity. While Lord Russell apparently did not have the benefit of these texts as evidence, I nonetheless suggest that he employs a strategic ignorance of the palpable s/m flavour of branding as he seeks to desexualize the practice of a man branding his initials on his wife's buttocks. Instead, he locates the Wilsons' activities within the more benign and conventional arena of adornment and jewellery.

Lord Russell further ignores the evidence in *Brown* that addressed branding. In describing the activities that qualified as assaults in *Brown*, Lord Templeman recounts, "In one case, a victim was *branded* twice on the thigh" (*R. v. Brown* 1993, 51; emphasis added). More generally, the lord laments, "The victims were degraded and humiliated sometimes beaten, sometimes wounded with instruments and sometimes *branded*" (51; emphasis added). In *Brown*, branding was clearly envisaged as an aggressive activity that supported the charge of assault. Lord Russell disregards these facts, instead concluding that he "cannot detect any logical difference between what the appellant did and what he might have done in the way of tattooing" (*R. v. Wilson* 1996, para. 13). He does, however, cite *Brown* to support the lawfulness of tattooing. "The speeches of Lord Templeman, at page 79, Lord Jauncey, at page 90, and the dissenting speech of Lord Slynn, at page 119, all refer to tattooing as being an activity which, if carried out with the consent of an adult, does not involve an offence under section 47" (para. 12). Lord Russell thus neglects to consider how the judges in *Brown* viewed the practice of branding, instead analogizing it to tattooing in his effort to exploit their acknowledgment that tattooing is lawful, despite the fact that it causes injury.

In building on his tattoo analogy, Lord Russell posits that the accused in *Brown* were engaged in much more risky activity than the Wilsons. He seizes upon Lord Templeman's assessment of the dangers of gay s/m, stating, "In Brown, the appellants engaged in sadomasochism of the grossest kind, involving inter alia, physical torture, and as Lord Templeman pointed out: 'obvious dangers of serious physical injury and blood infection'" (*R. v. Wilson* 1996, para. 10). Lord Russell thus attempts to portray the activities in *Brown* as inherently dangerous, despite the fact that no medical attention was ever required after the s/m sessions. In contrast, when assessing the dangers of branding, he insists, "We do not think that we are entitled to assume that the method adopted by the appellant and his wife was any more dangerous or painful than tattooing" (para. 14). Lord Russell reaches this conclusion despite the fact that medical attention was sought a few days after the branding, and the examining doctor was concerned enough that he felt entitled to override the standard patient-doctor confidentiality relationship and contact the police.[4] But since the judge had already established that branding is analogous to tattooing, there was no need to hypothesize upon the risks to physical health in the way the lords had done in *Brown*.

This juxtaposition is particularly ironic when it is recalled that in *Brown*, the appellants' cognizance of the risks of their activities, and their vigilance in minimizing those risks, was used to indict them, never mind the fact that their precautions attenuated those risks. In *Wilson*, Mr Wilson appears to have had no training in erotic or decorative branding of human flesh. And as Califia has pointed out in his s/m guidebook, "Because burn scars spread, branding is very difficult to do properly and should be done by or learned from only an experienced body-modification artist" (1993b, 134). Granted, the judges in *Wilson* had no evidence to guide them about the possible dangers of branding.

Yet it was open to them to send the case back for a retrial with directions that the dangers of branding be assessed before a conviction or an acquittal could be reached. It therefore appears the "obviousness" of the dangers of the appellants' activities (including branding) in *Brown*, and the lack of obviousness of the dangers in Wilson branding his wife without any training, reveal a blatant judicial bias that favoured heterosexual marital activities.

Indeed, heterosexist and monogamist-centric assumptions of the sanctity of the marital home are evident in Lord Russell's final policy assessment of the impact of the trial ruling. He concludes, "[We] are firmly of the opinion that it is not in the public interest that activities such as the appellant's in this appeal should amount to criminal behaviour. Consensual activity between husband and wife, in the privacy of the matrimonial home, is not, in our judgment, a proper matter for criminal investigation, let alone criminal prosecution" (*R. v. Wilson* 1996, para. 15). In this statement, Lord Russell brings the Wilsons into the fold of the "public interest." Their marriage presumptively makes their activities licit. The court is sure to label the Wilsons with the culturally cherished roles of "husband" and "wife," thereby imbuing them with legitimacy. The activities took place, not just in private, but in the "privacy of the marital home." Although the appellants in *Brown* also conducted their affairs in private, a perception emerges that the marital home is more private and hallowed than other private areas, and therefore demands more deference and respect from the judiciary and the police system. Lord Russell thus implies that there is legal significance to the sexual identity and marital status differences between the appellants in *Brown* and the appellant in *Wilson*. Being unmarried, gay, and polyamorous allows the state to closely scrutinize your private activities and impose a pejorative interpretation on mutually fulfilling and consensual activities. In contrast, being married, heterosexual, and monogamous can whitewash activities that would otherwise be understood as suspect and perverse.

The desire to exonerate a husband for consensually branding his wife reflects the normative order of the cinematic treatment of s/m. Recall that in the few movies that portrayed s/m practitioners in a sympathetic light, the narrative always centred on a heterosexual couple that married or entered into a monogamous and committed relationship by the end. In *Secretary*, the couple gets married; in *Exit to Eden*, the couple gets engaged; and in *Preaching to the Perverted*, the couple reunites and has a baby, and the female protagonist apparently forsakes her previous polyamorous and bisexual ways. While the viewer in each of these films is encouraged to sympathize with the s/m protagonists, something that is not done in Lord Russell's denial of the s/m connotations to the Wilsons' branding, there is a common theme: in both cinema and law, marriage can act as a legitimating framework that incorporates the kinky couple into the terms of sexual citizenship and respectability.

R. v. Emmett (1999)

To avoid overstating the significance of the Wilsons' hetero-marital identity, I must mention a British case that followed *Brown* but involved a heterosexual couple that was cohabiting at the time of the material events. In *R. v. Emmett* (1999), a man was convicted of assault for two incidents of consensual s/m activity that caused physical injury. In the first incident, Emmett asphyxiated his female partner, causing subconjuctival haemorrhages in the eyes and bruising around her neck. In the second incident, he poured lighter fuel on his partner's breasts and ignited it, causing a serious burn that became infected. After both incidents, the female partner sought medical help at Emmett's insistence.

The Court of Appeal upheld the conviction, relying on *Brown* and clearly stating that the sexual orientation of the partners was irrelevant. Further, even though the couple had married before the trial (although after the material events in question), the court did not allow them to have recourse to the cherished "privacy of the marital home" shield to retroactively exonerate their past activities. This would seem to suggest that the primary issue when adjudicating the criminality of consensual activity causing physical injury is not sexual orientation or even marital status, but rather the perceived "extremity" of the activities, which the court in *Emmett* considered to have been extremely dangerous.

Yet two important aspects of the case should be noted. Emmett's sentence of eighteen months' imprisonment was suspended for two years at trial, and this was not altered on appeal. As a result, while Emmett was saddled with a criminal record, he was not incarcerated. This is in contrast to the convicted persons in *Brown*, some of whom served multiple-year jail sentences for participating in activities that never required anyone to seek medical attention. Furthermore, unlike some of the submissives in *Brown*, Emmett's partner was not charged with accessory to assault (on her own body). The *Emmett* court provided no explanation for the difference in sentencing practices, and there is no comment on the fact that the police or the Crown did not pursue charges against Emmett's partner. But one clue to the disparity may be gleaned from Justice Wright, the presiding judge in *Emmett*, who stated, "It is only right to recall that, since the events which formed the basis of this prosecution and since the prosecution was launched, they [Emmett and his partner] have married each other" (para. 6). What is the significance of this fact, such that it must be "recalled" in the written judgment? Justice Wright does not elaborate on his reasoning, but I posit that the heterosexual couple's current marital status assisted in mitigating Emmett's culpability. Although his conviction still stands, Emmett will not be expelled from the community through incarceration. Thus, while being married, heterosexual, and monogamous does not completely immunize a couple from conviction in Britain, it can apparently buy some leniency. If the activities happen to come before the judiciary, a soft lens will be employed to either normalize (as in *Wilson*), or at least mitigate (as in *Emmett*), any activities that might *spank* of perversion.

Sadomasochist Desires as Indicators of Sexual Aggression

The trilogy of British s/m cases considered above showed a tendency towards leniency where consensual s/m occurred within a heteronormative relationship. In Canadian case law, there is a less discernible bias based on sexual orientation or marital status. To the Canadian judicial gaze, s/m tends to be suspect, regardless of choice of partner. In this section, I look at how the term *sadomasochism* is used as a signifier of pathology and a synonym for violence. In particular, linguistic confusion abounds with the terms *sadism*, *masochism*, and *sadomasochism*.

Recall that in the list of paraphilias in the *DSM-IV-TR* and *DSM-V*, the conjoined term *sadomasochism* does not appear as a mental disorder. Yet case law that relies on medical or psychological experts has tended to blur the diagnostic landscape, aggregating sadism and masochism and confusing their medical definitions. Of course, people can suffer from multiple paraphilias according to this medical framework and as such be classified as sexual sadists and sexual masochists. Yet when the term *sadomasochist* is employed in the case law, the evidence rarely justifies the inclusion of *masochist* in the identification. Usually, the evidence supports only a finding of sadism, in which someone is aroused by inducing the non-consensual suffering of another person. Surprisingly, the confusion is not caused solely by laypersons unfamiliar with the medical definitions. Often, it seems that expert witnesses themselves perpetuate the misuse of *sadomasochism* as a proxy for sadism.

For example, in the 1992 case of *R. v. Cepicka*, the accused pleaded guilty to aggravated assault, abduction, and failing to comply with a no-contact order in relation to his ex-girlfriend. During the sentencing hearing, Brian Shustack, a chartered psychologist, gave evidence on Cepicka's mental state. The judgment directly quotes the doctor's report, which stated that the accused suffered from "issues of insecurity, anger and sado-masochism" (para.13). Yet the judgment does not indicate anywhere that Cepicka harboured any masochistic tendencies, or that he was interested in consensual s/m activities. Instead, all that is presented is his obsessive and aggressive behaviour towards his ex-girlfriend.

In the 1993 case of *R. v. MC*, a sixteen-year-old was convicted of sexually assaulting a young boy. The evidence included the testimony of Ruth Bray, a child and forensic psychologist who had examined M, the accused, as an expert witness for the defence. In reference to Bray's evidence, the presiding judge stated, "Her testing did not show him to be a homosexual paedophile nor a sadomasochist" (para. 25). In this instance, the judgment paraphrases the doctor's conclusions, so it is unclear whether she used the term *sadomasochism* in her report. What is clear is that at the very least, the judge used the expert witness testimony to aggregate the separate pathologies of sadism and masochism in the judgment. Since there was no evidence that M expressed masochistic proclivities or engaged in consensual s/m activities, it can be extrapolated that the term *sadomasochist* was used interchangeably with *sadist*.

In the 2004 case *R. v. Dee*, the accused pleaded guilty of committing sexual assault against a woman that entailed physical abuse, forced removal of a tampon, and an attempted rape. In sentencing, the defence called Giorgio Ilacqua, whom the court qualified as an expert of forensic psychology and criminal sexual rehabilitation. The presiding judge stated, "It is Dr Ilacqua's opinion that Mr Dee does not present with sadomasochistic fantasies, sexual fetishes or any other significant sexual deviance" (para. 27). As in *R. v. MC*, the judge paraphrases the doctor's conclusions, so it is unknown whether the term *sadomasochism* was used, or whether the judge imposed this term in his recap of the doctor's report. In either case, psychiatric discourse is deployed in the judgment to identify sadomasochism as "sexual deviance." And again, there was no evidence that would support a finding that Dee was masochistic or interested in consensual s/m.

In these three cases, it appears the term *sadomasochist* is used as a stand-in for *sadist*. The alleged facts of each case indicated sexual aggression and the desire to dominate, not to be the object of domination. The reduction of s/m to sadism reflects the feminist anti-pornography framework that construed masochism as an empty and irrelevant signifier in the aggregated term. Hence, even after the amendments to the *DSM* in the fourth and fifth editions effectively de-pathologized (some forms of) consensual sadism and masochism, expert psy discourse is still being used to perpetuate the view that s/m desire is equivalent to sadistic violence.

In Quebec, there seems to be additional medical authority for referring to sadomasochism as a paraphilia. The Office québécois de la langue française, a provincial body whose mandate is to promote the French language, includes sadomasochism as an example of a paraphilia (L'Office québécois de la langue française, n.d.). The 2004 judgment in *R. c. Cloutier* cites this official definition to clarify the use of the term *paraphilia* by a psychiatrist. In the 2005 case of *R. c. Dompierre*, a psychiatrist, Louis Morissette, testified that the accused did not suffer from a paraphilia, which she defined as "une préférence sexuelle déviante (sadisme, fétichisme, exhibitionnisme, sadomasochisme, etc.)" (18). In contrast to the English-Canadian case law, this definition does not conflate sadism with sadomasochism, but instead names both as separate examples of sexual deviancy. It can be extrapolated that from Morisette's perspective, both the imposition of sadistic acts upon a non-consenting person *and* mutual s/m activity indicate problematic mental disorders.

This view is reflected in the 2003 case of *R. c. St Aubin*, where the accused had engaged in s/m activities, and had later committed sexual assault upon a stranger. Before committing the sexual assault, the accused had apparently visited a psychiatric hospital because he was troubled by his s/m activities and fantasies. The court recounts that at the hospital, "Il décrit des pratiques sadomasochistes avec sa conjointe et d'autres personnes, et reconnaît la frontière mince entre ces scénarios et les scénarios de viol" (para. 23).[5] On his next visit to the hospital, he was again troubled by similar issues: "Il disait encore avoir des fantaisies de viol qu'il contrôlait et fréquenter toujours des soirées sadomasochistes" (para. 24).[6] With this background in mind, the court lamented the accused's denial of any connection between his s/m activities and his subsequent attack on a stranger: "Grégoire St-Aubin ne semble pas faire de lien entre ses pratiques sadomasochistes et l'agression commise, alors qu'il semble clair pour le médecin que, 'dans ce scénario (de viol), comme dans les scénarios sadomasochistes Monsieur visait un sentiment de contrôle et de domination'" (para. 27).[7] As such, in the court's view, which was supported by the medical expert witness, s/m is a slippery slope that can lead to non-consensual sexual aggression.

In *R. v. L. (A.C.T.)*, a 2011 Manitoba sentencing decision, law and psy experts again perpetuate the notion of a slippery slope between s/m activities and sexual assault. The accused was involved in a BDSM relationship with the mother of the victim. While the official crimes were sexual interference and assault with a weapon, the pre-sentence report also indicts the accused's consensual activities with the victim's mother: "His participation in the BDSM lifestyle led to an unwillingness to identify boundaries between appropriate and inappropriate sexual behaviour" (para. 7). In this statement, BDSM activities are blamed, in part, for the sexual abuse that ensued. The report later states, "Although Mr [S.] doesn't have a history of being charged with sexual inappropriate behaviour, he does have a personal history that demonstrates concerns about his ability to avoid risky sexual behaviour. This includes his history of interest in the BDSM lifestyle and the current charge in front of the Court" (para. 7). This pre-sentence report thus frames the accused's BDSM history as an indication of problematic sexual behaviour that is relevant for determining the appropriate sentence for his crime.

Admittedly, in the scenarios outlined in the above cases *R. c. St Aubin* (2003) and *R. v. L. (A.C.T.)* (2011), s/m activities do appear to map onto subsequent sexual crimes. Yet by simplistically and categorically linking s/m to sexual assault, the courts erase the boundary between mutuality and force in the realm of non-normative sexuality. Without relying on any empirical evidence, the courts imply that all people who indulge in s/m activities are budding rapists.

This juridical conflation between sexual dominance in an s/m context, and sexual sadism in a non-consensual context, reflects the truth-claims of a number of s/m films. Recall that the female dominant characters in *Basic Instinct* and *Body of Evidence* enjoy both taking the dominant position during consensual sexual encounters, and murdering people. The male protagonists who succumb to the femmes fatales' wiles are also infected with not just s/m desires, but sadistic impulses as well. After falling under the spell of their s/m lovers, both men perpetrate aggressive sexual encounters with other women that could easily be interpreted as date rapes. Similarly, in *Nine and a Half Weeks*, the dominant lover not only engages in consensual s/m activities with his girlfriend, but also forceful sexual encounters that again can be read as sexual assaults and coercive. This slippery-slope theme is also prevalent in the gay s/m films. In *Cruising*, the killer is both a sexual dominant and a homicidal maniac. In *Frisk*, the protagonist's s/m encounters lead him to eventually enact sexual violence and murder. And in *Pulp Fiction*, the two gay rapists and killers keep a sexual slave on hand, apparently for mutual s/m enjoyment. This is also reminiscent of some of the anti-s/m feminist discourse in the sex wars. For example, recall that according to Marissa Jonel's anecdotal evidence, the increased popularity of s/m among lesbians has a "direct connection" to battering and abuse-related deaths among lesbian couples (Jonel 1982, 19). The law's signification of the term *sadomasochism* as essentially sadistic thus runs parallel to many of the pejorative representations of sexual dominants in film and anti-s/m feminism.

The (Ineffectual) Consent Defence

In these Canadian cases that delved into the s/m tendencies of accused persons in sexual assault cases, consent was not claimed as part of the defence. Instead, s/m desires were used as a factor to assist in determining the culpability of the accused, or in measuring the level of danger that he posed to others. In this section, I consider the defence of consent in crimes of sexual assault, where the accused claims that the activity took place within the boundaries of a mutually agreed s/m encounter.[8] As in *Brown*, the claim of consent has generally been rejected as a defence, because the s/m activity in question is deemed inherently dangerous, degrading, exploitive, and/or psychologically unhealthy.

R. v. Jobidon (1991)

The Supreme Court of Canada's 1991 decision in *R. v. Jobidon* is the leading precedent in cases where an accused raises consent to s/m activity as a defence to a charge of assault. In that case, the court probed the limits of a consent defence in the context of a fist fight. It ruled that while section 265 of the *Criminal Code* defines assault as taking place "without the consent" of the other person, the common law has imposed limits on a consent defence, at least where physical fights are concerned. As Justice Gonthier wrote for a majority of the court, "The limitation demanded by s. 265 as it applies to the circumstances of this appeal is one which vitiates consent between adults intentionally to apply force causing serious hurt or non-trivial bodily harm to each other in the course of a fist fight or brawl" (para. 127).

Despite this precise holding, Justice Gonthier's policy considerations wander beyond the issue of consent in fist fights. He states a concern, related to the issue of deterrence in the context of consensual force, that the recipient of the force "may find that he derives some form of pleasure from the activity" (*R. v. Jobidon* 1991, para. 116). This pleasure is immediately pathologized by Justice Gonthier, as he continues: "It is perhaps not inconceivable that this kind of perversion could arise in a domestic or marital setting where one or more of the family members are of frail or unstable mental health" (para. 116). If there is any doubt that Justice Gonthier is referencing sexual pleasure, he then quotes criminal law theorist George P. Fletcher, who states, "If someone is encouraged to inflict a sado-masochistic beating on a consenting victim, the experience of inflicting the beating might loosen the actor's inhibitions against sadism in general" (para. 116). Although Justice Gonthier is quick to differentiate the situation in the case at hand from what Fletcher is describing, his approving citation clearly indicates a condemnation of consensual s/m activity. Without any reference to medical opinion or empirical evidence (although of course, the *DSM* would have supported this perspective), Justice Gonthier imposes a pathologizing gaze to unequivocally define the experience of pleasure derived from pain as a perversion suffered by people with "frail" or "unstable" minds. And again, s/m is definitively mapped onto sadism. The satisfaction that a dominant partner derives from a sadomasochist encounter is defined as an enjoyment in hurting another, not an enjoyment in pleasuring another in an unusual way (e.g., through infliction of physical pain or staged humiliation).

R. v. Welch (1995)

In the 1995 appellate case *R. v. Welch*, the possibility of consensual s/m activity is again reduced to sadistic activity. Speaking for the Ontario Court of Appeal, Justice Griffiths defined the central issue as "whether the consent of a complainant may be a valid defence to the offence of sexual assault causing bodily harm … consisting of a hurt or injury to the complainant that interferes with her health or comfort and is more than transient or trifling in nature" (para. 1). At the trial, the complainant and the accused gave vastly different accounts of what had occurred on the night of the alleged sexual assault, which consisted of restraint, being hit with a hand and a belt, and penetration of the vagina and rectum. The accused claimed that the complainant had consented to the activity and encouraged him throughout the encounter. The complainant attested that, on the contrary, she had objected and protested for the entire duration. The trial judge instructed the jury that the defence of consent was not available to a charge of sexual assault causing

bodily harm. After reviewing Canadian, English, and American jurisprudence and legal writing, Justice Griffiths found that the trial judge
had properly instructed the jury.

In his conclusion, Justice Griffiths re-inscribes sadism as the defining
feature in an s/m session. He refers to the encounter between the accused and the complainant as "sadistic sexual activity" (*R. v. Welch*
1995, para. 88). He then dismisses the agency of the (allegedly) submissive partner: "The consent of the complainant, assuming it was given,
cannot detract from the inherently degrading and dehumanizing nature
of the conduct" (para. 88). In finding that consent provides no exculpatory value, Justice Griffiths, in effect, rejects the agency and the erotic
choices of submissive lovers within his legal framework.

To support this conclusion, Justice Griffiths quotes an English academic article that advocated for restrictions and the criminalization of
certain s/m activities. William Wilson states, "A fundamental building
block of our moral society is the social taboo against the infliction of
injury on another. Remove this building block and not only do sensibilities stand to be damaged but, over time, perhaps our very commitment to the sanctity of life. To reduce this fundamental moral issue to
an issue about the presence or absence of consent may be to miss what
is really at stake, namely our humanity, as presently conceived. If sadism is allowable, if consented to, then it is consent rather than moral
conviction which polices the barrier between a society of would-be sadists and the kind of society most of us would like to inhabit" (1992,
395). In this excerpt, Wilson appears in the grips of a moral panic,
whereby a marginal group of people (sadomasochists) come to be defined as a major threat to cherished and fundamental societal values.
Indeed, Wilson is even more explicit than Justice Griffiths in constructing s/m as dehumanizing, suggesting (with considerable hyperbole)
that legal tolerance of consensual s/m will put our commitment to the
sanctity of life, and our very humanity, at risk. And again, as with the
feminist anti-pornography perspective, literal sadism is presented as
the operating drive that actuates consensual sadomasochism. Sadism,
apparently, is a contagious pleasure that needs to be policed. Wilson
implies that without the social and moral taboo against hurting one
another, we might all turn into sadists. This privileging of sadism is
made explicit earlier in the article, when he characterizes s/m as premised on "the values of the Marquis de Sade" (390). Needless to say,
Wilson never considers the values of Sacher-Masoch as another interpretive guide to the erotic dynamics of consensual s/m.

Although the pejorative construction of consensual s/m sexuality in *Welch* can be understood as both detrimental to s/m practitioners and a diminishment of the masochist piece in the erotic exchange, there are potential policy reasons for disregarding consent in cases of alleged sexual assault causing bodily harm. For example, the victim in *Welch* vigorously denied that consent had been given. However, establishing a lack of consent beyond a reasonable doubt will often prove difficult where the only witnesses to the activity were the accused and the complainant. Cheryl Hanna argues that removing the defence of consent when actual bodily harm results from a sexual encounter appropriately privileges the rights of victims of sexual violence over those of consensual sadomasochists (2001). Although she acknowledges a few cases where the police targeted consensual sadomasochists for ideological reasons, she concludes, "No doubt, there are far more people who have been victimized by sexual violence than those who have been held criminally culpable for engaging in safe, consensual S/M" (288–9).

From a victim's rights perspective, this stance is temptingly pragmatic. As I read the facts of *Welch*, I was persuaded that the complainant was telling the truth and the accused was presenting perjured evidence. Yet as Monica Pa has argued, "Although … there is a grave potential for abusing the S/M sex defense, such is the case whenever a consent defense is allowed. Several defenses have proof problems, including a consent defense in rape cases" (Pa 2001, 86). Why should accused rapists have recourse to a consent defence and not s/m practitioners? The underlying assumption is that s/m sex is fundamentally problematic, whereas non-kinky sex is innocent until proven guilty, i.e., until shown to have been forced.

Hannah realizes that it is not a principled position to simply assert that it is too onerous for the prosecution to prove non-consent in cases allegedly involving s/m activity, so she instead concludes her analysis by construing legal tolerance of s/m as a perilous route: "To follow the path of sexual autonomy will lead us to the path to violence" (2001, 290). Like Wilson, she invokes essentialist themes of humanity and civilization to justify legal restrictions on the sexual autonomy of sadomasochists: "To suggest that anyone should have the right to control, beat, or brutalize another and escape culpability under a theory of sexual consent violates our deepest notions of freedom, human rights, and civility" (ibid., 289). Note how the use of the word "our" otherizes sadomasochists who clearly do not believe they are violating "*our* deepest notions of freedom, human rights, and civility" when they participate in consensual s/m. In this moral panicked framework, sadomasochists' interest in sexual fulfilment is thus identified as a fundamental threat to societal values. And once again, the pleasures, freedom, and identity of the submissive partner are ignored, while the dominant partner is positioned as the pre-eminent player in an s/m exchange.

R. v. Hancock (2000)

In contrast to the erasure of potential submissive desires in *R. v. Welch* (1995), the court in *R. v. Hancock* (2000) could not help but acknowledge the desires of the submissive partner in a manslaughter trial involving s/m. The facts adduced at trial revealed that the victim, Davis, was a hardcore masochist who subjected his body to physical attacks at his own hands and those of others. The two accused testified that on a number of occasions they had participated in s/m encounters where Davis would outline in written scripts and detailed conversations exactly what kinds of physical experiences he desired. On the night of the alleged assault that led to the victim's death, Davis was slapped, whipped, kicked, punched, burned, anally penetrated with a fist, and penetrated with fish hooks by the two accused and three others (who were not parties to the trial). After the encounter, Davis declined an offer to be taken to a hospital, and the medical evidence indicated he died within a few hours.

A primary component of the defence was that Davis not only consented to the physical onslaught but had instructed and paid the accused to carry it out. As with the previous s/m encounters, he had composed a written script of the scene and had discussed the details with the accused. Defence counsel submitted that *Welch* was wrongly decided, as it violated the equality guarantee in section 15 of the *Canadian Charter of Rights and Freedoms* by discriminating against masochists on the basis of their sexual orientation.

Justice Edwards of the B.C. Supreme Court rejects this argument. On the basis of the logic of *R. v. Jobidon* (1991), he explains that the purpose of criminalizing consensual activity intended to cause bodily harm in this instance "is not the suppression of sexuality but the suppression of violence because it is dangerous to individuals and to public order" (*R. v. Hancock* 2000, para. 64). Thus violence, and not sex, is identified as the defining feature of an s/m encounter. Therefore it becomes easy for Justice Edwards to construct s/m as a slippery slope, stating, "If such violence is not condemned as criminal and wrong and is practiced with impunity, society and individuals become inured to it" (para. 66). And admittedly, the facts of the case do seem to indicate that the accused had become desensitized to the possibly fatal ramifications of their actions, after having engaged in a number of similar encounters with the victim over the years.

Yet Justice Edwards does not confine his censure of s/m to those extreme and reckless manifestations where serious bodily injury or death is foreseeable. Instead he cites the same passage by William Wilson previously used by the Ontario Court of Appeal in *Welch*. Recall that in that citation, Wilson issues the sweeping warning that tolerance of consensual s/m threatens our humanity. There is no attempt to differentiate between reckless and dangerous s/m and skilful and careful s/m. It is the mere fact that pleasure can be extracted from the meting out or receiving of pain that is presented as antithetical to a civilized society.

Justice Edwards later turns to the *Brown* decision and cites Lord Templeman's statement: "The violence of sado-masochistic encounters involves the indulgence of cruelty by sadists and the degradation of victims. Such violence is injurious to participants and unpredictably dangerous. I am not prepared to invent a defence of consent for sado-masochistic encounters which breed and glorify cruelty and result in offences" (*R. v. Hancock* 2000, para. 69). Recall that in that British case, a number of the dominant players were found guilty of assault charges and were sentenced to multi-year prison sentences, all despite the consent of the submissives, the fact that no medical attention was required, and the meticulous care taken by all parties. By citing this case with approval, Justice Edwards conflates life-threatening reckless sexual behaviour with experienced skilful sexual behaviour, based on the sweeping claim that s/m is quintessentially rooted in cruelty, not mutual sexual fulfilment.

R. v. R.D.W. (2006)

A similar understanding of s/m is found in the 2006 case *R. v. R.D.W.*, where the sixteen-year-old accused pleaded guilty to assault, despite the consent of his sixteen-year old girlfriend, the "complainant." It should be noted that the girlfriend "complainant" never complained to the police, did not assist the Crown with the prosecution, and had encouraged the accused to perpetrate the "assault." The indicted activity entailed scarification with a razor blade, which came about as part of the couple's mutual interest in s/m.

Since the court accepted the accused's guilty plea, its task was to issue an appropriate sentence. In this regard, a psychiatric report was presented that assessed the risk of whether the accused would reoffend.

According to Eaves, the risk was considered low, in part because the accused's current relationship did not involve s/m activity, and instead was described as "healthy and respectful" (*R. v. R.D.W.* 2006, para. 14). In its ruling, the court issued a conditional discharge, with one condition being that the accused undergo psychological or psychiatric counselling or monitoring.

The court thus adopted the psychiatric assessment of s/m as antithetical to a "healthy and respectful" relationship. Again, neither the court nor the psychiatric report attempted to differentiate cutting or mutilation from s/m activities that do not pose a serious risk of injury. More importantly, there was no reference to the *DSM-IV-TR*'s modern understanding of sadism and masochism as potentially non-pathological, if practised consensually, and without resulting in distress or impairment in life functioning. Although s/m is not criminalized as such, the judgment implicitly views it as inherently problematic, such that the accused had to be monitored by a medical expert to ensure that his current desires would not compel him to reoffend.

In these cases where alleged consent was vitiated in the context of s/m activity, the court did not consult any experts on the medical understanding of when sadism and masochism cross the line into pathology. This was not a debatable point, as it was presumed to be either "unhealthy" or "degrading." While there was a psychiatric assessment in the case of *R.D.W.*, the assumption was that sadomasochist tendencies are indicators of unhealthy proclivities. The role of the doctor was simply to assess whether the accused still harboured s/m desires – an approach that, as in the cases that conflated sadism with s/m, leaves no room for consensual healthy s/m sexuality.

R. v. J.A. (2008; 2010; 2011)

The issue of consent within an s/m context was further adjudicated in *R. v. J.A.*, an Ontario criminal case that began in 2008 and involved a couple who engaged in what BDSM practitioners refer to as "edgeplay" – that is, activities considered extreme or risky. The legal question of consent was particularly contested because the fact scenario involved a male partner who had been convicted of violent offences in the past, including domestic violence-related assault, and a complainant who gave conflicting accounts at the police station and in the courthouse. The case garnered diverse and split judicial rulings, with two overturned decisions and dissenting judgments at both the Court of Appeal and Supreme Court of Canada. In addition, the case attracted much attention from the feminist community, including a LEAF intervention. At the heart of this controversial case was the issue of whether the s/m activities in question engaged the right to sexual autonomy, or the need to protect against sexual exploitation.

The material events occurred on 22 May 2007, when the accused, J.A., and the complainant, K.D. – a couple with a history of kinky conduct – embarked on an edgy sexual course. After some initial foreplay, the couple moved onto erotic asphyxiation, with J.A. choking K.D. to unconsciousness. The complainant described this activity as a "fetish," used to intensify the sexual experience. During the period of unconsciousness (K.D. estimated it to be about three minutes), J.A. bound her hands behind her back and inserted a dildo into her anus. This penetrative activity continued for about ten seconds after K.D. regained consciousness, after which the couple had vaginal intercourse. Once they had finished this activity, according to K.D.'s testimony, she said their agreed safe word, and J.A. cut the ties. About seven weeks later, on 11 July 2007, K.D. went to the police and described these events. According to the police, K.D. alleged that she did not consent to the sexual activity that had taken place while she was unconscious. A videotape statement was created to this effect. J.A. was charged with several offences contrary to the *Criminal Code*, including sexual assault pursuant to section 246(a), and aggravated assault pursuant to section 268(2). At trial, K.D. recanted her police statement, explaining that her complaint had been motivated by an argument with J.A., in which he had threatened to seek sole custody of their son. As the trial judge explained, K.D. was clearly "on side" with the defence during the trial and maintained that all of the activities were consensual. While the Crown had the option of making a K.G.B. application,[9] which, if successful, would allow the introduction of K.D.'s police statement for the truth of its content, this course of action was abandoned following consultations with senior Crown counsel. It should thus be emphasized that there was no admissible testimonial evidence indicating that K.D. did not consent.

The trial judge, Justice Nicholas, found J.A. guilty of sexual assault, on the basis of a finding that K.D. did not consent to the anal sex on the night in question, but had only discussed its possibility in the past. She further found that even if K.D. had provided explicit consent to the anal sex, she could not legally consent to sexual activity that occurs while she is unconscious. On the count of aggravated assault based on the choking to the point of unconsciousness, Justice Nicholas found J.A.

not guilty because, on the basis of evidence adduced at trial, the unconsciousness that K.D. experienced was "transient" and thus did not amount to bodily harm. In the sentencing decision, Justice Nicholas reviewed J.A.'s criminal history, which included charges of drug trafficking and possession, thirteen convictions of weapons and/or violent offences (assaults and threatening), and three previous convictions related to domestic violence – two of them involving the complainant. Ultimately, J.A. was sentenced to eighteen months (less 115 days of pretrial credit), ordered to provide a sample of his blood for DNA profiling, and registered as a sex offender.

In a split 2–1 decision, the Court of Appeal overturned the sexual assault conviction on the basis of two determinations. On the finding that K.D. did not consent to the anal sex, the majority found that Justice Nicholas had ignored the gist of K.D.'s uncontroverted evidence that she had consented. The majority further found that one *can* legally consent to sexual activity expected to occur while unconscious; the dissent, on the other hand, found that such consent is rendered inoperative during the period of unconsciousness. On the charge of aggravated assault, the majority found that the trial judge had erred in law with her analysis of bodily harm. However, because the Crown had not charged J.A. with sexual assault causing bodily harm, the Crown could not rely on bodily harm to vitiate consent to erotic asphyxiation.

At the Supreme Court level, the only question to be decided was whether one can legally consent to sexual activity that occurs during a period of unconsciousness. Chief Justice McLachlin, writing for the six-judge majority, sided with the dissenting judge in the Court of Appeal dissent, finding that consent must be contemporaneous, ongoing, and conscious in order to be valid. Justice Fish, writing for the three-judge dissent, found that a conscious person can consent in advance to sexual activity that will occur after she has consensually been rendered unconscious.

As with many criminal cases involving s/m, the facts of this case are messy and make it challenging to figure out the extent to which the outcome depended on issues particular to the specific participants. In *R. v. J.A.*, both the accused and the complainant are problematic figures. The accused has a criminal record that significantly includes domestic assault convictions. The complainant's inconsistent statements undermine her credibility, either because one can view her police complaint as fallacious and strategic, or because one can view her court testimony as fallacious and symptomatic of battered spouse syndrome. But a close examination of this "hard case" suggests that the judges produced "bad law" – at least for those associated with s/m. The guilt of the accused was premised on linking s/m with harm, degradation, danger, and exploitation, and ignoring the s/m subcultural context and the possibility of edgeplay as an experience of desire, intimacy, trust, and sexual autonomy. In the following analysis, I offer alternate readings to the dominant judicial and feminist interpretation of the facts and their significance. Before I do so, let me take a cue from Janet Halley's careful qualifications when she rereads controversial cases, to make clear that I am not making any claims to the authentic interior truth of the real J.A. or K.D. or what happened on the night in question. Rather, I offer alternative interpretations of the legal *figures* "J.A." and "K.D." and the *narrative* of that night as they are produced in judicial, testimonial, and feminist discourse. Nonetheless, I do claim that how one interprets these discourses will affect the socio-legal imaginary and produce material effects on real people.

One of these effects was to imbricate s/m with harm and degradation, as is what happened with the trial decision's assessment of K.D.'s credibility, its use of precedent, and its evaluation of the meaning of the anal penetration. Recall that Justice Nicholas not only determined that K.D. could not *legally* consent to the anal penetration because of her state of unconsciousness, but found also that K.D. did not *factually* consent. Justice Nicholas comes to this conclusion despite K.D.'s testimony during both examination and cross-examination that she had consented to the anal sex. What stands out for the trial judge is that under examination, K.D. stated that they had never had anal sex before, but under cross, she modified her testimony, recalling that they had engaged in anal sex on a previous occasion. Justice Nicholas discounts this revised testimony, stating, "Human experience would dictate that she would not have to be reminded that anal penetration had occurred on other occasions. I find that she did not at any time consent to this penetration by the dildo in her anus" (*R. v. J.A.* 2008, para. 41). There appear to be two propositions underlying the judge's observations. First, the trial judge apparently views anal penetration as so exceptional that one experience with it will make an indelible mark on one's memory. Second, the judge assumes that if the couple had never had anal sex before, this indicates that the anal penetration on the night in question was non-consensual (despite K.D.'s claim to the contrary), because it was not explicitly brought up and agreed upon. Both propositions peculiarize anal sex and conceptualize it as requiring that consent be specifically worded. This perspective builds upon the long-standing judicial history of criminalizing anal sex as a sexual offence, an indecent act, or obscene representation. Recall also that anal sex is still technically criminalized in section 159 (1) of the *Criminal Code*, subject only to an "exception" that the law does not apply to "husband and wife," or any two people over the age of eighteen who do it in private, with privacy understood to be violated if more than two people are present. Anal sex is thus treated much more suspiciously than vaginal sex, which has an age of consent of sixteen years of age and has no corresponding provisions concerning privacy or group sexual activity. Besides the implicit homophobia of treating anal sex differently in this way, both the judicial history and Justice Nicholas's decision ignore the fact that for some couples, perhaps in particular kinky couples, anal sex may simply not stand out in a long roster of multiple and colourful sexual practices. In addition, the judge's invocation of the essentialist category "human experience" to explain her view of anal sex dehumanizes kinky practitioners who may have different understandings of what activities are so hardcore that they require explicit discussion.

Justice Nicholas also rejects another part of the complainant's testimony for reasons that demonstrate an essentialist conception of sexuality. The complainant testified that she and J.A. had a safe word – "Tweety Bird" – that could be uttered to halt an activity. According to her testimony, the complainant said "Tweety Bird" on that night after both partners had finished with the intercourse, but while she was still in bondage, at which time the accused cut her ties. Justice Nicholas deems K.D. to be lying or mistaken: "In my view, there was no need to use the safe word at the point she described as all manner of sexual activity was complete and she is disbelieved on that point" (*R. v. J.A.* 2008, para. 5). In this finding, the judge's assessment of what counts as "sexual activity" is circumscribed by a vanilla sensibility. While both may have "finished" with the sexual intercourse, from a kinky perspective, being in bondage can itself constitute a sexual activity. Justice Nicholas's incredulity about the complainant's use of their safe word, based solely on her own sense of logic (and not on any testimonial inconsistencies), betrays an investment in sexual normativity and a wilful disregard for the s/m context and the complainant's self-professed agency. Nothing explicitly turns on this finding. However, accepting K.D.'s testimony might have helped to establish her sense of control and her ability to use the safe word when she wanted an activity to cease. This might in turn have affected the assessment of consent – as it would be reasonable to assume that K.D. would have uttered the safe word immediately upon her return to consciousness, if she had subjectively experienced the anal penetration as non-consensual.

Justice Nicholas's citation of other cases further invalidates the potential partnership between submissive and dominant, conflating all s/m with unmitigated violence. In particular, her citation of the British House of Lords decision, *R. v. Brown* (1993), through her consideration of the Ontario Court of Appeal decision, *R. v. Welch* (1995), suggests a generalized pejorative view of s/m sexuality. Recall that in *Brown*, none of the submissive sexual partners complained to the police, none were rendered unconscious, and none required medical attention. Nonetheless, Justice Nicholas cites with approval the case's characterization of s/m as "violence which is inflicted for the indulgence of cruelty" and involves "the degradation of victims" (*R. v. J.A.* 2008, para. 16).

The moralistic rhetoric of this citation is repeated when Justice Nicholas characterizes the bondage and anal sex in the case before her. In the concluding paragraph of her decision, she states the complainant "was not legally capable of consenting to the sexual degrading acts that occurred to her," and later elaborates, "I find that the binding of her hands and the forceful insertion of the dildo to be degradation and dehumanizing acts in the circumstances of this case" (*R. v. J.A.* 2008, para. 45). Although Justice Nicholas's indictment is restricted to the "circumstances of this case," her twice-repeated use of the language of "degradation," combined with the anti-s/m case law she cites, suggests an objection not only to sexual activity when unconscious, but also to the general practice of this kind of kinky sexual activity.

As stated, the majority of the Court of Appeal overturned this decision, while the Supreme Court of Canada overturned the appeal and restored the conviction. Unlike the trial decision, the Supreme Court majority decision contains no overtly moralistic rhetoric regarding the "degrading" or "dehumanizing" nature of the sex in question. Instead, Chief Justice McLachlin writes a more abstract and legalistic ruling based on statutory interpretation and precedent, finding that consent requires a contemporaneous, conscious mind. Yet a close consideration of the ruling reveals a mistrustful view of sexual relationships, where the threat of exploitation pervades, and the right to sexual autonomy is passed over.

This is reflected in Chief Justice McLachlin's determination that the complainant did not subjectively consent to the bondage and anal penetration, despite her testimony that she had in fact done so before the period of unconsciousness, and that she had carried on with sexual activities after regaining consciousness. Timing was the linchpin to this finding. While the majority was seemingly concerned with wrongful acquittals in the case of victims who become inadvertently unconscious, for example, because of drink or drugs, or as the result of a disability, a sexual normative agenda was also reinforced. As Judith Halberstam argues, "Hegemonic constructions of time and space are uniquely gendered and sexualized" (2005, 8). As discussed below, the majority in *R. v. J.A.* perpetuates such a sexualized hegemonic construction, enforcing a temporal linearity that presumes a proper chronological order to an erotic encounter.

The non-normative practice of erotic asphyxiation and sexual activity while unconscious invokes what Halberstam calls "queer time." In the book *In a Queer Time and Place*, Halberstam defines *queer* in a manner that can inform the edgeplay of the lovers in *R. v. J.A.*, describing it as "nonnormative logics and organizations of community, sexual identity, embodiment, and activity in space and time" (2005, 6). In particular, "queer time" refers to models of temporality that disassociate from the hierarchical dyadic construction of "risk/safety" (6). In *R. v. J.A.*, the majority insisted that one cannot be allowed to consent to unconscious sexual activity, in part, because of the *risks*. One such risk is that the conscious lover may misinterpret the desires of the unconscious party, or may purposefully exceed the bounds of her consent. Yet a queer approach may find such a risk irrelevant, or even exciting. For the submissive edgeplayer, time is queered, such that immediate physical sensation and the possibility of monitoring one's partner is exchanged for the psychic satisfaction of imagining what will happen during future unconsciousness, and what did happen during past unconsciousness. In addition, regaining consciousness while in the middle – as opposed to the beginning – of a sexual activity perverts normative sexual chronology, yet can be experienced as highly pleasurable. As the respondent's factum suggests, even vanilla couples may request and enjoy being woken up to kisses or other sexual activity (*R. v. J.A.* 2011 Factum of the Respondent, para. 40).

While the majority decision properly rejects the notion that certain relationships of "mutual trust," like marriage, attenuate the risk of exploitation, what it fails to acknowledge is that some people may have a sexual bent that creates an entirely different relationship to risk and desire. As Lisa Downing suggests in her analysis of erotic asphyxiation,

"Wanting something dangerous *despite or because of* the lack of a guaranteed safety clause could be a valid version of an ethics of pleasure" (Downing 2007, 123). Indeed, in opposition to the more acceptable s/m credo of "safe, sane, and consensual," edgeplay practitioners often adopt a philosophy described as "risk-aware consensual kink" or RACK. This alternative not only asserts the right to engage in activities considered more "extreme" but also challenges the binary opposition between "safety" and "risk." While promoting s/m as "safe, sane, and consensual" will likely have more political traction with the mainstream, the RACK approach foregrounds the fact that all sexual activity – including vanilla sex – carries some risk. Halley offers a useful theorization of such ambivalent pleasures in the vanilla context of workplace sexual behaviour that may or may not be harassment: "It's a risky desire: acting on it places one in the way of having some unwanted sex" (Halley 2006, 300). Later in her analysis, Halley not only points out the difficulty in discerning wanted from unwanted sex, but through a queer lens, also dismantles this binary: "The edgy experience of unwantedness in sex is probably cherished by more people than are willing to say so" (302). Alex Dymock's theorization of female masochism that goes beyond the "safe, sane, and consensual" approach to s/m also offers an alternative lens from which to view K.D.'s subjectivity (2012). Dymock argues that desire and pleasure must be disaggregated in order for some edgeplay, like erotic asphyxiation, to become intelligible: "The problem of the desire–pleasure–acceptance mechanism is that sexual desire and pleasure are not one and the same, nor is pleasure always desire's aim or counterpoint" (62). While K.D. will not experience simultaneous pleasure during her period of unconsciousness, it does not mean that she does not desire it. Such a desire, however, becomes unacceptable because, as Dymock points out, the law refuses to recognize female masochists as sexual subjects when they transgress pleasure as well as safety imperatives.

If we thus take into account the challenges offered by queer theory and the RACK approach to s/m, it becomes apparent that the process of deciding which risks and desires will be considered unacceptable, and which will be ignored or naturalized, depends on sexual ideology that privileges vanilla risk aversion over non-normative desire – whether or not there is a claim or evidence of non-consent. The majority decision imposes a sexual normativity that disregards kinky understandings of acceptable or even desirable risk in queer time, where sensation and satisfaction can happen out of sequence. In their place, the context of domestic violence and sexual danger becomes the master narrative for interpreting erotic asphyxiation.

Feminist, pop cultural, and psychiatric accounts of edgeplay reflect and reinforce this master narrative. The LEAF factum for *R. v. J.A.* is a case in point (*R. v. J.A.* 2011 Factum of LEAF). In describing the relevant incidents, the factum portrays the accused's previous assault convictions as contiguous with the sexual activities in question: "This appeal involves an accused who has twice been convicted of assaulting the complainant and who this time strangled her into unconsciousness and then bound her hands behind her back and penetrated her unconscious body anally with a dildo" (para. 2). The couple's previous experiences with kinky sexuality, including erotic asphyxiation, are characterized as past incidents of "violent sexual acts" (para. 21). The complainant's testimony that she willingly participated in these acts, and her retraction of the police complaint, do not complicate LEAF's argument. Instead, K.D.'s testimony and behaviour are constructed as symptomatic of her victimization: "Women in relationships involving coercive control are required to be 'willing victims': they must accept the abusive spouse's domination, including by reporting that they agreed to, enjoyed, or are responsible for, the violence and abuse" (para. 21). The pathologization of the complainant as a battered spouse helps to discredit her and erase any possibility of her sexual agency. This erasure is further entrenched when LEAF characterizes the pleasures of erotic asphyxiation and unconscious sexual contact as extending solely to the benefit of a male conscious lover who wants to assault his partner. As with the dominant judicial gaze, there is no consideration of the pleasures of submissive sexuality and erotic contact that happens in queer time and out of sequence, or the satisfaction in giving your dominant lover such an experience. In this way, the LEAF factum for *R. v. J.A.* continues in the same ideological track as its factum for *R. v. Butler*; in both representation and practice, women who may enjoy kinky submissive sexuality are conflated with women who have been raped and sexually exploited.

While the LEAF factum expresses no concern for the impact such a decision may have on s/m practitioners, or on the legal understanding of s/m in general, two 2012 feminist law review articles do seek to take such issues into account: one by Karen Busby (2012) and the other by Lise Gotell (2012).[10] Although each article has its own agenda, both reckon with the possible ramifications of the case on female sexual agency and BDSM practitioners, both fault the judiciary for ignoring or misrepresenting some of the pertinent facts and issues, and both appear to support the conviction of J.A. While the articles seek to offer a remedial contextual analysis of the case, I argue that the process of contextualization is political, not self-evident. My analysis of both articles is informed by Halley's call to "take a break from feminism" in order to recognize alternate readings of ambiguous sexual interactions and challenge the feminist "politics of injury" (Halley 2006). Halley defines this feminist political position as an epistemological commitment to the following formula: female injury (woman is the injured party) + female innocence (woman is innocent or incapable of causing harm to man) + male immunity from harm (man is in a position of dominance and incapable of being injured or being in a position of vulnerability vis-à-vis women) = REALITY. In the next few paragraphs, I take issue with this legal feminist perspective.

A key issue that both articles address is the question of how to contextualize the relationship between J.A. and K.D. Both articles contend that media articles, queer commentary, and the judicial decisions (other than the sentencing decision) either minimized or ignored J.A.'s criminal record, particularly the three convictions based on domestic violence. In Gotell's words, K.D. and J.A. were in an "established and abusive heterosexual relationship" (2012, 369). In her indictment of J.A., Busby cites the sentencing decision, which characterizes him as a "serial abuser of women, and this woman in particular" (2012, 337). I take Busby and Gotell's critique seriously, and in fact revised my own description of the fact scenario after reading their articles, to ensure that I had not inadvertently euphemized J.A.'s documented history of violence. But the context that I think the feminist scholars downplay is that the couple was also in an established kinky relationship. According to K.D., they had engaged in "sado-type" behaviour before, including breath play to the point of unconsciousness, bondage, and "dirty talk." They had agreed on a safe word to halt activity and had previously discussed what was allowed and what was not. Bracketing the doctrinal issue of whether one can legally consent to sexual activity expected to occur while one is unconscious, the question of non-legal subjective consent (that is, K.D.'s own sense of whether she consented or not) poses some difficulties when we bear in mind the tension between the abuse and the kinky context. If one begins with the politics of injury, particularly the first part of the formula that is built on female injury, then the obvious answer (and Busby and Gotell's implicit answer) is that the abusive context trumps the kink context (or from LEAF's perspective, there is no contest, and the kink is evidence of the abuse). But if we "take a break" from the politics of injury to assess empowerment, agency, pleasure, danger, coercion, or violation in J.A. and K.D.'s sexual relationship in general, and that night in particular, then the kinky context seems to me to be at least as important as the previous incidents of violence.

How can we adjudicate between the contexts of domestic violence and s/m practice? The feminist tenet to listen to women's voices and the meanings they attribute to their own experiences offers one avenue. The problem is that K.D. gave two conflicting accounts about her subjective experiences. Her testimony at trial was that she did consent; the videotaped police statement was that she did not. Although the Crown abandoned its application to allow admission of the videotaped statement, it still stands as some non-admissible evidence that K.D. did not consent. As stated, K.D.'s explanation for her allegations at the police station was that she had had a fight with J.A. and he had threatened to seek sole custody of their child. Which account to believe? Busby and Gotell both object to judicial, journalistic, and queer academic discourse that accepted K.D.'s testimony at trial, which, in their view, implicitly entrenches the stereotype of "vengeful wives" (Busby 2012) and "lying and vengeful women and the threat of false allegations" (Gotell 2012, 386). What neither seems to note is that the "battered woman" is also a reified category that is susceptible to stereotyping. In particular, there are feminist stereotypes that women in abusive relationships cannot be trusted to tell the truth – if that truth involves defending their partners, or retracting or nuancing a claim of assault – because they are still under the power of, afraid of, or attached to their abuser. Thus the profile of the battered woman is also premised on the notion that women lie, notwithstanding the fact that those who traffic this construction also want to excuse their lying. So which "voice" should we listen to, and which stereotype do we perpetuate? If the starting point is the politics of injury, particularly the premise of female innocence, we of course listen to and place our trust in the videotaped statement, as Busby and Gotell do. In support, both scholars cite the trial judge, who found that K.D. was in distress when the videotaped statement was played at trial in front of the accused, and who was therefore said to fit the judicial construction of a "typical" recanting witness. Gotell reviews these facts, along with the couple's history of both domestic violence and "rough sex," to suggest that "informing this decision is a description of someone who is afraid of the accused and who may, in fact, be falsely recanting" (378). Yet this interpretation of K.D.'s distress is not the only plausible scenario. She could also be distressed because she is uncomfortable with the evidence of her previous false statements. Of course, such a hypothesis flies in the face of the politics of injury. As Halley states, the premise of female innocence casts women as incapable of harming, or of having the agency, will, or malice to cause injury to, others – particularly male others. However, if we "take a break" from the politics of injury, then there might be good reasons to put more weight on K.D.'s trial testimony, particularly after a close examination of the facts that night.

In recounting the material facts, neither Gotell nor Busby shares with readers what followed after K.D. awoke from the period of unconsciousness. This takes the anal penetration out of its sexual context and withholds evidence that might cast a more benign light on the sexual circumstances that night. As stated, after she awoke, the anal penetrative activity continued for about ten seconds, then segued into vaginal intercourse. K.D. testified that "once he was finished and I was finished," she said the safe word, and J.A. untied her. If we take this testimony seriously (and discount the trial judge's disbelief of K.D.'s use of the safe word as reflecting essentialist vanilla notions of sexual norms), it stands as evidence that K.D. did not subjectively experience the period of unconsciousness as a sexual assault. As I argued above, if she had felt assaulted, it seems plausible that she would have used the safe word soon after she had revived. In addition, her testimony about J.A. having "finished," which was then followed by her being "finished," could reasonably be interpreted as a reference to each achieving an orgasm. This would again provide some evidence that she did not experience the sexual activity that night as assaultive. Finally, the fact that it was over seven weeks from the incident to when K.D. went to the police also raises questions about whether the events of that night were experienced as incidents of sexual violation. Of course, it can be extremely challenging for sexual assault victims to go to the police, and that can explain the time delay between the assault and the complaint. And of course, women can continue to have consensual sex and orgasms right after an incident of assault (or even orgasm during the assault).[11] I am not saying that this evidence amounts to "proof." But it is something to think about. One would have to be completely devoted to a feminist politics of injury to not even consider that such facts might challenge the notion that K.D.'s phenomenological experience that night is best described as one of sexual victimization.

The final manifestation of the politics of injury that I want to address is Busby and Gotell's treatment of J.A., and its correspondence with the premise of male immunity from harm. Both Busby and Gotell spend much time providing context that they believe others have overlooked, in particular citing the sentencing decision, and underscoring J.A.'s criminal record. For example, Busby cites the trial judge's characterization of J.A. as a "dangerous and deviant man," and Gotell footnotes a lengthy quote from the sentencing decision that, in her view, demonstrates the "clear and unambiguous context of abuse within which the events in *J.A.* occur" (2012, 371). A closer examination of the facts, however, suggests that the relevance of this "context" is not as clear or unambiguous as Gotell makes out. Anally penetrating K.D. with a dildo during a period of consensually rendered unconsciousness (even if that "consent" is constrained or coerced within larger systems of gender inequality), and then continuing with mutual sexual activity until each one "finished," does not fit the past pattern of abuse against K.D. (if two incidents can be called a "pattern"). Neither Gotell nor Busby highlights the fact that among J.A.'s history of violent offences, none are sexual. The two incidents of domestic violence involving K.D. were in the context of heated arguments, not sexual interactions. Again, I am not suggesting this "proves" that no sexual assault took place, but rather that it undermines the seamless connection that some have sought to forge between the past assault and the sexual activities in question.

I think the reason that this connection seems so seamless to Busby, Gotell, LEAF, and the trial judge is that J.A. has been objectified as an "abuser" in their narratives. Within the politics of injury, which includes the presumption of male immunity from harm, J.A.'s identity as an abuser trumps his identity (and K.D.'s identity) as a kinky person. In this kind of feminist discourse, an abuser becomes an immutable character type; it is the core of J.A.'s identity.[12] He certainly cannot be a *victim* of a female partner who teams up with the police to craft a version of that fateful night that will send J.A. into the prison industrial complex. I know I may be skating on thin ice right now, if I have not already plunged into treasonous waters, so let's put aside the idea that J.A. could have been victimized, in part, by K.D. Even if Busby and Gotell think the man is legally guilty and morally repugnant, they express no concern for the harms and the failures of the criminal justices system *to men*. In this way, not only do their analyses adhere to the politics of injury, but both are also implicated in what Halley refers to as "governance feminism," and more specifically, what Elizabeth Bernstein calls "carceral feminism" (2010).

When Halley talks of governance feminism, she describes what could be read as neutral and even positive developments. In simple terms, feminism has a will to power, it has actual power, and it has done many good things with this power. The fact that rape is taken seriously as a harmful practice – even if not seriously enough – is one example. One of its neuroses, however, is its denial of the costs of feminist gains. As Halley states of feminism, "[It] has governance capacity to change social life, but it also avoids acknowledging the full range of its effects" (2006, 33). One of those unacknowledged effects is to strengthen the criminal justice system, a coercive and violent system that consistently harms those most vulnerable, on the basis of gender, racialization, and poverty, among other sites of oppression.[13] When governance feminism allies with a criminalizing state that purports to address systemic and social problems through punishment – with incarceration being its main tool – this is carceral feminism.

In my view, it is problematic that Busby and Gotell do not consider the carceral effects of the *J.A.* decision in their articles when each has sought out so carefully to provide "context" to the case. Neither mentions the endgame: J.A. was sentenced to eighteen months in jail, registered as a sex offender, and forced to provide a DNA sample – all despite K.D.'s protests and pleas for leniency at the sentencing hearing. Does either scholar think this was a good punishment from a retributive or utilitarian standpoint? Or is it irrelevant, because the feminist victory is the conviction, with other questions about the penal system deemed "outside the scope" of the legal and feminist question of guilt? Whatever the reason for omitting J.A.'s punishment, it represents a trend in governance feminism to ignore its will to power and decontextualize the material effects of such criminal convictions. This is ironic, because one of feminism's most important contributions to legal critique has been to expose the material effects of abstract rulings.

Beside J.A.'s individual objectification as a "criminal" and "abuser," in the spirit of providing "context," I think it is also important to acknowledge that his punishment more broadly legitimates the neoliberal criminal justice system, entrenches the prison industrial complex, and extends the criminalizing surveillance society.[14] To make such an acknowledgment does not mean that one does not take sexual violence seriously. For example, Rape Relief, a radical feminist organization and women's shelter, provides strong arguments against the collection of DNA samples as a means of addressing violence against women. In an online article, "Not in Our Name," Rape Relief argues that collecting

DNA samples from offenders works against the interests of most sexual assault survivors and diverts public resources away from services that assist victims, and towards the police – an institution complicit in violence against women. In addition, not just concerned with women, Rape Relief also addresses the impact on marginalized men: "Native men, men of colour and poor men are jailed in Canada at a rate far out of proportion with Canadian demographics. Because their DNA would dominate the DNA databank, using such a databank to identify perpetrators of crime would reinforce and even promote more inequality in our justice system" (Miller and Kubanek n.d.). Thus, on the basis of class and racial inequality, Rape Relief effectively breaks from a politics of injury to highlight male vulnerability and victimization within a decontextualized and neoliberal punishment scheme.

Besides not commenting on this penal realist context, Busby's article takes carceral feminism one step further. Not only is J.A.'s conviction claimed as a good thing, she also suggests we might need more criminal law. Over thirty American states have passed strangulation felony crimes, and Busby, citing a New York police media release, finds that this new crime appears to be an effective avenue for law enforcement. On the basis of this American model, she demonstrates her faith in a police and criminal-centred response by suggesting that Canada should consider creating its own strangulation-specific offence. No consideration is given to the prolific scholarship by critical race feminists about the ineffectiveness of allying with the state in response to intimate partner violence, increasing police powers, and diverting more funds into the prison system, and the harms such approaches can cause to both marginalized men and to female victims of male violence.[15] And of course, s/m players who participate in breath play will also be more vulnerable to criminalization under such a new law.

In contrast to Busby's implicit embrace of the penal state, Gotell does not advocate for a proliferation of criminalizing solutions. Instead, she challenges the affirmative consent discourse that portrays female victims of violence as neoliberal subjects who are themselves responsible for managing the risk of sexual danger. For the men, they are produced as "good masculine sexual subjects, defined through the imperatives of consent seeking and disciplined through the risk of criminalization" (2012, 366). However, while these aspects of Gotell's article seem to be deconstructing both the male and female neoliberal roles produced by law, other parts depict men as empowered liberal subjects who make meaningful (and harmful) choices. Indeed, most of Gotell's references to masculinity endow men with substantial agential power. This can be seen, for example, in her argument that insofar as cases like *R. v. J.A.* ascribe sexual subjectivity or autonomy to women, they effectively "obscure the stakes for men's sexual access and entitlement" (376), "hold women accountable for their own objectification," and "shield from view men's agency, interpersonal and relational coercion, and larger systems of sexist oppression" (381). In such descriptions, only men can wield power, agency, and desire to access sexual pleasure; it would thus be a mistake to take heed of any consent that women may give to submissive or risky sexual behaviour, as any such consent can only be the product of "larger systems of oppression." While Gotell is critical of the gendered neoliberal transactional model of sexuality (where legitimate sex can take place only after the male asks for consent and the woman gives consent), her framing of sexual interactions also reads as a neoliberal contract. The difference is that in Gotell's version, the bargainers have unequal power. The man's sexual access and entitlement is seen as having come at the unavoidable expense of the woman's right to be free from objectification. They are portrayed as having cross-purposes; if he wins, then she must lose. In contrast to this cynical and individualistic framing, a sympathetic reading of the s/m dynamic would not understand the interaction as contractual, but instead as one of mutuality, trust, intersubjectivity, and the symbiotic sharing of desire and pleasure.[16]

In addition, the unspoken assumption in Gotell's reasoning is that foregrounding a woman's sexual agency, adventurousness, or desires – even if this is supported by the woman's own testimony – denies structural constraints. Yet as Kathryn Abrams has argued, the recognition of structural constraints and systemic oppression might better be understood as a "critical description, rather than a life sentence of injury and passivity" (1995, 348). If the context of kinky sexuality *and* abusive incidents are acknowledged, it is possible to understand K.D. as someone who negotiates both pleasure and danger in her relationship with J.A. Moreover, recognizing that oppressive ideologies inform desire and action does not mean that criminalizing the male partner in risky power-play sexuality is the answer.

While Gotell has recently written on the limited effectiveness of criminal convictions as the primary or sole response to sexual assault in the context of gender inequality,[17] her 2012 article on *R. v. J.A.* does not address the neoliberal dimensions of the penal system or comment on the way the criminal justice system, and the sentencing decision, responsabilized J.A. as a rational actor who failed to correct his behaviour after his past convictions and stints in jail. There is no mention of the carceral system itself as a major player in inculcating violence and engendering misery. Indeed, in citing J.A.'s criminal record to establish the abusive context of his relationship with K.D., Gotell implicitly relies on the truth-value of criminalizing neoliberal discourse. As with Busby, no *context* is provided about the ways poverty, mental health issues, intergenerational trauma, colonialism, racism, *and* criminalization are linked to male violence in intimate partner settings.[18] Despite Gotell's interest in exposing neoliberal ideologies in this article, the politics of injury obscures J.A.'s reification as an abuser in a neoliberal framework, and his victimization at the hands of the penal system.

I realize that my engagement with the harms of criminalization goes outside of the scope of Busby's and Gotell's articles. This may be particularly unfair to Gotell's article, which focuses on the governing effects of the legal discourses at play in and around the *J.A.* decision. But working with state power and relying on criminalizing discourse involves political contradictions, entailing both benefits and costs; I think it important here to highlight some of those contradictions and costs. Sometimes, as Halley insists, it is a zero-sum game. Sometimes men and sexual minorities will bear the costs of ensuring that more sexual assault cases that should end in conviction (from a legal feminist perspective), do end in conviction. That might be a symbolic and political benefit. Some women, particularly those with more social capital, might be safer because of it. But one cost is that more men – and disproportionately, more marginalized men – will be funnelled into a bloated, failing, and violent penal system. Another cost is that sexual minorities, particularly BDSM edgeplayers, will become more vulnerable to criminalization. Busby's article goes to great lengths to deny any costs, insisting that moderate practitioners of "safe, sane, and consensual" BDSM have little to fear from the *J.A.* precedent. She's right. But edgeplayers are another story.

In the cinematic world, there appear to be few films that deal with consensual edgeplay. One exception is *Killing Me Softly*, which also associates erotic asphyxiation with abuse. Yet at the same time, unlike the feminist and judicial constructions, it paradoxically sells the practice as highly erotic. Recall that in the most explicitly kinky consensual scene, the female submissive lover, Alice, allows her partner, Alex, to tie a scarf around her neck while they engage in intercourse. He creates a rhythm in sync with his thrusts, alternately tightening and loosening the scarf around her throat. In her voice-over, Alice says of this sexual act, "I gave up all control and let him decide when I could breathe and when I couldn't. I loved it." The scene is played erotically, not suspensefully, drawing the audience into the sensuality of the moment. It is only later, when Alex becomes a prime murder suspect and begins to act in an obsessive and controlling fashion, that the erotic asphyxiation retroactively comes to signify the beginning of dysfunction and abuse. And the fact that the lovers part in the end – despite Alex's innocence (of murder at least) – suggests that their edgeplay s/m practice, while highly pleasurable, is incompatible with a sustainable loving relationship. In this way, *Killing Me Softly* supports a general negative view of erotic asphyxiation, particularly because its instigator – Alex – comes to be tainted with the taboo of incest.

Another film worth mentioning in relation to *R. v. J.A.* is Roman Polanski's masterpiece *Rosemary's Baby* (1968), not because it addresses s/m, but because it was highly acclaimed and features the sexual exploitation of a woman when she is unconscious. In this supernatural flick, Rosemary's husband drugs his wife on the night they are planning to conceive a child. In the morning, Rosemary's body is covered with deep scratches, and she has vague memories of a dream where she was being raped by something "inhuman." When she questions her husband, he explains that he did not want to miss out on "baby night," implying he had sexual intercourse with her unconscious body, which he describes as "fun, in a necrophile sort of way." What Rosemary later discovers is that her husband is a member of a cult, and while she was indeed raped, it was not by her husband, but rather by Satan himself. In a hyperbolic way, this film expresses many of the feminist and judicial concerns about advance consent. Before she passes out, Rosemary says, "We have to make a baby," which could be interpreted as advance consent. Furthermore, when she is unconscious, her husband takes advantage of her vulnerable state and allows another to rape her, while Rosemary remains unaware of this violation. Thus in this cinematic treatment, advance consent to sexual contact while unconscious is portrayed as leading not only to sexual abuse, but also to the conception of the devil's spawn!

In a less dramatic way, the *DSM-IV-TR* and the *DSM-V* also speak indirectly to the *R. v. J.A.* case, on the issue of erotic asphyxiation. In its definition of *sexual masochism*, the *DSM-IV-TR* states, "One particularly dangerous form of Sexual Masochism, called 'hypoxyphilia' [erotic asphyxiation], involves sexual arousal from oxygen deprivation" (American Psychiatry Association 2000, 572). According to Moser and Kleinplatz, this is a misleading statement, as they argue, "There is no empirical data correlating hypoxyphilia to masochism" (2005b, 104.) In contrast, however, Richard Krueger's review of the literature on paraphilic sexual masochism found that people who engaged in hypoxyphilia consistently fantasized about masochistic scenarios (2010, 7). He further found that fifty deaths a year can be attributed to this practice and recommended that the *DSM-V* retain sexual masochism as a paraphilic disorder, in part because "in a very small number of cases … masochistic fantasy and behavior result in severe harm or even death" (8). As the author has provided fatality statistics with regard to only one practice, hypoxyphilia, there is the suggestion that erotic asphyxiation is one of the key justifiers of the pathologization of sexual masochism. Krueger's perspective on the link between erotic asphyxiation and paraphilic masochism was adopted in the *DSM-V*. Recall that erotic asphyxiation, referred to in this edition as "asphyxiophilia," is referenced both in the diagnostic criteria as a specification and in the commentary on sexual masochism, where it warns "masochists are at risk of accidental death while practicing asphyxiophilia" (American Psychiatry Association 2000, 695). This alarming and disparaging view is replicated in the trial decision and LEAF factum in *R. v. J.A.*, which painted the consensual choking as symptomatic not only of the accused's desire for dominance, but also of the complainant's frail mental state.

The Criminalization of a Professional Dom and Law's Monopoly on Humiliation

R. v. Bedford (1998; 2000)

In this section, I consider the *R. v. Bedford* "bondage bungalow" case that began in 1998, where Terri Bedford, a professional dominatrix, was charged with keeping a bawdy house, contrary to section 210(1) of the *Criminal Code*. Many readers will be familiar with the 2013 decision involving Bedford, where the Supreme Court of Canada struck down three key prostitution-related criminal laws for violating the constitutional rights of sex workers, including section 210(1) (*Canada [Attorney General] v. Bedford* 2013 SCC 72). The earlier case that I now examine concerned the services that Bedford and her female employees provided to male clients at Madame de Sade's House of Erotica, run out of a bungalow in a residential zone in Toronto. Clients could choose from a variety of s/m themed sessions, ranging from erotic cross-dressing to bondage and whipping. Bedford also put limits on the permissible services. There was a clear rule conveyed to employees and potential clients: sexual intercourse, oral sex, and masturbation of a client by a mistress were prohibited on the premises. However, there was evidence that testicle massage was allowed if a client was masturbating himself and was having difficulty maintaining an erection or achieving orgasm.

The arrest happened in 1994, when fifteen police officers descended upon the location, executed a search warrant, and charged Bedford for keeping a common bawdy house, defined by the *Criminal Code* as "a place that is (*a*) kept or occupied, or (*b*) resorted to by one or more persons for the purpose of prostitution or the practice of acts of indecency" (*Criminal Code* 1985, s. 197(1)). Before trial, it was specified that the charge referred to Bedford keeping the bawdy house for the purposes of prostitution. The accused lost at both the trial and appeal, and her application for leave to appeal to the Supreme Court of Canada was denied. In this analysis, I will refer to the trial and appellate decisions, and to a few oral rulings made by the trial judge on procedural issues. The conduct of the police and the judgments in this case reveal a voyeuristic delight in delving into the details of the activities at the s/m establishment, as well as a jealous need to establish the justice system's monopoly on meting out humiliation.

The defence's main argument was that there had been no "prostitution," as understood by the law, because the s/m sessions offered by Bedford and her mistress employees did not constitute "sexual acts." Because of Bedford's prohibition of intercourse, oral sex, or masturbation by a mistress, the defence took the position that the s/m sessions offered were not primarily sexual in nature, but were more about power, pain, and humiliation, and therefore did not qualify as "prostitution" within the legal meaning. Finally, the defence argued that the police had violated Bedford's *Charter* rights during the arrest by using excessive force, performing an unnecessary strip-search, conducting themselves disrespectfully, and seizing a large number of items from the premises with the intent to put the accused out of business. The details of this behaviour, which were supported by the Crown's key witness, included officers pushing and shoving the female dominants, demanding that the accused call them "master," asking for a demonstration of boot-licking, and ridiculing the s/m props and clothes. In addition, the female occupants were all strip-searched on the premises by a female officer, allegedly to see if they were concealing weapons or money.

In an oral ruling rejecting the defence's request for a stay of proceedings because of abuse of process, Justice Bogusky focused exclusively on the justifications offered by the police for their conduct, and not on the experiences of the female accused (*R. v. Bedford* Ruling (re Charter application) 1998, 1378). For example, in considering the police "rowdyism," he downplays the seriousness of the behaviour by concluding in essence that boys will be boys. As stated by Justice Bogusky, "If you want to get a reaction from a bunch of young bucks present them with some imagery of the male anatomy, including images of penises plus equipment for cross-dressing and you might get a rather strange reaction. The reaction which flowed was almost predictable" (1379–80). In other words, the male gender of the police officers (the "young bucks") excuses their inappropriate behaviour, particularly because they were confronted with sex toys and emasculating cross-dressing attire. In reference to the allegation that the police engaged in rough-housing, Justice Bogusky states vaguely, "Now here, again, human nature says there is obviously an explanation" (1384). However, this statement is not followed by any elaboration on which aspects of human nature are being cited to explain what behaviour. And there is no clear ruling on whether the abuse took place at all, despite evidence from both Crown and defence witnesses that at least some unnecessary pushing and shoving did take place. Finally, with regard to the strip-search, Justice Bogusky does have some reservations about its necessity, initially stating, "It looks like a make-work project" (1386). However, after taking a brief adjournment, he comes back to state flatly, "The strip-search was felt necessary by the officer in charge of the search. The reasons for the search were given to the court. It was not done arbitrarily. I have to accept the reasons, therefore no remedy lies specifically on that" (1387–8). In other words, the court refuses to examine the superficial explanation proffered by the police, effectively abdicating its responsibility to assess whether that explanation is valid or lawful in the circumstances of the case.

Ultimately Justice Bogusky rejects all of the defence's *Charter* arguments. While he finds that Bedford "was not well done by" and that the police conduct was "shabby," he determines that even when added up, the police "indiscretions" did not warrant a stay of proceedings because of abuse of process (*R. v. Bedford* Ruling (re Charter application) 1998, 1389). A consideration of the consensual s/m at issue and the police conduct towards the female accused reveals an unjust quirk in the law: it was unlawful for Bedford to provide consensual and pleasurable degradation and humiliation, but lawful for the police to degrade and humiliate the suspects, all because it was "almost predictable" that male police officers would be unsettled by the accoutrement of the establishment and act inappropriately. The Court of Appeal ultimately agreed with this result, despite the appellate judgment's characterization that "the conduct of some of the officers was unprofessional and *demeaning* to the appellant" (*R. v. Bedford* 2000, para. 14; emphasis added). For the appellate court, this "demeaning" treatment was considered par for the course, and the harm to the dignity of the accused was overlooked.

I want to take a moment to specifically consider the strip-search in the context of this legal double standard on demeaning treatment. Recall that the police explained their conduct by saying they needed to ensure that the female occupants were not concealing weapons and money. However, given the nature of the bawdy-house charges being laid, there was no reason to search for concealed weapons. Further, while it is true that the exchange of money for sexual services is at the crux of the definition of prostitution, the police provided no reason to suspect that the women were hiding money on their bodies in this specific circumstance. What the police claimed was a right to strip-search as routine to a bawdy-house arrest.

Unfortunately for the accused, the *Bedford* appellate decision came out a year before the Supreme Court of Canada laid down important restrictions on the lawfulness of strip-searches in *R. v. Golden* (2001). I believe under that reasoning, the strip-search would have been deemed unlawful. Since the *Bedford* court did not have the benefit of the *Golden* precedent to guide its determination, I am not arguing that the strip-search question was necessarily wrongfully decided at the time. However, the Supreme Court of Canada's insights about the phenomenology of strip-searching sheds light on the ideological and gendered issues at play in *Bedford*. In *Golden*, the Supreme Court of Canada concluded:

> Strip searches are thus inherently humiliating and degrading for detainees regardless of the manner in which they are carried out and for this reason they cannot be carried out simply as a matter of routine policy. The adjectives used by individuals to describe their experience of being strip searched give some sense of how a strip search, even one that is carried out in a reasonable manner, can affect detainees: "humiliating," "degrading," "demeaning," "upsetting," and "devastating" (see *King, supra; R. v. Christopher*, [1994] O.J. No. 3120 (QL) (Gen. Div.); J. S. Lyons, Toronto Police Services Board Review, *Search of Persons Policy – The Search of Persons – A Position Paper* (April 12, 1999)). Some commentators have gone as far as

to describe strip searches as "visual rape" (P. R. Shuldiner, "Visual Rape: A Look at the Dubious Legality of Strip Searches" (1979), 13 *J. Marshall L. Rev.* 273). Women and minorities in particular may have a real fear of strip searches and may experience such a search as equivalent to a sexual assault (Lyons, *supra*, at p. 4). The psychological effects of strip searches may also be particularly traumatic for individuals who have previously been subject to abuse (Commission of Inquiry into Certain Events at the Prison for Women in Kingston, *The Prison for Women in Kingston* (1996), at pp. 86–89). (para. 90)

The Supreme Court of Canada thus understood that even lawful strip-searches are inherently traumatic, and described the experience in the language of sexual abuse.[19] Taking this into account, the conclusion in *Bedford* that the police strip-search was acceptable, but the s/m conduct was not, appears acutely ironic. In *Bedford*, "humiliating" and "degrading" treatment of women in the form of a strip-search was justified as a matter of routine policy, while the provision of sexual pleasure for men through the consensual uses of humiliation and degradation was deemed criminal. The law therefore displayed a greater tolerance for the occurrence of sexual trauma than the occurrence of sexual pleasure. The legal gaze saw harm to society where consensual sexual pleasure was not kept private and non-commercial, but did not see social harm in the non-consensual strip search of Bedford and her female employees; their complaints were individualized and irrelevant to the law. Ultimately, the justice system does not condemn humiliation and degradation; it simply seeks to monopolize its use. As Robert Cover states, "Legal interpretive acts signal and occasion the imposition of violence upon others … Interpretations in law also constitute justifications for violence which has already occurred or which is about to occur. When interpreters have finished their work, they frequently leave behind victims whose lives have been torn apart by these organized, social practices of violence" (1986, 1601). In *Bedford*, Cover's insights manifest. The law has no trouble doling out sexual humiliation and degradation, so long as it is routinized and framed within regulated social practices.

This "routine procedure" also specifically addresses gendered order. While the police could not offer a lawful compelling reason for ordering strip-searches in the circumstances of the specific case, there was an ideologically compelling reason to carry out the strip-search, which was to put the women back in their place. The dominatrix establishment created a social anxiety that caused the "young bucks" to get out of hand, to become rowdy, and ultimately to violate the dignity of the female suspects. By ordering that the women be stripped, as well as by pushing them around, mocking the s/m scenarios, and demanding a demonstration of boot-licking, the male cops re-established their top position in the gendered and sexual order.

Bearing this in mind, a consideration of the filmic representation of female dominants reveals overlapping normative orders. Recall that when professional dominants were represented, the narratives always included a moment where they would bottom for a man. In *Exit to Eden*, *Preaching to the Perverted*, and *Crimes of Passion*, the female dominants all take the bottom position during missionary sex towards the end of the film. In both law and film, professional female sexual dominance – while titillating and provocative – creates a crisis in gendered order. And in both arenas, the female dominants must be relegated back into a submissive sexual position, either coercively, as with the strip-searching and degrading treatment under police custody, or tacitly, as with the representation of female dominants who finally embrace hetero-normative sexual intercourse, and their feminine (i.e., submissive) position within it.

Another overlap between the *Bedford* judgments and filmic representation centres on the pleasures of vicarious kink and the utterances of disgust. Justice Bogusky explicitly expressed disgust in his ruling on the admissibility of testimony by defence expert witnesses on s/m. In explaining why he allowed them all to testify before determining if they had any relevant expertise or insight to assist the court, he stated, "If I exclude all of the so-called experts on the basis of non-relevancy, the court runs a risk of drawing a negative inference toward the facts or the accused because some of the evidence presented was, although initially entertaining, it ultimately began to progress to the bizarre and ultimately disgusting. To avoid this possibility, I require some assistance in putting a human face on the participants as they are members of our community. In other words, I can use all the help I can get" (*R. v. Bedford* Ruling (re experts) 1998, 1355). These expert witnesses, made up of social scientists, theorists, and psychologists, were attesting that s/m was not centred on sex but upon other things, such as power or emotional catharsis. However, Justice Bogusky suggests that for him, their primary purpose was to humanize s/m practitioners. His ruling attests both to the vicarious pleasure he derived from these articulations of kink, and to his own normalcy. By stating that ultimately the evidence ceased to be entertaining and became "bizarre" and "disgusting," he firmly erects a discursive border between himself and the s/m practitioners. And yet one could interpret his acknowledgment of s/m participants as "members of our community" as conversely blurring the discursive border slightly. While firmly establishing himself as a non-sadomasochist, Justice Bogusky still offers a token of fellowship in his oral ruling by placing s/m practitioners within the inclusive space of belonging in *our* community.

Unfortunately, in the *Bedford* trial and appellate decisions (as opposed to the oral ruling on the *Charter* application), no inclusionary gestures are made towards s/m practitioners. Instead, both decisions revel in the details of the s/m activities taking place in the establishment, reaping an epistemological pleasure in specifying the sexual taxonomies that justify conviction. In the *Bedford* trial decision, Justice Bogusky catalogues the different visual effects, moods, props, and body parts involved in the contested activities. He also brings the language of s/m to the scene by citing the labels used by practitioners themselves, such as by referring to "cock-and-ball" stimulation and "ass play." However, he then concludes his judgment by proffering an example of one form of s/m activity that he apparently feels can "sum up" the primarily sexual nature of impugned s/m behaviour: "Common sense allows no other interpretation of a scenario involving a naked male with a rope around his penis being attended to by a female, even more so when she is wearing lingerie" (*R. v. Bedford* 1998, para. 11).

The *Bedford* appellate decision replicates the trial decision's cataloguing of the s/m sexual services that were on offer. But appellate Justice Finlayson goes further to provide specific statistics on the activities and the arousal level of the clients. He states that according to the Crown's key witness, a female employee of the establishment, "Most clients (about 96%) got erections during erotica session and about 80% achieved orgasm" (*R. v. Bedford* 2000, para. 8). In the next paragraph he continues, "A specific activity conducted in the erotica room, in which 45–50% of the clients were involved, was called 'cock-and-ball stimulation' or 'cock-and-ball torture'" (para. 9). Offering specific percentages of clients engaged in particular activities getting erections and achieving orgasm lends the decision an almost scientific legitimacy. These empirical data buttress the epistemological pleasure embedded in the decision. The judge's vicarious textual renderings of these s/m scenes and experiences thus proliferate and expand the s/m terrain of pleasure. Through the process of criminalization, the law reaps the pleasures in knowing, understanding, naming, and pinpointing, down to the exact number of erections and orgasms, the alleged truth of these s/m sessions.

Yet *Bedford* articulates an ambivalent counter-truth-claim to the predominant legal construction of s/m. In the anti-s/m feminist literature and earlier cases that involve s/m pornography or practice, violence operates as the master narrative to explain such behaviours. The sexual and pleasurable aspects of s/m are suppressed as the anti-s/m gaze fixates on the ways the submissive body is restrained or marked within scenarios that will be read only as exploitive, regardless of any stated intentions of the participants. In *Bedford*, the sexual nature of s/m is foregrounded. Of course, in the case law the consistency in both truth-claims – s/m is violence or s/m is sex – is that the law appears to choose the one that will support criminalization. Nonetheless, a legal recognition of s/m as a sexuality does complicate the jurisprudence and may create unwitting discursive space for s/m practitioners to assert their own truth-claims about their desires.

An Interlude on Personal Narratives by Legal Academics and Advocates

I end this section by looking at another form of legal discourse that addressed *Bedford*, this time from an advocate's perspective. Lead counsel for Bedford and professor of law at Osgoode Hall Law School, Alan Young, examines the Canadian criminal justice system and, in one chapter, describes his defence strategies and experience in representing Bedford (2003). Young offers many astute observations in his analysis. For example, he highlights the trial and appellate courts' phallocentricism in determining the nature of the s/m sessions, stating that "legal professionals operated on a simple, mindless formula: hard-on = crime. The penis overwhelmed their field of vision and the thoughts and words of experts and practitioners fell on deaf ears" (92). Young's characterization enriches my earlier argument that both the trial and the appellate decisions seemed fixated on the penis, erect and/or ejaculating, as proof that the activities were primarily sexual.

I have deep respect for Young's commitment to advocating and defending adults engaged in consensual sexual and recreational drug activity, and I admire the irreverent stance he takes in *Justice Defiled* towards the criminal justice system. In fact, I support every critique he puts forward against laws that interfere with consensual choices. However, one thing I find fascinating in his account of *Bedford* is that he seems compelled to use the lexicon of disgust and to erect an identity border between himself and the s/m practitioners, even as he passionately defends their rights. This strategy recalls the House of Lords dissenting judges in *R. v. Brown* (1993), who appeared compelled to reassure the reader that while they did not find the sadomasochists criminals, they did find them unappealing.

In beginning his discussion of *Bedford*, Young states, "I have never had trouble defending public sexuality, but in 1998 the boundaries of my tolerance were stretched when I was retained to defend sado-masochistic fantasy" (2003, 85). Here, Young establishes himself as somewhat reluctant in taking Bedford's cause. He then identifies himself as a vanilla-sex practitioner, describing his sex life as "Ordinary. Conventional. Plain" (86). He elaborates later, "I wasn't sure if I liked the issue. Sure, I had been championing the cause of sexual liberty for years, but that was all about vanilla sex. Personally, I had never approached the fringe, and the little I knew about S/M from movies and books creeped me out" (87). Young thus reveals the influence of popular culture and identifies himself as a non-sadomasochist who initially experienced disgust at the thought of s/m. But he later explains that this visceral reaction mostly faded away when he learned that "most of the S/M conduct pursued by aficionados was not very painful, and the humiliating aspects were so ritualized and scripted that the sting and degradation became muted" (87). The fact that Young begins his discussion of the *Bedford* case with his own emotional journey and a sexual self-identification as "vanilla" and "ordinary" has narrative significance. He may have done this to reassure the reader that he took the case because of legal principle and not because of personal investment. He might have believed that his advocacy for the rights of s/m providers and practitioners would be taken more seriously if he shared with the reader the feelings of being "creeped out" by the thought of s/m. When he narrates that he eventually embraced their cause, his legal stance perhaps has more credibility to a reader who feels distaste towards s/m.

Yet after he finishes his analysis of *Bedford*, Young's final musing on s/m again communicates to the reader that he has no interest in kinky practices. He states, "Despite my championing of the S/M cause, I always had a bit of sadness when I thought about some of the characters inhabiting this sub-terranean world. It's somewhat pathetic that someone has to dress up as Louis XV or as an infant in a soiled diaper and yell '*Vive la France*' or whimper 'Mommy, don't hurt me too bad' in order to get a sexual buzz. I find this sad because I still believe that vanilla sex is one of the most magnificent and oceanic experiences available in life's repertoire. Who needs the costumes and the humiliation? Well, I guess some people do" (2003, 97). Here, Young takes on a slightly condescending tone towards s/m practitioners. It is "sad" and "pathetic" that they need these "costumes and humiliation" to get a sexual buzz. He uses examples that would likely be foreign and disgust-provoking from a conventional sexual standpoint, in particular the adult-baby role playing. Young further feels compelled to share with the reader his personal sexual desires. He wants us to know that he experiences "vanilla sex" as "magnificent" and "oceanic," such that *he* certainly does not need any of the s/m props or role playing to feel sexual pleasure. Perhaps having informed the reader that he had only vanilla sex before he began the case, he also needed the reader to know that his desires were not converted by his proximity to s/m during his advocacy work.

Young thus frames his analysis of *Bedford* with his own visceral distaste for s/m and assertions of his vanilla subjectivity. From my reading, what is operating in this rhetorical strategy is, in part, a management of the contagiousness of disgust. As Miller has argued, utterances of disgust, while they create a social community, also risk contaminating the speaker (1997, 5, 194).[20] By providing his personal perspective on s/m and vanilla sex, Young ensures that the reader includes him in the social community that feels an aversion to s/m, and by giving details of his own "ordinary" but "oceanic" sexual trajectory, he further attenuates the risk of being contaminated by his cause.

I don't necessarily disagree with Young's rhetorical strategy in general, as I am acutely aware of the identity politics at stake when one writes about s/m from a sympathetic viewpoint. It feels like a no-win situation. If you acknowledge a personal interest in s/m, your critique seems biased; you can be dismissed as being too close to the issue to be objective. If you identify as a non-sadomasochist or as vanilla, then you can be accused of objectifying s/m practitioners or appropriating sadomasochist causes without truly understanding the subculture's dynamics or the larger social marginalization. My screenplay prelude for this book clearly engages with this conundrum by attempting to entice the reader with clues about the origins of my interest in the topic of s/m. My story further parallels Young's, as both begin with the suggestion that we were initially disturbed by the thought of s/m. Although we have different agendas, Young's deployment of autobiographical storytelling is not so different from my own. My understanding of *Justice Defiled* is that Young seemed to be most concerned with the possibility that the reader might mistake his advocacy of s/m as an attraction to s/m, hence the need to elaborate upon his sexual preferences. My use of personal anecdotes is premised on the hope that disclosing a familiarity with s/m will work to de-stigmatize the practice. But in both cases, an epistemology based on personal revelations is at play.

S/M outside Criminal Regulation and inside Other Legal Contexts

Family Perversions

So far, the issue of parenting and youth in connection to s/m has come up only sporadically in the cases I have examined. In *Brown*, one method of vitiating the consent of the submissive partners was to represent them as "youth" who had been corrupted by older perverted men. In *Loyalist*, the arbitration board decided that a college professor's interest in BDSM pornography, and his defence of those desires as a lifestyle choice, were sufficient indicators that he was an unsuitable role model to his students. In *R.D.W.*, both the dominant and the submissive were sixteen-year-old minors whose s/m desires were seen as unhealthy but, perhaps because of their youth, still fixable. By contrast, in *Price*, although addressing s/m pornography, the court accepted the defence evidence that constructed s/m practice as normal and healthy. And interestingly, the court gave a sympathetic portrayal of witness Sylvia Schneider, a self-proclaimed enthusiast of s/m practice, despite the fact that she had a teenage daughter who was apparently aware of her mother's sexual interests. As such, while most of the case law is unsettled by the affiliation of s/m with youth, *Price* was exceptional in this regard. As I demonstrate in this subsection, when the main issue is the capability of an s/m practitioner to parent, the tolerant perspective in *Price* continues to stand out as an exception.

NOVA SCOTIA (MINISTER OF COMMUNITY SERVICES) V. A.C. (2003)
The 2003 Canadian family law case *Nova Scotia (Minister of Community Services) v. A.C.* exemplifies how s/m, though not explicitly criminalized, and technically de-pathologized under some circumstances, can still operate as a damning blight on a person's character. The case involves an application by the minister of community services for permanent care and custody of two children pursuant to the *Children and Family Services Act*. The respondent, A.C., was the mother of the two children, who was "prepared to do anything to get the children back" (para. 8). During all material times, A.C. was living with or involved

with J.C., who was the stepfather of the two children, C.A.T. and P.T. The facts of the case present an unequivocal picture of childhood abuse and neglect. The children's physical, emotional, and educational needs were recklessly ignored, they were physically abused and subjected to unhygienic living conditions, and they witnessed domestic violence. On those facts alone, the judge appears to have had sufficient reason to grant the application. Yet she spends a significant chunk of the judgment interrogating the sexually "deviant" behaviours and characteristics of A.C. The case shows that along with her incompetence as a parent, what ends up being put on trial is the truth of A.C.'s sexuality.

A brief timeline of events demonstrates how A.C. began to practise s/m and how this affected her parental rights. In about 1994, A.C. was twenty years of age and became intimately involved with J.C. She had two children from previous relationships. Early in their relationship, A.C. was informed both by the Children's Aid Society of Halifax (The Society) and by J.C. himself that J.C. had a record of sexual assault upon minors. Undaunted by his history of abusive paedophilic behaviour, A.C. married J.C. in 1996. In her summary of the facts, Justice Dellapinna details that about this time, A.C. and J.C. began to participate in "deviant sexual behaviour," including "extreme sadomasochism, bondage, and eventually bestiality and the involvement of third parties including prostitutes" (*Nova Scotia v. A.C.* 2003, para. 18). In the judicial discourse that follows, these sexual practices became a linchpin upon which to justify the granting of the application for a permanent care and custody order with no order for access. A.C. lost all rights to be with her children ever again.

The assertion that A.C.'s sexual proclivities were relevant to the assessment of her capacity to parent was based on a specific concern about exposing the children to sexual deviance, and on some underlying assumptions about the contagiousness of deviance. Experts supposedly knowledgeable in the field of sexual perversion were called upon to dissect A.C.'s sexuality to determine whether she was constitutionally deviant or had been coerced into it by a dysfunctional relationship, and to assess the risks of recidivism.

Though Justice Dellapinna never fully decided whether A.C. was inherently deviant or had been coerced, the judge determined that as a result of A.C.'s history, she could not be trusted to put her children's needs over her own or her partner's sexual needs.

As mentioned above, the main reason for indicting A.C.'s participation in s/m sexuality was the determination that she had exposed her children to it. However, there was no direct evidence brought forward that indicated the children had witnessed their mother and stepfather engaging in any sexual activity. Further, A.C. testified that the children were never exposed to their sexual practices. Valorie Rule, a registered clinical and forensic psychologist who contributed to a parental assessment of A.C., countered this evidence. She attested, "It is not socially appropriate to engage in bondage and sadomasochism and bestiality in a two-bedroom mobile home where children are present. It is unlikely that the children did not witness some of these behaviours" (*Nova Scotia v. A.C.* 2003, para. 32). Justice Dellapinna echoes this sentiment, stating, "It is hard to believe [that the children never witnessed the s/m activities] given the very small premises in which the parties and the children lived" (para. 22). In her assessment of the evidence, the judge preferred the expert's extrapolation over A.C.'s first-hand account of what was likely to have occurred within the six years that the couple were together and participating in s/m.

Yet a two-bedroom home should have theoretically allowed for privacy during any kind of sexual contact – at least to the same extent as exists for the many non-kinky couples who also live with children in two-bedroom mobile homes. Yet s/m sexuality is presumed to be more blatant and more visible, and inherently less likely to be performed outside of the children's view. There is an implication that a couple practising s/m could not or would not hide their "deviance" from the children. Yet what should be at issue is whether the parents were able to maintain healthy boundaries between their sex life (whatever form it may take) and their children. After all, it is also presumably not in the best interests of a child to witness her non-kinky parents engaging in sexual activity in open spaces, like the living room. Yet the judgment does not focus on this broader issue of A.C.'s ability to maintain healthy boundaries with her children within the confines of her home. Instead, her "deviant" sexuality itself becomes evidence that she has not prioritized her children. Justice Dellapinna's and Rule's conclusions are s/m is a deviance and an indulgence that A.C. could not afford to pursue while her children were residing with her in such a humble abode.

Once Justice Dellapinna finds that the children must have been exposed to their parents' deviance, the finding becomes conflated with the issue of abuse. Rule states, "It is the consultant's opinion that Ms A.C. does not display any appreciable level of empathy for the experiences of her children in regard to her sexual deviant behaviour and/or the use of corporal punishment" (*Nova Scotia v. A.C.* 2003, para. 32). The structure of this statement parallels the participation in sexual deviance with the physical abuse of children. Debra Garland, another expert who also contributed to a Parental Capacity Assessment, stated one of the main concerns was "that the children had been exposed to domestic violence and varied and extensive sexual behaviour of the parents" (para. 35). Here, the notion that the children were exposed to physical violence becomes akin to the children being exposed to non-normative sexual behaviour. In the opinion of both experts, sexual behaviour and deviance comes to be equated with the physical abuse of the children. S/m is construed as an inherently abusive practice, in this case not to the participants, but to the children who may become damaged by its proximity.

A significant portion of the judgment is devoted to deciphering A.C.'s true sexual self. Was she sexually aroused by the deviant behaviour, or was it simply a strategy to maintain her relationship with J.C.? Rule's services as a clinical psychologist were sought so she could "assess the impact on and risk to the children resulting from the sexual deviant behaviour that Mr and Ms A.C. were charged with" (*Nova Scotia v. A.C.* 2003, para. 26). Although A.C. denied seeking out or enjoying the s/m sex, and although there was evidence that J.C. at other times was emotionally and physically abusive, Rule concludes "that Ms A.C. has a degree of sexual deviance that will need to be addressed through psychotherapeutic intervention" (para. 32). She later recommends that A.C. consult the services of "a trained Psychologist who is expert in sexual behaviours and in particular, paraphilias" (para. 33). Despite A.C.'s protests to the contrary, Rule determines that A.C. must have extracted sexual pleasure from the s/m activity, and thus suffers from a mental disorder. As previously noted, such blanket condemnations of s/m desire effectively contradict the *DSM-IV-TR*'s more narrow diagnostic criteria for determining paraphiliac sadism and masochism.

There is one interesting quirk to the facts that may explain why Rule rejected A.C.'s denials of pleasure. According to the outlined facts of the case, throughout most of the C.s' s/m activities, A.C. performed the dominant role. Recall that the *DSM-IV-TR* views sadism as a sexual pathology that can be imposed on another, while masochism is not so conceived. There is an underlying assumption that literal activity and passivity correspond to the respective roles of sadist and masochist. Yet if A.C.'s unwavering assertion that she was not inclined towards sexual dominance is accepted, then she was indeed forced into adopting the top position. Her testimony regarding her spouse's coercive sexual demands is antithetical to the *DSM-IV-TR*'s diagnostic criteria for the paraphilia of masochism. From the *DSM-IV-TR*'s perspective, it would have been impossible for J.C. to have forced A.C. to indulge *his* masochistic tendencies. Thus Rule concludes that A.C. must have exercised some agency and derived some pleasure from her dominant role. Had A.C. been forced into playing the submissive role, the judge might have more easily believed that she had been coerced since, as with *Butler* and *R. v. J.A.*, submissive sexuality, even when consensual, is still often dismissed as fallacious by the language of degradation and dehumanization.

In contrast to Rule's assessment of A.C.'s deviance, there was conflicting testimony from Valerie O'Day, a registered professional counsellor who had been seeing A.C. in the year leading up to the trial. The judge acknowledged, "It was Ms O'Day's opinion that Ms A.C. was not sexually deviant – although she took part in sexually deviant behaviours. Rather, she took part in her husband's sexual fantasies because she wanted to be loved by Mr J.C." (*Nova Scotia v. A.C.* 2003, para. 45). O'Day does acknowledge that A.C. had adopted the dominant role in their s/m activities, but she describes it as A.C. being "relegated to the role of J.C.'s private dominatrix" (para. 43). Her choice of the word "relegate" implies that a superior had assigned A.C. into a subordinate position. O'Day later elaborates, "It is possible to understand the sexually deviant behaviours Ms A.C. sometimes willingly participated in as being a function of her husband's intense sexual preoccupations combined with her own determination to accommodate this man rather than risk her marriage and end up alone … even if she was degraded and abused herself" (para. 45). Notice that O'Day's use of the term "degraded" invokes the term normally associated with being on the submissive end of s/m encounters. In addition, O'Day attempts to explain A.C.'s sexual behaviour by drawing upon the more familiar gendered narrative of a woman desperate for love and terrified of being abandoned. As a witness for the respondent, she attempts to normalize A.C. by desexualizing her behaviour, or rather to pathologize her in a different way, as an abused woman who was coerced into sexual behaviour in order to satisfy her husband.

Both Rule and O'Day are employed by the state in order to arrive at the truth of A.C.'s sexuality. Both are invested in superimposing a psychiatric archetype over the actions of A.C. to make sense of her abnormal sexual behaviour. Rule labels A.C. as a victim of a paraphiliac disorder who needs psychological assistance to overcome her sexual abnormalities. O'Day positions A.C. as a battered woman who needs psychological assistance to strengthen her self-integrity. The law thus required experts to excavate A.C.'s psyche to understand the impetus behind her scandalous acts. As Foucault has pointed out, "It is no longer a question simply of saying what was done – the sexual act – and how it was done; but of reconstructing, in and around the act, thoughts that recapitulated it, the obsessions that accompanied it, the images, desires, modulations, and quality of the pleasure that animated it" (1990, 63). The court is bent on getting at the psychic interior of A.C. through expert analyses that reify A.C.'s sexuality as an object of knowledge.

For her part, A.C. attempted to fit herself into O'Day's framework of the battered woman who was coerced into deviance. In response to the allegations that she willingly participated, she stated she only did so "in order to keep her husband happy" (*Nova Scotia v. A.C.* 2003, para. 55). She claimed that "she received no sexual gratification from the deviant sexual behaviour with Mr J.C. and … the thought of what she did now sickens her" (para. 55). In order to merit gaining access to her children, A.C. justified her participation in s/m by stressing that she was motivated solely by a fear of losing her husband.

In claiming to now be sickened at the thought of those deviant behaviours, A.C. employs the language of disgust in an attempt to assure those in authority that she is normal and as such participates in a shared visceral repulsion towards deviance. As Miller has argued, "Disgust signals our being appalled, signals the fact that we are paying more than lip-service; its presence lets us know that we are truly in the grip of the norm whose violation we are witnessing or imagining" (1997, 194). Using disgust rhetoric, A.C. attempts to add credibility to her regret and shame regarding her previously deviant behaviour. She wants to convey that she has now internalized the community's normative standards of behaviour on a corporeal level. It's not just that she thinks the behaviour is wrong; she is also disgusted by it.

And yet Justice Dellapinna never arrives at a complete determination of whether A.C. was ultimately a sexual deviant or a battered woman. The justice does accept, however that, "had it not been for the cravings of Mr J.C., it is highly unlikely that Ms A.C. would have initiated the deviant behaviour that was so prevalent during their marriage" (*Nova Scotia v. A.C.* 2003, para. 74). Thus to a certain extent, the narrative that prevailed in the end constructed A.C. as not inherently abnormal but corrupted by her husband. The ease with which this explanation was accepted recalls Krafft-Ebing's general assumptions that men are more driven by their libido, and women by their desire for love and/or security. Despite the fact that A.C. had participated in s/m sexuality for years, the judge finds it easier to believe that she did it for love.

Yet the legal significance of this determination is unclear in Justice Dellapinna's closing remarks. In deciding that A.C. will permanently lose custody with no access to her children, she asserts in a concluding statement, "If the children were returned to Ms A.C., they would be exposed to unacceptable risks. Those risks include risk of physical harm, emotional harm, the possibility of sexual abuse, exposure to domestic violence as well as physical and emotional neglect" (*Nova Scotia v. A.C.* 2003, para. 81). In this summation, Justice Dellapinna does not directly cite the issue of exposing the children to sexual deviance. On the surface, it appears that there was no need to arrive at the truth of whether A.C. did or did not enjoy the s/m activity. Yet several pages of the twenty-page judgment are devoted to summarizing the testimony of Rule and O'Day on this question. As such, this juridical imperative to perform an excavation into the libido of A.C. is imbricated in part with "the pleasure that comes of exercising a power that questions, monitors, watches, spies, searches out, palpates, brings to light" (Foucault 1990, 45) the truth of A.C.'s sexual self. Further, the judgment seems to harvest the shock value of A.C.'s sexual practices to justify the order that permanently denied A.C. custody or access to her children, despite the fact that there was never any evidence that those sexual practices were made visible to or had an impact on them.

SMITH V. SMITH (2003)

While the *A.C.* decision demonstrated how a judge might fixate on the s/m tendencies of a parent in the context of child neglect and abuse, the 2003 American case *Smith v. Smith* reveals how, even without evidence of child mistreatment, s/m activities themselves can be taken as evidence of parental incompetence.[21]

The case addresses the custody of Ed, an eleven-year old child born of Ann and Bob Smith, who had divorced after twenty-seven years of marriage. Joint custody rights were awarded. Ed's primary residence was with Mr Smith, but Ms Smith had generous visitation rights, and Ed resided with her when Mr Smith was travelling for business. Some time after their divorce, Ms Smith moved in with Mr Jones, with whom she developed a relationship that involved s/m activities.

The problem arose when Ms Smith informed Mr Smith that Ed, who had a congenital condition, had suffered from a faecal impaction during his last visit. Ed had experienced this problem on earlier occasions. Mr Jones, who had worked as a medical technician and had learned how to relieve faecal impaction, proceeded to dis-impact Ed with Ed's and his mother's permission. Ed was grateful for the relief this provided. Mr Smith, on the other hand, viewed Mr Jones's intervention as child sexual abuse and petitioned to prevent Mr Jones from having further contact with Ed.

Blair, a court-appointed forensic and clinical psychologist, was asked to evaluate the parental fitness of the adults and to determine whether the dis-impaction constituted abuse. While he found that the dis-impaction was not abuse, he seized on Ms Smith and Mr Jones's s/m relationship as proof of their incapacity and incompetence as parental figures. According to Klein and Moser, who scrutinized Blair's expert's report, there was no evidence that Ed was aware of the couple's s/m interests, that Ed suffered any abuse or neglect while in their care, or that Ed experienced any unusual social or psychological issues (Klein and Moser 2006, 236–9). By Blair's account, Ed enjoyed positive parent–child relationships with both Ms Smith and Mr Jones, and furthermore was doing well in his school and social life. Nonetheless, Blair was convinced the situation was dangerous for Ed. He diagnosed Ms Smith as suffering from sexual masochism and Mr Jones as suffering from sexual sadism, despite the absence of evidence that either suffered distress or dysfunction, something that, as Klein and Moser pointed out, is a necessary criterion for such diagnoses in the *DSM-IV-TR* (237). Further, Blair asserted that the s/m activities constituted domestic violence. The fact that Ms Smith defended the s/m activities thus rendered her an incompetent parent, too "clouded or confused" to recognize the dangers both to herself and to her son (239). Blair further speculated that Mr Jones's sexual sadism would likely lead to paedophilia, despite the fact that there was nothing in Mr Jones's history to support this view.

The judge was apparently convinced by Blair's report and adhered to the recommendations made. Mr Jones was banned from having any contact with Ed, even though Blair acknowledged that Ed had a better relationship with Mr Jones than with his biological father, Mr Smith. Ms Smith's visitation rights were curtailed and she not only lost all spousal support from Mr Smith, but was also ordered to attend thirty psychotherapy sessions to address her involvement in "domestic violence." As Klein and Moser observe, "One can only conclude that the court decided that Ms Smith was a domestic violence victim and her reported interest in SM was a justification or denial of her abuse" (2006, 240). The juridical truth of s/m was that it constituted violence, and as in most of the previous judicial decisions, consent was not a defence, but rather proof of mental incompetence.

Both Klein and Moser report having been consulted in other cases where a parent's s/m interests were deemed a relevant issue in determining custody (2006, 240). The results of these cases disclose a judicial perception that s/m and parenting are incompatible. The authors state, "We know of no cases where the parent admitting to SM interests obtained or retained custody of the minor" (241). If Blair's report is any indication, the psychological and psychiatric fields are complicit with the law to render parents interested in s/m as unfit, inappropriate, and/or potentially abusive.

Conversely, on the silver screen, a few films have portrayed s/m practitioners in parenting roles. In *Preaching to the Perverted*, recall that Tanya and Peter have a baby at the end of the film and are supported by loving friends and family. In *Exit to Eden*, when Lisa accepts Elliott's marriage proposal, she muses that their future will include having children. Furthermore, if I can stray outside of the cinematic realm for a moment, the 2012 *Fifty Shades* trilogy of best-selling erotic novels pays credence to the possibility that a couple engaged in "kinky fuckery" – in the words of the protagonist – can also play Mommy and Daddy, for real (James 2012a; 2012b; 2012c). I will briefly address this phenomenal pop cultural intervention into s/m truth-claims in the conclusion to this book. For now, suffice it to say that popular fiction appears to be ahead of the law in contemplating the viability of s/m practitioners as suitable parents.

R. v. M. (P.) (2011)

But it is not all bad news when it comes to s/m in the context of family and youth. A 2011 case from Ontario that addresses youth sexuality, agency. and the question of exploitative parental relations shows a more promising and contextual understanding of s/m (*R. v. M. (P.)* 2011). In this criminal case, Y.H., a sixteen-year-old female, left her family home to move in with M.P., a man twenty-nine years older. After a few months of platonic engagement, M.P. and Y.H. began a sexual relationship, which lasted for approximately eighteen months. Both parties maintained that the sex was entirely consensual, but the authorities were contacted when the couple attempted to fly overseas together. M.P. was charged with touching a young person with whom he was in a relationship of dependency for a sexual purpose, contrary to section 153(a) of the *Criminal Code of Canada*. In order to prove the charging requirement that Y.H. and M.P.'s relationship constituted one of dependency, the Crown submitted emails in which Y.H. referred to the accused as

"Daddy," and to herself as his "little girl." On its face, this could be fairly strong evidence that M.P. had assumed a parental role with Y.H. But Justice Theo Wolder took heed of other aspects of the e-mails, indicating that Y.H. and M.P.'s sexual relationship involved s/m, and read the comments in that context. He first demonstrates an open-minded attitude towards BDSM, which he defines as "being a continuum of erotic practice and expression involving the consensual use of restraint, intense sensory stimulation, and fantasy power role-play" (*R. v. M. (P.)* 2011, para. 22). Just this definition alone is remarkably progressive, as it uses neutral or even favourable language and avoids the common but morally laden words of "violence," "bondage," "pain" and "dominance/submission," all of which carry a derogatory tenor, in a vanilla semiotic system. Turning specifically to the terms "Daddy" and "little girl," Justice Wolder contextualized their use using BDSM norms: "After having reviewed the various emails, I am satisfied that there is no suggestion that the accused treated the complainant as his 'daughter.' There is absolutely no evidence of a parent/child type of relationship between the accused and complainant. In the context of all the emails, it appears that both parties did enjoy and participate in this type of sexual behaviour, usually initiated by the complainant and responded to by the accused, but not to the point of persistence. I am not at all satisfied that the language by the accused in the various emails is anything more than a reflection of his participation in the BDSM role-playing. Therefore I am not satisfied that the language used in the various emails suggest that the accused was in any way exploiting the complainant in the manner in which they interacted" (para. 24). This nuanced understanding of the couple's interactions assisted in securing an acquittal. This finding is surprising, as there are a number of reasons why a judge might have cast the relationship as one of dependency, and therefore exploitative. For example, Y.H. had moved in with the accused just after she turned sixteen; she left her family home because of quarrels with her parents; the accused was the father of one of her friends; there was a significant age disparity, such that one could call the couple inter-generational; Y.H. had suffered from depression and self-harmed through cutting, and after she moved in with the accused, he convinced her to get treatment. Despite these factors that could have indicated particular vulnerability of Y.H. and parental-like behaviour of the accused, Justice Wolder went against the judicial trend of viewing BDSM as inherently suspect or even pathological, particularly when associated with youth, as in *R. v. R.D.W.* (2006). Indeed, it was partly through the lens of BDSM that the couple's sexual relationship was ultimately absolved.

Sadomasochists as Human Rights Bearers: Hayes v. Vancouver Police Department and Barker (2005; 2006; 2008; 2010)

While the cases discussed above address the possible criminalization of those associated with s/m, the human rights case of *Hayes v. Vancouver Police Department and Barker* (2005; 2006; 2008) indicates that some practitioners are trying to use the law to legitimate their sexuality. In May 2005, Peter Hayes filed a human rights complaint on the basis of religion and sexual orientation, alleging that Constable Kevin Barker of the Vancouver Police Department denied him a chauffeur's permit because of his BDSM and pagan identity. In an interim decision dated 28 December 2005, the British Columbia Human Rights Tribunal accepted the filing of Hayes's complaint of discrimination on the basis of sexual orientation, stating that a full hearing was required in order to decide if Hayes's BDSM identity could fit within that ground. The City of Vancouver petitioned for a judicial review of this decision, but it was upheld by the B.C. Supreme Court in 2006, and by the B.C. Court of Appeal in 2008.

The case provides even more splintering and specifying of categories of sexual identity and practices. Although the tribunal used the term "BDSM" to cover Hayes's activities and identity, it acknowledged that he referred to himself using different vocabulary. According to the tribunal, Hayes wished to distance himself from the term BDSM, preferring the terms "natural dominants and natural submissives," or "D/s lifestylers" (which the tribunal assumed to mean "Dominant/submissive") or "M/s lifestylers" (which the tribunal assumed to mean "Master/slave") (*Hayes v. Vancouver Police Department and Barker* 2005, para. 18). Hayes's sexual identity provides a new lexicon, new "secret" desires to probe and confess, new sexual deviations to adjudicate, and ultimately new opportunities to speak of sex.

The most patent example of this compulsion to speak sex was determined by the legal process itself. For the tribunal to accept Hayes's complaint, he had to fit his experience of discrimination within the terms of the B.C. *Human Rights Code*, which provides an exhaustive list of possible grounds of legal protection (1996, c. 210). Accordingly, it was not enough to analogize his sexual identity or practices to sexual orientation; he had to conceptualize his identity to actually fit within that definitional field. As such, Hayes made arguments similar to those traditionally made by gay and lesbian complainants seeking protection on the grounds of sexual orientation. Most notably, he argued that people like him "did not choose to be the type of person who can only carry out fulfilling intimate relationships within the context of BDSM (D/s and/or M/s). They were born with that predisposition and cannot change the way their minds and bodies react" (*Hayes v. Vancouver Police Department and Barker* 2005, para. 41). This justification invokes the constitutionally accepted notion of immutability as a factor that attracts protection of human rights violations. Yet as Carl Stychin has pointed out, "Under the immutability approach the personal characteristic becomes an (unfortunate) deviation from a static norm" (Stychin 1995, 56). There is a sense that Hayes must apologize for this unfortunate birth condition; he did not choose it, nor can he change it. The norm, that of non-BDSM desire, gets retrenched and solidified as the unspoken benchmark against which all other deviations are judged.

And yet, as Stychin acknowledges, there are potential gains to be made when sexual minorities can mould themselves to conform to legal categories, even if the fit is Procrustean. Looking back again at *Butler* and the LEAF factum, those who engaged in sexuality involving domination and submission were erased from the realm of the human. In their effort to combat the dehumanization of women, these texts effectively dehumanized those who enjoy and consent to conscious role playing or power playing in their sexuality. This effective erasure of sadomasochists from humanity's embrace makes Hayes's assertion – that his BDSM identity should be protected as a *human* right – all the more audacious and important. As Judith Butler has argued, "The failure of the norm is exposed by the performative contradiction enacted by one who speaks in its name even as the name is not yet said to designate the one who nevertheless insinuates his or her way into the name enough to speak 'in' it all the same" (1997, 91). Attempts to preclude s/m sexuality from *human* sexuality helped to create the possibility that the marginalized sexual minorities would appropriate the language of humanity in order to wheedle their way into a normative legal framework.

Yet using the "master's tools" involves seizing a double-edged sword. On 23 November 2010 the British Columbia Human Rights Tribunal found that the evidence did not support a finding of discrimination on the basis of religion or sexual orientation, but hedged on the issue of whether Hayes's BDSM lifestyle could qualify in principle as a sexual orientation (*Hayes v. Vancouver Police Department and Barker* 2010). Remaining on the fence, the tribunal explained, "For the purposes of our decision, we have assumed, without deciding, that BDSM could constitute a 'sexual orientation' protected by the *Code*" (para. 19). The decision is accordingly written as if BDSM *is* a sexual orientation but refuses to commit to this interpretation, preferring instead to dismiss the complaint on other grounds.

In the circumstances, the outcome could be interpreted as an ambivalent win-loss. The "loss" manifests in the tribunal's decision to dismiss the complaint, which was based primarily on its assessment of the conflicting witness testimony and a finding that Hayes was simply less credible than Constable Barker. For example, Hayes alleged that Constable Barker made discriminatory remarks, including accusing him of being involved with a "sex cult." Constable Barker testified that he never made any such remark, but rather reviewed the applicant's police record and denied the licence on the basis of "harm reduction" and "determinations of risk." Although Hayes did not have a criminal record, he did have three police reports in his history. The first involved a 1994 incident where Hayes was charged, tried, and acquitted of four counts of sexual offences against a person under fourteen. The second report addressed a 2003 complaint that led to an investigation of allegations that Hayes had posed naked in his bedroom in view of his neighbours, but did not result in any formal charges. The third account also dated from 2003, and involved police attending at Hayes's home because of a domestic dispute he was having with his partner, L.B. Again, no charges were laid. The next day, L.B. met with the police, not because she wanted them to lay charges, but so that she could "put on record her side of the incident." In this report, she alleged that Hayes had manipulated her into a "cult"-type relationship based on a "master/slave" dynamic that she experienced as abusive. Although none of these incidents resulted in convictions, the Vancouver Police Department's Guidelines on chauffeur permits allow a constable to take into account whether an applicant has been investigated or charged with a *Criminal Code* offence involving sex. Constable Barker testified that he relied on Hayes's police reports in determining that Hayes posed an unacceptable risk towards vulnerable clients. The tribunal accepted that sexual orientation was not a factor in the determination, and that the constable had relied solely on evidence that Hayes may have engaged in the sexual exploitation of youth, indecency, and/or domestic violence. While this determination was a loss for the complainant, other aspects of the case leave space open for s/m sexual subjectivity in future cases.

Once again, Charles Moser provided expert testimony that the tribunal deemed helpful. Moser not only explained BDSM from a non-pathological perspective, he also contributed to the production of sexual knowledge and allowed vicarious access to s/m. For example, Moser differentiates between BDSM lifestylers, where BDSM affects all areas of one's life, and kinksters, whose practices involve discrete encounters that do not infiltrate daily activities. This taxonomy sheds light on the diversity of the subculture, inadvertently advertises the possible pleasures associated with s/m sexuality, and can feed voyeuristic satisfaction in learning about perverse s/m identities. Yet at the same time, as Stychin reminds us, there are costs to making sexual alterity intelligible within a legal framework. Moser's categories could be used to compartmentalize different communities, where, for example, discrimination against a "kinkster" might not be considered a violation of her human rights, because s/m would not be deemed an inherent or immutable part of her identity.

But despite the cost of legitimating confining categories, and despite Hayes's ostensible loss at the tribunal, the case has helped to bring the issue of s/m into public discourse and provided an alternative lens through which to view s/m as a sexual orientation, rather than a pathology. Furthermore, in *Hayes*, a sadomasochist audaciously interpolates himself into a human rights framework. *Hayes* thus reveals the ways a marginalized identity can appropriate the legal system, so often used in the process of subjugation, as a forum for articulating a normative framework that is at once familiar (everyone has a right to be free from discrimination) and utterly radical (I am a sexual dominant and I am part of a community of rights bearers).

The Right to Kinky Privacy: Mosley v. News Group Newspapers Limited (2008)

The penultimate case examined in this chapter circles back to England, where another s/m practitioner, Max Mosley, has also asserted his rights in court – but this time, with success. In 2008, Mosley, then the president of the Fédération Internationale de l'Automobile, engaged in an s/m encounter with five dominatrices in a private residence. Unbeknownst to Mosley, or four of the women, one dominatrix had made secret arrangements with *News of the World* to sell information about the night. To gather evidence of Mosley's sexual affairs, *News of the World* equipped her with undercover video recording equipment.

Two days later, the newspaper published an article entitled "F1 Boss Has Sick Nazi Orgy with 5 Hookers," which included pictures captured from the clandestine video, and a link to some footage. Mosley filed a civil lawsuit against the newspaper and was eventually vindicated by the judgment in *Mosley v. News Group Newspapers Limited* (2008). Finding in Mosley's favour, Justice Eady reasoned that a close inspection of the video revealed that there were no Nazi signifiers during the incident, and that Mosley had held a reasonable expectation of privacy during this sexual encounter. Mosley was awarded £60,000 in damages based on a breach of confidence and a violation of his right to privacy.

In reaching his decision, Justice Eady makes several findings that humanize s/m and its practitioners, breaking down the differences between s/m and vanilla, while rejecting sexual moralism as a guiding principle in adjudication. When interpreting the s/m scenarios, Justice Eady refused to impose a Nazi flavour on the scenes or a criminal intent to the practitioners, based simply on the s/m nature of the party. He stated that it was "vital to have in mind the particular and most unusual context in which these events took place. Beatings, humiliation and the infliction of pain are inherent to S and M activities. So too is the enactment of domination, restraints, punishment and prison scenarios. Behaviour of this kind, in itself, is in this context therefore merely neutral" (*Mosley v. News Group Newspapers Limited* 2008, para. 48). This interpretation departs from the majority of judicial utterances concerning s/m, where activities that include beatings, humiliation, domination, and pain have been seen as inherently nefarious. The idea that these elements of an incident are merely "neutral" helps to de-stigmatize s/m, particularly because deference is paid to a hermeneutic based on the sexual subculture's *own terms*.

Yet while recognizing the specificity of the s/m subculture, Justice Eady also emphasizes that Mosley's rights fall under universal principles, and that his desires are not, in essence, any different from others'. The decision stated that Mosley's right to privacy flows from Article 8 of the *European Convention on Human Rights and Fundamental Freedoms*, which provides that "everyone has the right to respect for his private and family life, his home and his correspondence." Justice Eady elaborates that the purpose of this article is "to prevent the violation of a citizen's autonomy, dignity and self-esteem" (*Mosley v. News Group Newspapers Limited* 2008, para. 7). The use of the term "dignity" in relation to s/m practitioners is a radical departure from most case law that addresses s/m, where the activity is generally presumed to be a violation of dignity. Justice Eady is aware of this societal bias, stating, "One should be careful not to dismiss matters going to personal dignity because a particular sexual activity or inclination itself may seem undignified. After all, sexual activity is rarely dignified" (para. 215). By acknowledging commonalities across most manifestations of sexuality, Justice Eady deconstructs the barrier between s/m and vanilla, revealing the shared interest in the protection of dignity for all sexual agents. This de-exceptionalization of s/m also recalls the counter-hegemonic arguments made by Moser and Kleinplatz, whose scholarship and advocacy have demonstrated the unscientific basis of singling sadomasochism out for pathologization.

Several times in his decision, Justice Eady further advances the jurisprudence by calling attention to the unprincipled use of sexual moralism to judge s/m activities and practitioners. Cautioning both journalists and judges, he states, "It is not for journalists to undermine human rights, or for judges to refuse to enforce them, merely on grounds of taste or moral disapproval. Everyone is naturally entitled to espouse moral or religious beliefs to the effect that certain types of sexual behaviour are wrong or demeaning to those participating. That does not mean that they are entitled to hound those who practise them or to detract from their right to live life as they choose" (*Mosley v. News Group Newspapers Limited* 2008, para. 127). Justice Eady's principled stance again stands out as exceptional within the case law, where judges have habitually ignored the rights of s/m practitioners, on the basis of subjective opinions that the activities or desires were inescapably "demeaning." The judgment thus serves as an important intervention in the jurisprudence, by encouraging future judges to be self-reflective about the impermissible use of personal taste or sexual morality when dealing with parties associated with s/m.

While the decision opens up more space for s/m to be understood as what Gayle Rubin calls "benign sexual difference," the judgment still retreated from legitimating more edgy forms of sadomasochism. Justice Eady determined that had Mosley actually been participating in Nazi-themed scenarios, this would have tipped the balance of competing interests in favour of the newspaper's right to freedom of expression. He states, "I have come to the conclusion (although others might disagree) that if it really were the case, as the newspaper alleged, that the Claimant had for entertainment and sexual gratification been 'mocking the humiliating way the Jews were treated,' or 'parodying Holocaust horrors,' there could be a public interest in that being revealed at least to those in the FIA to whom he is accountable" (*Mosley v. News Group Newspapers Limited* 2008, para. 122). Similar to the anti-s/m feminist position in the sex wars, the idea of appropriating the Nazi Holocaust for s/m ritual was cast as inherently problematic. From Justice Eady's perspective, this is particularly true because of Mosley's prominent public position. There is a sense that the verisimilitude of Nazi scenarios within s/m role playing comes too close to genuine violent anti-Semitism, even if done in private. As Mosley maintained that he never incorporated Nazi signifiers into his s/m play, the radical suggestion by a few s/m defenders that such an appropriation could signify other things besides mockery, such as the processing of past trauma, was not advanced or considered. Justice Eady's contextual understanding of the s/m subculture's codes and meanings thus did not extend to the resignification of the Nazi atrocity. But because there was no evidence suggesting that Mosley's activities invoked Nazism, he was able to find in favour of the right to privacy in s/m play.

In response to the newspaper's claim that Mosley had been engaging in criminal activities, Justice Eady distinguished Mosley's activities from those of the accused in *R. v. Brown* (1993). Recall that in *Brown*, criminal charges were laid not just against the dominant lovers, but also against the submissive lovers, who were accused of assault occasioning bodily harm *on their own bodies*. The newspaper made a similar accusation here, relying on *Brown* to argue that Mosley could be indicted for assault occasioning actual bodily harm towards himself, as he had allowed the dominatrices to mete out a rigorous spanking that apparently discoloured his buttocks. Justice Eady rejected the argument, determining that sexual activity between consenting adults in private does not attract criminal liability. He distinguished the facts from *Brown*, finding that the court in that case was concerned with extremely dangerous behaviour and the possible corruption of young people, neither of which was a relevant consideration before him. Justice Eady, of course, must defer to the *Brown* House of Lords decision, so it was not open to him to reject its reasoning outright. Nonetheless, its citation reinforces the continuing influence of the decision and indicates what a touchstone the case has become for trials involving s/m. Until that precedent is abolished, it is likely to continue to be cited, reinforcing anti-s/m ideologies not just in England, but – as with *R. v. J.A.* – in Canada as well.

The Investigation of Cpl James Charles Brown and His Civil Lawsuit (2012–)

I end this chapter with the ongoing case of Corporal James Charles Brown, who – like Hayes and Mosley – has been stigmatized by association with s/m and is using the law to fight back. In July 2012, the RCMP placed Corporal Brown on administrative duties, pending a code of conduct investigation into allegations that he had posted s/m-themed photos of himself with a woman on the kinky social networking site Fetlife. The photos depict Brown in various positions of dominance over the woman and include images of bondage and of someone wearing black boots and brandishing a knife. Of particular significance was the fact that, before his suspension, Brown had played a minor role in the investigation of serial killer Robert Pickton, who has been convicted of murdering six women and is connected to the deaths of over forty others. When the story broke, the media coverage used sensationalist language to describe the s/m-themed photos and quoted authority figures who cast the s/m pictures as suspicious, unethical, and deviant. In the *Globe and Mail* newspaper, for example, the pictures are described as "disturbing, graphic photos of himself and women engaged in simulated acts of bondage and torture" (Mickleburgh 2012). The article quotes Assistant Commissioner Randy Beck, who ordered the investigation, stating, "I am personally embarrassed and very disappointed that the RCMP would be, in any way, linked to photos of that nature" (2012). Drawing on the persuasiveness of psy authority, the article also quoted Mike Webster, a former Mountie and current expert on police psychology, who stated, "If it was my neighbour, fine. But this is a policeman, and the public places its trust in this individual, and now he behaves in this way" (2012). Webster further censured the RCMP for not having launched its code of conduct investigation immediately upon learning of the existence of the photos: "They make it worse. They downplay, they minimize unacceptable conduct. They sweep it under the rug" (2012). Provincial Justice Minister and Attorney-General Shirley Bond was quoted as being "clearly unhappy" and "disappointed" with the situation, stating, "It's important that British Columbians have confidence in the men and women who serve in our communities every day, as police officers" (2012). Finally, Commissioner Wally Oppal, who led the inquiry into the police handling of the Robert Pickton murders, stated, "These are serious allegations concerning Brown's conduct, and I just want to make sure that there isn't any link between that and the Pickton investigation" (2012). What is interesting about all of these quotes is that the purported wrongness of Brown's actions is not elaborated upon, it is assumed. No one spells out the obvious assumption, which is that an interest in BDSM sexual dominance indicates sexually violent tendencies, or at least an inability to take sexual violence seriously. Brown is rendered abject, contaminating the "blue line" with associations of sexual deviance.

In contrast to the above commentators, who stopped short of expressly condemning Corporal Brown for his s/m sexuality, Cameron Ward – a lawyer who represented a number of families of the missing and murdered women connected to Pickton – had no such qualms. In a blog post entitled "RCMP Officer Jim Brown Is a Sexual Sadist – So What's the Big Deal?" Ward tells us what "the big deal" is, stating, "Cpl Jim Brown isn't just a police officer who is a sexual deviant on his own time and who likes to connect with other like-minded individuals to share their twisted experiences" (2012). In support of this comment, Ward states that Brown's minor role in the Pickton investigation helped to produce a police informant named Ross Caldwell, and raises questions about possible connections between the two: "The women whose remains were found at the pig farm were likely the victims of a group of sexual sadists and torturers, who likely included convicted murderer Willy Pickton himself. How did Cpl Jim Brown meet informant Ross Caldwell? Was Cpl Jim Brown one of the sexual sadists frequenting Piggy's Palace [a drinking establishment on the Pickton property]?" (2012). Ward's comments use disgust rhetoric to pathologize and castigate Brown for being a "sexual sadist" who enjoys "twisted experiences" and go further to demonstrate the hallmarks of moral panic. Brown's s/m sexuality, which involves staged and consensual photography, is now represented as a deep threat to society, with an insinuation that Brown himself may have been an accessory to the Pickton murders.

Brown is now challenging this insinuation, alleging he is the one who has been wronged. In November 2012, Brown launched a civil suit, claiming damages for defamation and/or breach of privacy. The first named defendant is Grant Wakefield, who is alleged to have created a fake profile on Fetlife to gain membership, befriended Brown, accessed his pictures, and then mixed those photos with others not of Brown (including one in which a knife is being held to the throat of a woman), before presenting them to the RCMP and the media as if they were all of Brown (Woodward 2012). The second named defendant is Ward, who is alleged to have republished Wakefield's false statements, and who, in the words of Brown's lawyer, "amplified and expanded on the false and malicious personal attack on Cpl Brown's integrity by tying him to Canada's most notorious serial killer, Willy Pickton" (Baynham and Reid 2012). As of January 2014, the case is still ongoing.

Brown, like Mosley, is thus seeking recourse through the law, asserting his individual rights to be free from defamation and breach of privacy.[22] It is particularly poignant that Brown is claiming a right to privacy, considering that he is being condemned, in part, for breaching the public/private divide through his own Internet postings on Fetlife. Even though access to the Fetlife website is restricted to members who have agreed to its privacy terms, it was characterized in most of the media coverage as a fully open and public space. In the circumstances, the case will likely have to involve some consideration of where social networking activities and websites properly fall on a public-private spectrum.

Whatever comes of Corporal Brown's lawsuit, it encapsulates well the contested place that s/m holds in the Canadian socio-legal imaginary. On the one hand, being associated with s/m casts you as suspect, someone who is engaging in wrong, if not necessarily criminal, behaviour. Moral panics and abject anxieties can ensue, especially if the s/m practitioner also happens to be a figure of state authority and respect. In such cases, sexual kink can meld with sexual violence and even murder in the socio-legal imaginary. Turning to the liberal forum for adjudicating wrongs, Brown appropriates the law for his own purposes, asserting his status as victim in civil court. Such claims can, inadvertently, marginalize more edgy play. For example, what if – contrary to the claims made in his lawsuit – Corporal Brown is the person who enacted a fantasy role play that involved the staged use of a knife held up to a woman's throat? Should a police officer's ability to participate in kinky social networking depend on whether the s/m scenarios he depicts are judged to be "mild" or "extreme"? If the answer to this question is yes, then there is an assumption that such depictions have a fixed and easily discernible meaning. In this regard, it is useful to return to some of the issues that were previously discussed in my chapter on s/m pornography. Indeed, Corporal Brown's case speaks to the porn-phobic idea that representation is mimetic of practice, such that those who produce or consume texts that stage sexual violence within a fantasy context inevitably betray an interest in enacting such violence within a literal context. Of course, if Brown had played a sexually violent character in a non-pornographic forum, such as in a community theatre production, there would be no such literal interpretation. Objections to Brown's photographs signify a commitment to sexual exceptionalism in the socio-legal imaginary, where representation deemed to be for the purpose of arousal appears more suspect and potentially harmful than representation deemed to be for the purpose of intellectual stimulation.

Conclusion

S/m practice is regulated, criminalized, pathologized, and tolerated in a variety of legal contexts. The evaluation of the three British cases (*Brown, Wilson,* and *Emmett*) showed that disgust with s/m can be amplified if the practitioners are also gay, and that this could have an impact on the punitive attitude of the judges. In *Brown,* the majority's perspective on s/m viewed sadism as its driving force, while the submissives' consent was contemptuously discounted. The cinematic and legal gazes overlap here, as the gay s/m subject emerges in both discourses as an elicitor of disgust, as well as a bearer of temptation. Criminal sanctions are justified based on both of these truth-claims. Disgust of gay s/m validates a sense of its moral repugnance, while concerns regarding its perverse allure explain the necessity of punishing and incarcerating gay sadomasochists to prevent further contamination of the male population.

The Canadian judgments that address genuine or alleged s/m behaviour generally disavow submissive pleasure or construct it as mental illness, while condemning the dominant partner as actually or potentially sadistic in a non-consensual fashion. What is perhaps surprising is that expert witnesses trained in the psy sciences frequently fail to enlighten judges about the differences between consensual s/m and behaviour that falls under the category of a paraphilic disorder. As such, the psy discourse is deployed to perpetuate the truth-claim that all manifestations of s/m desire are pathological, despite the fact that clinical definitions in the *DSM-IV-TR,* and now, in the *DSM-V,* identify mental disorder only when practised with a non-consenting partner, or where the desires cause significant distress or interfere with major life functioning. In addition, some of these experts seemed to use the term *sadomasochism* interchangeably with *sadism.* This semantic conflation reflects the feminist anti-s/m discourse that depicted sadism as the primary pleasure being enacted, with masochism being at best a product of unhealthy conditioning, and at worst a ploy to justify the violence. Much of the legal and feminist discourse of *R. v. J.A.* perpetuated this perspective, as the female submissive's claims of consent were disregarded as fallacious, pathological, or structurally coerced, and the male dominant was construed as a sexual opportunist who committed acts of violence purely for his own gratification.

Yet in the dominatrix case of *R. v. Bedford*, the enduring legal construction of s/m as violence and not sexuality was inverted. Bedford's services were deemed sexual, thus justifying her criminalization under the bawdy-house provisions. Furthermore, the law's hypocrisy towards the uses of pain and humiliation was laid bare in the decisions. While consensual and pleasurable infliction of pain and humiliation in a commercial context was indicted as criminal, the police officers' coercive infliction of emotional pain and sexual humiliation upon female suspects was exonerated. A comparable ideology is thus found in both law and film, where the female dominant must, at some point in the narrative, submit to a male figure. In film, he can be represented as a lover, a police officer, or a prosecutor. In *Bedford*, though the police were mildly chastised for their unnecessary and invasive force, their behaviour was excused through a naturalization of their gender anxiety. In addition, though the court did have the benefit of expert defence witnesses, some of whom were trained in the psy disciplines, these testimonies ultimately were deemed moot. As such, the law is not deferential to psy truth-claims regarding s/m in all cases but appears more likely to internalize those that justify the regulation or suppression of s/m. The *Bedford* judgments also revealed a voyeuristic pleasure, delighting in specifying the details of gender-transgressive practices, but ending on the cathartic satisfaction of finding Bedford guilty. Even though her sentence did not include incarceration, such a verdict symbolically expels the professional dominatrix from the community.

Cases that deal with s/m beyond the criminal context still, more often than not, perpetuate a pathologizing perspective, particularly if children are involved. Both *A.C.* and *Smith* suggest that during custody and access litigation, the sexuality of parents who are s/m practitioners is viewed in and of itself as an indication of incompetence and mental illness. In both cases, virtually all of the psy experts perpetuated an essentialist view of s/m pleasure as definitively pathological and symptomatic of parental incapacity. This judgment is in contrast to a few pop cultural representations, namely *Preaching to the Perverted*, *Exit to Eden*, and most recently, the *Fifty Shades* trilogy, where s/m and parenting are reconciled. However, *R. v. M. (P.)* indicates the variegated judicial response to BDSM in the context of potentially abusive familial practices. Despite a number of factors that could be interpreted as exploitative between a young person and a man twenty-nine years her senior, their BDSM activities were exculpated.

Another promising arena for sadomasochist subjectivity may be the realm of human rights, both domestic and international. On the domestic front, the *Hayes* decision has opened up a small door in the legal imaginary to think of s/m differently. The recognition that s/m feelings and practice may receive protection under the category of sexual orientation allows the s/m subject to appropriate the language of dignity and human rights. Yet while this may create future opportunities for s/m subjects to use the law to advance certain individual rights, the cost of casting oneself as a liberal legal subject can be to reify identity, uphold the sexual chauvinism of the status quo, and displace abjection onto other, more marginalized subjects.[23]

On the international human rights front, *Mosley* stands out from the other legal matters discussed in this chapter, in that it not only recognized the specific context of fantasy and force in the s/m subculture but also highlighted shared dignity and internationally protected privacy interests for both vanilla and s/m practitioners. England thus provides us with the worst construction of s/m as abject, disgusting, and in need of expulsion from the body politic (*Brown*), and – in my view – the most progressive rendering of s/m as benign, but vulnerable to stereotyping and discrimination (*Mosley*). While there may be multiple reasons accounting for these different approaches – *Brown* is a criminal case involving gay men, edgier s/m activities, and a police investigation, while *Mosley* was a civil case involving a heterosexual man, less extreme activities, and a moralistic profit-motivated newspaper making sensationalist accusations – the disparity still points to the contested status of s/m in the law. Furthermore, it should be remembered that unlike the accused in *Brown*, Mosley was a sex trade client who was committing "adultery," which might have been expected to heighten his deviant status.

The ongoing case of Corporal Brown shares many of the features of the *Mosley* case. A man in a prominent position (Mosley as the former president of the Fédération Internationale de l'Automobile, Brown as an RCMP officer) is outed by a private actor (for Mosley a news agency, for Brown a private citizen), and sensationalist claims are made about his s/m interests. In both cases, the s/m-contaminated subject fights back in civil court on the basis of defamation and privacy breaches. The investigation of Corporal Brown for a code of conduct violation because of his Fetlife photos also recalls the *Loyalist* arbitration decision discussed in chapter 4. In that case, an arbitration tribunal upheld a professor's dismissal because of his unapologetic interest in BDSM pornography. In both cases, a professional in a position of trust (in *Loyalist* a professor, with *Brown* a police officer) is accused of abusing or compromising his authority and integrity because of his s/m interest and activities. Thus, while practitioners of mild s/m may be gaining more tolerance in criminal law, the stigma can lead to workplace consequences and, in the case of Corporal Brown, to an alleged public smear campaign.

But however one calculates the level of stigma associated with different s/m activities, it seems the most humanizing decisions come from lower courts. While s/m subjects have had few successes, the trial decisions in cases like *Little Sisters* (regarding gay and lesbian s/m representation), *Price* (regarding heterosexual s/m on the Internet), *R. v. M. (P.)* (regarding the BDSM practices of an inter-generational couple), and *Mosley* (regarding the right to sexual privacy) share certain features. Importantly, they credit s/m practitioners as authorities who can define the meaning of their own practices and pay attention to the shared interests of s/m and non-s/m practitioners in expressive freedom and sexual privacy. Perhaps one reason these decisions cut against the legal grain is that at the trial level, the decision-makers hear oral testimony from living and breathing s/m subjects. By contrast, judges at the appellate level focus more squarely on transcripts, documents, and abstract and disembodied principles, without having comparable opportunities to meet the human beings whose practices are at issue. Although it should be noted that many trial decisions reinforce the abject status of s/m, the court of first instance nonetheless provides a promising generative arena for the performance of more complicated sexual subjects.

Conclusion: Epistemic Violence, Epistemic Pleasures

Now do you want me or don't you because
we've got walls to press up against,
restraints to buckle, harnesses to strap,
and skin to cut – I wanna know you like that.

I wanna see you in a black latex mini dress,
long black gloves,
a leather garter belt,
your calves in combat boots and black seamed stockings,
sitting with your thighs spread,
hat on your head,
elbows on your knees,
smoking a cigarette, waiting for me to take you.

I wanna shave you bald,
yank your head back,
tie your arms above you,
clamp your nipples,
spread your legs,
hold a dildo in my hands,
and fuck you from the bottom up.

You inspire me to desire and vision
Can I cut a line down your back?
Can I run a finger along it later,
when you lay on top of me,
and call it mine?

Trish Thomas

In her poetic-colloquial style, Thomas seduces her new lover with incisive detail, opening windows into future erotic moments while closing the door on her lover's past. In her imagined tryst, she specifies a desire to engage with bondage, cutting, force, pain, role playing, sex toys, multiple orifice penetration, and other non-normative behaviour. The socio-legal imaginary is both fascinated and repulsed by such a sexual display. And when the law gets involved, such activities could be deemed assault, and the representation could be deemed obscene. As evidenced by the analysis of *R. v. Scythes* (1993) in chapter 4, another piece of Thomas's erotica has already been found to be obscene under the provisions of the *Criminal Code* (1985, s. 163). Thus while Thomas muses that her lover inspires "desire and vision," the hegemonic vision traced throughout this book would likely only see violence, degradation, dehumanization, and pathology.

Constructing s/m as fundamentally violent inflicts, as Califia argues, "hidden violence to dissidents and perverts" (1988b, 9). It is an instance of epistemic violence. The knowledge produced in the socio-legal imaginary denies the agency, the humanity, the understandings, and the feelings of s/m practitioners. And as Robert Cover suggests, in law, interpretive acts "signal and occasion the imposition of violence upon others" (1986, 1601). Under the auspices of the law, s/m subjects are convicted, incarcerated, fined, stripped, humiliated, shoved, mocked, infantilized, pathologized, dehumanized, censored, trivialized, erased, dismissed from their jobs, and denied all or partial access to their children. Cover urges us to be cognizant of the material effects of legal interpretation; the process does not merely convey semantic deliberation, but "is joined with the practice of violent domination" (1604). He further suggests that because a judge perpetrates violence vicariously through other actors in the social organization, the violence of law is often camouflaged. The cruel irony then is that the dominant script in the socio-legal imaginary casts s/m as violent, while the violence imposed by the law upon the bodies and subjectivities of s/m practitioners happens offstage, outside of the narrative.

At the same time, these hegemonic discourses reap epistemic enjoyment in discerning, delineating, and determining the truth of s/m. While often being repressive and punitive, socio-legal discourses on s/m effectively proliferate pleasure as they traffic in the excitement and the incitement of new knowledges of sex. In other words, not only is knowledge power, knowledge is also pleasure.[1] But this indulgence in the voyeuristic process of meaning-making still creates abject anxiety, which is often followed by a pronouncement of disgust and the expulsion of the sexual deviant from the social body.

Yet even in ostensible legal losses, there are gains to be had. The ambivalence of such legal outcomes was exemplified in the *Hayes* Human Rights Tribunal decision. Although Hayes's complaint was ultimately dismissed, the tribunal's decision to proceed as if s/m desire fell within the rubric of a sexual orientation supports Butler's Foucauldian observation that "every juridical form of power has its productive effect … to become subject to a regulation is also to become subjectivated by it, that is, to be brought into being as a subject precisely through being regulated" (2004, 41). While juridical-psy-cinematic-feminist articulations have often criminalized, demonized, or pathologized s/m desire, they have conversely created an identity that can be appropriated by the maligned subject to reverse the normative agenda. Hayes takes up the mantle of sadomasochist to assert the legitimacy of his desires within the terms of a liberal legal subject, contributing to both the intelligibility and the reification of s/m identity.

Artistic forms of resistance can also render s/m more intelligible, while undermining sexual chauvinism. During the sex wars, s/m lesbians cleverly appropriated anti-s/m feminist ideology, turning swords into sexual fantasies. Popular films sympathetic to s/m subjectivity, like *Preaching to the Perverted*, further dramatize the sadistic hypocrisy of the law's treatment of consensual s/m, while creating an erotic plot that features a young man's conversion from legal moralist to sexual outlaw. Yet it should be remembered that s/m practitioners, both real and fictional, who seem to access legitimacy often align with other normative ideals and contain their sexual practices within private domains. One of the most progressive judicial decisions to address s/m, *Mosley v. News Group Newspapers Limited*, provided legal vindication to a white, economically privileged, heterosexual man, based on his fundamental right to privacy. One of the most progressive films to address s/m, *Secretary*, delivers a happy ending for a white, middle-class, young, heterosexual, conventionally attractive, non-disabled couple who move their s/m practice from the workplace to their marital home.

As Eleanor Wilkinson argues, the mainstreaming and increased visibility of s/m generates both dangers and possibilities (2009). Two recent cultural phenomena exemplify this ambivalence: Rihanna's 2011 hit single and video "S&M," and E.L. James's 2012 erotic trilogy, *Fifty Shades*, continue the project of recuperating kinky sexuality through an appeal to popular sentiment. Although *Vicarious Kinks* has not focused on musical or literary creations, I want to take a moment to consider how these two texts challenge as well as reinforce hegemonic truth-claims in the socio-legal imaginary, and the kinds of regulatory and critical responses they have induced.

The *Fifty Shades* trilogy is a prime example of the ways that s/m representation can be both hegemonic and transgressive. Made up of three novels, *Fifty Shades of Grey, Fifty Shades Darker*, and *Fifty Shades Freed*, E.L. James's trilogy tells the love story of a seasoned sexual dominant, Christian Grey, and an inexperienced college graduate, Anastasia Steele. Though the attraction between the two is instant and intense, they clash over how to proceed. The romantic conflict builds around Grey wanting a contractual dominant/submissive relationship, and Steele wanting a conventional boyfriend/girlfriend relationship. This incompatibility is ultimately overcome when Grey forsakes total control for mutual intimacy, and Steele embraces mild BDSM activities for mutual pleasure. By the end of the third instalment, the protagonists get to have their kink and monogamous reproductive marriage too.

The BDSM trilogy has experienced unprecedented success, with over forty million copies sold worldwide (Singh 2012). While it began as a piece of fan fiction for the vampire series *Twilight*, James has said in an interview that the BDSM plot was inspired after she came across Califia's anthology, *Macho Sluts* (Newman 2012). Despite this queer genesis, *Fifty Shades* has been dubbed "mommy porn," an oxymoronic genre that conveys its popularity among a female readership – housewives, mothers, suburban dwellers – that is not usually associated with the racy, explicit, or kinky. The book trilogy is also credited for having spurred dramatic increases in the sale of sex toys and enrolment in how-to sex workshops, indicating it has not only stirred readers' fantasy lives but has also affected their sexual practices (Elejalde-Ruiz 2012). On a surface reading of its success and impact, *Fifty Shades* can be interpreted as not just including BDSM practitioners within the terms of sexual citizenship, but as breaking down the barriers between kink and vanilla on both a theoretical and embodied level.

On the other hand, some critics have condemned the trilogy for eroticizing and justifying domestic violence (Flood 2012). For example, recalling the book burnings of Samois texts by anti-s/m feminist groups, Wearside Women in Need, a British women's shelter, initially suggested that *Fifty Shades* be burned, along with an effigy of Christian Grey, the dominant romantic hero. But perhaps in reaction to criticisms that it had adopted fascist tactics to express its disapproval, the shelter now states it will instead use pages of the books as toilet paper and compost (Kim 2012). This sensational reaction to the novel aptly summarizes the theoretical frame used in *Vicarious Kinks*. First, the BDSM representation incited prolific and heated discourse from the shelter, and also from feminist analysts, literary pundits, and editorial pieces. Second, the shelter's intense condemnation of the trilogy appeared to rest on abject anxiety: the representation of activities that resemble (or replicate – depending on your point of view) the dynamics of intimate partner violence were placed within the context of an erotic love story. Third, the shelter drew on the moralizing impact of disgust discourse, quite literally, when its director, Clare Phillipson, castigated the book as "disgusting" and "vile" (2012). Her repugnance for the trilogy is explained by the purported fact that it "normalizes abuse, degrades women and encourages sexual violence" (2012). However, utterances of disgust alone were not sufficient to signal the shelter's condemnation. Thus finally, in a gesture of symbolic expulsion, the shelter sought first to burn the books – and then concretized the metaphor of discharging social waste by announcing plans to use them as toilet paper! Such a strategy exemplifies Kristeva's point that the anal rejection is not limited to the childhood stage of development, but rather continues as a way to manage the abject and symbolically reconstitute categorical borders.

Not all detractors of the trilogy come from this essentialist anti-s/m position. From a "sex critical" perspective, Lisa Downing problematizes *Fifty Shades* as a "faux transgressive trilogy" (2012, 98). In her deconstructive article Downing exposes how the trilogy perpetuates the pathologization of kinky orientations and administers the familiar cure of gender and hetero-normative romance, marriage, and babies. In this way, one can read it as nothing more than a spiced up conversion narrative, where the good girl tames the BDSM bad boy. Critiquing some of the anti-s/m feminist reactions to the trilogy, Downing further juxtaposes the safe, consensual, and negotiated BDSM depicted in the novel to the domineering, non-consensual, and abusive control that Grey wields over Steele outside of the bedroom. This juxtaposition highlights how the truly insidious patriarchal message of the narrative resides in the abusive non-sexual practices that are excused – and even romanticized – within the larger storyline.

Although I would call *Fifty Shades* ambivalent rather than "faux transgressive," I do want to build upon Downing's analysis but turn the critical lens upon the ways abjection is displaced. As Downing points out, the narrative suggests that the aetiology of BDSM desire is childhood trauma. In Grey's case, the trauma comes from his biological mother, a sex worker who was addicted to drugs. Grey's mother was neglectful and did not protect Grey from her violent pimp, who extinguished cigarettes on Grey's chest, triggering associations between motherly love, sex, and pain. This trite explanation for Grey's proclivities not only oversimplifies and pathologizes BDSM, it also projects deviant status onto the maligned and caricatured figures of sex worker and sex-work manager. Indeed, Grey refers to his mother with the hateful epithet "the crack whore," as does Steele, on occasion. Justification for Grey's sexuality thus rests not only on blaming a "shitty mother" and a "savage" pimp but also turns in a symbolic sense on abject transference towards the stigmatized sex industry.

Grey's mother is not the only woman blamed for his BDSM bent. When he was fifteen, Grey began a sexual relationship with an older woman, Elena Lincoln, a dominatrix who initiated him into kinky sex. At that point in his life, Grey was a troubled teenager, getting into fights and skipping out of school. Grey explains to Steele that Elena's intervention probably saved him from following in the footsteps of his biological mother, who died of a drug overdose. Despite this positive impact, Steele despises the woman, blaming her for turning Grey into an emotionally stunted pervert. Steele refers repeatedly to her derogatorily as "Mrs Robinson," a "pedophile," an "evil witch," and "the bitch troll." While Grey defends their affair as a positive experience for almost the entire story, in the last few pages of the third book, when Steele is pregnant with his child, he changes his mind. As Grey considers his imminent role as a parent, he feels for the first time that the affair with Elena was "wrong." This repro-normative epiphany confers a superior moral sense on a parent, specifically a superior sexual moral sense. Reflecting much of the cinematic representations addressed in chapter 3, the female top/male bottom BDSM dynamics are disparaged, while the reversed gender configuration is romanticized. Grey's BDSM desires are thus blamed partly on BDSM contamination, an older female dominatrix, and a presumed damaging impact of inter-generational sexuality for the younger party.[2]

Fifty Shades thus represents an ambivalent intervention. On one hand, it has incited erotic imaginations and increased awareness of certain aspects of BDSM culture, codes, and vocabulary. On the other hand, the protagonists that the trilogy celebrates adhere to privileged conventions in virtually every respect (coupled, monogamous, married, reproductive, heterosexual, white, upper-class, non-disabled, male top/

female submissive, practitioners of mild s/m), and are rendered acceptable in part by the vilification of *bad* female sexual subjects (e.g., sex workers and female dominatrices) who transgress gender, monogamy, and romance imperatives. In this sense, the trilogy also entrenches what Eleanor Wilkinson refers to as s/m normativity (2009, 187).

Rihanna's song and video "S&M" does a better job of featuring a diverse set of transgressive sexual practices, directly confronting pathologizing and misogynist accusations through parody and sexual satire. In the opening lyrics and in the chorus of "S&M," Rihanna uses the juxtaposition of "bad" and "good" to reverse the stigmatizing gaze on the sexual deviant and blatantly flaunt the erotic experience of transgression: "Feels so good being bad/There's no way I'm turning back"; and "'Cause I may be bad, but I'm perfectly good at it." Against her imagined detractors, Rihanna takes pleasure in her badness, and pride in her sexual prowess. Later in the chorus, she outlines explicit sensory detail: "Sex in the air, I don't care, I love the smell of it." The bawdy invocation of sexual aromas further revels in the abject carnality of s/m. But the final line of the chorus is the song's pièce de résistance: "Sticks and stones may break my bones/But chains and whips excite me." Rihanna appropriates the first half of the familiar childhood saying, but replaces "but words can never hurt me" with "but chains and whips excite me," thus demonstrating the polysemic nature of violent motifs. While nonconsensual violence is symbolically represented by "sticks and stones," the reference to "chains and whips" fetishizes these props of domination for sexual excitement. This brazen line is particularly poignant because of Rihanna's well-known experiences of family violence as a child, and intimate partner violence with her on-and-off-again boyfriend Chris Brown (Eells 2011). Far from disaggregating her history of trauma from her sexual kinks, in a candid interview with *Rolling Stone*, Rihanna unapologetically forges a link: "I do think I'm a bit of a masochist ... I think it's common for people who witness abuse in their household. They can never smell how beautiful a rose is unless they get pricked by a thorn" (2011). Like some feminist defenders of s/m practice during the sex wars, Rihanna makes use of the pathologizing gaze, but refuses its anti-kink mandate.

The video for the song also rebuts anti-s/m ideology, with a sexual carnivalesque bonanza that features Rihanna in roles including an aristocratic dominatrix walking her man-dog, to a naughty girl in bondage having a tantrum (see figure A).

Figure A: Rihanna as a sexy child

This vacillation between top and bottom is significantly played out in other parts of the video that dramatize Rihanna's interactions with the press. The first scene begins with Rihanna wearing a newsprint dress and being pulled by reporters onto a stage, kicking and screaming. She is then fixed to the wall with thin ClingWrap and tape. As Rihanna sings her seductive lines of defiance, the reporters are scribbling down notes, with such epithets as "slut," and diagnoses like "Daddy issues." The newsprint dress also brands Rihanna as a "slut," but significantly, the word "Barbados" is splayed across the corset section of her intertextual garment (see figure B).

Such an imbrication highlights the way that misogynist labels of hypersexual women often overlap with racialized markers. Yet signalling their own perversity and subservience to a larger social order, some reporters are themselves sporting ball gags in their mouths (see figure C).

And in subsequent scenes, the reporters' submissiveness is further underscored as they are seen struggling in bondage or fawning over the diva, while Rihanna asserts her dominance and control.

In these dizzyingly quick-cut scenes, Rihanna makes a mockery of the fluctuating dynamics between pop star and paparazzi, exposing the vicarious perversity of a press that viciously feeds off of a celebrity's past trauma, as well as her sadomasochistic tendencies, while ostentatiously worshipping her as a goddess.

Yet such a graphic sexual satire could not escape the censor's attention. England's online *Daily Mirror* reported that the video was banned in eleven countries, and that the BBC prohibited the song from being played on its music station Radio 1 before seven p.m. (Rainbird 2011). YouTube further restricts the video to viewers who attest they are

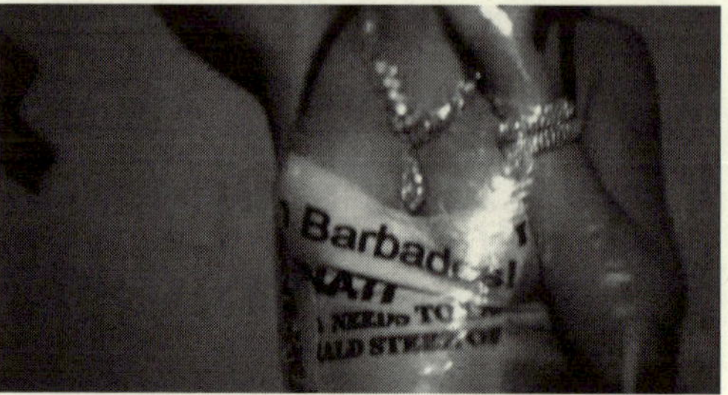

Figure B: Rihanna's intertextual newsprint dress

Figure C: Members of the press with ball gags in their mouths

eighteen years old or older. It is notable that while Rihanna's "S&M" video is thus censored, videos like Kanye West's "Monster," which features dead women hanging from meat hooks, enjoy unrestricted play on YouTube. Interestingly, Rihanna may have foreseen that her celebration of kinky practice would provoke such a sexual chauvinist response, as her music video also shows her sporting a tube top with the word *Censored* written across her chest (see figure D).

   In turning the threat of censorship into a sexualized piece of lingerie, Rihanna increases the transgressive currency of her video, and at the same time declares that the "sticks and stones" of censors not only fail to hurt her, but can be put to work in sexual and artistic practice. The song's remarkable success, hitting #1 on the Billboard Pop Chart, suggests that this sexy strategy has made an intervention in the social imaginary. Music, as an aphrodisiac in itself, and videos that blur the line between entertainment and erotica, may hold particular force to challenge anti-s/m ideology, because they appeal not only to rational argument, but also to visceral reactions. As s/m practitioners had done

Figure D: Rihanna sexualizing censorship

during the sex wars, Rihanna's music video advances a corporeal epistemology through its catchy beat and seductive imagery.

While this conclusion has recapitulated the epistemic violence and epistemic pleasure of vicarious kinks, it has also highlighted the strategies used by sadomasochist subjects to resist their own dehumanization and to insist on their existence and their desires. The image of the sadomasochist is hardly stable in the socio-legal imaginary, and yet there are persistent truth-claims born out of the inter-penetrative discourses I have surveyed and interrogated. Two of the most enduring truth-claims seem to be that s/m is risky, and it is sexy. The dominant discourses tend to portray both these characteristics as negatives, with risks routinely exaggerated to include mental health problems, physical abuse, and even death, and a perception of addictive and dangerous sexiness that can cloud the rational mind. Yet as theorists and popular culture continue to grapple with these themes, the resulting expansion of discourse on s/m can be paradoxically affirming. As Oscar Wilde has said, the only thing worse than being talked about is *not* being talked about. Sadomasochists in particular may share his point of view, given their ability to appropriate shaming rituals from which to generate erotic fantasy, role playing, and political critique.

Notes

Introduction

1 I define sexual citizenship as the processes by which members of society are judged and constituted on a continuum between belonging and not belonging, based on how and with whom they have sex. See, generally, Brenda Cossman (2007), particularly 1–20, where Cossman surveys the theoretical literature on citizenship and sexual citizenship.

2 See Patrick Califia (formerly Pat Califia), who defines a "bottom" as "someone who temporarily cedes control, within consensual and negotiated limits, to their top" (1993a, 133). A "top" is defined as "someone who temporarily takes control, within consensual and negotiated limits, from his or her bottom. Responsible tops are people who have eroticized taking responsibility for the bottom's emotional and physical state and well-being during the scene" (152). As is evident from these definitions, when the term is used, it is generally by parties who are either pro s/m or neutral on the topic, as is Sumner.

3 See, for example, Moser and Kleinplatz (2006, 3): "So what is SM? It is sometimes easier to say what it is not. It does not entail violence and it is not nonconsensual."

4 See, for example, Hanna (2001, 239), who takes it for granted that s/m is about violence when she states in the first line of her article, "In sadomasochism, sex and violence intersect, becoming intertwined and indistinguishable."

5 See Deleuze (1991, 14): "It is no accident that the names of two writers were used as labels for these two perversions. The critical (in the literary sense) and the clinical (in the medical sense) may be destined to enter into a new relationship of mutual learning."

6 Taylor (2004, 23) defines the term *social imaginary* as an epistemic discursive site that addresses "the ways people imagine their social existence, how they fit together with others, how things go on between them and their fellows, the expectations that are normally met, and the deeper normative notions and images that underlie these expectations." Particularly pertinent to the social imaginary are the ways "images, stories and legends" constitute a naturalized social order in the minds and hearts of ordinary people. In my research, I have carved out a region in the social imaginary, which I have dubbed the socio-legal imaginary. This term is meant to convey two things. First, I add the *legal* to include not just how ordinary people imagine their social existence, but also to include how elites – judges, lawyers, and law professors – imagine ordinary people's existence. Second, I conjoin these two realms, the *social* and the *legal*, to emphasize the interlocking relationship between the two corresponding imaginaries.

7 I should be clear that by drawing exclusively on Freud's theory of the anal stage of sexual development, the scope of my Freudian appropriation is limited. This may seem irresponsible, particularly to people who adhere to holistic models of knowledge, but in being opportunistic with Freud, I am only following in his footsteps. His most famous "redoubling" would be that of Sophocles's tragedy, *Oedipus Rex*, which he used to create a model of childhood sexual development. Freud certainly didn't deal with all the details of the story, or all of its implications. He instead took a narrative and fashioned it into a further narrative to tell the tale of the libido. Similarly, I will be unabashedly selective in excising out only what is useful to me and leaving out the vast majority of Freud's theories and certainly his conclusions. I employ this narrative on anality and sexual/ psychic development not to prove a transcendental truth, but rather as a psychoanalytic and semiotic *construction* that assists me in deciphering adult sexual perversion inherent in the consumption of vicarious kink.

1. Who's Your Daddy? S/M's Founding Fathers

1 See René Descartes ([1637] 1992), a foundational thinker in dichotomizing the mind and body, as well as Plato's chariot allegory, *Phaedrus* (360 BCE), section 246b.
2 See Miller (1997, 104), where he suggests that "the metaphor of penetration [in heterosexual intercourse] is in a way a desperate male defense against the male fear of being engulfed."
3 Note that Wilhelm Stekel, a contemporary of Freud who wrote extensive case studies of sadism and masochism, challenged the notion that sadism

naturally attaches to males and masochism to females, most significantly, using the animal world as evidence: "In the animal world the female is sometimes the aggressive member. Aggressiveness may reach such a degree in certain of the arachnids that the female devours the male during copulation" (Stekel, 1929, 58). His view, however, did not seem to penetrate the popular imaginary.

4 It is interesting to note that Krafft-Ebing interprets these suitor trials as proof of male *sadism*, not masochism, because in his view, men must have sadistic drives in order to have the requisite aggressiveness to fight for their woman. So Krafft-Ebing and Ellis come to opposite conclusions about what pleasures are engaged when men rival for a woman's hand.

5 U 05 Sexual Sadism Disorder, "Rationale" tab, http://www.dsm5.org/ProposedRevision/Pages/proposedrevision.aspx?rid=188# (no longer available online).

6 Ibid.

2. Feminists Divided: The Battle over S/M in the Sex Wars

1 See Duggan and Hunter (2006, 1).

2 For some overviews of the sex wars controversy see Duggan and Hunter (2006), Healey (1996), and Rich (1986).

3 Many, but not all, of these "neutral" feminists identified as socialist-feminists. A good example would be Ardill and O'Sullivan, who identify as such in "Upsetting an Applecart: Difference, Desire and Lesbian Sadomasochism" (1986).

4 In a phone interview I conducted 13 April 2007 with Varda Burstyn regarding her experiences with the "porn wars" in Canada, she suggested that a heterosexual feminist who dared identify as a sadomasochist would have likely suffered censure from the feminist community in the 1980s. She suggested that self-identifying heterosexual sadomasochists perhaps avoided participating in the women's movement for this reason.

5 A notable exception to this tendency is Gayle Rubin, whose writings made a point of drawing connections between kinky heterosexuals and other sexual minorities.

6 This observation was confirmed by conversations with Varda Burstyn and Marianne Valverde in 2007–8.

7 I piece together this history from various sources, but mostly from Hunter (2006), Rubin (1987), Rich (1986), and Chenier (2004).

8 For example, Joan Bridi Miller (1976), *Gay Community News*, and Janet Schrim (1979).

9 Patrick Califia (formerly Pat Califia) currently identifies as a transman, so I will refer to him using male pronouns. However, during the sex wars, he did not identify as trans, but as lesbian.

10 It appears that NOW's current website does not include this 1980 resolution in its web archives. See Blasius and Phelan (1997, 468–9) for a copy of the 1980 resolution. In 1999, through the efforts of the S/M Policy Reform Project, NOW withdrew its official position against s/m and passed a new resolution: The 1999 Delineation of Lesbian Rights; see National Organization for Women, http://www.now.org/nnt/fall-99/resolutions.html#delles.

11 The 1970 manifesto "The Woman-Identified Woman" was a nascent text that helped formulate lesbian feminism by Radicalesbians (1970).

12 For an overview of the conflict, see Marcia Pally (1982).

13 See, for example, MacKinnon (1987; 1989); Gubar and Hoff (1989); and Itzin (1993).

14 Mind you, this claim was not necessarily contested by lesbian sadomasochists. Indeed both Califia and Rubin acknowledge the connection of lesbian s/m to gay s/m. What is different here is that anti-s/m feminists believed that this connection compromised s/m's feminist status.

15 Apparently, not all Jewish feminists objected to the use of Nazi symbols within the context of s/m. Irish cultural critic Cherry Smyth told Emma Healey about "one Jewish woman talking very powerfully and passionately of her right to use Nazi imagery in her lovemaking as a way of taking control of the fact that she has lost most of her family in the concentration camps" (Healey 1996, 108). In this instance, identity politics are again being put to use to defend even the most shocking s/m appropriations. And since the defender was a Jewish woman whose family was victimized by Nazism, the anti-s/m position that sadomasochist lesbians were privileged individuals who "played" with power at the expense of ethnic minorities is directly challenged. The diversity of those who engage with s/m is also established.

16 An appropriate example is that of *The Story of O* (Réage 1966), a sadomasochistic novel written by "Pauline Réage," a pseudonym used to protect the identity of the real author. Another example is *Nine and a Half Weeks: A Memoir of a Love Affair* (McNeill 1978) written under the pseudonym "Elizabeth McNeill," and upon which the movie *9½ weeks* was based. For a helpful discussion of the use of pseudonyms to heighten narrative appeal, see Felicity A. Nussbaum (1989, 86).

17 This claim that the Fringe romanticized categories of deviance also seems strange, considering the fact that the Sexual Fringe included non-sadomasochists, particularly celibates.

18 See Jarrett (2000), Jenkins and Maier-Katkin (1992), and Cohen (2002, xiv–xv).

19 Healey also ridicules and exaggerates lesbian feminism, for example by claiming that it promoted "sexless wimmin-loving where women come as a result of political penetration – mind fuck" (1996, 106).

20 For a current example of a diplomatic article that, in my view, arguably overstates the sex-radical position, see Deckha (2007, 442), where the sex-radical position is characterized as "naivete in celebrating all forms of S/M as resistance or empowerment." Notably, no citation is offered to support this characterization.

21 It is interesting to see how Healey's narrative attempts to mitigate this violent attack. After describing the incident, she states, "No doubt the threat to the poor sm girls that night was greatly exaggerated" (1996, 129). Healey doesn't explain why being threatened by angry protesters wielding crowbars would not be a terrifying experience, but instead relies on sarcasm when describing the "poor sm girls" to do the work of downplaying the seriousness of what happened.

22 This does not hold true in *Unleashing Feminism* (Reti 1993b), in which the authors lament that lesbian sadomasochists have gained influence and acceptance in the 1990s.

23 The author's identity is revealed in an addendum to the article, where Barbara Ruth identifies herself. Sadomasochists' use of pseudonyms is not unlike the ex-sadomasochists' use. In both cases, s/m is construed as an edgy and taboo practice. The difference is that the ex-sadomasochists condemn the lesbian sadomasochists for promoting it, while the lesbian sadomasochists condemn the anti-s/m feminists for policing it.

24 Incidentally, Patrick Califia is the only pro-s/m writer I have found who directly defends the use of Nazi symbols. It should be noted, however, that Califia does not defend or address the public use of Nazi symbols in s/m play. Emma Healey (1996) refers to someone who uses Nazi signifiers within a therapeutic context.

25 Seven years after Califia's article was published, Leo Bersani would continue this seductively unsentimental understanding of sexuality as a positive thing in its most antisocial form: "The inestimable value of sex as – at least in certain of its ineradicable aspects – anticommunal, antiegalitarian, antinurturing, antiloving" (1987, 215). Interestingly, Bersani derives this conceptualization, in part, from Catharine MacKinnon and Andrea Dworkin's analyses, but he reverses the normative evaluation; instead of indicting these sexual dynamics, he extols them.

26 This statistic was a distortion of a statement made by Boyd Stephens, a coroner who estimated that 10 per cent of San Francisco's homicides were sex related, which included being gay/queer-bashed.

27 Incidentally, in my research on the sex wars, I have not found any literature from the anti-s/m side that would rebut any of the factual claims made by either Rubin or Califia, or any explanations that would justify this hostile and anti-dialogic treatment. If my research is correct, it is simply not addressed in their literature.

28 Lucy's account is notable not just because she claims s/m to be "cathartic and healing," but also because she is a committed anti-pornography feminist and separatist. Her position exemplifies that there was some criss-cross between the supposedly separate camps of radical feminists and sex-radicals.

29 Califia as well speaks of "eros" as "impeccably honest" and contends that "it takes courage to hear its demands and follow them" ([1980a] 1994, 114).

30 For a recent incarnation of the argument that s/m should be assessed as a cultural identity, see Deckha (2011).

31 In a similar invocation of culture, Califia explicates on the cultural meaning behind the title of his book of erotica, *Macho Sluts*. He states, "In this country, machismo is a survival mechanism by which minority men try to preserve their self-esteem and their culture" (1988b, 20). By appropriating the term *macho*, Califia likens his sadomasochist lesbian characters to "minority men" who are struggling to maintain their dignity within a context of cultural imperialism.

32 Most notably in Butler (1990) and Sedgwick (1990).

33 The absurdity of this charge unfortunately bears an uncanny resemblance to a real charge brought against the submissive partners in the British case *R. v. Brown*, (1993) 97 Cr. App. R. 44, which I discuss in detail in chapter 5. For now, suffice it to say that bottoms in a consensual sadomasochist encounter were charged *and* convicted of accessory to assault upon themselves.

34 In the last fifteen years, a number of academics and writers have given sympathetic treatment to s/m in practice or in pornography, including Shannon Bell in a number of articles (see 2002), Brenda Cossman (2004), Monica Pa (2001), Carl F. Stychin (1994), to a degree, Vera Bergelson (2007), and Stacey May Fowles (2008). From a more anti-s/m perspective, there is Sheila Jeffreys (2003); Cheryl Hanna (2001), Janine Benedet (2001). And taking a more measured and reconciliatory approach are Maneesha Deckha (2007) and (2011).

35 Halley's analysis centres on *Oncale v. Sundowner Offshore Services, Inc.* - 523 U.S. 75 (1997), the American Supreme Court decision that established that federal employment anti-discrimination law applies to sexual harassment in the context of same-sex interactions.

3. S/M in Showbiz

1 See, generally, Comolli and Narboni (1992).

2 See Austin (2002), 2, where the author argues, "In the inter-discursive encounters between audiences and film texts within specific contexts, film viewers are productive agents in the creation of meaning, pleasure and use. But these activities are neither autonomous from textual mechanisms, institutional practices, material and discursive settings, nor innocent from the operations of power." See also Sobchack (1992), who posits the dialectical and dialogic experience of film.

3 I direct the reader to check out the queer romantic comedy *Better Than Chocolate* (1999), which dramatizes the censorship struggles that Little Sisters Bookstore has had with Customs Canada because of the intersection of s/m and homophobia. While the main lesbian couple do not engage in s/m practices, there is still engagement with the issue of s/m as a freedom of expression issue. Also, recall in chapter 2 where I discuss Emma Healey's report that the lesbian film *She Must Be Seeing Things* (1987) incited anti-s/m protests in parts of England because it supposedly contained implicit s/m themes. Unfortunately, I was not able to review the film, as it is not readily available.

4 For a humorous version of this plot line, see the *Seinfeld* episode #313, "The Subway," which originally aired on 8 January 1992. In this episode, George gets picked up by a beautiful woman on the subway and recklessly decides to skip a job interview to go with her to a hotel. In the room, she handcuffs a nervous but eager George to the bed, and then proceeds to empty his wallet and steal all of his clothes.

5 "Loco de Amor," a song by David Byrne and Celia Cruz.

6 One could argue that the two other confirmed female killers in the movie, Hazel Dobkins and Roxy, also used phallic weapons to kill. Dobkins killed her entire family with a knife she had received as a wedding present, and Roxy appropriated her *father's* razor blade to kill her two brothers.

7 See Freiberger (2000), who argues that Catherine is a symbol of Nick's death instinct.

8 Deleyto (1997) at paragraph 9 references Weinrichter (1992, 25), who suggests that "what saves [Nick] Curron is his satisfactory sexual performance … As long as he can keep it up, he has nothing to fear, but, just in case, Catherine always has her own very special dildo at hand."

9 Interestingly, in both scenes, the man is positioned behind the woman, i.e. they have sexual intercourse in "doggy" style. There is a sense that this kind of violent s/m-inspired sex is more animalistic.

10 Gray extends Laura Mulvey's analysis of woman as the object of the male
    gaze, arguing that comedy "positions the woman not simply as the object
    of the male gaze but of the male laugh – not just looked-at but to-be-
    laughed-at." Carl, as a feminized subject, becomes interpolated in this
    project, not necessarily because of a male gaze, but because of a normal-
    izing gaze – one that reduces sexual minorities, particularly emasculated
    male subjects, to objects of fun. Jenny Barrett (2007) links this concept,
    to be laughed at, to the s/m subject.

11 Another comedy in which sadomasochists form the basis of humour is the
    1982 ironic film *Eating Raoul*, which portrays s/m practitioners as danger-
    ous, pathetic, and ridiculous. In this film, a very straight-laced couple,
    the Blands, cook up a scheme in which they lure sexual fetishists to their
    house and then kill them for their money. The humour is derived by
    portraying the fatal demise of the sexual perverts as well as from portray-
    ing how the most "normal" people in the film are, in fact, unrepentant
    killers (and in the end, become cannibals, to dispose of a body).

12 See generally, Cossman (2007).

13 At the same time, this splitting of maternal roles does simultaneously
    present a counter-hegemonic picture of womanhood. In other words,
    the baby operates as an ambivalent trope in the narrative.

14 See specifically: "Within the Western tradition … the love story [between
    sex worker and client] has at its heart a rescue fantasy" (Campbell 320).

15 Although, of course, *Basic Instinct* and *Body of Evidence* came out after
    9½ Weeks, so it might be more accurate to say that *Basic Instinct* and *Body of
    Evidence* were making an intertextual linkage to *9½ Weeks* and the violent
    and rapacious consequences of indulging in s/m.

16 Miller initially makes this claim about male sexuality, but acknowledges
    that women too can have a desire to "[indulge] their own fascination with
    the contemptible and the disgusting" (1997, 131).

17 In addition, recall Califia's short story, "The Hustler," where the sex scene
    takes place in an alley with garbage strewn around (1988a, 177).

18 Makarushka argues that Elizabeth "is horrified at the recognition of an
    otherness within herself, an otherness she cannot name" (1995, 147), and
    later she states of Elizabeth, "Overcome with revulsion, she vomits, and
    her self-loathing is transformed into resolution" (148).

19 This vomiting scene also comes right after Elizabeth witnesses a crowd
    of people over-indulging in alcohol and food at a gallery opening.

20 Foster (2003) refers the reader to Cripp (1993a; 1993b).

21 An interesting inter-textual reference is found in *Basic Instinct*, where one
    scene features *Hellraiser* playing on Nick's television while he is passed
    out on the couch.

22 I discerned only one quick shot of a woman of colour in a crowd scene that lasts for less than a second.

23 Dyer (1997, 2) writes that white people enjoy the status of not being associated with the particularity of a racial category; they can stand in for all of humanity because their racial identity is construed as "neutral."

24 I derive this insight from Chanter, who argues that "to entrench ourselves in the language of gender or race – even to inhabit those discourses in ways that are intended to be liberatory – is to endorse a reification of such concepts that is bound to overlook the abjection of other subject positions that are relegated to background phenomena, and rendered insignificant by the very elucidation or critical deployment of one concept rather than another" (2008, 28).

25 Califia recounts that the "vanilla" lesbians and gay men protested *Cruising* because they were embarrassed by leathermen and thus wanted to keep them under the mainstream radar. Califia objected to the film because it allegedly created the belief that "if you went home with someone wearing leather, they would tie you up and stab you to death" (1987, 270–1).

26 It should be noted that the *DSM-V* (2013) does not perpetuate the truth-claim that sexual sadism usually increases in severity over time.

27 According to Wikipedia, the term *gimp*, in the context of sadomasochism, "is a usually derogatory term used to refer to a (male or female) sexual submissive person, typically dressed in black leather (or rubber), often in a gimp suit, and wearing a bondage hood or mask of the same material" (1913). I could not find a more reliable source for the definition, but it seems an apt description of the "Gimp" character in *Pulp Fiction*.

28 In my research, it is unclear whether Tarentino coined the term *gimp* as an s/m identity in *Pulp Fiction* or if the term existed beforehand in any BDSM context. If it did exist before, it does not seem to be a common word, as it is not listed in older BDSM glossaries, such in the one provided by Califia (1993a). A.J. Withers (2012, 7) cites Miller, Parker, and Gillinson, who define disablism as "discriminatory, oppressive or abusive behavior arising from the belief that disabled people are inferior to others" (2004, 9).

29 Deckha's analysis of the book upon which the film is based suggests that the narrative offers a helpful case study through which to consider agency, consent, and feminist and legal responses to s/m (2007). From my perspective, because the ideological bent of the story is so deeply s/m phobic, and the depiction of its characters is so derogatory, the use of it as a hypothetical scenario to make normative claims about s/m is problem-atic. In its representation, the story has already judged the practice as dysfunctional and destructive.

30 See Khan (2009), where I pull together my cinematic analysis of professional dominatrices, including a more sustained engagement with *Shortbus*, and compare that to the case *R. v. Bedford* (2000), 184 D.L.R. (4th) 727, 143 C.C.C. (3d) 311; 2000 CarswellOnt 839 (C.A.) (WestlawCarswell).

4. The Legal Fondling of S/M Pornography

1 Brenda Cossman makes a similar observation in her analysis of the *Butler* decision (1997, 115): "The Court does not tell us what makes sex good; it only tells us what makes sex bad."

2 It is worth noting that such obligations are not imposed on other genres. No one expects science fiction to be faithful to scientific empiricism. No one expects comedies to portray the human condition in all of its complexity and contradictions. Yet pornography, because it appeals to our sexual hormones and not our funny bone, is seen as somehow more dangerous and more responsible to uphold a particular idealized and literal vision of human conduct.

3 Duggan, Hunter, and Vance make a similar observation concerning MacKinnon's disgust with images of women enjoying ejaculation in their mouths and on their faces: "The notion that the female character is 'used' by men suggests that it is improbable that a woman would engage in fellatio of her own accord" (1985, 138).

4 See, generally, Cossman (2007).

5 I found a copy of Trish Thomas's outlawed story in Findlay (1996), 195. It is fascinating to note that nowhere in the story does the submissive express reluctance or resistance to the encounter. In fact, in numerous parts of the narrative, she directs the sexual activities.

6 For a pop cultural commentary on this case, see the movie *Better than Chocolate* (1999), a romantic comedy that dramatizes the struggles Little Sisters Bookstore has encountered with Customs censorship, under the fictional name "Ten Percent Books." The film is particularly interesting for the ways it links day-to-day homophobia and violence with bureaucratic systemic discrimination.

7 Gilles Deleuze's analysis of the differences between the sadist and the masochist would support this view: "A genuine sadist could never tolerate a masochistic victim" (1991, 40).

8 Justice Low does respectfully explain, though, that at the time of *Butler*, the Supreme Court of Canada justices would have had no way to predict the impact of the Internet on Canadian society since 1995 (para. 93).

9 My translation: "show a woman in a degrading and dehumanizing manner and in this sense, they constitute harmful material to society, notably for women."

10 I borrow the description "tolerated residuum" from Kennedy (1993, 137), to indicate the ways society acknowledges certain unjust practices by trivializing the rights at stake because of other social priorities.

5. The Legal Fondling of S/M Practice

1 The accused were charged under the *Offences against the Person Act 1861, Chapter 100, Acts Causing or Tending to Cause Danger to Life or Bodily Harm*, ss. 20 and 47. Some theorists have speculated that the police felt compelled to lay charges to justify the exorbitant costs of their investigation. See Thompson (1994, 2).

2 For a consideration of the tropes of (un)manliness, see Stychin (1994).

3 The judicial naturalization of "male community life" in *R. v. Jones (Terence)* (1986) 83 Cr.App.R. 375 (CA Crim. Div.) mentioned above, reveals a pointed tolerance of aggression and serious injury when it occurs in non-sexual arenas. The children who were "bullied" in *R. v. Jones (Terence)* suffered serious injury where one child suffered a ruptured spleen that needed surgery for its removal. The other child suffered a broken arm. Both children protested throughout the encounter and tried to get away. The accused children were acquitted.

4 See Griffith (n.d.), which states that the doctor's actions in the *Wilson* decision determine that confidentiality can be breached in cases of "iniquity."

5 My translation: He described engaging in sadomasochistic practices with his common-law partner and with other people and recognized the thin line between these scenarios and rape scenarios.

6 My translation: He again described having rape fantasies and having attended sadomasochistic social events.

7 My translation: Grégoire St-Aubin does not seem to make the connection between his sadomasochistic practices and his aggressive act, whereas it seems clear to the doctor that with the rape scenario, as with the sadomasochistic scenario, Mr St-Aubin experiences feelings of control and domination.

8 This section does not address cases where there is no air of reality to the claim of consent to "rough sex." For a useful survey of this case law, see Busby (2012). I engage with the normative claims of this article in the subsection that addresses the case, *R. v. J.A.* [2011] 2 S.C.R. 440.

9 See *R. v. B (K.G.)*, [1993] 1. S.C.R. 740.
10 Another 2012 article that addresses the *J.A.* decision is Olson (2012).
   In this piece, Olson uses a blended liberal-queer framework to analyse
   the contemporary community standard of tolerance test, autonomy and
   consent in the *J.A.* case. I do not reckon with this article in this section of
   Vicarious Kinks, as my focus here is on how some feminist arguments work
   to erase s/m subjectivity, and Olson basically arrives at a conclusion similar
   to mine in her article, albeit through a different theoretical trajectory.
11 For a useful overview of this issue, see Levin and van Berlo (2004).
12 For an exploration of the reification of "the batterer" and the problematic
   reductionist effects of this label, see Corvo and Johnson (2003).
13 There are numerous books that track the harm of criminalization and its
   discriminatory impact. For two examples, see Sudbury (2005) and
   Wacquant (2009).
14 See Meiners (2009).
15 For commentary on the problems of criminal justice responses to domestic
   violence for both males and females, see, for example, Crenshaw (2012),
   Gruber (2012), and Miccio (2005).
16 For an example of this viewpoint from the perspective of an edgeplayer,
   see Juno and Vale (1993, 44), where Bob Flanagan, performance artist and
   extreme masochist, addresses the "incredible amount of trust" required
   for extreme play, including erotic asphyxiation.
17 See Gotell, "Canadian Sexual Assault Law" (n.d.).
18 See Sokoloff and Dupont (2005) and Incite! Women of Color against
   Violence (2006).
19 Note that the appellant's factum states that as a child, Bedford suffered
   physical abuse at the hands of her foster mother and repeated sexual
   abuse at the hands of her adopted brother (Appellant's Factum, 21
   October 1999, para. 28). From the Supreme Court of Canada's reasoning,
   because of this history of abuse, the experience of a strip-search may have
   been particularly traumatic for Bedford.
20 Miller states, "To study disgust is to risk contamination; jokes about his or
   her unwholesome interests soon greet the disgust researcher" (1997, 5),
   and, "Disgust has … powerful communalizing capacities and is especially
   useful and necessary as a builder of moral and social community" (194).
21 The facts of this case are derived from Klein and Moser (2006), 233. Dr
   Klein was consulted as an expert witness in support of Mr Jones and Ms
   Smith. While the authors refer to the decision, no citation is provided. I
   have been unable to locate the case in electronic and print databases.

22 The RCMP are now also investigating Ward for an alleged criminal offence of defamatory libel.
23 For a thorough and persuasive argument against the use of law and individual rights claims as vehicles for social justice, see Spade (2011).

Conclusion: Epistemic Violence, Epistemic Pleasures

1 This observation, of course, also taps into the alternate meaning of "knowledge," that is, to know someone is to have had sexual intercourse with her.
2 I find it incredibly ironic that a story that banks on the stigmatizing stereotype of the predatory older female was so popular with middle-aged women.

References

Jurisprudence

Brodie v. The Queen, [1962] S.C.R. 681.

Glad Day Bookshop v. Deputy Minister of National Revenue, [1992] O.J. No. 1466 (Ct. J. (General Div.)) (QL).

Hayes v. Vancouver Police Department and Barker, [2005] BCHRT 590 (QL).

Hayes v. Vancouver Police Department and Barker, 2006 BCSC 1217.

Hayes v. Vancouver Police Department and Barker, 2008 BCCA 148.

Hayes v. Vancouver Police Department and Barker, 2010 CarswellBC 3299, 2010 BCHRT 324, [2011] B.C.W.L.D. 1115, [2011] B.C.W.L.D. 1114, [2011] B.C.W.L.D. 1104.

Laskey, Jaggard and Brown v. United Kingdom (Application Nos. 21627/93, 21826/93, 21974/93) (1997) 24 E.H.R.R. 39 (E.C.H.R.).

LEAF. 1991. "Factum of the Intervenor, Women's Legal Education and Action Fund." *Butler v. R.*, [1992] 1 S.C.R. 452, [1992] 8 C.R.R. (2d) 1.

LEAF. 2000. "Factum of the Intervenor, Women's Legal Education and Action Fund." *Little Sisters Book and Art Emporium v. Canada (Minister of Justice)*, 2000 SCC 69, [2000] 2 S.C.R. 1120.

Little Sisters Book and Art Emporium v. Canada (Minister of Justice), 2000 SCC 69, [2000] 2 S.C.R. 1120.

Little Sisters Book and Art Emporium v. Canada (Commissioner of Customs and Revenue), 2007 SCC 2, [2007] 1 S.C.R. 38.

Loyalist College of Applied Arts & Technology v. O.P.S.E.U., Local 420 (2004), CarswellOnt 4536 (Ont. Arbitration Board).

Mosley v. News Group Newspapers Limited, [2008] EWHC 1777 (QB).

Nova Scotia (Minister of Community Services) v. A.C., [2003] N.S.J. No. 184 (S.C. (Fam. Div.)) (QL).

Oncale v. Sundowner Offshore Services, Inc. – 523 U.S. 75 (1997).

R. c. Cloutier, [2004] J.Q. No. 13601 (Cour du Québec (Chambre criminelle et pénale) District de Montréal) (QL).

R. c. Dompierre, [2005] J.Q. No. 17553 at para. 18 (Cour du Québec (Chambre criminelle et pénale) District de Longueuil) (QL).

R. c. Laliberté, [1992] O.J. No. 1346 (Ct. J. (Prov. Div.)) (QL).

R. c. Latreille, [2004] J.Q. No. 10097 (Cour municipale de Montréal (Québec)) (QL).

R. c. Latreille, [2006] J.Q. No. 1201 (Que. S.C.) (QL).

R. c. Latreille (2007), CarswellQue 9142 (Que. C.A.) (Westlaw).

R. c. St Aubin, [2003] J.Q. No. 5766 (Cour du Québec (Chambre criminelle et pénale) District de Montréal) (QL).

R. v. A. (J.) 2008 ONCJ 195 (Trial decision); *R. v. A. (J.)* 2010 ONCA 226, 253 C.C.C. (3d) 153 (Court of Appeal decision,); *R. v. J.A.,* [2011] 2 S.C.R. 440 (Supreme Court of Canada decision).

R. v. B (K.G.), [1993] 1. S.C.R. 740.

R. v. Bedford, [1998] O.J. No. 4033 (Ct. J. (Prov. Div.)) (QL)

R. v. Bedford, Ruling (re Charter application) (August 21, 1998) 1378 for Bedford trial.

R. v. Bedford, Ruling (re experts) (August 21, 1998) 1354 for Bedford trial.

R. v. Bedford (2000), 184 D.L.R. (4th) 727, 143 C.C.C. (3d) 311; 2000 CarswellOnt 839 (C.A.) (WestlawCarswell).

R. v. Bedford (2000), Appellant's Factum, (October 21, 1999).

R. v. Brown, Central Criminal Court (U.K., Manchester, December 1990) Justice Rant presiding (unreported).

R. v. Brown, [1992] 2 All E.R. 552 (U.K. High Court).

R. v. Brown (1993), 97 Cr. App. R. 44, 1993 WL 963434 (HL), (1993) 157 J.P. 337, [1994] 1 A.C. 212, [1993] 2 All E.R. 75 (U.K. House of Lords).

R. v. Butler 1990 CarswellMan 228, [1991] 1 W.W.R. 97, 1 C.R. (4th) 309, 60 C.C.C. (3d) 219, 5 C.R.R. (2d) 68, 73 Man. R. 197, 3 W.A.C. 197, 73 Man. R. (2d) 19.

R. v. Butler, [1992] S.C.J. No. 15; [1992] 1 S.C.R. 452.

R. v. Cepicka (1992), CarswellAlta 502, 131 A.R. 138, 25 W.A.C. 138 (Alta. Prov. Ct.) (WestlawCarswell).

R. v. Close, [1948] V.L.R. 445 (New Zealand).

R. v. Dee (2004), W.C.B.J. 16682; 63 W.C.B. (2d) 94 (Ont. Ct. J.) (QL).

R. v. Emery (1991), 4 O.R. (3d) 344 (Ct. J. (Prov. Div.)).

R. v. Emery, [1992] O.J. No. 640; 8 O.R. (3d) 60 (Gen. Div.).

R. v. Emmett (18 June 1999), EWCA Crim 1710 (U.K. C.A. Crim. Div.) (QL).

R. v. Erotica Video Exchange Ltd (1994), 163 A.R. 181 (Alta. Prov. Ct.) (QL).

R. v. Golden, [2001] 3 S.C.R. 679, 2001 SCC 83.

R. v. Hancock, [2000] B.C.J. No. 2750 (Sup. Ct.) (QL).

R. v. Hicklin (1868), L.R. 3 Q.B. 360.

R. v. J.A., [2011] 2 S.C.R. 440. Factum of LEAF 2011.

R. v. J.A., [2011] 2 S.C.R. 440. Factum of the Respondent 2011.

R. v. Jobidon, [1991] 2 S.C.R. 714.

R. v. Jones (Terence) (1986), 83 Cr. App. R. 375 (U.K. CA Crim. Div.).

R. v. Kouri, 2005 SCC 81, [2005] 3 S.C.R. 789.

R. v. Labeye, 2005 SCC 80, *Jane Sexes It Up* [2005] 3 S.C.R. 728.

R. v. L. (A.C.T.) 2011 CarswellMan 692, 2011 MBQB 316, 272 Man. R. (2d) 132, 99 W.C.B. (2d) 382.

R. v. MC, [1993] O.J. No. 3240 (Ct. J. (Prov. Div.)) (QL).

R. v. M. (P.) 2011 CarswellOnt 8292, 2011 ONCJ 401, 98 W.C.B. (2d) 395.

R. v. Price, [2004] B.C.J. No. 814 (Prov. Ct.) (QL).

R. v. Ramsingh (1984), 14 C.C.C. (3d) 230 (Man. Q.B.).

R. v. R.D.W., [2006] B.C.J. No. 1451 (Prov. Ct.) (QL).

R. v. Scythes, [1993] O.J. No. 537 (Ct. J. (Prov. Div.)) (QL).

R. v. Wagner (1985), 43 C.R. (3d) 318 at 331 (Alta. Q.B.).

R. v. Welch, [1995] CarswellOnt 987 (Ont. C.A.) (WestlawCarswell).

R. v. Wilson (16 May 1995), (U.K. Crown Court at Doncaster) (unreported).

R. v. Wilson, [1996] E.W.J. 4692 (U.K. C.A. Crim. Div.).

Towne Cinema Theatres Ltd v. The Queen, [1985] 1 S.C.R. 494.

Legislation and Reports

British Columbia, *Human Rights Code*, (R.S.B.C. 1996, c. 210).

Canadian Charter of Rights and Freedoms, Part I of the *Constitution Act, 1982*, being Schedule B to the Canada Act 1982 (U.K.), 1982, c. 11 [Charter] s. 2(b).

Criminal Code, R.S.C. 1985, c. C-46.

The Convention for the Protection of Human Rights and Fundamental Freedoms as amended by Protocol No. 11; *European Convention of Human Rights* (Rome 4 November 1950).

Offences against the Person Act 1861, Chapter 100, Acts Causing or Tending to Cause Danger to Life or Bodily Harm, ss. 20 and 47 (U.K.).

The Report of the Standing Committee on Justice and Legal Affairs (MacGuigan Report) (1978).

Books, Articles, Artistic Writing

Abrams, Kathryn. 1995. "Sex Wars Redux: Agency and Coercion in Feminist Legal Theory." *Columbia Law Review* 95 (2): 304–76.

Allen, Frances. 2013. "DSM-5 Writing Mistakes Will Cause Great Confusion." *Huffington Post*. TheHuffingtonPost.com, 11 June 2013.

American Psychiatric Association. 1942. *Statistical Manual for the Use of Hospitals for Mental Diseases*. Utica, NY: State Hospitals.

– 2013. *Diagnostic and Statistical Manual of Mental Disorders: DSM-5*. Washington, DC: American Psychiatric Association.

American Psychiatric Association, Committee on Nomenclature and Statistics. 1968. *DSM-II: Diagnostic and Statistical Manual of Mental Disorders*, 2nd ed. Washington, DC: American Psychiatric Association.

American Psychiatric Association, Committee on Nomenclature and Statistics of the American Psychiatric Association. 1952. *Diagnostic and Statistical Manual of Mental Disorders*. Washington DC: American Psychiatric Association.

American Psychiatric Association, Task Force on DSM-IV. 1994. *DSM-IV: Diagnostic and Statistical Manual of Mental Disorders*, 4th ed. Washington, DC: American Psychiatric Association.

– 2000. *DSM-IV-TR: Diagnostic and Statistical Manual of Mental Disorders*, 4th ed., text rev. Washington, DC: American Psychiatric Association.

American Psychiatric Association, Task Force on Nomenclature and Statistics. 1981. *DSM-III: Diagnostic and Statistical Manual of Mental Disorders*, 3rd ed. Washington, DC: American Psychiatric Association.

Anderson, Benedict. 1991. *Imaginary Communities*. New York: Verso.

Ardill, Susan, and Sue O'Sullivan. 1986. "Upsetting an Applecart: Difference, Desire and Lesbian Sadomasochism." *Feminist Review* 23:31–57.

Atkinson, Ti-Grace. 1982. "Why I'm against S/M Liberation." In Linden et al., 90–2.

Austin, Thomas. 2002. *Hollywood, Hype and Audiences: Selling and Watching Popular Film in the 1990s*. Manchester, UK: Manchester University Press.

Bailey, Cameron. 1988. "Nigger/Lover: The Thin Sheen of Race in 'Something Wild.'" *Screen* 29 (4): 28–43.

Barrett, Jenny. 2007. "'You've Made Mistress Very, Very Angry': Displeasure and Pleasure in Media Representations of BDSM." *Particip@tions* 4 (1). http://www.participations.org/Volume%204/Issue%201/4_01_barrett.htm.

"Basic Instinct, Trivia." 1992. IMDb, Internet Movie Database. http://www.imdb.com/title/tt0103772/trivia.

Baynham, Bryan, and Daniel Reid. 2012. "Bryan Baynham Interviewed by the Province and Other Media Outlets; Mountie Fights Back – Sues Fraudster and Cameron Ward." Harper Grey LLP, 5 November. http://www.harpergrey.com/news/2012/11/article487/.

Bell, Shannon. 2002. "Liquid Fire: Female Ejaculation and Fast Feminism." In Johnson 2002b, 327–45.

Benedet, Janine. 2001. "Little Sisters Book and Art Emporium v. Minister of Justice: Sex Equality and the Attack on *R. v. Butler.*" *Osgoode Hall Law Journal* 39:187–205.

Bergelson, Vera. 2007. "The Right to Be Hurt: Testing the Boundaries of Consent." *George Washington Law Review* 75:165–236.

Bernstein, Elizabeth. 2010. "Militarized Humanitarianism Meets Carceral Feminism: The Politics of Sex, Rights, and Freedom in Contemporary Antitrafficking Campaigns." *Signs* 36 (1): 45–71.

Bersani, Leo. 1987. "Is the Rectum a Grave?" *October* 43:197–222.

Bland, Lucy, and Laura L. Doan. 1998. *Sexology Uncensored: The Documents of Sexual Science.* Chicago: University of Chicago Press.

Blasius, Mark, and Shane Phelan. 1997. *We Are Everywhere: A Historical Sourcebook of Gay and Lesbian Politics.* New York: Routledge.

Burstyn, Varda. 1985a. "Political Precedents and Moral Crusades, Women, Sex and the State." In Burstyn 1985b, 4–31.

– ed. 1985b. *Women against Censorship.* Vancouver: Douglas & McIntyre.

Busby, Karen. 1994. "LEAF and Pornography: Litigating on Equality and Sexual Representations." *Canadian Journal of Law and Society* 9:165–92.

– 2012. "Every Breath You Take: Erotic Asphyxiation, Vengeful Wives, and Other Enduring Myths in Spousal Sexual Assault Prosecutions." *Canadian Journal of Women and the Law/Revue femmes et droit* 24 (2): 328–58.

Butler, Judith. 1990. *Gender Trouble: Feminism and the Subversion of Identity.* New York: Routledge.

– 1997. *Excitable Speech: A Politics of the Performative.* New York: Routledge.

– 2004. *Undoing Gender.* New York: Routledge.

Califia, Patrick. (1979) 1994. "A Secret Side of Lesbian Sexuality." *Advocate*, 27 December, 19–23. Reprinted in Califia 1994, 19–23.

– (1980a) 1994. "Among Us, against Us – the New Puritans: Does Equation of Pornography with Violence Add Up to Political Repression?" Reprinted in Califia 1994, 113–22.

– (1980b) 1994. "Feminism and Sadomasochism." *Heresies* 12.3 (1981): 30–4. Reprinted in Califia 1994, 165–74.

– 1987. "A Personal View of the History of the Lesbian S/M Community and Movement in San Francisco." In Samois 1987, 245–82.

– 1988a. "The Hustler." In Califa 1988b, 177–210.

– 1988b. *Macho Sluts.* Boston: Alyson Publications.

– 1988c. *Sapphistry: The Book of Lesbian Sexuality*, 3rd ed. Tallahassee, FL: Naiad.

– 1993a. "Glossary." In *Sensuous Magic*, 131–53.

– 1993b. *Sensuous Magic.* New York: Richard Kasak Books.

– 1994. *Public Sex: The Culture of Radical Sex.* Pittsburgh: Cleis.

Califia, Patrick, and Robin Sweeney, eds. 1996. *The Second Coming: A Leatherdyke Reader*. Los Angeles: Alyson Publications.

Campbell, Russell. 2006. *Marked Women: Prostitutes and Prostitution in the Cinema*. Madison: University of Wisconsin Press.

Chanter, Tina. 2008. *The Picture of Abjection: Film Fetish and the Nature of Difference*. Bloomington: Indiana University Press.

Chenier, Elise. 2004. "Lesbian Sex Wars." *glbtq: An Encyclopedia of Gay, Lesbian, Bisexual, Transgender & Queer Culture*. http://www.glbtq.com/social-sciences/lesbian_sex_wars.html.

Cohen, Stanley. 2002. *Folk Devils and Moral Panics*, 3rd ed. London: Routledge.

Cole, Susan G. 1989. *Pornography and the Sex Crisis*. Toronto: Amanita Publications.

Corvo, Ken, and Pamela J. Johnson. 2003. "Vilification of the 'Batterer': How Blame Shapes Domestic Violence Policy and Interventions." *Aggression and Violent Behavior* 8 (3): 259–81.

Cossman, Brenda. 1997. "Feminist Fashion or Morality in Drag? The Sexual Subtext of the Butler Decision." In Cossman et al. 1997, 107–51.

– 2004. "Sexuality, Queer Theory and 'Feminism After': Reading and Rereading the Sexual Subject." *McGill Law Journal* 49:847–76.

– 2007. *Sexual Citizens: The Legal and Cultural Regulation of Sex and Belonging*. Stanford: Stanford University Press.

Cossman, Brenda, Shannon Bell, Lise Gotell, and Becki L. Ross, eds. 1997. *Bad Attitude/s on Trial: Pornography, Feminism and the Butler Decision*. Toronto: University of Toronto Press.

Coughlin, Ann. 1995. "Regulating the Self: Autobiographical Performances in Outsider Scholarship." *Virginia Law Review* 81:1229–340.

– 2002. "Representing the Forbidden." *California Law Review* 90:2143–83.

Cover, Robert M. 1986. "Violence and the Word." *Yale Law Journal* 96 (8): 1601–29.

Creet, Julia. 1991. "Daughter of the Movement." *Differences* 3 (2): 135–59.

Crenshaw, Kimberle W. 2012. "From Private Violence to Mass Incarceration: Thinking Intersectionally about Women, Race, and Social Control." *UCLA Law Review* 59:1418–73.

Cripp, Thomas. 1993a. *Making Movies Black*. Oxford: Oxford University Press.

– 1993b. *Slow Fade to Black*. Oxford: Oxford University Press.

Crosby, Lynne, ed. 1993. *The Girl Wants To: Women's Representations of Sex and the Body*. Toronto: Coach House.

Daley, Chris. 2002. "Of the Flesh Fancy: Spanking & the Single Girl." In Johnson 2002b, 127–38.

Darwin, Charles. 1871. *The Descent of Man: And Selection in Relation to Sex*. Volume 2. London: John Murray. Digitized by Google.

– (1872) 2001. *The Expression of Emotion in Man and Animals*. Electronic reproduction, NetLibrary.

Davis, Katherine. 1987. "Introduction: What We Fear We Try to Keep Contained." In Samois 1987, 7–13.

Deckha, Maneesha. 2007. "Pain, Pleasure, and Consenting Women: Exploring Feminist Responses to S/M and Its Legal Regulation in Canada through Jelinek's *The Piano Teacher*." *Harvard Journal of Law and Gender* 30:425–59.

– 2011. "Pain as Culture: A Postcolonial Feminist Approach to S/M and Women's Agency." *Sexualities* 14 (2): 129–50.

Deleuze, Gilles. 1991. *Coldness and Cruelty*. New York: Zone Books.

Deleyto, Celestino. 1997. "The Margins of Pleasure: Female Monstrosity and Male Paranoia in 'Basic Instinct.'" *Film Criticism* 21 (3): 20–42.

Descartes, René. (1637) 1992. *A Discourse on Method: Meditations on the First Philosophy; Principles of Philosophy*, translated by John Veitch. London: Dent.

Doane, Mary Ann. 1991. *Femmes Fatales: Feminism, Film Theory, Psychoanalysis*. New York: Routledge.

Douglas, Mary. (1966) 2003. *Purity and Danger*. New York: Routledge.

Downing, Lisa. 2007. "Beyond Safety: Erotic Asphyxiation and the Limits of S/M Discourse." In *Safe, Sane and Consensual: Contemporary Perspectives on Sadomasochism*, ed. Darren Langdridge and Meg Barker, 119–32. London: Palgrave.

– 2012. "Safewording! Kinkphobia and Gender Normativity in Fifty Shades of Grey." *Psychology & Sexuality* 4 (1): 92–102.

Downs, Donald Alexander. 1989. *The New Politics of Pornography*. Chicago: University of Chicago Press.

Duggan, Lisa, and Nan D. Hunter, eds. 2006. *Sex Wars: Sexual Dissent and Political Culture*, 10th anniversary ed. New York: Routledge.

Duggan, Lisa, Nan Hunter, and Carole S. Vance. 1985. "False Promises: Feminist Antipornography Legislation in the U.S." In Burstyn 1985, 130–51.

Dyer, Richard. 1986. *Heavenly Bodies: Film Stars and Society*. New York: St Martin's.

– 1997. *White*. London: Routledge.

Dymock, Alex. 2012. "But Femsub Is Broken Too! On the Normalisation of BDSM and the Problem of Pleasure." *Psychology & Sexuality* 3 (1): 54–68.

Ebert, Roger. 1984. Review of *Crimes of Passion*. RogerEbert.com, 1 January http://www.rogerebert.com/reviews/crimes-of-passion-1984.

– 1986. Review of *Nine and a Half Weeks*. RogerEbert.com, 21 February. http://www.rogerebert.com/reviews/9-12-weeks-1986.

– 1994. Review of *Pulp Fiction*. RogerEbert.com, 14 October. http://www.rogerebert.com/reviews/pulp-fiction-1994.

Eells, Josh. 2011. "Queen of Pain." *Rolling Stone*, 14 April, 41–2, 44–5, 80.

Elejalde-Ruiz, Alexia. 2012. "Pull Down the Shades, Pull Out the Toys. As 'Fifty Shades of Grey' Goes Mainstream, Sex Toy Sales Are Heating Up Too." *Chicago Tribune*, 24 July. http://articles.chicagotribune.com/2012-07-24/features/sc-fam-0724-sex-toys-20120724_1_fifty-shades-bdsm-babeland.

Ellis, Havelock. 1972. *Psychology of Sex: A Manual for Students*, 2nd ed. New York: Emerson Books.

Evans, Jamie Lee. 1993. "Rodney King, Racism and the SM Culture of America." In Reti 1993, 74–8.

Farr, Susan. 1987. "The Art of Discipline: Creating Erotic Dramas of Play and Power." In Samois 1987, 183–91.

Findlay, Heather, ed. 1996. *A Movement of Eros: 25 Years of Lesbian Erotica*. New York: Richard Kasak.

Flood, Alison. 2012. "Fifty Shades of Grey Condemned as 'Manual for Sexual Torture.'" *Guardian*, 24 August. http://www.guardian.co.uk/books/2012/aug/24/fifty-shades-grey-domestic-violence-campaigners.

Forster, E.M. 1927. *Aspects of the Novel and Related Writings*. New York: Harcourt Brace.

Foster, Gwendolyn. 2003. *Performing Whiteness: Postmodern Re/constructions in the Cinema*. New York: State University of New York Press.

Foucault, Michel. 1990. *An Introduction*. Vol. 2 of *The History of Sexuality*. Translated by Robert Hurley. New York: Vintage Books.

Fowles, Stacey May. 2008. "The Fantasy of Acceptable 'Non-Consent': Why the Female Sexual Submissive Scares Us (and Why She Shouldn't). In *Yes Means Yes!: Visions of Female Sexual Power & a World without Rape*, edited by Jaclyn Friedman and Jessica Valenti, 117–25. Berkeley, CA: Seal.

Freeman, Jo. 1975. "Political Organization in the Feminist Movement." *Acta Sociologica* 18 (2–3): 222–44.

Freiberger, Erich D. 2000. "In the Beginning Was the Act: *Basic Instinct* as the Cinematic Image of Freud's Death Drive." *Literature and Psychology* 46:1–25.

Freud, Sigmund. 1961. *Beyond the Pleasure Principle*. Translated by James Strachey. London: Hogarth.

– 1962. *The Interpretation of Dreams*. Translated by James Strachey. New York: Penguin Books.

– 1975. *Three Essays on the Theory of Sexuality*. Edited and translated by James Strachey. New York: Basic Books.

– 1981a. "A Child Is Being Beaten: A Contribution to the Study of the Origin of Sexual Perversions." In *The Standard Edition of the Complete Psychological Works of Sigmund Freud*, edited and translated by James Strachey, 17:175–204. London: Hogarth.

– 1981b. "The Economic Problem of Masochism." In *The Standard Edition of the Complete Psychological Works of Sigmund Freud*, edited and translated by James Strachey, 19:159–70. London: Hogarth.

– 1981c. "Instincts and Their Vicissitudes." In *The Standard Edition of the Complete Psychological Works of Sigmund Freud*, edited and translated by James Strachey, 16:109–40. London: Hogarth.

– 1981d. "Negation." In *The Standard Edition of the Complete Psychological Works of Sigmund Freud*, edited and translated by James Strachey, 19:233–40. London: Hogarth.

Gandal, Keith. 2007. *Class Representation in Modern Fiction and Film*. New York: Palgrave Macmillan.

Garber, Marjorie B. 1995. *Vice Versa: Bisexuality and the Eroticism of Everyday Life*. New York: Simon & Schuster.

Geddes, Patrick, and John Arthur Thomson. 1889. *The Evolution of Sex*. London: W. Scott.

Gotell, Lise. 1997. "Shaping Butler: The New Politics of Anti-Pornography." In Cossman et al. 1997, 48–106.

– 2012. "Governing Heterosexuality through Specific Consent: Interrogating the Governmental Effects of *R. v J.A.*" *Canadian Journal of Women and the Law/Revue femmes et droit* 24 (2): 359–88.

– n.d. "Canadian Sexual Assault Law: Neoliberalism and the Erosion of Feminist-Inpired Law Reforms." Academia.edu. http://www.academia .edu/322349/Canadian_Sexual_Assault_Law_Neoliberalism_and_the_ Erosion_of_Feminist-Inspired_Law_Reforms.

Gray, Frances. 1994. *Women and Laughter*. Hampshire, UK: Macmillan.

Green, Les. 2000. "Pornographies." *Journal of Political Philosophy* 8 (1): 27–52.

Griffith, Richard. n.d. "Legal Aspects of Confidentiality." http://healthlaw .swan.ac.uk/resource_files/Medical%20School/confidentiality%20and% 20information%20sharing%20-%20med%20sch.rtf.

Gruber, Aya. 2012. "A 'Neo-Feminist' Assessment of Rape and Domestic Violence Law Reform." *Journal of Gender Race and Justice* 15:583–615.

Gubar, Susan, and Joan Hoff, eds. 1989. *For Adult Users Only: The Dilemma of Violent Pornography*. Bloomington: Indiana University Press.

Halberstam, Judith. 2005. *In a Queer Time and Place: Transgender Bodies, Subcultural Lives*. New York: New York University Press.

Halley, Janet. 2006. *Split Decisions: How and Why to Take a Break from Feminism*. Princeton: Princeton University Press.

Halperin, David. 2007. *What Do Gay Men Want? An Essay on Sex, Risk, and Subjectivity*. Ann Arbor: University of Michigan Press.

Hanna, Cheryl. 2001. "Sex Is Not a Sport: Consent and Violence in Criminal Law." *Boston College Law Review* 42:239–90.

Harris, Elizabeth. 1982. "Sadomasochism: A Personal Experience." In Linden et al. 1982, 93–5.

Healey, Emma. 1996. *Lesbian Sex Wars*. London: Virago.

"Hellraiser, Trivia." 1987. IMDb, Internet Movie Database. http://www.imdb .com/title/tt0093177/.

Hirschman, Elizabeth. 1991. "Possession and Commoditization in *Fatal Attraction, Blue Velvet,* and *Nine and a Half Weeks.*" 86 (1–2) *Semiotica* 1–42.

Holmlund, Chris. 1994. "'Cruisin" for a Bruisin': Hollywood's Deadly (Lesbian) Dolls." *Cinema Journal* 34 (1): 31–51.

Hoople, Terry. 1996. "Conflicting Visions: SM, Feminism, and the Law; A Problem of Representation." *Canadian Journal of Law and Society* 11:177–220.

Incite! Women of Color against Violence. 2006. *Color of Violence: The Incite! Anthology*. Cambridge, MA: South End.

Itzin, Catherine, ed. 1993. *Women, Violence and Civil Liberties: A Radical New View*. Oxford: Oxford University Press.

James, E.L. 2012a. *Fifty Shades Darker*. New York: Vintage.

– 2012b. *Fifty Shades Freed*. New York: Vintage.

– 2012c. *Fifty Shades of Grey*. New York: Vintage.

Jarrett, Kelly Jo. 2000. "Strange Bedfellows: Religion, Feminism, and Fundamentalism in the Satanic Panic." PhD dissertation, Duke University.

Jeffreys, Sheila. (1986) 1993. "Sadomasochism: The Erotic Cult of Fascism." Reprinted in Jeffreys 1993, 171–89.

– 1993. *The Lesbian Heresy: A Feminist Perspective on the Lesbian Sexual Revolution*. London: Women's Press.

– 2003. *Unpacking Queer Politics: A Lesbian Feminist Perspective*. Cambridge, UK: Polity.

Jenkins, Philip, and Daniel Maier-Katkin. 1992. "Satanism: Myth and Reality in a Contemporary Moral Panic." *Crime, Law and Social Change* 17 (1): 53.

Johnson, Merri Lisa. 2002a. "Jane Hocus, Jane Focus." In Johnson 2002b, 1–11.

– ed. 2002b. *Jane Sexes It Up: True Confessions of Feminist Desire*. New York: Thunder's Mouth.

Jonel, Marissa. 1982. "Letter from a Former Masochist." In Linden et al. 1982, 16–22.

Juno, Andrea, and V. Vale. 1993. "Bob Flanagan: Supermasochist." *Re/Search* 1:6–126.

Kennedy, Duncan. 1993. *Sexy Dressing Etc*. Cambridge, MA: Harvard University Press.

Khan, Ummni. 2009. "Putting a Dominatrix in Her Place: The Representation and Regulation of Female Dom/Male Sub Sexuality." *Canadian Journal of Women and the Law/Revue Femmes et Droit* 21 (1): 143–75.

Kim, JuJu. 2012. "Domestic Abuse Charity to Use *Fifty Shades of Grey* as Toilet Paper." Time Newsfeed, 7 November. http://newsfeed.time.com/2012/11/07/charity-to-use-50-shades-of-grey-as-toilet-paper/.

Klein, Marty, and Charles Moser. 2006. "SM (Sadomasochistic) Interests as an Issue in a Child Custody Proceeding." *Journal of Homosexuality* 50 (2–3): 233–42.

Kleinplatz, Peggy J., and Charles Moser. 2005. "Is SM Pathological?" *Lesbian and Gay Psychology Review* 6 (3): 255–60.

– eds. 2006. *Sadomasochism: Powerful Pleasures*. Birmingham, NY: Haworth.

Krafft-Ebing, Richard von. 1965. *Psychopathia sexualis, with Especial Reference to the Antipathic Sexual Instinct; a Medico-Forensic Study*, 12th ed. Translated by Franklin S. Klaf. New York: Stein and Day.

Kristeva, Julia. 1982. *Powers of Horror: An Essay on Abjection*. Translated by Leon S. Roudiez. New York: Columbia University Press.

– 1994. *Revolution in Poetic Language*. Translated by Margaret Waller. New York: Columbia University Press.

Krueger, Richard. 2010. "The DSM Diagnostic Criteria for Sexual Masochism." *Archives of Sexual Behavior* 346–56.

Langdridge, Darren, and Meg Barker, eds. 2007. *Safe, Sane and Consensual: Contemporary Perspectives on Sadomasochism*. New York: Palgrave Macmillan.

Lederer, Laura, ed. 1980. *Take Back the Night: Women on Pornography*. New York: Bantam Book.

Lesh, Cheri. 1982. "Hunger and Thirst in the House of Distorted Mirrors." In Linden et al. 1982, 202–4.

Levin, R. J., and W. van Berlo. 2004. "Sexual Arousal and Orgasm in Subjects Who Experience Forced or Non-Consensual Sexual Stimulation: A Review." *Journal of Clinical Forensic Medicine* 11 (2): 82–8.

Lewis, Reina, and Karen Adler. 1994. "Come to Me Baby or What's Wrong with Lesbian SM." *Women's Studies International Forum* 17:433–41.

Linden, Robin Ruth. 1982. "Introduction: Against Sadomasochism." In Linden et al. 1982, 1–15.

Linden, Robin Ruth, Darlene R. Pagano, Diana E.H. Russell, and Susan Leigh Star, eds. 1982. *Against Sadomasochism: A Radical Feminist Analysis*. East Palo Alto, CA: Frog in the Well.

L'Office québecoise de la langue français. n.d. s.v. "paraphilie." http://gdt.oqlf.gouv.qc.ca/ficheOqlf.aspx?Id_Fiche=8871430.

Lucy, Juicy. 1987. "If I Ask You to Tie Me Up, Will You Still Want to Love Me?" In Samois 1987, 29–40.

MacGuigan Report. 1978. *The Report of the Standing Committee on Justice and Legal Affairs*.

MacKinnon, Catherine. 1982. "Feminism, Marxism, Method, and the State: An Agenda for Theory." *Signs* 7 (3): 515–44.

– 1983. "Feminism, Marxism, Method, and the State: Toward Feminist Jurisprudence." *Signs* 8 (4): 635–58.

– 1987. *Feminism Unmodified: Discourses on Life and Law*. Cambridge, MA: Harvard University Press.

– 1989. *Toward a Feminist Theory of the State*. Cambridge, MA: Harvard University Press.

– 2001. *Sex Equality*. New York: Foundation.

Madonna. *Sex*. 1992. New York: Warner Books.

Makarushka, Irena. 1995. "Women Spoken For: Images of Displaced Desire." In *Screening the Sacred: Religion, Myth, and Ideology in American Popular American Film*, edited by Joel W. Martin and Conrad E. Ostwalt Jr, 142–51. Boulder, CO: Westview.

Manatu, Norma. 2003. *African American Women and Sexuality in the Cinema*. Jefferson, NC: McFarland.

McClintock, Anne. 1993. "Maid to Order: Commercial Fetishism and Gender Power." *Social Text* 37:87–116.

McNeill, Elizabeth. 1978. *Nine and a Half Weeks: A Memoir of a Love Affair*. New York: Perennial.

Meiners, Erica R. 2009. "Never Innocent: Feminist Trouble with Sex Offender Registries and Protection in a Prison Nation." *Meridians: Feminism, Race, Transnationalism* 9 (2): 31–62.

Miccio, G. Kristian. 2005. "A House Divided: Mandatory Arrest, Domestic Violence, and the Conservatization of the Battered Women's Movement." *Houston Law Review* 42:237–323.

Mickleburgh, Rod. 2012. "'Embarrassed' RCMP Brass Launch Probe of Officer's Bondage Photos." *Globe And Mail*, 6 July. http://m.theglobeand mail.com/news/british-columbia/embarrassed-rcmp-brass-launch-probe-of-officers-bondage-photos/article4393814/?service=mobile.

Miller, Fiona, and Julia Kubanek. n.d. "DNA Evidence and a National DNA Databank: Not in Our Name." Vancouver Rape Relief and Women's Shelter. http://www.rapereliefshelter.bc.ca/learn/resources/dna-evidence-and-national-dna-databank-not-our-name.

Miller, Joan Bridi. 1976. "Sado-Masochism: Another Point of View." *Gay Community News*.

Miller, William. 1997. *The Anatomy of Disgust*. Cambridge, MA: Harvard University Press.

Miller, Paul, Sophia Parker, and Sarah Gillinson. 2004. *Disablism: How to Tackle the Last Prejudice*. London: Demos.

Mills, Bart. 1986. "Hard Core, Soft Sell." *American Film* 11 (6): 46–51.

Miriam, Kathy. 1993. "From Rage to All the Rage: Lesbian-Feminism, Sadomasochism and the Politics of Memory." In Reti 1993, 7–70.

Moser, Charles, and Peggy J. Kleinplatz. 2005a. "Does Heterosexuality Belong in the DSM?" *Lesbian and Gay Psychology Review* 6 (3): 261–7.

– 2005b. "*DSM-IV-TR* and the Paraphilias: An Argument for Removal." *Journal of Psychology & Human Sexuality* 17 (3–4): 91–109.

– 2006. *Sadomasochism: Powerful Pleasures*. New York: Harrington Park.

Moser, Charles, and J.J. Madeson. 1996. *Bound to Be Free: The SM Experience*. New York: Continuum.

Murray, Thomas E. 1989. *The Language of Sadomasochism: A Glossary and Linguistic Analysis*. New York: Greenwood.

National Coalition for Sexual Freedom. 2010. "The APA Paraphilias Subworkgroup Agrees: Kinky Is NOT a Diagnosis." 16 February. http:// archive.constantcontact.com/fs003/1102908923221/archive/1103050720626 .html.

Newmahr, Staci. 2011. *Playing on the Edge: Sadomasochsim, Risk, and Intimacy*. Bloomington: Indiana University Press.

Newman, Rebecca. 2012. "Mommy Porn? How Dare Men Put Down Women's Sexual Fantasies." *Telegraph*, 7 December. http://www.telegraph.co.uk/ culture/books/9729588/Mommy-Porn-How-dare-men-put-down- womens-sexual-fantasies.html.

Nichols, Jeanette, Darlene Pagano, and Margaret Rosoff. 1982. "Is Sadomasochism Feminist? A Critique of the Samois Position." In Linden et al. 1982, 137–46.

Nix. 2002. "Killing Me Softly (2002) Movie Review." Beyond Hollywood, 8 July. http://www.beyondhollywood.com/killing-me-softly-2002-movie- review/.

NOW. 1999. "The 1999 Delineation of Lesbian Rights." http://archive.is/JCvvH.

Nussbaum, Felicity A. 1989. *The Autobiographical Subject: Gender and Ideology in Eighteenth-Century England*. Baltimore: Johns Hopkins University Press.

Nussbaum, Martha C. 2004. *Hiding from Humanity: Disgust, Shame and the Law*. Princeton: Princeton University Press.

Olson, Ingrid. 2012. "Asking for It: Erotic Asphyxiation and the Limitations of Sexual Consent." *Jindal Global Law Review* 4:171–200.

Oxford English Dictionary, 2nd ed., s.v. "encounter."

Pa, Monica. 2001. "Beyond the Pleasure Principle: The Criminalization of Consensual Sadomasochistic Sex." *Texas Journal of Women & the Law* 11:51–92.

Pally, Marcia. 1982. "The Fireworks at the Sexuality Conference: Whom Should Feminists Fuck?" *New York Native*, 24 May.

Plato. 360 BCE. *Phaedrus.* http://www.perseus.tufts.edu/hopper/text?doc=Perseus%3Atext%3A1999.01.0174%3Atext%3DPhaedrus.

Radicalesbians. 1970. "The Woman-Identified Woman." http://library.duke.edu/rubenstein/scriptorium/wlm/womid/.

Rainbird, Ashleigh. 2011. "Rihanna Causes Controversy with S&M Video." *Daily Mirror*, 2 February. http://www.mirror.co.uk/celebs/news/2011/02/02/rihanna-causes-controversy-with-s-m-video-115875-22892349/.

Réage, Pauline. 1966. *Story of O.* Translated by Sabine d'Estree. New York: Grove.

Reti, Irene. 1993a. "Remember the Fire: Lesbian Sadomasochism in a Post-Holocaust World." In Reti 1993b, 79–99.

– 1993b. *Unleashing Feminism: Critiquing Lesbian Sadomasochism in the Gay Nineties.* Santa Cruz, CA: HerBooks.

Rich, Adrienne. 1979. *On Lies, Secrets, and Silence: Selected Prose, 1966–1978.* New York: Norton.

– 1980. "Compulsory Heterosexuality and Lesbian Existence." *Signs* 5 (4): 631–60.

Rich, Ruby. 1986. "Feminism and Sexuality in the 1980s." *Feminist Studies* 12 (3): 525–61.

Ridge, George Ross. 1961. "The 'Femme Fatale' in French Decadence." *French Review* 34 (4): 352–60.

Richters, Juliet, Richard O. De Visser, Chris E. Rissel, Andrew E. Grulich, and Anthony Smith. 2008. "Demographic and Psychosocial Features of Participants in Bondage and Discipline, 'Sadomasochism' or Dominance and Submission (BDSM): Data from a National Survey." *Journal of Sexual Medicine* 5 (7): 1660–8.

Rozin, Paul, and A. Fallon. 1987. "A Perspective on Disgust." *Psychological Review* 94 (1): 23–41.

Rozin, Paul, Jonathan Haidt, and Clark R. McCauley. 2000. "Disgust." In *Handbook of Emotions*, edited by Michael Lewis, 2nd ed., 637–53. New York: Guilford.

Rubin, Gayle. 1987. "The Leather Menace: Comments on Politics and SM." In *Coming to Power: Writings and Graphics on Lesbian S/M*, edited by Samois, 194–229. Boston: Alyson Publications.

– 1989. "Thinking Sex: Notes for a Racial Theory of the Politics of Sexuality." In Vance 1989b, 267–319.

Sasha. 2003. "Love Bites." *Eye Weekly*, 4 September. http://contests.eyeweekly .com/eye/issue/issue_09.04.03/plus/lovebites.php.

Samois. 1979. *What Color Is Your Handkerchief? A Lesbian S/M Sexuality Reader*. Berkeley, CA: Samois.

– ed. 1982. *Coming to Power: Writings and Graphics on Lesbian S/M*. Boston: Alyson Publications.

Schrim, Janet. 1979. "SM and Feminism." In *A Woman's Touch: An Anthology of Lesbian Eroticism and Sensuality for Women Only*, edited by Cedar and Nelly, 67–72. Eugene, OR: Womanshare Books.

Sedgwick, Eve Kosofsky. 1990. *Epistemology of the Closet*. Berkeley: University of California Press.

"Sex Issue, The." 1981. Special issue of *Heresies* 12.

Sims, Karen, Rose Mason, and Darlene Pagaon. 1982. "Racism and Sadomasochism: A Conversation with Two Black Lesbians." In Linden et al. 1982, 99–105.

Singh, Anita. 2012. "50 Shades of Grey Is Best-Selling Book of All Time." *Telegraph*, 7 August. http://www.telegraph.co.uk/culture/books/ booknews/9459779/50-Shades-of-Grey-is-best-selling-book-of-all-time.html.

Sokoloff, Natalie J., and Ida Dupont. 2005. "Domestic Violence at the Intersections of Race, Class, and Gender Challenges and Contributions to Understanding Violence against Marginalized Women in Diverse Communities." *Violence against Women* 11 (1): 38–64.

Sobchack, Vivian. 1992. *The Address of the Eye: A Phenomenology of Film Experience*. Princeton: Princeton University Press.

Spade, Dean. 2011. *Normal Life: Administrative Violence, Critical Trans Politics, and the Limits of Law*. Cambridge, MA: South End.

Stallybrass, Peter, and Allon White. 1986. *The Politics and Poetics of Transgression*. Ithaca, NY: Cornell University Press.

Star, Susan Leigh. 1982. "Swastikas: The Street and the University." In Linden et al. 1982, 131–6.

Stein, Marc, ed. 2003. *Encyclopedia of Lesbian, Gay, Bisexual, and Transgender History in America*. New York: Charles Scribner's Sons.

Stekel, Wilhelm. 1929. *Sadism and Masochism: The Psychology of Hatred and Cruelty*. Vol. 1. New York: Liveright.

Stokes, Mason. 2001. *The Color of Sex: Whiteness, Heterosexuality, & the Fictions of White Supremacy*. Durham: Duke University Press.

Stoller, Robert J. 1991. *Pain & Passion: A Psychoanalyst Explores the World of S & M*. New York: Plenum.

Stoltenberg, John. 1982. "Sadomasochism: Eroticized Violence, Eroticized Powerlessness." In Linden et al. 1982, 124–30.

Stychin, Carl F. 1994. "Unmanly Diversions: The Construction of the Homosexual Body (Politic) in English Law." *Osgoode Hall Law Journal* 32 (3): 503–36.

– 1995. "Essential Rights and Contested Identities: Sexual Orientation and Equality Rights Jurisprudence in Canada." *Canadian Journal of Law & Jurisprudence* 8 (1): 49–66.

"The Subway." 1992. *Seinfeld* episode #313. http://www.seinfeldscripts.com/TheSubway.htm.

Sudbury, Julia. 2005. *Global Lockdown: Race, Gender, and the Prison-Industrial Complex.* New York: Routledge.

Sumner, L.W. 2004. *The Hateful and the Obscene: Studies in the Limits of Free Expression.* Toronto: University of Toronto Press.

Taylor, Charles. 2004. *Modern Social Imaginaries.* Durham: Duke University Press.

Thomas, Trish. 1993. "Fuck Your Ex-Lover." In *The Girl Wants To: Women's Representations of Sex and the Body*, edited by Lynn Crosbie, 180–1. Toronto: Coach House.

– 1996. "Wunna My Fantasies." In *A Movement of Eros: 25 Years of Lesbian Erotica*, edited by Heather Findlay, 195–200. New York: Richard Kasak Book Edition.

Thompson, Bill. 1994. *Sadomasochism: Painful Perversion or Pleasurable Play?* London: Cassell.

Van Iquity, Sister Dana. 2007. "Cruising: This Time It Might Change Your Mind." *San Francisco Bay Times*, 6 September. http://www.sfbaytimes.com/index.php?article_id=6815&sec=article.

Vance, Carole S. 1984a. "Epilogue." In Vance 1989b, 431–9.

– ed. 1984b. *Pleasure and Danger: Exploring Female Sexuality.* London: Pandora.

– 1993. "More Danger, More Pleasure: A Decade after the Barnard Sexuality Conference." *New York Law School Law Review* 38:289–318.

Wacquant, Loïc. 2009. *Punishing the Poor: The Neoliberal Government of Social Insecurity.* Durham, NC: Duke University Press Books.

Walker, Alice. 1982. "A Letter of the Times, or Should This Sado-Masochism Be Saved?" In Linden et al. 1982, 205–8.

Walker-Crawford, Vivienne. 1982. "The Saga of Sadie O. Massey." In Linden et al. 1982, 147–52.

Walters, Barry. 1996. "Don't Even Risk 'Frisk' Tale of Crazed Gay Killer, Revised Version Still No Better Than Disastrous Premiere." *San Francisco Examiner*, 29 March. http://www.sfgate.com/cgi-bin/article.cgi?f=/e/a/1996/03/29/WEEKEND2044.dtl.

Ward, Cameron. 2012. "RCMP Officer Jim Brown Is a Sexual Sadist – So What's the Big Deal?" *Native News North*, 6 July. http://groups.yahoo.com/group/NatNews-north/message/22886.

Wayne, Linda. 1996. "S/M Symbols, Fascist Icons, and Systems of Empowerment." In Califia and Sweeney 1996, 242–51.

Weinberg, Thomas S. 2006. "Sadomasochism and the Social Sciences: A Review of the Sociological and Social Psychological Literature." In Kleinplatz and Moser 2006, 17–40.

Weinrichter, Antonio. 1992. "Instinto Basico: Gatillazo fatal." *Dirigido* 204:22–5.

Weiss, Margot Danielle. 2011. *Techniques of Pleasure: BDSM and the Circuits of Sexuality*. Durham: Duke University Press.

White, Hayden. 1987. *The Content of the Form: Narrative Discourse and Historical Representation*. Baltimore: Johns Hopkins University Press.

Wilkinson, Eleanor. 2009. "Perverting Visual Pleasure: Representing Sadomasochism." *Sexualities* 12 (2): 181–98.

Williams, Linda. 1993. "Second Thoughts on *Hard Core*: American Obscenity Law and the Scapegoating of Deviance." In *Dirty Looks: Women, Pornography, Power*, edited by Pamela Church Gibson and Roma Gibson, 46–61. London: British Film Institute.

– 1999. *Hard Core: Power, Pleasure and the "Frenzy of the Visible."* Berkeley: University of California Press.

– 2004. "Porn Studies: Proliferating Pornographies On/Scene: An Introduction." In *Porn Studies*, edited by Linda Williams, 1–23. Durham: Duke University Press.

Wilson, Alexander. 1981. "Friedkin's Cruising, Ghetto Politics, and Gay Sexuality." *Social Text* 4:98–109.

Wilson, Erin Cressida. 2003. *Secretary*. New York: Soft Skull.

Wilson, William. 1992. "Is Hurting People Wrong?" *Journal of Social Welfare & Family Law* 14 (5): 388–87.

Withers, A.J. 2012. *Disability, Politics, and Theory*. Halifax: Fernwood.

Wright, Susan. 2010. "Depathologizing Consensual Sexual Sadism, Sexual Masochism, Transvestic Fetishism, and Fetishism." *Archives of Sexual Behavior* 39 (6): 1229–30.

Wood, Robert E. 1993. "Somebody Has to Die: Basic Instinct as White Noir." *Post Script* 12 (3): 44–51.

Woodward, Jonathan. 2012. "Mountie in Bondage Photos Fights Back against Fraudster." *CTV News*, 1 November. http://bc.ctvnews.ca/mountie-in-bondage-photos-fights-back-against-fraudster-1.1021312#ixzz2IWqYchQ0.

Young, Alan N. 2003. *Justice Defiled: Perverts, Potheads, Serial Killers and Lawyers*. Toronto: Key Porter Books.

Young, Lola. 1996. *Fear of the Dark: "Race," Gender, and Sexuality in the Cinema.* London:

Wikipedia. 2013. s.v. "Bondage Suit [Gimp Suit]." http://en.wikipedia.org/wiki/Gimp_%28sadomasochism%29.

Zanghellini, Aleardo. 2004. "Is Little Sisters Just Butler's Little Sister?" *University of British Columbia Law Review* 37:407–47.

Index